The Golden Age of Cinema

The Golden Age of Cinema

Hollywood, 1929–1945

Richard B. Jewell

Blackwell Publishing

BLACKWELL PUBLISHING
350 Main Street, Malden, MA 02148-5020, USA
9600 Garsington Road, Oxford OX4 2DQ, UK
550 Swanston Street, Carlton, Victoria 3053, Australia

First published 2007 by Blackwell Publishing Ltd

1   2007

Library of Congress Cataloging-in-Publication Data

Jewell, Richard B.
    The golden age of cinema : Hollywood, 1929–1945 / Richard B. Jewell.
        p.   cm.
    Includes bibliographical references and index.
    ISBN 978-1-4051-6372-9 (hardcover : alk. paper)
        ISBN 978-1-4051-6373-6 (pbk. : alk. paper)   1. Motion pictures—United States—
History.   2. Motion picture industry—United States—History.   I. Title.

PN1993.5.U6J49 2007
791.430973—dc22
                                    2007010757

A catalogue record for this title is available from the British Library.

Set in Futura and 10.5/13 pt Minion Pro
by The Running Head Limited, Cambridge, www.therunninghead.com
Printed and bound in Singapore by C.O.S. Printers Pte Ltd

The publisher's policy is to use permanent paper from mills that operate a sustainable
forestry policy, and which has been manufactured from pulp processed using acid-free and
elementary chlorine-free practices. Furthermore, the publisher ensures that the text paper
and cover board used have met acceptable environmental accreditation standards.

For further information on
Blackwell Publishing, visit our website:
www.blackwellpublishing.com

For Annie B.

Contents

Illustrations

Acknowledgments

While I take responsibility for the content of this book, I would be remiss if I did not thank the many people who contributed to *The Golden Age of Cinema: Hollywood, 1929–1945* during its lengthy gestation period. One of the most mannerly traditions of publishing is the opportunity afforded authors to acknowledge the many different kinds of assistance that enabled them to complete the best work possible. Herewith, I take full advantage of this tradition.

First, I lift my glass filled with the finest champagne to my special friends, the professionals who worked in Hollywood during the years covered in this book and who generously shared their knowledge and reminiscences with me. Sadly, they are all now deceased, though I often think of them, particularly when I am rewatching one of their extraordinary movies: Pandro Berman, John Brahm, Frank Capra, Edward Dmytryk, Jane Greer, June Haver, Fred MacMurray, Rouben Mamoulian, David Raksin, Ginger Rogers, George Sidney, James Stewart, Charles Walters, Billy Wilder, Robert Wise and Fred Zinnemann.

This book began as a collaborative effort with my colleague Drew Casper. During the writing phase, he quickly sprinted ahead of me, and so we decided to split the texts apart and publish them separately. To my amazement, both books will now arrive from the same company and in the same year. I am indebted to Drew for his friendship, support and, particularly, his encouragement during the dark days when I questioned whether I would ever be able to complete the project.

I am particularly grateful to Lisa Majewski, my former student and teaching assistant, who helped me research several of the chapters and read and offered useful comments on the entire manuscript. Lisa is, without question, the kindest and most sympathetic person I know. Anyone fortunate enough to have earned her friendship is indeed blessed.

Around the mid-point of the book's development, Chris Cooling read and provided discerning feedback on several of the chapters. During the 10-year period when I served as Associate Dean for Academic Affairs of the USC School of Cinema-Television, I was fortunate to work with three very able assistants: Joyce Hirayama, Stacey Zackin and Daphne Sigismondi. They helped to facilitate the project and propped up my spirits when I found myself bogged down in the quicksand of academic administration.

My boss during those years, Dean Elizabeth Daley, was always sensitive to my scholarly ambitions and kindly allowed me to take a semester off to complete one of the chapters. After I gave up the Associate Dean position, Dean Daley provided a one-year sabbatical, enabling me finally to complete the manuscript.

Two eminent scholars – Charles Maland of the University of Tennessee and Dana Polan of New York University – reviewed the book and offered many excellent suggestions. The work has improved markedly because of their input, and I am deeply indebted to both of them.

Several people helped me to procure the illustrations. Ned Comstock of the USC Cinema-Television Library demonstrated total commitment to the project as he searched through various collections looking for the best images. Dace Taube of the USC Doheny Library staff and my sterling ex-student, Barbara Hall of the Academy of Motion Picture Arts and Sciences Library, also located some wonderful stills for me. Charles Uy, Curator of the Wolper Center in the Doheny Library, provided additional timely assistance.

After an exasperating experience with another publishing company, I was fortunate to send my manuscript to Jayne Fargnoli of Blackwell. She seized it and ran with it like Reggie Bush runs with a football. No author ever had a finer champion than Jayne. I am also thankful to Ken Provencher who has helped to make my continuing relationship with Blackwell thoroughly harmonious and satisfying.

I would definitely be remiss if I did not mention five friends whose good works, as well as their stimulating conversations, have inspired me: Lawrence Bassoff, Leonard Maltin, Woody Omens, Frank Rosenfelt and David Shepard.

I am privileged to hold the Hugh M. Hefner Chair for the Study of American Film at the University of Southern Caliornia. Mr. Hefner is much more than just a benefactor; his knowledge and love of Hollywood movies from the 1930s and 40s are boundless and unqualified. Thus, in one sense, this book was written for him. I very much hope he finds it of value because no one's opinion of this history means more to me than his.

The Golden Age of Cinema: Hollywood, 1929–1945 was also written for my students. Over the years, I have had the great good fortune to teach Hollywood cinema during its Classical Period to many undergraduates and graduate students. Their enthusiasm and thirst for knowledge have inspired me to be a better historian, a better writer and a better teacher. This book has benefited in incalculable ways from my interactions with so many lively, fertile young minds.

Finally, I must acknowledge my supreme debt to my wife Lynne – the person who has tolerated my quirks, my tantrums, my often intolerable behavior for more years than she will allow me to mention. Without her unfaltering support, this book would not have been written.

Richard B. Jewell
The Hugh M. Hefner Professor of American Film
University of Southern California
School of Cinematic Arts
Los Angeles, CA 90089–2211

Introduction

Born at the end of the period covered by this book, I grew up watching (and loving) the movies of the 1950s and 1960s. My early experiences in various movie theaters were supplemented by television viewings of films made in the 1930s and 1940s. I liked these films as well, but did not truly appreciate them until I began to study film in a serious fashion. Soon, I came to understand why the period is often called the "golden age" of cinema – a time when the sound film rapidly developed into a prominent and influential business, cultural product and art form.

The term "Classical Hollywood Cinema" is now widely used by academics to describe films made during this time, and the term will recur throughout this book. And yet while it may be argued that American theatrical filmmaking passed through its most dominant, authoritative and significant years between 1929 and 1945, those years were hardly serene. Bookended by the Great Depression and World War II, they represent arguably the most unstable, tension-filled era of the twentieth century. But great works of the human imagination rarely arise during periods of relative tranquility. As Harry Lime (Orson Welles) says in *The Third Man* (London Film/Selznick, 1949): "In Italy for 30 years under the Borgias they had warfare, terror, murder, bloodshed, but they produced Michelangelo, Leonardo da Vinci and the Renaissance. In Switzerland, they had brotherly love and 500 years of democracy and peace and what did they produce? The cuckoo clock." Thus, the worldwide upheaval of the 1930s and 1940s engendered a fertile environment for the production of many exceptional American films – films that are still being enjoyed and studied and remade more than 50 years after they were released.

And yet, to my astonishment, there exists no single book devoted to this extraordinary period in Hollywood history. For years I have been teaching courses on Classical Hollywood without a satisfactory textbook. While several excellent books on the early sound period have been published, none provides the foundational knowledge and breadth of coverage that I believe my students need to appreciate the films of the era. So, like many other professors, I have written *The Golden Age of Cinema: Hollywood, 1929–1945* out of my own sense of pedagogic frustration.

As the title suggests, this work does not cover all of the films made in America during the period. It omits the documentary, experimental, avant garde, exploitation, educational and industrial work that was done in the United States during these years. Nor does it do full justice to Hollywood; there is scant information about the animated films, newsreels and shorts which the studios produced in abundance. I have chosen, instead, to focus on the theatrical feature. Even so, I make no claim that the book is comprehensive or encyclopedic. The Hollywood companies made several thousand feature films between 1929 and 1945. I am able to discuss only a fraction of them.

This book is, therefore, introductory in nature. It presupposes no knowledge of the subject and is written in clear and straightforward prose, without reliance on academic jargon. Its goal is to help the reader achieve a fairly sophisticated understanding of the key cinematic and extra-cinematic elements that shaped the production of Hollywood motion pictures during the period. The extra-cinematic factors include the social, political, economic and cultural changes that occurred between the onset of the Depression and the end of World War II, as well as the other leisure time activities that competed with and, in many cases, were adapted and exploited by the Hollywood production machine. These elements are taken up primarily in chapter 1 but reappear in other chapters as well. The remaining chapters cover the principal cinematic influences: Hollywood business practices, technological developments, censorship restraints, narrative and stylistic issues, genre thinking and the star system.

Organizing historical material by topic rather than in a traditional chronological fashion has disadvantages. It requires a certain amount of repetition and may produce the misleading assumption that each chapter covers a discrete, self-contained topic rather than one that is intimately intertwined with all of the others. However, I believe the structure also has advantages. Primary among them is that it provides a multifaceted understanding of the films – why they were made, how they changed over time and what their impact on the American public was. The arrangement of the chapters should have a cumulative effect on the reader, increasing his or her understanding of the levels of influence that impacted the production of every Hollywood feature. One's viewing of any film from this period should be richer and more informed after reading this book, whether the picture is a Technicolor blockbuster like *Gone with the Wind* (Selznick/MGM, 1939) or a cheap black-and-white "B" western such as *Scarlet River* (RKO, 1933).

Although I must reiterate that the book is not intended to be exhaustively comprehensive, it does mention many film titles. As in the final sentence of the last paragraph, my approach will be to identify them when first mentioned in any chapter by the studio that distributed them and the year of their initial release. When, as in the case of *Gone with the Wind*, the film was produced independently and then distributed by one of the major studios, both the producer and the distributor will be indicated. This method of identifying films is nonstandard and will likely cause some controversy, but I believe it most accurately reflects the production practices of the time. The book illuminates the "studio system" era, a period when eight major studios dominated the theatrical film business in the United States. These studios controlled the flow of movies from their West Coast studios to theaters throughout America and around the world. Studio executives and producers enjoyed "final cut"; they, rather than the directors who worked as their employees, made all the final decisions about their company's releases. Furthermore, the making of Hollywood movies during the period was intensely collaborative. Seven of the eight majors (United Artists was the exception) each employed hundreds of talented, creative people who worked together and contributed to a large number of films each year. Assigning credit for a picture to one of these individuals (typically the director) strikes me as a dubious and misleading practice. I have, therefore, ascribed "authorship" of each film to its studio rather than to any particular individual.

While I make no apologies for this decision, I hope it will not be misconstrued. I remain an ardent admirer of such brilliant directors as John Ford, Howard Hawks, Charles Chaplin, Ernst Lubitsch, William Wyler, Rouben Mamoulian, Alfred Hitchcock, Frank Capra, Preston Sturges, Orson Welles and Billy Wilder. They created distinctive and personal films – films that reflected their own taste and sensibility – and many fashioned their best work while toiling as "hired guns" for the studios. Still, the achievements of these "great men" have received more than their fair share of attention. This book will look at Hollywood from a variety of different perspectives, pushing the "auteur" directors to the periphery in order to emphasize more powerful forces that shaped the motion pictures of the period.

1

Historical Overview

The period from 1929 to 1945 was marked by a series of traumatic events that shook the very foundations of American society. An economic cataclysm which began in autumn 1929 ushered in an era of deprivation, anxiety and despair that lingered for more than a decade. Developments in Europe during the 1930s led to the possibility of a world controlled by a group of tyrants whose authoritarian, racist philosophy inspired them to commit the most heinous acts of the twentieth century. The Nazis ignited World War II and came frighteningly close to winning it. But America's entrance into the conflict in late 1941 brought an end to the country's economic problems and helped assure the final victory of the Allies. By the end of 1945, the United States was clearly the world's most powerful nation, having triumphed over its own economic difficulties as well as the enemies of freedom and tolerance. After years of focusing almost exclusively on life within the US, American leaders widened their purview and accepted a leadership role in a new world, now complicated by the existence of atomic weapons.

Major Historical Events

The years that preceded the Depression were filled with contradictions and excess. In many ways a reaction to the Puritanistic origins of the country, the repressive Victorian atmosphere of the late nineteenth and early twentieth centuries and the horrific bloodshed of World War I, the 1920s were marked by the emergence of a "consumer culture" and bold rejection of past beliefs. Lured by abundant job opportunities and dazzled by the enticements of urban life, approximately six million rural Americans moved to cities where they were introduced to such technological marvels as automobiles, radios, telephones and movies, and to an animated life that rarely slowed its pace. People who had been taught to work hard and save their earnings were now encouraged by the rapidly emerging world of advertising to spend money on the new technological wonders. They were likewise persuaded to loosen up, dance the Charleston, wear snappy suits or short skirts, smoke and have a few drinks. One of the era's most glaring contradictions was Prohibition, which made the sale and consumption of alcoholic beverages illegal beginning in 1920. This unpopular law backfired on its ascetic sponsors who watched in horror as hundreds of thousands of Americans frequented speakeasies, trafficked with bootleggers and, in other ways, flagrantly disobeyed the law.

Underpinning the optimistic liberation of the 1920s was a general prosperity and a growing sense that riches were within the reach of anyone smart enough to grab them. The stock market became the obsession of many would-be millionaires. Buoyed by the steady rise of the Dow Jones Industrial Average (DJI), they borrowed money, bought shares of stock (often on margin) and watched euphorically as the market broke into a bullish charge in 1928, which carried over to 1929. Stocks worth $27 billion at the beginning of 1925 had grown in value to $87 billion on October 1, 1929. The run up of certain securities was spectacular. Radio Corporation of America rose from $85 per share to $420 in one year; American Telephone and Telegraph climbed from $209 to $303 in a matter of months, Wright Aeronautical gained $34.75 in one week.

Blinded by the uninterrupted good news, most investors completely missed the danger signals: the overexpansion of major industries, the weak banking structure, the swollen credit balloon, the unsound and unregulated policies of the market itself. In September 1929, stocks began to fluctuate alarmingly. In October, the market collapsed, causing many to lose fortunes much faster than they had made them. It struck bottom in June 1932. At that point, US Steel had fallen from $262 to $22, General Motors from $73 to $8, Montgomery Ward from $138 to $4. The entire stock market declined 86.2 percent between September 1929 and June 1932; it would take more than 22 years to recover the losses. But the biggest loser was not the stockholder, it was America itself: its capitalistic economy had suddenly plunged into a state of near meltdown.

One year after the stock market crashed, six million American workers were looking for jobs. Many plants were operating at a fraction of capacity, many others had closed down. President Herbert Hoover, a Republican who had defeated Democrat Al Smith in 1928, believed the problems were temporary and called on local government initiative and private charity to alleviate the suffering. But the situation proved to be anything but temporary.

By 1932, one-third of the workforce was unemployed. In the large industrial centers of the northeast and midwest, the figures were even worse. Chicago had 600,000 jobless, New York one million. Fifty percent of the workers in Cleveland had no employment; in Akron, the figure was 60 percent; in Toledo, 80 percent. Farmers were also devastated. They saw wheat fall from $1.05 per bushel in 1929 to 39 cents in 1932, cotton from 17 cents a pound to 6 cents, corn from 81 cents a bushel to 33 cents. Many lost their farms and equipment when they failed to make their mortgage payments. A multitude of city dwellers suffered the same fate, evicted from their homes or apartments because they were broke. (Figure 1.1)

The homeless often built their own shelters out of packing crates and pieces of metal on the outskirts of large cities. These pathetic domiciles came to be known as "Hoovervilles" and symbolized the growing disaffection that Americans felt for their President. When Herbert Hoover became the nation's leader, he stated, "we shall soon with the help of God be in sight of the day when poverty shall be banished from this nation." He further promised, "two cars in every garage, a chicken in every pot." Few political promises have ever been buried so completely by the avalanche of historical change.

In fairness, it should be emphasized that Hoover was not an American Nero, fiddling while Washington fell apart. His administration did back legislation designed to ease the crisis, helping to create the Reconstruction Finance Corporation which was set up in 1932 to loan money to such businesses as banks, railroads, insurance companies and farm mortgage associations and thereby restore confidence in the country's beleaguered finance and credit institutions. It was spending $500 million in public works projects by the end of the year. But the President, a great believer in "rugged individualism," was more given to encouraging platitudes ("prosperity is just around the corner") than to bold action. And some of his administration's legislative initiatives actually made things worse. The Hawley-Smoot tariff bill of 1930, for example, was especially ill timed; it hastened the collapse of the European economy and caused a trade war to break out between the US and its international trading partners.

Hoover's reputation was further tarnished by his handling of the "bonus march" of 1932. Requesting payment of bonuses promised for their service in World War I (but not collectable until 1945), some 15,000 unemployed veterans congregated in Washington, DC. After the Senate denied their petition, many of the "forgotten men" stayed on, camping in and around the Washington area. In July, Hoover dispatched the Army, under the command of Douglas MacArthur, to scatter the veterans and destroy their "Hoovervilles." This method of "thanking" Americans who had risked their lives for their country left a bitter taste in many voters' mouths.

They expressed their contempt for the incumbent at the polls, electing

Figure 1.1 A breadline made up of hundreds of hungry men snakes down a New York street during the Depression. Courtesy of the USC Doheny Library Department of Special Collections.

Democrat Franklin D. Roosevelt by a landslide in 1932. Roosevelt carried all but six states. When he took control in March 1933, the new President immediately declared a national bank holiday, feeling that the battered American banking system represented the greatest cause for alarm. Five thousand banks had failed during the first three years of the Depression, wiping out the life savings of many and causing a panic run on financial institutions throughout the country. FDR promised Americans that each bank would be examined and allowed to reopen only when the government was certain it was a safe haven for depositors. The stratagem worked, people relaxed and started to put funds back into the vaults, rather than rushing to pull them out. This decisive action alerted the populace that Roosevelt would act, in all the necessary ways, to subdue the national emergency.

Act he did, bringing, for example, a quick end to Prohibition. Roosevelt and his "New Deal" colleagues never developed a clearly defined, systematic plan to eradicate the deep-seated problems they faced, but they were not afraid to experiment. "It is common sense to take a method and try it," he said. "If it fails admit it frankly and try another. But above all do something."

Soon enough the American government had erected a virtual alphabet city of federal acts, programs and offices to attack the major predicaments of the Depression. Among the more famous were: the Civil Works Administration (CWA), the Public Works Administration (PWA), the Civilian Conservation Corps (CCC) and the Works Progress Administration (WPA), all of which created government jobs for the unemployed; the Glass-Steagall Banking Act, which set up the Federal Deposit Insurance Corporation (FDIC), thus insuring all deposits up to $5,000 and restoring people's faith in America's banking institutions; the Securities and Exchange Commission (SEC), which began to monitor Wall Street activity and assure investors that the irregularities that contributed to the crash of 1929 would be prevented in the future; the Agricultural Adjustment Act (AAA) and the Resettlement Administration (RA), which were designed to subsidize farmers and enable them to earn an acceptable living; the Tennessee Valley Authority (TVA), which built dams and power plants to improve the lives of Americans living in one of the country's most backward areas; the Social Security Act, which provided old-age pensions; and the National Industrial Recovery Act (NIRA) and the National Recovery Administration (NRA), which were supposed to help business and labor by establishing industry-wide codes that would include minimum wages and maximum hours for workers and formulating production and price agreements. In 1935, the Supreme Court declared the NRA unconstitutional, but its basic agenda remained in place throughout the Roosevelt presidency. Indeed, the Wagner Act, passed by Congress in that same year, encouraged the growth of trade unionism by banning unfair labor practices and guaranteeing the right to organize, to bargain collectively, to picket and to strike. It also created the National Labor Relations Board (NLRB).

Franklin D. Roosevelt was a master politician who used the newly established mass medium of radio to full advantage. His "fireside chats" personalized the battle against the Depression "wolf," giving Americans a sense that order and stability would return to their lives. In the 1936 election, he easily defeated his Republican opponent Alf Landon, carrying every state except Maine and Vermont. And yet the New Deal could not make the Depression disappear. While life in America clearly improved after the terrifying 1932–33 period, the prosperity that many had enjoyed a decade earlier stubbornly refused to return.

Roosevelt's second term was much more difficult and vexing than his first had been. Angered because the Supreme Court had declared both the NRA and the AAA unconstitutional, FDR attempted a "court packing" gambit which would have given him more control over a body that he believed to be obstructionist. Howls of protest came from many corners (including some that had always supported the President before), and he was forced to abandon his hopes for court reform in July 1937. A similar attempt to deal with perceived enemies, his effort to "purge" the Democratic Party of conservative senators who had criticized aspects of the New Deal, backfired in 1938, further tarnishing the President's reputation. Walter F. George of Georgia, "Cotton Ed" Smith of South Carolina and Millard F. Tydings of Maryland, plus several other independent-minded Democrats, were all re-elected despite FDR's vigorous campaigns against them. But Roosevelt's greatest miscalculation was his decision to cut back sharply on relief programs in June 1937. Soon, the nation was mired in the "Roosevelt recession": stock prices plunged, unemployment rose by two million within three months, steel production fell by 75 percent, auto production by 50 percent.

Now a regular target of criticism from both the political left and the political right, FDR responded by pushing through new public works legislation as well as new agricultural initiatives. Roosevelt's deteriorating credibility was reflected in the 1938 elections where the Republican Party made a comeback, gaining seven Senate and 80 House seats. And the grip of the Depression was still firm: 10 million people, fully 15 percent of the workforce, remained unemployed in 1939. However, the disaffection did not mushroom – voters elected FDR to an unprecedented third term in 1940. Hesitant to change leadership in the face of continuing crises, the populace gave Roosevelt a solid victory over Wendell Willkie.

By that time the crises included World War II. While the United States wrestled with its formidable economic problems, Europe had witnessed the rise of National Socialism in Germany and Fascism in Italy. The German Nazi Party, led by Adolf Hitler, came to power in 1933 and immediately set about revitalizing a country that had been brought to its knees fewer than 15 years earlier by the First World War. Hitler espoused a pseudo-Nietzschean ideology based on the supposed superiority of the "true" (Aryan) Germans, the need to purify the race, the ill treatment that Germany had allegedly received as a conquered nation and the importance of reclaiming lands that had been taken from her in 1919. Openly violating the Versailles Treaty that ended World War I, the Nazis began to rearm and rattle their sabers. In 1935, they reclaimed the Saar Basin; in 1936, they moved into the Rhineland, and in 1938, they occupied Austria and the Sudetenland and made them part of the "Third Reich." Meanwhile, Benito Mussolini, Hitler's ally and leader of the Italian Fascists, had invaded and conquered Ethiopia in 1935, and both the Germans and Italians had aided the victory of Francisco Franco's Falange (Fascist) Party over the Loyalists in the bloody Spanish Civil War of 1936–39.

As Europe moved inexorably toward another conflagration, the United States remained stubbornly neutral. Many Americans believed their leaders had made a grave error in allowing American participation in World War I, and they were committed to keeping the country out of all future "foreign" wars. Evidence of this "isolationist" attitude, which took hold shortly after the end of World War I and remained strong for more than 20 years, included America's refusal to become a member of the League of Nations in 1920, despite the enthusiastic endorsement of that body by President Woodrow Wilson, and the passage of a series of Neutrality Acts in the 1930s which prevented the government from selling arms or making loans to belligerent nations. A 1937 public opinion poll showed that 94 percent of the populace felt US foreign policy should be directed at keeping the country out of all foreign wars.

In September 1939, the Nazis, having already taken control over much of Czechoslovakia without significant resistance from other European powers, overran Poland. England and France then honored their mutual protection pact with the Poles, declaring war on Germany. The Second World War had begun. The Nazis proved to be a frighteningly effective war machine, conquering Denmark, Belgium, Norway, the Netherlands, Luxembourg and France within a year.

"I have said this before, and I shall say it again and again and again. Your boys are not going to be sent into any foreign wars," Roosevelt assured Americans in 1940, but he and his advisors were clearly as alarmed by the German victories as they were suspicious of the Nazis' ultimate ambitions. In 1940, FDR signed an executive order leasing 50 over-age destroyers to Great Britain for 99 years. In return, the US was given several strategic naval bases from Newfoundland to British Guiana. The country had begun to sell arms to both

England and France the year before when Roosevelt convinced Congress to repeal the arms clause of the Neutrality Acts. A new approach was offered in 1941; the Lend-Lease Act gave the government the right to sell, lend, lease or give war materials to any nation resisting aggression. This included, of course, Great Britain and eventually the USSR. The Russians and Germans had signed a non-aggression treaty in August of 1939, but Hitler reneged, ordering his troops to attack Russia in June 1941. By that time, the US was, for all intents and purposes, involved in an undeclared war with Germany. (Figure 1.2)

Most Americans sided with their President and approved the assistance being provided to the perceived allies, but vociferous advocates of isolationism stepped up their attacks on FDR and others who, they claimed, were attempting to maneuver the country into the war. The Committee to Defend America First, led by famous aviator Charles Lindbergh and Robert E. Wood of Sears, Roebuck, plus powerful press baron William Randolph Hearst and congressional voices Burton K. Wheeler, Gerald P. Nye and Hamilton Fish, argued passionately against US intervention. A multitude of Americans agreed; as late as August 1941, 74 percent of the populace still opposed involvement in the battle with the Germans.

On December 7, 1941, the Japanese bombed Pearl Harbor in Hawaii and stilled the isolationist voices for good. This "unprovoked and dastardly attack" (as Roosevelt called it) on the American Pacific fleet was devastating. It destroyed or damaged 21 warships, demolished 188 aircraft and damaged 159 additional planes, killed 2,433 military personnel, wounded 1,178 more and, in its way, highlighted how strong the isolationist sentiment had been in the country up to that time. Despite the passage of the Selective Service Act in 1940, which enabled the government to draft young men into the armed forces, the US had only 1.5 million soldiers (approximately two-thirds of whom were only partially trained) on what Roosevelt labeled the "day that will live in infamy." The Japanese force, by contrast, numbered 2.4 million trained soldiers and 3 million trained reserves.

Japanese militarists, who had embarked on a policy of conquest and subjugation in Asia in 1931 and grown more and more vexed with the United States for openly opposing their objectives, took full advantage of America's obsession with non-involvement in their surprise attack upon Pearl Harbor. However, America's Pacific aircraft carriers were not at Pearl on December 7, and the attacking Japanese pilots overlooked massive amounts of fuel that were stored there. They also failed to attack dry docks where a number of the damaged ships would eventually be repaired. These strokes of American good fortune soon proved crucial in the Pacific conflict. Shortly after Roosevelt and

Figure 1.2 President Franklin D. Roosevelt broadcasts from the Oval Office of the White House in 1940. Courtesy of the USC Doheny Library Department of Special Collections.

Congress committed the nation to war on Japan, Germany and Italy honored their agreement with their Axis partner by declaring war on the United States. World War II had finally engulfed America.

Pearl Harbor and contemporaneous attacks on American troops in the Philippine Islands united the country in a way that no other event in American history ever had. Young men and women rushed to join the military, swelling its ranks to almost 3.9 million by the end of 1942 and to more than 9 million by the end of the following year. The Depression came to an abrupt end, laid to rest by the immediate need to build the machines of war and the determination of American industry to fill this need. Within six months of the Japanese attacks, 6 million workers found new jobs, many in the defense plants that manufactured tanks, aircraft, battleships, submarines and other machines of war. During the same period, federal procurement officers placed orders for $100 billion in equipment – more than the American economy had ever produced in a single year.

The first six months of the war were trying for the American military, but a breakthrough came in June 1942 when US forces engaged a large portion of the Japanese fleet near Midway Island. When the battle ended, the Japanese had lost four carriers, two large cruisers, three destroyers, several auxiliary craft and 300 airplanes. The Battle of Midway tipped the Pacific balance of power in the American direction.

In Europe, Hitler was finding his Russian enemies every bit as tough as the British to defeat. Frustrated at Moscow and the Caucasus and defeated and forced to retreat at Stalingrad, the Nazis were made to endure similar disappointments in North Africa, where they were beaten by the British at El Alamein.

With the United States contributing enormous amounts of war materials and manpower to the European theater of operations, the Allies took the offensive in 1942. From newly won bases in North Africa, they attacked Sicily in the summer of 1943 and, by September, had succeeded in knocking Italy out of the war. The Germans responded by sending troops to hold and defend the land of their principal ally, but American, British and Free French forces fought their way slowly up the Italian peninsula. Meanwhile, the Russians began to move westward, pushing the Nazis back toward their own borders.

In June 1944, the Allies launched the massive "D-Day" assault, landing troops on the Normandy coast of France and beginning the final phase of the European campaign. After withstanding a last counterattack by the Germans at the Battle of the Bulge in December 1944, they were able to bottle up the enemy troops inside their homeland which had been decimated by aerial bombing. On May 7, 1945, the Nazis surrendered.

The war in the Pacific would drag on for a few more months. The Philippines had been retaken from the Japanese in the spring of 1945 and Okinawa fell shortly thereafter. This cleared the way for a full-scale invasion of the main Japanese islands, which were already partially devastated and cut off from crucial raw materials. Despite their extreme vulnerability, the Japanese leaders refused to surrender. New American President Harry S. Truman, who had taken over when the country's only four-term President, Franklin D. Roosevelt, died in April 1945, contemplated his options. They were essentially two: either a full-scale invasion, which would undoubtedly cost many American as well as Japanese lives, or the employment of a fearsome secret weapon recently invented by American scientists. Truman decided to use the atomic bomb, ordering the Army Air Corps to drop one on Hiroshima on August 6. Following the first test explosion of the bomb, one of the weapon's inventors, J. Robert Oppenheimer, was reminded of a passage from the *Bhagavad-Gita*, a Sanskrit poem integral to the Hindu religion: "Now I am become Death, the shatterer of worlds." The attack on Hiroshima was certainly shattering to the Japanese who lost 78,000 people and endured a second A-bomb blast on Nagasaki on August 9. The country surrendered on August 14.

A few days after the surrender, British leader Winston Churchill said, "America stands at this moment at the summit of the world." His statement was accurate from a variety of perspectives. As historian Godfrey Hodgson has pointed out, the US had the world's most powerful economy. At its wartime peak in late 1944, American industry was working at a rate that would have enabled it to equip a power equal to the USSR in no more than a few days. The gross national product of the US, which settled at $56 billion in 1933, moved beyond $210 billion in 1945. During the war years, national income, national wealth and industrial production all doubled or more than doubled. The war also cost other countries much more than it had the US. American battle losses totaled fewer than 300,000, significant enough but small compared to the 50 million Asians and Europeans who perished. In fact, more Americans died of pneumonia and tuberculosis during World War II than were killed in combat. Furthermore, no one could contest the military might of the United States in 1945 since it, and it alone, had nuclear weapons.

Most significantly, the United States emerged from the war with a very different attitude toward the rest of the world than it had exhibited on Pearl Harbor day. Hanging up the cloak of isolationism, Americans accepted the challenge of leadership in the new world. This commitment was signaled by the country's willingness to admit tacitly that it had been wrong in disassociating itself from the League of Nations; it now strenuously supported the League's evolution into the United Nations. That body took shape in meetings at Dumbarton Oaks in Washington, DC between Great Britain, the USSR and the US in August and September of the same year. During a San Francisco conference that lasted from April to late June 1945, the representatives of more than 50 countries hammered out the charter of the organization which officially came into force on October 24, 1945. The General Assembly held its first meeting in London in January 1946, where it was decided that UN permanent headquarters would be in the United States. The construction of the UN buildings on the East River in New York City became a fitting, concrete representation of America's movement from a passive to an active posture with respect to world affairs.

Economic Situation

US economic history between 1929 and 1946 was bracketed by two periods of relative tranquility surrounding a long, nightmarish ordeal of hardship and uncertainty. Explosive technological growth during the 1920s changed American lives in a variety of ways. By the end of the decade, 70 percent of US homes had electricity, and more than half contained telephones and phonographs and had an automobile parked outside. Charles Lindbergh's solo flight across the Atlantic in 1927 fired the imagination of his countrymen; if Americans could pull off such feats, some reasoned, they were capable of anything – utopia was truly within reach. The breakthroughs of technology and the dizzying run up of stocks near the end of the "roaring" era made the economic free fall which began in the last three months of 1929 seem totally shocking and unfathomable.

Economists generally view the stock market crash of October 1929 as the beginning of the Depression. The performance of the market during the remainder of the period ignited few celebrations. After reaching a high of 381.17 on September 3, 1929, the DJI bottomed out at 41.22 on July 8, 1932. The market, like most economic indicators, did improve during the war years, but it would not approach its pre-crash level again until 1954. It was hardly a time for the faint-of-heart to be dabbling in stocks; of the 10 worst single days in the twentieth-century history of the DJI, six occurred between 1929 and 1937.

The Depression was not confined to America; soon enough it became a worldwide phenomenon. Kreditanstalt, Austria's biggest bank, collapsed in 1931, marking the beginning of an economic calamity that soon engulfed Europe and spread to other continents. The aforementioned Hawley-Smoot Tariff, signed into law by President Hoover, exacerbated the situation, freezing foreigners out of the American market and making it nearly impossible for US businesses to sell their products overseas. The worldwide Depression also provided a fertile atmosphere for the growth of dictatorships in Germany, Italy and the USSR.

Although millions of Americans suffered during the Depression, surprisingly few seriously questioned their country's basic political and economic systems. The American Socialist Party, for example, which had polled 879,000 votes in the 1912 election and seemed a plausible answer to Depression woes in the early 1930s, had totally fallen apart by 1938. The American Communist Party did grow to perhaps 80,000 members by 1939, but the signing of the Soviet–German non-aggression pact by Stalin and Hitler in August of that year split the membership, leaving the Party in disarray and causing its ranks to decline.

Likewise, the efforts of individuals offering radical solutions to the hard times never developed significant momentum. "Kingfish" Huey Long, the often outrageous governor of Louisiana, concocted a "Share-Our-Wealth" scheme which promised to buy every family a house, a car and other basic items by taxing income over $1 million a year at 100 percent and confiscating fortunes of more than $5 million. By 1935, nearly 5 million Americans had grown sympathetic to Long's ideas, but an assassin's bullet felled him in September of that year and his famous slogan, "Every man a king," soon faded into history.

Father Charles Coughlin, a Catholic priest with a substantial radio following, began to promote the "National Union for Social Justice" in the mid-1930s. His sensationalistic broadcasts were filled with vituperative attacks on a wide range of targets including bankers, labor unions, Jews, Communists, President Roosevelt and, of course, the New Deal; they implied that an American Fascist state might be the proper medicine for a sick nation. An effective rabble rouser and fundraiser, Coughlin formed the National Union Party and threw his support behind the candidacy of William Lemke of North Dakota in the 1936 election. However, Lemke attracted only 892,000 votes, deflating the Coughlin movement. The "radio priest" did, however, remain on the air into the next decade, spouting even more inflammatory rhetoric and ultimately endorsing the anti-Semitic ideology of Adolf Hitler.

Less demonstrative but ultimately more effective than either Long or Coughlin was Dr. Francis E. Townsend of California. Shocked by the spectacle of many penniless, aged Americans living as hobos, Townsend called for the creation of old-age pensions, proposing that every person over 60 receive a monthly stipend of $200, so long as the individual agreed to spend the entire amount each month and earn no other income. According to the retired physician, this plan would revitalize the economy, as well as help the elderly, because their purchases would stimulate the job market. Soon more than 5 million people had joined Townsend Clubs. Roosevelt and his advisors paid attention to these geriatric voters; in 1935, the Social Security system became law.

Throughout FDR's first administration, he believed, like Herbert Hoover before him, that balancing the federal budget was one of the keys to pulling the country out of the Depression. But early in his second term, he began to listen to such advisors as Harry Hopkins of the WPA and Secretary of the Interior Harold Ickes who were fascinated by the theories of British economist John Maynard Keynes. Keynes hypothesized that deficit spending would stimulate factory production, create jobs and put enough money into people's pockets that they would pick up their level of consumption. In short, Keynes reasoned that governments could spend their way out of economic tailspins. Following the disastrous decision to curtail federal spending programs in 1937 and the resultant recession, Roosevelt finally agreed to heavy deficit spending and, in April 1938, the New Deal pushed a $3.75 billion public works bill through Congress.

The work projects developed and funded by the government were spectacular in their variety, from the building of hospitals, roads and schools to the composing of songs, the writing of plays and the painting of murals. It was a time when a multitude of artists, as well as bureaucrats, teachers, unskilled laborers and scientists, picked up paychecks from Uncle Sam.

One of the most volatile relationships of the 1930s and 1940s involved labor and management. Generally speaking, the Roosevelt administration supported the union movement. The New Deal put an end to child labor, established minimum wages and maximum hours and guaranteed the right of workers to organize and bargain collectively. The National Labor Relations Act of 1935 (called the "Wagner Act" after its sponsor, Senator Robert Wagner of New York) and the Fair Labor Standards Act of 1938 formalized these rights and stimulated the growth of union membership. Approximately 3.6 million workers belonged to unions in 1934; that number had grown to more than 9 million in 1941.

Despite these laws, the gains of organized labor did not come without recalcitrant, often angry, opposition from management. The first "sit down" strikes were called by the United Auto Workers against General Motors in 1936. Refusing to bargain, GM executives expressed outrage over the disruption of their assembly lines and the illegal seizure of their property. There were also episodes of violence during the 44-day shutdown, but the union eventually won. Much bloodier battles were fought before the steel industry finally acquiesced to unionization and collective bargaining. President Roosevelt, shocked by the bloodshed and stung by critics from the business world who accused him of "creeping socialism," retreated, refusing to support labor's 1937 drive to organize new industries.

Internecine strife also affected labor's own house. In 1935, John L. Lewis of the United Mine Workers and officials of the garment trade unions formed the Committee for Industrial Organization (CIO) and began to organize unskilled laborers into a union that would disregard craft lines. This move was in direct defiance of the conservative American Federation of Labor (AFL), the large "roof organization" under which a number of different unions cohered. Unions supporting the CIO were suspended by the AFL in 1936; they soon came together in their own umbrella structure, one which represented the automobile, steel, rubber and other industries. By 1938, the CIO had changed its name to the Congress of Industrial Organizations, its unions had fought some of the most violent and successful battles with intransigent managements and its membership had skyrocketed, making it a formidable rival to the hidebound AFL.

Perhaps America's most important group of workers – its farmers – had no large labor organization to help them through a period of continuing difficulties. While the 1920s were an exciting and prosperous time for many Americans, they were anything but happy years for those who earned their livings from the soil. Even though agricultural prices declined rapidly after the close of World War I, the Republicans in power at the time made almost no effort to aid agrarian interests. It is little wonder that so many rural Americans abandoned their farms for city life during the decade.

The onset of the Depression brought further price erosion and continuing inaction from the Hoover administration. The New Deal, of course, did implement a number of initiatives, including the controversial Agricultural Adjustment Act of 1933 which attempted to boost crop prices by requiring farmers to curtail output and subsidizing them for their cooperation. In a public relations gaffe, Secretary of Agriculture Henry A. Wallace decided to pay farmers to destroy crops and slaughter swine in 1933. Many jobless individuals, worried about the source of their families' next meals, were outraged by the tactic.

Although the Supreme Court declared the AAA unconstitutional in 1936, the New Deal continued to assist one of Roosevelt's most loyal political constituencies. It gained Congressional approval for the Soil Conservation and Domestic Allotment Act, which accomplished a lot of the same things that the AAA had, and both the Tennessee Valley Authority and the Rural Electrification Administration (REA) helped farmers obtain cheap electricity and other benefits. For many, this support was still not enough. A horrific drought afflicted the midwest from 1934 to 1936, forcing thousands to abandon the

"Dust Bowl." Their migration westward became a journey of disappointment for farmers who believed they would find a better life in California. Many found, instead, a world almost as bleak as the one they had left behind.

The war finally turned things around for farmers, as it did for so many others. Agricultural output and income both doubled between 1941 and 1945, in response to heavy demand for products from both the military and civilian sectors. By the end of World War II, farmers' incomes had reached an all-time high.

A triumphant time for the advocates of Keynesian theory, the World War II era saw the national debt balloon from $49 billion in 1941 to almost $260 billion when the Japanese surrendered in 1945. This money and more, much of it spent on superheated production of combat machinery, helped create millions of new jobs. Unemployment was quickly banished from the American scene, and the Depression, an unwelcome guest who had stubbornly refused to depart for more than a dozen years, was suddenly booted out of the national door. As President Roosevelt put it, "Dr. New Deal" had become "Dr. Win-the-War." The medicine dispensed by the latter proved to be far more popular and effective than any of the prescriptions offered by the former.

The industrial output of the United States during the war years was extraordinary. Henry J. Kaiser's shipbuilding company, for example, required 355 days to produce a Liberty ship in 1941. Before the war's conclusion, Kaiser workers had cut the average delivery time of these basic cargo vessels to 56 days; they even managed to complete one Liberty ship in two weeks. During this period, US factories built 71,000 warships, 300,000 aircraft, and 2.4 military trucks. Without question, America won World War II in the plants at home as well as on the battlefields abroad.

Deficit spending could not pay for everything. Taxes, which had risen throughout the Depression, especially on corporations and upper-income Americans, were increased substantially during the war. By 1945, yearly incomes over $200,000 were being taxed at a rate of 94 percent and excess profits at 95 percent. In addition, taxes were imposed for the first time on many lower-income workers. In 1939, only 4 million people earned large enough salaries to pay taxes; in 1945, 42.7 million belonged to the tax-paying ranks. Since the money was going to the defense of their country, few spoke out against the levies. The implementation of the payroll deduction system, which required employers to withhold a portion of each individual's yearly assessment from his or her paycheck, helped the treasury collect the needed revenues and made the process more palatable to most wage earners. More than 40 percent of the cost of winning the war was covered by taxes.

Government and private enterprise formed a remarkable partnership that was responsible for the leap in productivity during the war. Labor contributed mightily as well. There were few strikes during the initial period, though work stoppages did escalate as time went on and it became clear that the US would be victorious. In 1945, 38 million production hours were lost to strikes, whereas they only consumed a bit more than 4 million hours in 1942. Union membership continued its propulsive growth. By the end of World War II, 15 million Americans belonged to labor organizations, setting the stage for a highly aggressive post-war movement on behalf of workers.

The years between Pearl Harbor and Nagasaki provided a multitude of challenges to America's creative scientists. These inventive minds delivered radar, synthetic rubber, new plastics, new vaccines, DDT, high frequency shortwave radio, jet airplanes, atomic energy and a host of other breakthroughs that would help to hasten the war's end and affect life after 1945 in profound ways.

When V-J Day finally came, Americans were producing half of the world's goods and had the highest standard of living on the planet. Despite these facts and the spirit of unity and achievement that animated the times, life at home during World War II was not without its hardships. Many items, including gasoline, tires, shoes and various foodstuffs, were rationed, severely limiting opportunities for vacation travel and other forms of pleasurable relaxation. Inflation began to rise early in the era; although the government attempted to keep it in check through the imposition of wage and price controls, it remained a reality, taking a solid bite, along with the income taxes, out of disposable income. Additionally, a numbing fear hovered over the nation throughout the war – the fear that the Depression would return to America as soon as the conflict concluded. While the post-1945 world would contain a number of unpleasantries, this dire scenario, thankfully, would not be among them.

Societal Issues

The "Lost Generation" of American writers began publishing messages of angst and disillusionment in the 1920s. F. Scott Fitzgerald, Ernest Hemingway, T.S. Eliot, William Faulkner, Ezra Pound and others, most of them residing in Europe, expressed outrage over the brutal carnage of World War I and cheerlessly predicted an even more difficult and inhumane future. Their works would become cornerstones of twentieth-century literary and intellectual history.

At home, however, these apocalyptic warnings were lost on the majority of their countrymen and women. Proud to have been on the victorious side in the war and dazzled by a world filled with rapidly expanding possibilities, most Americans viewed their lives to come with optimism.

One of the greatest social changes of the decade was wrought by the automobile. Heretofore considered a luxury item, cars became affordable in the mid-1920s when Henry Ford's innovative mass production methods reduced the cost of a Model T to $280. The rapid development of the auto as a consumer product caused the government to embark on a highway building program that resulted in the creation of more than 750,000 miles of blacktop by 1929.

The social impact of the "automobile culture" was wide-ranging. In addition to stimulating a variety of industries (petroleum, glass, rubber, trucking, insurance, travel, etc.) and creating thousands of jobs, it provided a new and special sense of freedom for Americans. Rural areas were no longer isolated, leisure time activities were enlarged and the courting habits of teenagers were changed forever. The 1920s migration from farms and small towns to the metropolis was partially inspired and accomplished by the bracing mobility that cars provided. By the end of the decade, 26.5 million vehicles cruised through the landscape.

The love affair between Americans and their cars was just one aspect of the rapidly developing consumer consciousness already mentioned in earlier sections. This, like many other aspects of life in the 1920s, was a rebellion against the Victorian repression and self-denial which had dominated society before World War I. Other visible manifestations of the replacement of the old temperance by a new pleasure ethic included falling church attendance, the emergence of jazz music, increasingly frank approaches to sexuality, a fascination with Freud's revolutionary ideas about the unconscious mind and its effect on human behavior and, of course, the flagrant defiance of Prohibition by many Americans.

The fervent embrace of change was perhaps best reflected in the appearance of the "new" woman. This "flapper" now had the right to vote (she had won that right in the suffrage amendment of 1920), but she appeared more interested in the right to party – to smoke cigarettes, drink bootleg liquor, wear silk stockings and knee-length, loose-fitting dresses and dance the Charleston and Black Bottom in urban speakeasies. Her devotion to hedonistic pursuits, combined with similar predilections on the part of many males, took a toll on traditional family life; by 1929, the divorce rate was triple its 1890 level.

Another flamboyant indication of the new order was the sudden appearance of the criminal-as-celebrity, as larger-than-life embodiment of overnight success. For many gangsters like Al(phonse) Capone of Chicago, Prohibition was the most wonderful constitutional amendment ever enacted in the country's history. They made millions supplying the needs of alcohol-consuming Americans who had no intention of obeying this particular legal deterrent. Many members of the "bathtub gin" crowd viewed Capone and his ilk as Robin Hood figures who took the risks and deserved the rewards of their dangerous profession. They seemed no worse than the corrupt politicos who were unmasked in Washington during the same era, profiting from such scandals as Teapot Dome and Elk Hills. Romanticized views of Capone and other criminals overlooked the brutal methods that they used to establish and hold their respective turfs and the more unsavory activities that complemented their distribution of illegal booze. Nevertheless, many members of the public marveled at the ability of big-time mobsters to avoid prosecution and the government's inability to thwart their unlawful businesses.

Not everyone approved, however, of the flapper with her bobbed hair or idolized the bejeweled gangster, nor was every American persuaded to join the new army of consumers and acquire all the new gadgets on display in their local department stores. Millions of more conservative citizens watched the changing social scene in utter dismay. Members of this traditionalist constituency had fought for Prohibition in the first place and continued to support it, despite its evident failure.

Protestant fundamentalists, repelled by most of the new ideas and fads, were especially disturbed by Charles Darwin's theory of evolution. Darwin's belief that humans evolved from lower life forms, rather than being created by God as detailed in the Biblical book of Genesis, caused an uproar, especially when teachers began tentatively to discuss Darwin in their classrooms. The battle between fundamentalists who believed only in "divine creation" and progressive thinkers who accepted Darwin's theories climaxed in the famous Scopes trial of 1925. The trial in Dayton, Tennessee turned into a fascinating philosophical debate between former Presidential candidate and Biblical scholar William Jennings Bryan and liberal attorney Clarence Darrow, with a technicality allowing both sides to claim final victory. The actual outcome forbade John Thomas Scopes and other Tennessee educators from presenting the evolutionary doctrine to their students. Fundamentalist Christians would perhaps be the least surprised members of their society when the Depression enfolded America; to them, the economic crisis represented a fitting punishment for the repudiation of formerly cherished beliefs and values by their fellow Americans. Although far removed from the "Lost Generation" in practically every way, these bedrock conservatives viewed the future with the same degree of trepidation as the expatriate authors.

The 1930s brought widespread disillusionment to the country. The Great

Depression was obviously catastrophic from an economic standpoint, but its psychological impact was every bit as acute. "The only thing we have to fear is fear itself," said Franklin D. Roosevelt in his first inaugural address. The line may seem rather facile when one considers the homes, possessions, savings and livelihoods that many Americans had lost by the time FDR uttered these famous words in 1933. But Roosevelt intuitively understood the level of fright that afflicted so many lives when he became President and recognized that one of the New Deal's primary missions would be to restore his people's confidence and their hopes for the future. Americans had to believe there would be a happy ending to all this hardship.

Roosevelt's "brain trust" of university-educated advisors set about creating an active and visible government that soon began to touch individual citizens in many tangible ways, while the President spoke regularly and reassuringly to them over the radio. The "fireside chats" were part information and part politics, but mostly they were therapy – psychological counseling for a nation suffering through a collective nervous breakdown. Studs Terkel's oral history of the Depression, *Hard Times*, is replete with the memories of people ashamed of their inability to handle the contemporary difficulties. Although bewildered about the causes of the crisis, they often seemed to feel personally responsible for their plight, as if they had brought it on themselves and were the only ones incapable of restoring order to their lives. Roosevelt had to help these people overcome their feelings of inadequacy and shame, and he did it the best way he could – by putting as many of them as possible to work. Once individuals were productive again, once they were able to provide for themselves and their families, their psychological dejection began to lift.

Many of the New Deal programs were innovative and quite radical compared to legislation enacted by previous administrations. But this was not a time for indulgence or risk-taking by most members of society. The spirit of the 1920s had been individualistic, iconoclastic and animated; the spirit of the 1930s was communal, conformist and tempered. Trying times practically demanded a return to traditional family values, to abstinence and thrift. People indulged their dreams of wealth and power by playing "Monopoly," one of the most popular board games of the era, instead of the stock market. They studied Dale Carnegie's *How to Win Friends and Influence People*, which taught them to stifle their own egos and make others feel important as a means to achieve personal success. They became "joiners" – of clubs, groups, teams, unions. Being part of a collective was reassuring; it provided a sense of identity, of belonging, and it separated them from the period's most wretched individualists, its hobos and vagabonds.

The nation's most obstreperous entrepreneurs – its high-profile criminals – continued to make headlines. Prohibition was over by the end of 1933, but legal liquor could not immediately cancel the Robin Hood image of the racketeer. The Capone mob, for example, set up soup kitchens to feed hungry Chicagoans during the worst days of the Depression. It was difficult to condemn a group who seemed to care more about your welfare than anyone else did.

Another bunch of nonconformists who amazed the public with their recklessness – the itinerant bank robbers – represented the most extreme solution to Depression want. John Dillinger, "Pretty Boy" Floyd, "Baby Face" Nelson, Bonnie and Clyde and the "Ma" Baker gang all gained notoriety by seizing the assets of the country's most disliked white-collar genus – the banker. Floyd is reputed to have burned mortgages whenever he knocked over a bank, thereby earning the gratitude of local farmers and homeowners.

Vying with these outlaws for public attention was the emerging Bureau of Investigation (later the Federal Bureau of Investigation/FBI). Although the Bureau had been in existence since 1908, its agents were not allowed to carry guns until 1933. As soon as his troops were armed, Bureau chief J. Edgar Hoover began a public relations campaign to glorify the crime fighter and de-glamorize the criminal. He established the "Public Enemies" list, plastering miscreants' pictures in public places and loudly celebrating whenever one of his most wanted crooks was brought to justice. At the end of 1935, Capone was in prison and Dillinger, Floyd, Nelson, Baker and her son Fred and Bonnie and Clyde were all dead, most killed by the G-Men. By that time, Hoover had succeeded in turning his agents into national heroes, while the concept of the law breaker as Robin Hood seemed as dead as the legendary British outlaw himself.

Even though the Civil War had ended more than 60 years earlier, African Americans continued to live as second-class citizens throughout the 1930s. Segregated housing, schools, restaurants and public transit were the norm in the southern US and commonplace in other parts of the nation as well. For blacks, the Depression was even more devastating than it was for other segments of the population; the level of black unemployment consistently exceeded that of white unemployment, and blacks who did work were generally forced to accept a lesser wage than that earned by whites for identical toil. New Deal programs carried on this discriminatory practice, as well as excluding blacks from some of the advantages of the agricultural initiatives and segregating those who were hired by the CCC, the TVA and other agencies.

President Roosevelt's record on civil rights was basically a blank page, yet African Americans venerated him and became enthusiastic members of his political coalition. Deserting the Republican party of Abraham Lincoln, which had been responsible for their liberation from slavery, they supported FDR and the Democrats because they believed the New Deal was doing more for them than the previous succession of Republican administrations ever had and because of the outspoken advocacy they received from Roosevelt's wife, Eleanor.

Mrs. Roosevelt championed the rights of African Americans throughout her years in the White House and afterwards. Her efforts almost certainly did have a positive impact on the hiring and advancement of blacks by the government and helped to elevate their status throughout the society. One incident is telling: in 1939, the Daughters of the American Resolution (DAR) refused to allow Marian Anderson to give a concert in Washington's Constitution Hall. Mrs. Roosevelt resigned from the organization and arranged for the black singer to perform on federal property near the Lincoln Memorial. A few months thereafter, the First Lady presented Anderson with the Springarn Medal, an award for achievement given by the National Association for the Advancement of Colored People (NAACP). While her politically astute husband, ever mindful of the votes of white southerners, tempered whatever feelings he had for black causes, Eleanor Roosevelt was persistently vocal on their behalf.

African Americans became more militant during World War II. Although expected to contribute wholeheartedly to the unified effort, they still faced discrimination at every turn. This fundamental irony was not lost on them – they were being asked to commit themselves to a crusade against a blatantly racist enemy in order to protect a society that gave only lip service to the cherished belief that "all men are created equal." Examples of the discriminatory practices of the time: the military welcomed black soldiers, then funneled them into their own segregated units; black blood plasma was distinguished from white plasma, even though there was no medical reason for this and the process for storing the life-giving component had been discovered by black doctor Charles Drew; blacks found new jobs in the defense plants, but rarely received training in highly skilled positions or were promoted to supervisory posts.

Some positive change did occur over time. The CIO, which had begun enrolling black members in the 1930s, added thousands to its ranks during the war. The Navy integrated the crews of 25 vessels, the Air Corps commissioned some 600 black pilots and the Army ordered its training camps desegregated in 1944, though not all of them were. Still, these and other efforts to give a fair shake to African Americans and additional minority groups (such as Hispanics and Native Americans) were halfhearted at best. Angry, emphatic calls for change, foreshadowed by the enormous growth of the NAACP and by violent race riots in Detroit, New York and Los Angeles during the war years, would come after America's enemies had fired their final shots.

The battle against the Axis provided a positive psychic antidote to Depression anxiety for most Americans. Whether they were in uniform or not, worked in a defense plant or some trade unrelated to the war effort, all Americans were made to feel part of the great crusade. War bonds, the Red Cross, the United Service Organizations (USO), union no-strike pledges, rationing, newspaper reports of combat developments, FDR's radio chats, posted reminders that "loose lips sink ships" and innumerable other cues combined to create a wartime consciousness that challenged every individual to contribute to the victory team. Moreover, as the great battles began to be won and Uncle Sam's factories began to outstrip even the government's optimistic production estimates, a feeling of noble accomplishment and satisfaction spread through the land. The fact that most people had jobs and spending money in their pockets didn't hurt either. The war gave Americans back their self-confidence.

This self-confidence was reflected in a striking increase in marriages and births. The US population, which had grown by only 3 million during the 1930s, shot up by 6.5 million during the first half of the 1940s. Unfortunately, the divorce rate also rose markedly, perhaps as a result of many rushed and ill-advised unions prompted by the departure of soldiers for the combat zone.

World War II made an especially powerful impact on American women. In response to the predominantly male military buildup and the need to boost production, approximately 8 million females entered the workforce between 1940 and 1945. Many labored in defense plants that built submarines, tanks and fighter planes and a number proved they could handle jobs that had previously belonged only to men, such as riveting, welding and heavy machine operation. At first, many members of the "Rosie the Riveter" brigade viewed their efforts as just another sacrifice for the cause; they had no intention of continuing to work when the war ended. But as time went on, more and more came to enjoy the blandishments their salaries bought them, as well as the feeling of independence and achievement that work added to their lives. By 1945, the thought of giving up their positions and incomes for a return to the domestic sphere was not so appealing to many women workers. They had tasted liberation and liked its flavor (see Figure 1.3).

An unfortunate byproduct of the entry of thousands of mothers into the labor force was the growing absence of supervision for their children. During the war, many youngsters came home from school to an empty house or apartment. Lacking guidance and discipline from their elders, they were soon on the streets with predictable results. Juvenile delinquency soared, especially in cities like San Diego where defense plants operated 24 hours a day.

Another disturbing aspect of World War II was the nation's venomous

Figure 1.3　A female worker tightens down the engine cowling of a P-38 fighter plane at the Lockheed plant in the Los Angeles area, 1943. Courtesy of the USC Doheny Library Department of Special Collections.

hatred of the Japanese. Although the US was also at war with Germany and Italy, Americans were infinitely more tolerant of people with German and Italian blood than they were of the Japanese enemy. Much of the loathing had its roots in the "sneak" attack on Pearl Harbor, but it was also a racist response to a culture that few understood or cared to understand. The Japanese were consistently stereotyped as sub-human by the media; the most popular incarnation was the buck-toothed, slant-eyed monkey, apparently spawned by the devil.

Sadly, Japanese Americans were not exempted from the vicious propaganda. General John L. DeWitt, head of the West Coast Defense Command, put it this way: "A Jap's a Jap . . . It makes no difference whether he is an American citizen or not. I don't want any of them . . . There is no way to determine their loyalty." Similar thinking prompted the government to order the relocation of more than 100,000 Japanese Americans to 10 camps in seven western states where they were kept under guard. The similarities between these camps and the concentration camps of America's enemies remain among the war's crueler ironies. Despite the fact that no proof of their disloyalty was ever offered, these people lost their jobs, their homes, most of their possessions. Many were psychologically traumatized by the experience. Even the achievements of the 442 Regimental Combat Team, a Japanese American unit that fought valiantly during the Italian campaign, had little impact on prevailing attitudes. Antagonism toward the Japanese and Japanese Americans would continue, even after the war ended and the camps were cleared. Given the fact that World War II was fought, at least partially, to smash the contemptible racist beliefs of the Nazis, the ugly Japanese stereotyping and unjustified relocation seem especially ill-conceived. They are, perhaps, the most lamentable aspects of this generally unified and laudable period in American social history.

Hollywood Responds to the Crises

Buoyed by the novelty of sound movies, movie companies enjoyed fulsome profits in 1929 and 1930. Indeed, early in 1930 some of their leaders began to believe that their business was "Depression-proof." By the end of that year, however, it was clear that the troubled economic situation was going to have a significant negative impact on theater attendance. The years 1932 and 1933 were terrible for Hollywood, as well as for the rest of American commerce. Studios responded by dismissing many employees, cutting salaries, closing theaters and reducing the average cost of their productions. But even these measures could not prevent RKO and Paramount from falling into receivership. The accounting ledgers of other major studios were also glutted with red ink.

Many studies of Hollywood during the Depression suggest that its product was overwhelmingly "escapist," i.e. designed to provide a couple of hours of mindless relief from the miseries of the decade. On one level this is true; very few feature films depicted the "hard times" in realistic or penetrating fashion. But it would be wrong to infer that Hollywood filmmakers pretended the economic convulsion didn't exist in their creations. In fact, the Depression was a major shaping force on many 1930s motion pictures.

These efforts were remarkably varied. The gangster films offered characters who refused to accept the limited prospects of the period but paid dearly for their decision to take a shortcut to success. Similarly, the "fallen woman" pictures of the early 30s featured protagonists who compromise their virtue and reputations for money. Money was also a near obsession in many contemporary comedies. *We're Rich Again* (RKO, 1934), which focused on a family desperately scrambling to return to the realm of the millionaires, was a typical title. *My Man Godfrey* (Universal, 1936) attempted to suggest a strategy whereby the well-to-do could help the poor without resorting to charity. Musicals such as *Top Hat* (RKO, 1935) were among the most escapist pictures of the time, but some, like *42nd Street* (Warner Bros., 1933) and other backstage stories did dramatize contemporary realities. They suggested that unity, teamwork and perseverance were viable solutions to the challenges of the time. More radical ideas, from American acceptance of a political dictatorship (*Gabriel over the White House*, MGM, 1933) to a socialistic approach to land management (*Our Daily Bread*, Viking/United Artists, 1934), were greeted with considerably less enthusiasm by the public. Much more palatable was the benevolent altruism proposed by Longfellow Deeds in *Mr. Deeds Goes to Town* (Columbia, 1936).

All the major studios survived the worst days of the Depression. As the decade drew on and tickets sales slowly began to increase, most of the studios began making profits again. But their leaders had not forgotten the dark days of the early 30s. They kept costs under control and continued to feed the public a steady diet of uplifting, reassuring motion pictures. In the romantic realm of 1930s Hollywood entertainment, heroes triumph, villains are punished, love conquers all, benevolent political leadership is assured and dreams come true. Even though surely confounded and disillusioned by the staying power of the Depression, movie patrons never stopped going to the movies and never stopped believing in these movie myths.

The transition from a public obsession with the Depression to a public obsession with the war took place in the late 30s and early 40s. In February 1939, Pandro Berman, head of production at RKO, sent a telegram to director George Stevens informing him that corporate president George Schaefer had vetoed his request to make *The Mortal Storm* or *Address Unknown*. Since both literary works were anti-Fascist, Schaefer's reasons were politically motivated. As Berman told Stevens, the president was "afraid [to] commit us to any picture that is propaganda against anything."

George Schaefer's attitude was shared by most of the other studio executives. Fearful of the isolationist convictions of most of their domestic customers and determined to protect their foreign markets, the men who made the movies had no enthusiasm for screen stories dealing with the rapidly deteriorating European situation. The industry's self-censorship apparatus, the Production Code Administration (PCA), also actively discouraged the production of such pictures (see chapter 4).

Nevertheless, a few Hollywood insiders managed to fashion films that bucked the trend. The leaders in this regard were Harry and Jack Warner of Warner Bros. Appalled by the Nazis' anti-Semitic policies, the Warners stopped exporting their films to Germany in 1936. In 1939, they made the first true anti-Nazi picture, *Confessions of a Nazi Spy*, which opened four months before the outbreak of World War II. Following their lead came such titles as *Escape* (MGM, 1940), *The Mortal Storm* (MGM, 1940), *The Great Dictator* (Chaplin/United Artists, 1940), *Four Sons* (Twentieth Century-Fox, 1940), *The Man I Married* (Twentieth Century-Fox, 1941), *Underground* (Warner Bros., 1941) and a handful of other unflattering portrayals of Hitler and Mussolini and their followers. With the exception of *Confessions of a Nazi Spy*, none was particularly realistic or hard-hitting, though *The Great Dictator* was a major success at the box office.

Even though the progress of the war had cost Hollywood most of its European markets by the end of 1940, the studio heads remained reticent to dramatize the biggest story of the day. Acutely aware that a majority of Americans were determined to keep their country out of the conflict, they cranked out hundreds of features that contained no reference to Europe or to war at all.

Despite the industry's timidity, a few politicians became upset by the films that did depict the European "problem." Senators Gerald P. Nye from North Dakota, Burton K. Wheeler from Montana and Bennett (Champ) Clark from Missouri, egged on by the isolationist America First Committee, interpreted these movies as an overt effort to steer the United States into World War II. Calling Hollywood "a raging volcano of war fever," Nye prodded Congress into conducting an investigation into "pro-war" propaganda in motion pictures.

The Senate Subcommittee on War Propaganda began its "preliminary hearings" in September 1941. In addition to the anti-Fascist productions, it also focused on films that it considered "pro-war" such as *I Wanted Wings* (Paramount, 1941), *Sergeant York* (Warner Bros., 1941) and *Dive Bomber* (Warner Bros., 1941). The industry mounted a spirited defense, based primarily on free speech issues and spearheaded by former Presidential candidate Wendell Willkie. This defense, combined with the disorganized and poorly presented government case, caused the hearings to fall apart in October. Though the investigation could technically have continued at a later date, it was emphatically put to death by the bombing of Pearl Harbor in December 1941.

Signaling the beginning of a new period of unprecedented cooperation between the government and Hollywood, President Roosevelt stated shortly after the Japanese attack, "The American motion picture is one of our most effective mediums in informing and entertaining our citizens." By that time, studio heads had begun to rethink their production plans. They instinctively recognized that the public, as well as the government, would expect to see movies that foregrounded the war effort, underlining the importance of the battle against the European and Pacific enemies and the necessity for all Americans to unite and contribute to the effort. (Figure 1.3)

And in a remarkably short time, the studios came through. The 1942 and 1943 release years were crowded with topical dramas and comedies. Formerly moribund genres, such as the war film and the espionage drama, came roaring back to life and nearly every genre found ways to accommodate the nation's overarching obsession with the conflict (see chapter 6). This was a time when everyone from Sherlock Holmes (*Sherlock Holmes and the Secret Weapon*, Universal, 1942), and the invisible man (*The Invisible Agent*, Universal, 1942) to cowboys (*Riders of the Northland*, Columbia, 1942) and gangsters (*Seven Miles from Alcatraz*, RKO, 1942) battled the Germans and Japanese on theater screens.

The number of war-themed pictures began to decline in 1944. Audiences indicated a growing weariness with the topic and a desire for more movies that would take their minds off contemporary events. Still, perhaps to keep the government happy, the studios continued to produce a significant number of combat films and home front stories. The Hollywood executives were richly rewarded for their efforts. With spending money in their pockets and few entertainment alternatives, stateside workers flocked to their local theaters. Consequently, several of the studios posted record profits during the war years.

This is not to suggest that the period between 1942 and 1945 was without difficulties for studio executives. Production units were hit hard by the rationing of set building materials and raw film stock. This forced industry leaders to cut back on their productions and re-jigger their release patterns. By the end of the war, the studios were turning out about 30 percent fewer films than they had been at its beginning. But audiences did not seem to mind; films stayed in theaters longer than they had in previous years, and some members of the audience watched their favorites again and again.

A more formidable problem was the loss of hundreds of studio employees who enlisted or were drafted into the military. Even though motion pictures were considered an essential industry by Selective Service, a majority of male studio workers eschewed deferments and put on uniforms. These included such top-ranked talents as actors Clark Gable, James Stewart, Henry Fonda, Tyrone Power, Mickey Rooney and Robert Montgomery and directors Frank Capra, John Ford, William Wyler, John Huston and George Stevens. While the actors were certainly missed, the studios responded by making good use of the male stars who remained in Hollywood (Errol Flynn, Cary Grant, John Wayne, Gary Cooper, Bob Hope, Bing Crosby, Humphrey Bogart) and introducing some fresh new faces who were quickly embraced by the public (Gregory Peck, Van Johnson, Dana Andrews, Gene Kelly, Alan Ladd, Robert Walker). The production heads also gave opportunities to a number of inexperienced directors; some, like Vincente Minnelli, Fred Zinnemann, Billy Wilder, Robert Wise and Mark Robson, made the most of those opportunities.

The industry's commitment to the war effort stretched far beyond the creation of patriotic, morale-boosting movies. Hollywood professionals made training films and public service shorts. Its newsreel subsidiaries dispatched reporters and cameramen to the battle zones; their reports, screened in theaters on a regular basis, provided the only visual record of what American soldiers were accomplishing. Many stars, including Bob Hope, Dorothy Lamour, Bing Crosby, Marlene Dietrich and Hedy Lamarr, toured the country selling war bonds and were ubiquitous on radio broadcasts, hawking the bonds and exhorting the folks at home to contribute to the war effort in a multitude of ways. They also staffed the "Hollywood Canteen," where off-duty soldiers lucky enough to be stationed in southern California could dance with Joan Leslie or eat a meal served by Bette Davis. Hollywood personalities also traveled overseas to entertain the men and women in uniform. Even if soldiers never made it to the Hollywood Canteen or to a USO show featuring their favorites, they received a psychological boost from the pin up photographs provided by the studios. Sent out by the millions, these cheesecake pictures of Betty Grable, Rita Hayworth, Jane Russell and others were treasured by the men at arms who hauled them along to their foxholes and painted facsimiles of the American beauties on the noses of bomber planes. For many GIs, these gorgeous women epitomized what they were fighting for.

The government responded in kind, providing military advisors and, sometimes, military equipment and personnel to upgrade the quality and "realism" of the studios' battle pictures. It also set up an office in the movie capital (the Office of War Information Bureau of Motion Pictures) to help screenwriters fashion scripts that would strengthen the war effort (see chapter 4). And it suspended its investigation into the alleged monopolistic distribution practices of the companies that owned theater chains. Hollywood and Washington, in effect, were "married" for the duration of World War II. The union would not endure, but it would certainly benefit both parties while it lasted.

Other Leisure Activities

Moviegoing was a highly popular activity between 1929 and 1945, but there were other forms of entertainment that actively competed with Hollywood for the public's money and leisure time. Some of these involved minimal costs; crossword puzzles, for example, were a fad in the 20s and jigsaw puzzles became fashionable in the frugal 30s. Throughout the period, participation in swimming, tennis, softball and other sports became increasingly commonplace.

Much more closely related to film were such entertainment alternatives as radio, vaudeville, popular music, popular fiction and nonfiction, comic strips and comic books, live theater and spectator sports. These forms often intersected with Hollywood, affecting the film business and being affected by it. The following is a brief survey of developments in each of these leisure industries.

Radio

By the end of the 1920s, radio was well on its way to becoming the mass medium of American life. Dating from November 2, 1920 when station KDKA in Pittsburgh presented the first public program, radio broadcasting grew at a breathtaking pace during its formative years. Hundreds of stations popped up across the nation and hundreds of millions of consumer dollars were spent to acquire home receivers. Beginning in 1927, one could even have a radio installed in the car, and many drivers did.

The problem of how to turn radio into an income-generating enterprise was solved by the introduction of "commercials" – sponsored advertisements for products and services interjected into program content. That content was mostly music at first, but soon widened to encompass news, sports, comedy and drama. RCA, a leader in the production and sale of radio sets, also became a pioneer in the networking of stations. In the last half of the 20s, RCA strung together two national chains, known as NBC-Blue and NBC-Red; increased penetration meant better programming and the creation of a broad-based, homogenized listening audience that clicked on its favorite programs nearly every day. The end of the decade saw three major networks, as CBS emerged to compete with the two NBC aggregates.

By that time radio had its first "blockbuster" show: "Amos 'n' Andy." Freeman Gosden and Charles Correll, two white dialect comedians who played a variety of black characters on their NBC program, took the nation by storm. Though its popularity would level off in the 1930s, "Amos 'n' Andy" remained a staple broadcast offering for more than 20 years. Other early shows that developed enthusiastic followings included "The Rise of the Goldbergs" (later, "The Goldbergs"), an ethnic comedy set in the Jewish ghetto of New York City, and "The Rudy Vallee Show," a breakthrough variety program that featured crooner Vallee, his "Connecticut Yankee" band and appearances by top comedians, actors and vocalists.

The Depression affected radio, though much less harshly than it impacted most other US industries. Sales of sets declined in the early 1930s and so, apparently, did the size of the listening audience (audience measuring devices at this time were so primitive that it is impossible to be sure). However, radio's dog days were short-lived. By 1934, NBC was grossing more than $28 million and CBS almost $15 million. In that year a fourth network – the Mutual Broadcasting System – joined the competition.

Radio prospered by offering a varied menu of programs that appealed to every class, sex, age and ethnic group, and by introducing a flock of new stars whose shows attracted huge followings. Kids thrilled to the adventures of "Buck Rogers in the 25th Century," "Jack Armstrong," "Frank Merriwell," "Rin-Tin-Tin," "Superman," "Captain Midnight" and "The Lone Ranger." Mom followed the tribulations of her favorite soap opera characters on "One Man's Family," "The Romance of Helen Trent," "Stella Dallas," "The Guiding Light" and "Ma Perkins." Dad tuned in to the exploits of such smart, tough crime fighters as "Ellery Queen," "Bulldog Drummond," "The Shadow" and "Mr. District Attorney." The whole family was likely to gather round for favorite comedians Jack Benny, Fred Allen, Bob Hope, Fibber McGee and Molly, George Burns and Gracie Allen and ventriloquist Edgar Bergen and his acerbic dummy, Charlie McCarthy. Equally popular were variety shows hosted by Eddie Cantor, Bing Crosby, Kate Smith, Al Jolson and George Jessel, and the serious dramatic offerings of "The Lux Radio Theatre" (hosted by Cecil B. DeMille), "Mercury Theatre of the Air" (hosted by Orson Welles), "The Columbia Workshop" and "Campbell Playhouse."

When new trends arose, radio embraced them enthusiastically. The popularity of "Major Bowes' Original Amateur Hour," introduced in 1935, prompted a number of similar programs on both network and local stations. The nation's infatuation with swing music, beginning in 1936, resulted in the creation of new shows featuring the big band sounds of Tommy Dorsey, Benny Goodman, Duke Ellington, Glenn Miller, Guy Lombardo and others. Quiz programs were the hottest fad of the late 30s; they ranged from "Information, Please!" with Clifton Fadiman and "The World Game" with Max Eastman to musical puzzlers such as "Kay Kyser's Kollege of Musical Knowledge" and "Beat the Band" with Ted Weems. There were even satirical parodies: "It Pays to be Ignorant" and "Can You Top This?"

Americans also became heavily dependent on radio for news of world affairs. As mentioned, President Roosevelt used the medium to provide New Deal updates mixed with psychological reassurance from 1933 on. The kidnapping of Charles Lindbergh's baby in 1932, the abdication of British King Edward VIII in 1936, the tragic explosion of the German dirigible "Hindenberg" in 1937, the outbreak of World War II in 1939 and other momentous events of the time were reported and analyzed by such newsmen as Robert Trout, Lowell Thomas, Gabriel Heatter, Edward R. Murrow and H.V. Kaltenborn. Indeed, by 1938 the public was so conditioned to accept the veracity of radio news that the "Mercury Theatre of the Air" dramatization of H.G. Wells' *War of the Worlds*, presented as a fast-breaking radio "scoop," created a panic throughout a sizable portion of the northeast. Many actually believed that Martians had invaded their planet.

In May 1938, *Billboard* estimated that 26,666,500 American families, some 82 percent of the nation's total, owned radios. While no one could argue with its success as a medium of entertainment and information, radio was hardly daring or socially progressive. With a few notable exceptions, the networks evaded the pressing societal problems of the 1930s. Depression realities were certainly conveyed by the news reports and by the outlandish oratory of Long, Coughlin and others, but they were rarely addressed in the era's dramatic shows. These preferred to focus on the achievements of principled heroes and heroines capable of overcoming any criminal or romantic difficulty; in this respect radio's output was similar to the romantic style and approach of the Classical Hollywood film. Similarly uplifting were the comedy and music shows, which suggested that people could laugh or sing away Depression blues, and the amateur contests and quiz programs, which gave every person a chance to win money or prizes and, thereby, rise above the gloom. Radio thus played its part in the confidence-building project that FDR and the New Deal turned into a priority during the decade.

Two days after Pearl Harbor, 90 million Americans listened to Roosevelt discuss the crisis over approximately 800 stations. Like so many other aspects of American life, radio was instantly transformed by the US entry into World War II. Patriotic messages became part of every broadcast. It was not enough for established shows to encourage the purchase of war bonds, whole new programs were created for the same purpose: "Treasury Star Parade," "Music for Millions," "Millions for Defense." Established heroes (Tom Mix, Captain Midnight, Jungle Jim, The Hornet, Superman, Jack Armstrong), new heroes (Hop Harrigan), and resurrected heroes (Terry and the Pirates, Don Winslow of the Navy) battled the enemy abroad and at home. "The Army Hour," "The Navy Hour" and "Stage Door Canteen" entertained servicemen, as well as sending personal news from the home front to the front lines and back again. "Command Performance" granted the wishes of lucky soldiers – one might receive words of encouragement from his favorite movie star while another could listen to the cries of his newborn child. And there was the news, breathlessly reported from the world's most dangerous locales by Charles Collingwood, Eric Sevareid, Cecil Brown, George Hicks and Edward R. Murrow, among others.

Through it all, the stars of radio continued to prosper. Bob Hope's globe-trotting tours to entertain the troops made him even more popular than before. Fibber McGee and Molly, Rudy Vallee, Jack Benny, Bergen–McCarthy and Amos 'n' Andy retained their loyal listeners while a new star emerged – the disc jockey. With radio stations relying more on popular records than ever before, the DJ, who had been around since the 1930s, became a celebrity. By war's end, nearly 1,000 stations were broadcasting in the US, and more than 56 million sets maintained prominent locations in its homes. Although radio's position as a fixture in the life of the nation would never completely disappear, its importance eroded quickly during the post-war era because of the rapid development of its natural heir, television.

Vaudeville

Vaudeville entertainment – diversified programs of song, dance, comedy and novelty acts – enjoyed its last hurrah in the 1920s. The Keith and Albee chain and the Orpheum circuit included hundreds of theaters throughout the US where audiences applauded such stars as Will Rogers, Bert Lahr, Al Jolson, Ed Wynn, Fannie Brice, Ray Bolger and Eddie Cantor, and sometimes even stage luminaries like the Barrymores and the Lunts. The mecca for vaudeville per-formers was the Palace Theater in New York, which posted a profit of $500,000 in 1923.

However, the increasing popularity of film and radio began to erode vaudeville attendance in the mid-20s. Feature-length films were integrated into many variety bills, and soon it seemed that customers came mainly to watch the picture rather than the acts. Radio not only kept people at home, it lured the top performers away. A raft of the fledgling medium's earliest stars – Cantor, Benny, Wynn, Rogers, Burns and Allen, Jolson, etc. – had developed their talents and personas in front of vaudeville crowds.

In 1926, Keith-Albee somewhat arbitrarily declared 1926–27 "vaudeville's centennial year" and promised an "epoch-making period" in its history. Sadly, the only "epochal" aspect of vaudeville's performance would be its decline. To streamline operations and gain greater control over the marketplace, Keith-Albee merged with Orpheum, giving the combine 75 percent of the nation's variety theaters. Ominously, Keith-Albee-Orpheum was taken over by the newly formed film company RKO in 1928. National vaudeville grosses dropped by 70 percent from 1927 to 1932. In July 1932, two-a-day performances ended at the Palace and, in January of the next year, the legendary house converted to a straight film policy.

By the end of 1939, RKO had only one vaudeville theater left, the Golden Gate in San Francisco. A few other theaters in big cities continued to offer mixed film–vaudeville programs into the 1940s, but the glory days of this exuberant form of show business were clearly past. The public's appetite for more technologically-based diversions – movies and radio – and the chilling effects of the Depression caused vaudeville to disappear from the American scene in a relatively short time.

Popular music

Phonograph records, introduced in the first decade of the twentieth century, had become a thriving business by the early 20s with sales topping $100 million per year. The rapid development of radio, however, convinced many music lovers to curtail their purchases. Why buy recordings, they reasoned, when one could listen to the latest songs over the airwaves for free? By 1925, sales had fallen to $59 million per year. Technical improvements in recording and playback equipment, introduced in 1925, did provide a boost in sales; they climbed back to $75 million in 1929.

The energy, spontaneity and optimism of the 1920s were reflected in its jazz music, dance crazes (particularly the Charleston) and in its popular songs. People sang, "Ain't We Got Fun?," "Runnin' Wild," "I'm Sitting on Top of the World" and "Great Day," as well as such wacky nonsense tunes as "Yes, We

Have No Bananas," "Who Ate the Napoleons with Josephine When Bonaparte Was Away?" and "Does the Spearmint Lose Its Flavor on the Bedpost Overnight?" It was a time of high hopes and high spirits, captured wonderfully in the musical creations of Irving Berlin, Jerome Kern, Vincent Youmans, George and Ira Gershwin, Richard Rodgers and Lorenz Hart, among others.

The mood changed rapidly after October 1929. Record sales plummeted, hitting bottom in 1933 when only $5 million worth of discs were purchased. The public continued to listen to songs over the radio; now, however, they heard "Brother, Can You Spare a Dime?", "Ten Cents a Dance," "I've Got Five Dollars," "I Found a Million Dollar Baby in a Five-and-Ten Cent Store" and "Pennies from Heaven." Many songwriters tried to hoist up people's spirits, putting a hopeful spin on the lyrics of "Wrap Up Your Troubles in Dreams," "Now's the Time to Fall in Love" and "On the Sunny Side of the Street." Two of the era's biggest hits were "Happy Days Are Here Again," which was appropriated by the Democratic Party as the theme song of FDR's 1932 Presidential campaign, and "Who's Afraid of the Big Bad Wolf?", composed for a 1933 Disney cartoon. It became the optimist's favorite lyric of Depression defiance.

Record sales began to rise slowly in the mid-1930s. The proliferation of juke boxes in restaurants, cafés and bars had a good deal to do with the improvement, as did the introduction (by Decca) of discs that cost 35 cents, less than half the price of most other companies' offerings. America's love affair with the Big Bands also helped; soon every audiophile identified "Moonlight Serenade" with Glenn Miller, "Begin the Beguine" with Artie Shaw, "I'm Getting Sentimental over You" with Tommy Dorsey and "You're Driving Me Crazy" with Guy Lombardo. In 1938, record sales moved past the $25 million mark again.

European developments did not go unnoticed by composers of the 30s. Irving Berlin's "God Bless America," first sung by Kate Smith as part of her 1938 Armistice Day show, was enthusiastically embraced by Americans concerned about escalating Nazi militarism. "God's Country" and "This Is My Country" also underscored the public's swelling sense of patriotism. After the World War broke out, "There'll Always Be an England" and "The White Cliffs of Dover" were often heard as sympathy with the British cause increased, and "The Last Time I Saw Paris" by Oscar Hammerstein II and Jerome Kern became a well-loved, affecting lament following the German occupation of France in 1940.

The entrance of the United States into global hostilities brought an immediate musical response. "Remember Pearl Harbor," "We Did It Before" and "Goodbye Mama, I'm Off to Yokohama," conveyed the nation's determination to win, as well as its rambunctious spirit. A dose of divine intervention was conjured up in Frank Loesser's immensely popular "Praise the Lord and Pass the Ammunition" and in "Say a Prayer for the Boys over There" and "Comin' in on a Wing and a Prayer." This period of heartrending separation also turned a bevy of sentimental ballads into big hits: "You'll Never Know," "I'll Be Seeing You," "I'll Walk Alone," etc. Even Irving Berlin's "White Christmas" took on a special poignancy when heard by soldiers fighting in the steamy jungles of the South Pacific.

Prior to the war years, radio and the recording industry had generally been at odds. Record company executives blamed radio for lessening the public's appetite for home discs, and they bristled at radio's refusal to pay fees for broadcasting recorded music. This animosity lessened in the 1940s, thanks to the growing popularity of "Your Hit Parade," a program that helped create a pop music consciousness, plus the pervasive influence of the disc jockey. Capitol Records, a new company launched in 1942, quickly grew successful by wooing DJs and thereby gaining greater airtime for its artists. Largely because of radio, record company grosses began to skyrocket. The two industries would become intensely (some might argue incestuously) symbiotic after the war ended.

The Big Bands, devastated by Uncle Sam's call to arms, lost many of their members and their dominant position in the world of pop. Taking their place were individual singers, most former vocalists for one or more of the bands. Frank Sinatra led the way, becoming king of the "bobby sox" crowd. In 1943, some 30,000 fans showed up to squeal their way through his performances at New York's Paramount Theater. Among the other star singers in 1945 were Doris Day, Perry Como, Peggy Lee, Dick Haymes, Jo Stafford, Kay Starr, Dinah Shore and veteran Bing Crosby, whose public adulation peaked during World War II.

Popular fiction and nonfiction

American readers in the 1920s embraced Sinclair Lewis' satirical dissections of midwestern life (*Main Street, Babbitt, Elmer Gantry*), the detective stories of S.S. Van Dine (*The Green Murder Case, The Bishop Murder Case*), fictional tales of adventure set in exotic locales (*Beau Geste* and *Beau Sabreur* by P.C. Wren, *The Sea-Hawk* by Rafael Sabatini), nonfiction tales of adventure set in exotic locales (*White Shadows in the South Seas* by Frederick O'Brien, *Revolt in the Desert* by T.E. Lawrence, *Trader Horn* by Alfred Aloysius Horn and Ethelreda Lewis) and two books about the life of Christ, one of which (Bruce Barton's *The Man Nobody Knows*) presented Jesus as the ultimate salesman and father of "modern business." Naturally, the public devoured stories about rebellious "modern" characters, especially if they contained forthright discussions of their sexual activities. Edith M. Hull's *The Sheik*, Gertrude Atherton's *Black Oxen*, Michael Arlen's *The Green Hat*, Percy Marks' *The Plastic Age* and Vina Delmar's *Bad Girl* described titillating behavior heretofore unrecorded in popular fiction. Numerous biographies also became bestsellers of the 20s, among them Lytton Strachey's *Queen Victoria*, Emil Ludwig's *Napoleon*, André Maurois' *Disraeli* and Francis Hackett's *Henry the Eighth*.

Surprisingly, the public also made time for such heady books as *The Outline of Science* by J. Arthur Thompson, *The New Decalogue of Science* by Albert E. Wiggam and *The Story of Philosophy* and *The Mansions of Philosophy*, both by Will Durant. Two popular works that left their readers pondering were H.G. Wells' *The Outline of History* and Hendrik Willem Van Loon's *The Story of Mankind*. Wells conceived human development as a steady ascendance, inspired movement toward a utopian state, whereas Van Loon believed that "modern" men and women were not far removed from their caveman ancestors. There was plenty of evidence in this decade to support both positions.

The 1930s fostered a passion for historical fiction (*Cimarron* by Edna Ferber, *Anthony Adverse* by Hervey Allen, *Gone with the Wind* by Margaret Mitchell, *Northwest Passage* by Kenneth Roberts). Stories imbued with religious inspiration also captured a substantial readership, with former clergyman Lloyd C. Douglas (*Magnificent Obsession, Green Light, White Banners, Disputed Passage*) being one of the most successful authors of the period. Seeking answers to the tribulations of Depression life, many people turned to self-help books. By far the biggest seller was Dale Carnegie's *How to Win Friends and Influence People*, but Vash Young's *A Fortune to Share*, Walter B. Pitkin's *Life Begins at Forty*, Edmund Jacobson's *You Must Relax*, Dorothea Brande's *Wake Up and Live!* and Marjorie Hillis' *Live Alone and Like It* also attracted enthusiastic readers.

John Steinbeck's *The Grapes of Wrath* was the only bestseller to deal realistically with the tragic consequences of the Depression; instead, most popular books featured reassuring stories about characters whose faith and perseverance enable them to overcome near-insurmountable odds. Scarlett O'Hara in Mitchell's phenomenally successful *Gone with the Wind* was one example; others included O-Lan in Pearl Buck's *The Good Earth*, Ada Fincastle in Ellen Glasgow's *Vein of Iron*, Langdon Towne in Roberts' *Northwest Passage*, Gilbert Martin in Walter D. Edmonds' *Drums Along the Mohawk*, even Ma Joad in *The Grapes of Wrath*. The strength and tenacity of the human character became a favorite inspirational theme during these troubled times.

The increasingly problematic world situation began to intrude in popular works from the mid-1930s on. Sinclair Lewis' *It Can't Happen Here* dealt with the threat of homegrown Fascism, while Phyllis Bottome's *The Mortal Storm* depicted a family torn apart by Nazism. Nora Wain's *Reaching for the Stars* was an eyewitness account of the moral deterioration of Germany under National Socialism, and *Escape* by Ethel Vance (a pseudonym for Grace Zaring Stone) concerned the rescue of a woman from her captors in the land of Hitler. Even the Führer himself cracked the bestseller lists in 1939 when a complete, translated version of *Mein Kampf* showed up in bookstores.

Still, perhaps because of the country's determined commitment to isolationism, few "war" books attracted mass sales until the bombing of Pearl Harbor. From that point until the end of the war, the nonfiction lists were glutted with them. Personalized descriptions of men at war included W.L. White's *They Were Expendable*, Richard Tregaskis' *Guadalcanal Diary*, Quentin Reynolds' *The Curtain Rises* and two highly popular books by beloved reporter Ernie Pyle, *Here Is Your War* and *Brave Men*. Those anxious to find a little humor in the life-and-death world of the military grabbed Marion Hargrove's *See Here, Private Hargrove*, Bob Hope's *I Never Left Home*, Juliet Lowell's *Dear Sir* and cartoonist Bill Mauldin's *Up Front*. The more serious-minded could ruminate upon the strategic and political analyses of Major Alexander P. de Seversky's *Victory Through Air Power*, Walter Lippman's *US Foreign Policy* and Sumner Welles' *The Time for Decision*. Former Presidential candidate Wendell Willkie fired the imagination of many optimists in *One World*, calling for the end of colonialism and a new unity among nations once the war was over.

A few bestselling fictional works dealt with the war, such as Steinbeck's *The Moon is Down*, Pearl Buck's *Dragon Seed* and John Hersey's *A Bell for Adano*, but most readers during the period clearly preferred religious novels (A.J. Cronin's *The Keys of the Kingdom*, Franz Werfel's *The Song of Bernadette* and Lloyd C. Douglas' *The Robe*), historical romances (*Green Dolphin Street* by Elizabeth Goudge, *Forever Amber* by Kathleen Winsor, *Captain from Castile* by Samuel Shellabarger) and a variety of other stories that provided some relief from the intense wartime fixation. The best and most popular World War II novels would be published several years after the culmination of hostilities.

Comic strips and comic books

Newspaper comic strips were a popular and well-established form of American cultural expression by the early years of the twentieth century. The first strips – "The Katzenjammer Kids" by Rudolph Dirks, "Alphonse and Gaston" by Frederick Burr Opper, "Krazy Kat" by George Herriman, among others – were primarily humorous in intent. During the 1910s and 20s, a blending of comedy with the domestic life became modish, as evidenced by such series as George McManus' "Bringing Up Father," Sydney Smith's "The Gumps" and Frank King's "Gasoline Alley."

Just before the arrival of the Depression, action/adventure established itself as the dominant comic strip genre. "Tarzan" (by Harold Foster, based on the books by Edgar Rice Burroughs) and "Buck Rogers" (by Philip Nowlan and Dick Calkins) made the initial breakthrough in 1929. Soon, "Dick Tracy" (by Chester Gould), "Terry and the Pirates" (Milton Caniff), "Charlie Chan" (Alfred Andriola), "The Lone Ranger" (Charles Flanders), "Prince Valiant" (Harold Foster, after he turned over "Tarzan" to Burne Hogarth in 1936), plus "Secret Agent X-9," "Jungle Jim" and "Flash Gordon" (all originally drawn by Alexander Raymond) were competing with one another in a race to create the most intriguing characters and suspenseful situations. Air adventures, at least partially inspired by the exploits of Charles Lindbergh, were also well received: "Scorchy Smith" (Frank Robbins), "Tailspin Tommy" (Hal Forrest), "Ace Drummond" (Clayton Knight and Eddie Rickenbacker), "Barney Baxter" (Frank Miller), etc.

Comic books were introduced in the mid-30s, but did not gain wide popularity until the end of the decade. Recognizing the public preference for adventure, the most successful pioneer authors offered hyperbolized protagonists who were, by and large, godlike and indomitable. "Superman" (by Jerry Siegel and Joe Schuster) appeared in 1938 and quickly became the first megastar of the new form of publishing. Following the "Man of Steel" into the hearts of America's youth came "Batman" (Bob Kane and Bill Finger), "Captain Marvel" (Bill Parker and C.C. Beck) and "Wonderwoman" (William Moulton Marston and Harry Peter).

While the adventure strips and comic books featured heroes to cheer in cheerless times, the comics also included more mundane characters who, nevertheless, provided a tonic to Depression audiences. "Little Orphan Annie" (by Harold Gray) debuted in 1924, but her self-reliance, courage and spunk made her an ideal 30s heroine. Likewise, Walt Disney's ever-optimistic "Mickey Mouse" and "Chic" Young's Dagwood Bumstead (of "Blondie"), who never lost his positive attitude despite an unending series of minor catastrophes (mostly self-induced), kept readers amused and hopeful.

Most of the adventure heroes of 30s comics battled the criminal underbelly of American society, though some took on foreign troublemakers as well. A few of the more politically-minded artists openly challenged the fervent isolationism that prevailed in the US before Pearl Harbor. In 1937, Milton Caniff pitted his stalwarts against the treacherous Japanese in "Terry and the Pirates." "Secret

Agent X-9" (drawn by Austin Briggs, the successor to Alexander Raymond) concentrated his efforts on a group of spies whose nationality was never specified but whose leader, the arrogant Captain Ludwig, was clearly coded as German. In May 1940, Ham Fisher's "Joe Palooka" passionately called his fellow Americans to arms against the Axis.

In 1941, Joe Palooka enlisted in the Army. After Pearl Harbor, he would be joined in his battle against the enemy by characters from almost every strip and comic book. Dick Tracy, Superman, Charlie Chan, Captain Marvel, even Tarzan took up the cause, as did new military heroes "Buz Sawyer" (by Roy Crane) and "Johnny Hazard" (Frank Robbins). The era gave birth to other strips conceived for the men in uniform: "G.I. Joe" (by Dave Breger), "The Sad Sack" (Sergeant George Baker) and "Male Call" (Milton Caniff).

Consumers of comic books welcomed Will Eisner's "Blackhawk" series, about a group of guerrilla fighters determined to sabotage the foes of the Allies, and "Captain America" (by Jack Kirby and Joe Simon), a red, white and blue-costumed good guy who thwarts the enemy at night and on weekends. During regular working hours, he is just another G.I. named Steve Rogers. "The Young Allies," a spin-off from "Captain America," focused on a group of kids and their contributions to the winning of the war.

Like so many other visible aspects of American culture during the World War II period, comic books and strips conveyed the national obsession with contemporary events and the all-consuming hunger for victory. Indeed, they were so popular that during a New York newspaper strike in 1945, Mayor Fiorello La Guardia invited his constituents to gather their families around the radio and then broadcast a dramatic reading of the strips that would have run on that day.

Theater

The 1920s were a rousing, fertile period for the American stage. While regional theater declined somewhat, Broadway boomed, mounting a record number of new productions. Comedies and dramas and musicals of all kinds were introduced, as well as provocative experiments like Elmer Rice's expressionistic *The Adding Machine* and 13 probing, psychological plays by Eugene O'Neill, including *The Emperor Jones, The Hairy Ape* and *Desire Under the Elms*.

The czars of Broadway were the Shuberts, who owned 30 New York theaters and 50 more in Boston, Philadelphia, Chicago and other cities. Millions of dollars in profits flowed into Shubert accounts before the business suddenly turned sour at the end of the decade.

The biggest hit of the 20s was the sentimental comedy *Abie's Irish Rose* by Anne Nichols which attracted enthusiastic playgoers for six consecutive seasons. Other notable successes ranged from Shakespeare's *Hamlet* with John Barrymore and Bram Stoker's *Dracula* with Bela Lugosi to Ferenc Molnar's *The Guardsman* with Alfred Lunt and Lynn Fontanne, Maxwell Anderson and Laurence Stallings' *What Price Glory?* and Ben Hecht and Charles MacArthur's *The Front Page*. While an abundance of popular musicals appeared, such as *Lady Be Good!* starring Fred and Adèle Astaire, *The Cocoanuts* featuring the Marx Brothers and *Whoopee* with Eddie Cantor, the most important of them was *Show Boat* by Edna Ferber, with its landmark Jerome Kern–Oscar Hammerstein II score. It lasted for two years at the Ziegfeld Theater and moved the form toward a more unified integration of music and story elements.

In 1927, 280 shows opened on Broadway, setting a record that has never been equaled. However, the growing popularity of radio and movies soon affected theatrical attendance and decline set in even before the onset of the Depression. Many Broadway theaters closed after 1930, others converted to film programs. The once mighty Shubert organization lost more than $3 million in 1931 and plunged into receivership. Actors' Equity estimated that 5,000 performers and 15,000–25,000 directors, designers, costumers, stagehands and other support personnel were out of work in the early 30s.

One revitalizing force was the Group Theatre. Formed in 1931, this leftist collective of actors and directors modeled itself on the Moscow Art Theatre and popularized the Stanislavsky method of inner-driven acting that would prove to be so important to American film in the post-World War II period. Such influential figures as Elia Kazan, Clifford Odets, Stella Adler, Lee Strasberg, Harold Clurman, Franchot Tone and Morris Carnovsky would emerge from the group, and it would produce important plays by Sidney Kingsley, Maxwell Anderson, Irwin Shaw, William Saroyan and, most notably, former actor Clifford Odets.

Another altogether extraordinary effort to rejuvenate American drama was the Federal Theatre Project, organized in 1935. As part of the WPA, it succeeded admirably in achieving its goal of putting unemployed theater people back to work. Between 1936 and 1939, the Federal Theatre staged 63,000 performances of 1,200 different productions for audiences that totaled nearly 30.4 million. Among its most famous presentations were T.S. Eliot's *Murder in the Cathedral*, a dramatized version of Sinclair Lewis' novel *It Can't Happen Here*, Paul Green's *The Lost Colony* and Shakespeare's *Macbeth*, produced by Orson Welles and John Houseman and set in Haiti with an all-black cast.

The Federal Theatre was eventually brought low by politics. Conservatives such as North Carolina senator Robert Reynolds, who smelled Communist propaganda in some of the productions, marshaled enough votes to cut off the project's funding in the summer of 1939. Although the Federal Theatre did have a radical wing, most of its efforts were rather subdued compared to the hard-edged social commentary and heated agitprop that characterized a good deal of 30s drama. At a time when other forms of leisure entertainment charted a safe course around the period's desperation, the stage confronted it with surprising boldness. The Depression spawned a theater of ideas, messages, even occasional calls to arms.

Clifford Odets' *Waiting for Lefty* was one example. A 1935 multi-scene play, it dramatized the exploitation of cab drivers by their brutal employers and, in its finale, urged all workers to strike. The yawning gulf between society's haves and have-nots was examined in Sidney Kingsley's *Dead End*. Marc Blitzstein's anticapitalist musical *The Cradle Will Rock*, which the Federal Theatre attempted to suppress and ultimately disavowed, was a blunt call for revolution. Other overtly ideological plays included *The Last Mile*, John Wexley's indictment of American prison conditions; *Winterset*, Maxwell Anderson's blank verse tragedy about the injustices visited upon the nation's poor and ignorant; *Idiot's Delight*, Robert Sherwood's warning against Fascism and plea for peace in a deteriorating world; and *The Little Foxes*, Lillian Hellman's withering dissection of capitalist greed.

Though Depression realities (*Face the Music*), political commentary (*I'd Rather Be Right*) and glorifications of trade unionism (*Pins and Needles*) even popped up in some of the musicals of the time, theater in the 1930s was not devoid of escapism. More traditional musical hits included Fred and Adèle Astaire in *The Band Wagon*, Ethel Merman in *Anything Goes*, Bob Hope in *Roberta*, Jimmy Durante in *Billy Rose's Jumbo* and Ray Bolger in *On Your Toes*. The public appetite for comedies was satisfied by Noel Coward's *Private Lives*, George F. Kaufman and Edna Ferber's *Dinner at Eight*, Kaufman and Moss Hart's *You Can't Take It with You*, John Murray and Allen Boretz's *Room Service*, Philip Barry's *The Philadelphia Story* and *Hellzapoppin'*, a surrealistic farce written by and starring former vaudeville performers Ole Olsen and Chic Johnson. Jack Kirkland's sensationalistic adaptation of Erskine Caldwell's novel *Tobacco Road* proved to be the longest-running play of the period. This melodramatic tale of Jeeter Lester and other denizens of the Georgia backwoods held on for seven and a half years.

World War II brought prosperity back to Broadway, which witnessed a steady increase in the number of produced plays during the first half of the 40s. Although serious works about the war were mounted (none, however, with an anti-war theme), the public clearly preferred stage versions of contemporary events to be delivered in quixotic packages, e.g. the farcical (*Strip for Action*), the sentimental (*Winged Victory*), the romantically humorous (*Jacobowsky and the Colonel*). One of the biggest hits was Irving Berlin's all-soldier revue, *This Is the Army*, which eventually raised more than $10 million for the Army Relief Fund.

"That's entertainment!" was also the motto of the period's other successes. Far removed from 30s social protest drama, these shows offered patrons a few hours of total relief from their turbulent world. The premiere musical triumph of the decade, Rodgers and Hammerstein's *Oklahoma!*, was one example; other escapist musicals included *By Jupiter*, *One Touch of Venus*, *Song of Norway* and *Carousel*. The black farce *Arsenic and Old Lace*, the fantasy *Harvey*, the homespun portrait *I Remember Mama* and the domestic comedy *Life with Father* (which opened in 1939 and played until well after the war ended) were also highly popular. Thornton Wilder's Pulitzer Prize-winner, *The Skin of Our Teeth*, provided just the right note of reassurance; its fractured narrative asserted that the human species is indestructible, despite its multiple faults and foibles. Finally, in 1944 and 1945, the chill breeze of topical realism began to blow again in such productions as *Soldier's Wife* and *Foxhole in the Parlor*, which dramatized the psychological impact of the war on both soldiers and civilians.

Spectator sports

Babe Ruth, Red Grange and Jack Dempsey were three of the heroic names that induced many Americans to become sports fanatics in the 1920s. Attendance rose throughout the decade, as radio and newspapers provided greater coverage of athletic events. Colleges went on a stadium-building spree to accommodate their football crowds. When the University of Illinois opened its new stadium in 1924 against Michigan, 67,000 showed up to watch Fighting Illini running back Grange score four touchdowns in the first 12 minutes. Seasonal attendance for the New York Yankees climbed from a previous high of 600,000 to over one million a year after the baseball team acquired slugger Ruth in 1920. And an incredible 104,000 people jammed Chicago's Soldier Field in 1927 to witness the heavyweight fight between Dempsey and Gene Tunney. Gate receipts totaled more than $2.5 million.

The Depression brought a quick finish to the exhilarating expansion. Professional baseball attendance, which reached 10.2 million in 1930, fell back to 6.1 million in 1933. Managers and players, even the big stars, took salary cuts.

An All-Star game between the two leagues became an annual event in 1933, the Cincinnati Reds introduced night baseball in 1935, the Hall of Fame was established in 1936, but these and a raft of promotional gimmicks at the ballparks had minimal impact on the downward trend. Weaker franchises like the St. Louis Browns were especially hard-hit. Attendance at Browns' games fell below 100,000 in 1933, 1935 and 1936. Even their more successful National League counterparts, the St. Louis Cardinals, only managed to attract 325,000 fans in 1935 when they finished in first place.

College football weathered the 30s fairly well. While there was some initial decline in attendance, especially in the east and midwest, it returned to pre-crash levels in 1935 when *Time* magazine estimated that 20 million fans were showing up for gridiron contests. Jay Berwanger of the University of Chicago, Sammy Baugh of Texas Christian, Don Hutson of Alabama, Byron "Whizzer" White of Colorado and Tom Harmon of Michigan became the biggest names of the era.

Professional football was forced to fight for its life. The National Football League (NFL) contained more than 20 teams in 1926; only eight were left in 1932. The refusal of collegiate stars Berwanger and Harmon (at first) to play pro ball diminished the League's stature, but tenacious owners like George Halas of the Chicago Bears, Timothy J. Mara of the New York Giants, George Preston Marshall of the Washington Redskins and Curly Lambeau of the Green Bay Packers held on. By 1940, the game had become more innovative and exciting, business had risen and the NFL was positioned for further growth and success.

Even though boxing attracted no 100,000-plus crowds during the Depression, it remained popular and produced a great champion: Joe Louis. This black heavyweight from Detroit won 27 consecutive bouts before losing to Germany's Max Schmeling in 1936. A lot was riding on the Louis–Schmeling rematch, including Nazi pronouncements about the supremacy of the "Aryan" race. These racist notions had already been challenged when black American track star Jesse Owens won four gold medals at the 1936 Olympics, hosted by Hitler himself in Berlin. Louis provided additional proof of the fallacy of Nazi ideology by pummeling Schmeling into submission in the first round of their June 1938 battle. Called the "Brown Bomber," Joe Louis became a legitimate hero of both black and white Americans in the 1930s.

In some ways, World War II upset the world of sports even more than the Depression had. Travel restrictions and player shortages caused upwards of 300 colleges to give up football, including perennial powers Alabama, Stanford and Fordham. After Joe Louis entered the Army, the heavyweight championship was placed in suspended animation, pending completion of his military obligations. And, even though President Roosevelt stated that baseball "provided relaxation for the hard working populace" and supported the continuation of professional play, he would not offer deferments to its players. Consequently, more than half of the major leaguers were wearing military uniforms by the end of 1942; in 1945, the figure had risen to 90 percent.

The sportsmen who donned baseball uniforms during World War II were a motley assortment of 4-Fs, old-timers (most of whom had retired years before) and imports from Cuba, Puerto Rico and other countries south of the US border. Even a one-armed outfielder, Pete Grey, could find a spot on a big-league roster; he appeared in 77 games for the St. Louis Browns. The level of play was hardly major league caliber (owner Alva Bradley of the Cleveland Indians called it "a low form of comedy"). Nonetheless, the public retained its enthusiasm, mainly because of the aura of patriotism that enveloped the sport. Teams admitted servicemen free, sponsored salvage drives and publicized the fact that players had pledged a percentage of their salaries to purchase war bonds. Despite being jampacked with embarrassing plays, the 1945 World Series between the Detroit Tigers and Chicago Cubs drew almost 335,000 fans and set a record for gate receipts.

The NFL situation paralleled that of baseball. With more than 600 professional football players entering the service, the League carried on by reducing its rosters, bringing former stars like Broncho Nagurski out of retirement and finding "day jobs" in essential industries for many of its performers. Pro football also raised money for the war effort, and its attendance posted substantial gains from 1942 on.

Basketball was the one college sport whose popularity rose dramatically during the war. Its smaller squads were not seriously affected by the military buildup, making basketball especially attractive to crowds of alumni who had few other games to cheer. Teams like Stanford, Utah, Kentucky, Oklahoma A & M and DePaul dominated intercollegiate play. *Time* named basketball America's number one sport in 1945, with an estimated attendance of 75 million. Yet there was still no professional league; that would come soon enough in the post-war era.

2

Film Business

In 1929, the American film industry was in the late stages of its conversion to sound. The changeover was enormously expensive, but it did not alter the composition of the business profoundly. Some years before, the industry had settled into a structure dominated by a few large, powerful companies (e.g., Paramount, Fox, MGM). The cost of sound conversion (see chapter 3) helped to solidify this structure, leaving eight dominant studios and a mere handful of smaller, struggling outfits to compete for the public's moviegoing dollars. A number of marginal, undercapitalized production firms (Chadwick, Inspiration, Tiffany, Producers Distributing Corp, etc.) could not manage the transition to sound and soon disappeared, while some of the larger companies (First National, FBO, Pathé) were, or soon would be, absorbed by the surviving giants.

The structure of the industry was stable throughout the Classical Period. But business was hardly smooth. After posting solid profits in 1929 and 1930, thanks primarily to the novelty of talking pictures, several of the major studios experienced heavy losses between 1931 and 1935. These companies had made themselves vulnerable to the onset of the Depression by taking on substantial debt in order to re-tool their studio facilities for the production of sound movies and to acquire new theaters and wire them for sound. As a consequence, Paramount and RKO were both in receivership by the end of 1933 with Warner Bros., Fox and Universal hovering just outside the doors of bankruptcy court. Business did begin to pick up around the middle of the decade, and all the major companies survived after considerable cost cutting and reorganization.

While the Depression hit Hollywood slightly less hard than it hit most other American industries, its impact was still dramatic. Suddenly, many people couldn't afford to go to the movies. Box office attendance dropped by 25 percent and gross revenues by almost 30 percent between 1929 and 1933, forcing thousands of theaters to close their doors. The industry responded to the crisis by slashing admission prices and, eventually, by offering a variety of showmanship gimmicks to entice the customers back. The major stratagem was the widespread deployment of the double feature, wherein customers viewed two films for the price of one. Others included Bank Night, when cash prizes would be given to lucky ticket holders, several variations on Bingo (Screeno and Banko were two of the names used) and giveaway evenings when patrons received a piece of crockery or silverware, or some other useful culinary item. In the production arena, studios laid off employees, required others to take pay cuts and ruthlessly pared filmmaking costs.

Attendance rose slowly. By 1937, moviegoing was once again a regular habit for many Americans. While the "Roosevelt recession" that year did affect business, its bite was minimal compared to the chilling impact of the early Depression era.

World War II caused some initial concern about foreign markets. By 1940, practically all of Europe, except for Great Britain, was off-limits to US pictures, yet even this did not damage business substantially. The studios began to cultivate other foreign territories (especially Central and South America) more intensively and managed to squeeze additional revenue from the domestic market.

After America entered the war, the film business became a bonanza. Flush with cash from the newly expanded job market, Americans at home looked to movies as a preferred method of diversion. Their options limited by rationing, millions flocked to their local theaters where newsreels provided a visual sense of the war's progress, and theatrical films, often larded with patriotic sentiment, offered reassurance that the American spirit was too strong to be broken by any challenge from abroad. Film company profits soared, peaking in 1946 when an incredible $1.7 billion was recorded in the industry's ledger books. This magical year, however, would mark the end of the boom era; soon, most Americans would rely on television for their visual entertainment and movies would become an occasional pastime, rather than a regular habit.

The Studios

Hollywood's major studios produced around 60 percent of the films that were seen on domestic screens during the era, but managed to collect approximately 95 percent of the film rentals generated in the United States. The largest companies, commonly referred to as the "Big Five" (MGM, Paramount, Warner

Bros., Twentieth Century-Fox and RKO), had production, distribution and exhibition arms; these vertically integrated outfits were able to control the manufacturing, marketing and retailing of their product more completely than the so-called "Little Three." Of these, Columbia and Universal both lacked theater chains (Universal owned about 60 domestic theaters until 1933), while United Artists functioned solely as a distribution company for independently made productions.

Each of the majors had its business headquarters in New York. Except for United Artists, each maintained studio facilities in the Los Angeles area where most of their motion pictures were produced. Feature length films (running 55 minutes or longer) comprised the primary business, but the companies also provided theaters with short subjects (lasting 30 minutes or less), and some offered cartoons and/or newsreels as well.

The principal executives of most of the companies were well-established industry veterans by the time the Classical Period began. Some, like Carl Laemmle of Universal and Adolph Zukor of Paramount, had been guiding architects of the business from its earliest days; others, like Jack and Harry Warner of Warner Bros. and William Fox of the Fox Film Corporation, had championed the coming of sound and profited handsomely from their innovative zeal; still others, such as Irving Thalberg of MGM, Harry Cohn of Columbia and Darryl Zanuck of Twentieth Century-Fox, prided themselves on their ability to choose the right film projects and then shepherd them through the creative process. These film company executives – often called "moguls" – were a group of highly motivated visionaries who developed and shaped the film business to satisfy the desires of an audience entranced by moving picture entertainment.

Metro-Goldwyn-Mayer

The most consistently profitable of the studios, MGM never so much as flirted with a losing year during the Classical Period. Even the Depression caused only a slight downturn in the profits of this show business juggernaut.

With Nicholas Schenck as financial head in New York and Louis B. Mayer overseeing studio operations in Hollywood, the company was generally viewed as the best in the industry. Although its production and distribution operations were actually subsidiaries of the Loew's chain of theaters, it was renowned for its films and, especially, its stars. MGM's famous slogan was "More stars than there are in heaven," and it backed up the boast by offering pictures that featured Clark Gable, Greta Garbo, Joan Crawford, Marie Dressler, Wallace Beery,

Robert Taylor, Jean Harlow, Spencer Tracy, Norma Shearer, Lionel Barrymore, William Powell, Myrna Loy, Jeanette MacDonald, Nelson Eddy, Mickey Rooney, Judy Garland, James Stewart, Greer Garson, Lana Turner, Elizabeth Taylor and other household names.

Superintending the MGM films in the 1920s and early 30s was Irving Thalberg, whose reputation as the most creative production chief in Hollywood never changed until his death in 1936 at the age of 37. After that, Mayer took a more active hand in filmmaking decisions and the company's success continued unabated, though the critical reputation of its productions declined somewhat. MGM specialized in all-star vehicles that showcased its top-heavy roster of acting talent (*Grand Hotel*, 1932; *San Francisco*, 1936; *Boom Town*, 1940), comedies (*Red Headed Woman*, 1932; *Libeled Lady*, 1936; *Too Hot to Handle*, 1938; *The Women*, 1939; *The Philadelphia Story*, 1940), musicals (*Broadway Melody*, 1929; *The Great Ziegfeld*, 1936; *The Wizard of Oz*, 1939; *Babes in Arms*, 1939; *Meet Me in St. Louis*, 1944), adventure pictures (*Trader Horn*, 1931; *Mutiny on the Bounty*, 1935; *Test Pilot*, 1938), woman's films (*Susan Lenox (Her Fall and Rise)*, 1931; *Letty Lynton*, 1932; *Queen Christina*, 1934), series pictures ("The Thin Man," "Andy Hardy," "Dr. Kildare") and, during World War II, war movies (*Bataan*, 1943; *A Guy Named Joe*, 1943; *Thirty Seconds over Tokyo*, 1944). It also produced more than its share of literary (*Anna Karenina*, 1935; *Captains Courageous*, 1937; *Mrs. Miniver*, 1942) and stage adaptations (*Strange Interlude*, 1932; *Romeo and Juliet*, 1936; *Idiot's Delight*, 1939). The studio's biggest hit was *Gone with the Wind* (1939), a film produced independently by David O. Selznick but distributed by MGM. (Figure 2.1)

Paramount

Paramount controlled more theaters than any of its competitors. The theaters were a great asset when business was good, but they drained the company's coffers and pulled it into receivership during the worst years of the Depression. It emerged in 1935 after considerable reorganization and was reasonably successful until the war years when its fortunes soared. The $39.2 million profit Paramount recorded in 1946 was an industry record.

Adolph Zukor, often credited with developing vertical integration in the film business, stood atop Paramount's trademark mountain for more than 50 years. The studio's head of production changed with surprising frequency; between 1929 and 1938, Jesse L. Lasky, B.P. Schulberg, Emmanuel Cohen, William LeBaron and director Ernst Lubitsch each had his chance to run filmmaking

Figure 2.1   Irving Thalberg, the "boy wonder" who supervised production at MGM from 1924 until 1932. He then became one of the studio's unit producers until his death in 1936. Courtesy of the USC Cinema-Television Library.

operations. They were succeeded by Y. Frank Freeman who took control in 1938 and held the job until 1959. Another important Paramount executive was theater expert Barney Balaban who became president in 1936 when Zukor assumed the chairmanship of the board.

Paramount's star roster was the only one that offered MGM some challenge. It included Gary Cooper, Marlene Dietrich, Carole Lombard, Maurice Chevalier, Mae West, W.C. Fields, the Marx Brothers, George Raft, Joel McCrea, Barbara Stanwyck, Fred MacMurray, Claudette Colbert, Paulette Goddard, Bing Crosby, Bob Hope, Veronica Lake, Alan Ladd and Ray Milland.

Its comedies (*Trouble in Paradise*, 1932; *I'm No Angel*, 1933; *Duck Soup*, 1933; *Easy Living*, 1937; *Midnight*, 1939; *The Lady Eve*, 1941; *Sullivan's Travels*, 1941) were especially memorable, but it also produced woman's films (*Honor Among Lovers*, 1931; *Blonde Venus*, 1932; *Jennie Gerhardt*, 1933), musicals (*Monte Carlo*, 1930; *Love Me Tonight*, 1932; *College Swing*, 1938; *Holiday Inn*, 1942), adventure films (*The Lives of a Bengal Lancer*, 1935; *The General Died at Dawn*, 1936; *Beau Geste*, 1939), noir films (*This Gun for Hire*, 1942; *Double Indemnity*, 1944; *The Lost Weekend*, 1945) and the most popular Hollywood series of the 1940s, the "Road" movies, starring Bing Crosby and Bob Hope. In addition, the studio was home to a unique talent, Cecil B. DeMille, whose stirring historical epics (such as *The Sign of the Cross*, 1932; *Cleopatra*, 1934; *The Crusades*, 1935; *The Buccaneer*, 1938; *Union Pacific*, 1939; *Reap the Wild Wind*, 1942) brought him fame that rivaled any of the studio's actors.

Warner Bros.

Warner Bros. reaped the benefits of introducing sound features like *The Jazz Singer* (1927) and *The Lights of New York* (1928), and became one of the most powerful studios by the end of the 1920s. Its acquisition of First National Pictures and a large chain of theaters caused the company to suffer substantial losses between 1931 and 1934, but it survived the lean years and prospered from then on; the company was very profitable during World War II.

The two executives who ran Warner Bros. were Harry Warner, in charge of the New York office, and Jack Warner, who superintended studio operations in California. A third brother, Albert, was the corporate treasurer. Jack Warner was nominally in charge of production, but most of the important creative decisions were made by Darryl F. Zanuck (until 1933) and then Hal B. Wallis, who succeeded Zanuck and remained in place until 1944.

Warner Bros. had a solid contingent of stars, though it contained more character actors than glamour types. The biggest names were Bette Davis, James Cagney, Errol Flynn, Paul Muni, Olivia de Havilland, Humphrey Bogart, Edward G. Robinson, Kay Francis, Dick Powell, Joan Blondell, Claude Rains, George Brent, Ann Sheridan, Jane Wyman, Ida Lupino and Ronald Reagan.

While most studios specialized in a fairly narrow range of productions, Warner Bros. produced memorable films in nearly every genre. For example, the gangster film (*Little Caesar*, 1931; *The Public Enemy*, 1931; *The Roaring Twenties*, 1939), the woman's film (*Dark Victory*, 1939; *Now, Voyager*, 1942; *Mildred Pierce*, 1945), the adventure film (*Captain Blood*, 1935; *The Adventures of Robin Hood*, 1938; *The Sea Hawk*, 1940), the biography (*The Story of Louis Pasteur*, 1936; *The Life of Emile Zola*, 1937; *Juarez*, 1939), the musical (*42nd Street*, 1933; *Footlight Parade*, 1933; *Yankee Doodle Dandy*, 1942), the social problem film (*I Am a Fugitive from a Chain Gang*, 1932; *Black Fury*, 1935; *They Won't Forget*, 1937), the western (*Dodge City*, 1939; *Santa Fe Trail*, 1940; *They Died with Their Boots On*, 1941), the war film (*Sergeant York*, 1941; *Air Force*, 1943; *Objective, Burma!*, 1945). In addition, *Casablanca* (1943), their Academy

Award-winning romantic drama set in North Africa during World War II, became one of the most beloved films of the studio era.

Twentieth Century-Fox

The last of the majors to be formed, Twentieth Century-Fox came into being through a merger of independent Twentieth Century Pictures and the venerable Fox Film Corporation in 1935. The driving force behind the latter company was William Fox, one of the most active and entrepreneurial executives of the silent era. But Fox endured a series of setbacks after the Wall Street crash of 1929 and lost control of his company in the early 30s. It languished until the management team that had formed Twentieth Century in 1933 – business chief Joseph Schenck and production expert Darryl F. Zanuck – took over and began to run the combined organizaton. From 1935 until the end of the Classical Period, Twentieth Century-Fox was highly successful.

At first, the studio had only two bona fide stars, moppet Shirley Temple and folksy humorist Will Rogers. Rogers perished in an airplane accident in 1935, but Zanuck soon built a formidable stable of acting talent. It included Tyrone Power, Alice Faye, Don Ameche, Henry Fonda, Loretta Young, George Sanders, Betty Grable, Maureen O'Hara, Gene Tierney, Gregory Peck, Linda Darnell and Carmen Miranda.

The company's specialties were biographies (*Young Mr. Lincoln*, 1939; *The Story of Alexander Graham Bell*, 1939; *Wilson*, 1944), adaptations of novels (*The Grapes of Wrath*, 1940; *How Green Was My Valley*, 1941; *Jane Eyre*, 1944), musicals (*Alexander's Ragtime Band*, 1938; *Tin Pan Alley*, 1940; *The Gang's All Here*, 1943; *Coney Island*, 1943), westerns (*Jesse James*, 1939; *The Return of Frank James*, 1940; *Belle Starr*, 1941; *Western Union*, 1941; *The Ox-Bow Incident*, 1943), adventure films (*The Mark of Zorro*, 1940; *The Black Swan*, 1942; *Son of Fury*, 1942), noir films (*Laura*, 1944; *Fallen Angel*, 1945; *Hangover Square*, 1945) and war films (*Guadalcanal Diary*, 1943; *The Immortal Sergeant*, 1943; *A Walk in the Sun*, 1945).

Radio-Keith-Orpheum

Radio-Keith-Orpheum was created in 1928 by the Radio Corporation of America (RCA) to showcase its sound-on-film equipment and to compete with the well-established industry giants. This studio was much more volatile than the other majors, enduring regular changes of management and shifts in filmmaking philosophy. Like Paramount, it suffered substantial losses during the Depression and was forced into receivership in 1933. It took seven years for the corporation to emerge although, after 1935, its prolonged stay was caused by reorganization complications rather than perilous financial difficulties. The best years for RKO occurred during World War II.

RKO's initial management team consisted of Hiram Brown (New York) and William LeBaron (Hollywood). They would be succeeded by Merlin Aylesworth and David O. Selznick, Merlin Aylesworth and Pandro S. Berman, Leo Spitz and Sam Briskin, Leo Spitz and Pandro S. Berman, George Schaefer and Harry Edington, George Schaefer and Joseph I. Breen, and N. Peter Rathvon and Charles Koerner.

The RKO stars included Irene Dunne, Richard Dix, Constance Bennett, Ann Harding, Katharine Hepburn, Fred Astaire, Ginger Rogers, Victor McLaglen, Lucille Ball, Orson Welles, Robert Ryan and Robert Mitchum. Fluctuation throughout this roster had heavy impact on the filmmaking trends of the studio. In the 1930s, a majority of female stars led RKO to emphasize the woman's film; by the 40s, however, a greater number of male-oriented pictures was produced.

The studio's biggest hits were its Astaire–Rogers musicals (*The Gay Divorcée*, 1934; *Top Hat*, 1935; *Follow the Fleet*, 1936; *Shall We Dance*, 1937), but it also produced solid comedies (*Bringing Up Baby*, 1938; *Bachelor Mother*, 1939; *My Favorite Wife*, 1940), woman's films (*Christopher Strong*, 1933; *In Name Only*, 1939; *Kitty Foyle*, 1940), literary adaptations (*Of Human Bondage*, 1934; *Alice Adams*, 1935; *The Hunchback of Notre Dame*, 1939), adventure pictures (*The Lost Patrol*, 1934; *She*, 1935; *Gunga Din*, 1939), series pictures ("Hildegarde Withers," "The Saint," "The Falcon"), horror films (*Cat People*, 1943; *I Walked with a Zombie*, 1943; *The Body Snatcher*, 1945) and two of the most important and influential works of the period, *King Kong* (1933) and *Citizen Kane* (1941). The company also distributed the films of independent producers Walt Disney (beginning in 1936) and Samuel Goldwyn (beginning in 1941).

Universal

Although Universal's history dates from 1912 and its founding mogul, Carl Laemmle, is often credited with the invention of the star system, the studio had a difficult time in the 1930s, losing money every year except 1931 and 1934, when it posted modest surpluses, and 1939 when it managed a profit of $1.2 million. Its fortunes improved in the 40s when it generated steady, if unspectacular, profits through the war years.

Laemmle, utilizing his son Carl Laemmle Jr. as production chief, ran Universal until 1936 when an investment group headed by J. Cheever Cowdin took control. R.H. Cochrane became the new president with Charles R. Rogers functioning as head of production. Two former RKO theater executives, Nate Blumberg and Cliff Work, replaced this team in 1938. (Figure 2.2)

While Universal did own a small chain of theaters, it was forced to sell them in 1933 to escape receivership. Thus, it existed without a guaranteed exhibition outlet for most of the Classical Period. The company's biggest stars were juvenile songstress Deanna Durbin in the late 30s and the comedy team of Bud Abbott and Lou Costello in the 40s. Other members of the Universal acting company were Lew Ayres, Margaret Sullavan, Boris Karloff, Bela Lugosi, John Boles, Lon Chaney Jr., Basil Rathbone, Maria Montez, Jon Hall, Robert Cummings, Ella Raines and Yvonne DeCarlo.

In general, the studio made fewer big-budget pictures than its rivals (excepting Columbia), concentrating instead on inexpensive westerns, comedies, horror films and serials. Its most fondly remembered and influential productions were the horror films (*Dracula*, 1931; *Frankenstein*, 1931; *The Mummy*, 1932; *The Wolf Man*, 1941), but it also made contributions to the woman's film (*Back Street*, 1931; *Imitation of Life*, 1934; *Magnificent Obsession*, 1935), the comedy (*My Man Godfrey*, 1936; *The Bank Dick*, 1940; the Abbott and Costello films), the musical (*King of Jazz*, 1930; *Show Boat*, 1936; *One Hundred Men and a Girl*, 1937), the series ("Sherlock Holmes," "The Cohens and the Kellys"), the western (*Destry Rides Again*, 1939; *When the Daltons Rode*, 1940; *The Spoilers*, 1942; plus more than 100 low-budget cowboy movies starring Hoot Gibson, Buck Jones, Johnny Mack Brown and others), noir films (*Shadow of a Doubt*, 1943; *Phantom Lady*, 1944; *Scarlet Street*, 1945) and the serial ("Flash Gordon," "Buck Rogers"). Perhaps the studio's most famous critical success was the antiwar *All Quiet on the Western Front*, the Academy Award-winner of 1930.

Columbia

Columbia was even more cost-conscious than Universal, concentrating on the production of modestly budgeted program pictures, plus a handful of more expensive and ambitious films each year. Steering this very tight ship from the silent era to the 1950s was Harry Cohn, the blustery president and head of production. Cohn's brother Jack headed up the New York office.

At a considerable disadvantage because it owned no theaters and had few stars under exclusive contract, Columbia's thrifty philosophy nonetheless paid off. While its profits did not rival those of MGM, it never had a losing year. Even during the toughest days of the Depression, Columbia made money.

By far the company's most highly esteemed creative talent during the 1930s

Figure 2.2 Carl Laemmle, president of Universal, and his son Carl Laemmle Jr., the head of production at the studio in the early 1930s. Courtesy of the USC Doheny Library Department of Special Collections.

was director Frank Capra, whose timely productions (*It Happened One Night*, 1934; *Mr. Deeds Goes to Town*, 1936; *You Can't Take It with You*, 1938; *Mr. Smith Goes to Washington*, 1939) brought in millions and provided the studio with a level of respectability that it would not have otherwise enjoyed. Jean Arthur, Rosalind Russell, Jack Holt, Rita Hayworth, Grace Moore, Ralph Bellamy, Lloyd Nolan, Ann Sothern, Melvyn Douglas, Glenn Ford, Larry Parks and Ann Miller were other members of the Columbia acting company.

The studio's forte was comedy. Besides the Capra pictures, it produced such memorable films as *Twentieth Century* (1934), *The Awful Truth* (1937), *Holiday* (1938), *His Girl Friday* (1940) and *The More the Merrier* (1943). It also left its mark on the musical (*One Night of Love*, 1934; *You Were Never Lovelier*, 1942; *Cover Girl*, 1944), the woman's film (*Forbidden*, 1932; *Craig's Wife*, 1936; *Penny Serenade*, 1941), the series ("Blondie," "The Lone Wolf," "Boston Blackie"), the war film (*Sahara*, 1943; *Destroyer*, 1943; *Counter-Attack*, 1945) and the serial ("Captain Midnight," "Batman," "The Shadow"). In addition, Columbia released more than 175 inexpensive westerns during the period, starring Tim McCoy, Ken Maynard, Charles Starrett and others.

United Artists

A very different business enterprise, United Artists had no stars, no studio facilities, no theaters. It functioned solely as a distribution outlet for independently-made productions.

Formed in 1919 by Mary Pickford, Douglas Fairbanks, Charlie Chaplin and D.W. Griffith both to market their pictures and to protect their creative autonomy, the company soon opened its doors to other suppliers. By the beginning of the Classical Period, it was handling the films of Samuel Goldwyn, Howard Hughes, Gloria Swanson and Joseph Schenck, as well as Pickford, Fairbanks and Chaplin. The careers of Miss Pickford and Mr. Fairbanks faltered in the early sound era, but the company picked up the slack by bringing Walt Disney, Twentieth Century (before the merger with Fox), Alexander Korda, David O. Selznick, Walter Wanger and others into the fold.

Although United Artists was never highly profitable, it had only two losing years between 1929 and 1945, primarily because its overhead was low compared to other studios that maintained much larger staffs. However, during the World War II period when profits came easily to most of the movie companies, the performance of United Artists was desultory. The bulk of the company's problems derived from management. Joseph Schenck guided UA skillfully through the worst years of the Depression, but after he left to form Twentieth

Century-Fox with Zanuck, the organization never found an adequate replacement. The owners – especially Pickford and Chaplin – feuded constantly and eventually its most important filmmakers, Disney and Goldwyn, found new homes for their releases. The company's leadership woes would continue until the early 1950s when Robert Benjamin and Arthur Krim took control and transformed UA into one of the most dynamic studios of the post-World War II era.

United Artists was originally conceived as a prestige studio that would distribute many of the industry's most notable and expensive pictures. It maintained this reputation into the 1940s when more and more low-budget movies were added to the mix in order to keep the distribution exchanges busy. Nevertheless, the company philosophy of allowing independents to make their films without interference from the front office had its rewards. The following titles, with their producers, are evidence: *Hell's Angels* (Hughes, 1930), *City Lights* (Chaplin, 1931), *Scarface* (Hughes, 1932), *Our Daily Bread* (King Vidor, 1934), *Dodsworth* (Goldwyn, 1936), *Modern Times* (Chaplin, 1936), *A Star Is Born* (Selznick, 1937) *You Only Live Once* (Wanger, 1937), *Stella Dallas* (Goldwyn, 1937), *The Prisoner of Zenda* (Selznick, 1937) *Dead End* (Goldwyn, 1937), *Stagecoach* (Wanger, 1939), *Wuthering Heights* (Goldwyn, 1939), *Rebecca* (Selznick, 1940), *The Thief of Bagdad* (Korda, 1940), *The Great Dictator* (Chaplin, 1940), *Foreign Correspondent* (Wanger, 1940), *To Be or Not to Be* (Korda–Ernst Lubitsch, 1942), *Since You Went Away* (Selznick, 1944), *The Story of G.I. Joe* (Lester Cowan, 1945), *Spellbound* (Selznick, 1945).

Minor studios

A small group of other companies carved out a special niche in the industry during the Classical Period. Producing pictures (mainly westerns) on very tight budgets, they aimed their product primarily at rural Americans. Some of these operations maintained their own domestic distribution exchanges, while others utilized states' rights outfits to market their movies in different sections of the country. Overseas distribution of their films was not widespread.

Republic Pictures was the most famous and profitable of the minors. Formed in 1935 when Herbert Yates merged three companies (Mascot, Monogram and Liberty) with his Consolidated Film Laboratories, Republic specialized in westerns (*The Singing Cowboy*, 1936; *In Old Monterey*, 1939; *Robin Hood of the Pecos*, 1941) and western series ("The Three Mesquiteers"). It also released numerous serials "(Dick Tracy," "Red Ryder," "Captain Marvel"), mysteries (*The Spanish Cape Mystery*, 1935; *The Leavenworth Case*, 1936; *Who Killed Aunt Maggie?*,

1940) and musicals (*Follow Your Heart*, 1936; *Sitting on the Moon*, 1936; *The Hit Parade*, 1937 and its sequels in 1940, 1947 and 1950). The company made an occasional A-budget production (*Man of Conquest*, 1939; *Dark Command*, 1940); indeed, after World War II, it would begin to spend more on its pictures, commissioning works directed by such major industry figures as John Ford, Orson Welles, Frank Borzage and Nicholas Ray. John Wayne appeared in many Republic films before he became a star, and some afterward. The studio's other "name" performers included singing cowboys Gene Autry and Roy Rogers, and Vera Hruba Ralston, a Czech ice skater who eventually married chief executive Herbert Yates.

Monogram, also primarily a producer of westerns, was formed in 1930 by W. Ray Johnston and production head Trem Carr. Johnston became Republic's first president in 1935, but he eventually decided that the merger had been a mistake and resigned. He and Carr revived Monogram in 1937. Besides the many westerns (*The Mexicali Kid*, 1938; *The Ghost Rider*, 1935; *Phantom Ranger*, 1938; etc.) the company favored series films ("Charlie Chan," "Joe Palooka," "The Cisco Kid," "Renfrew of the Royal Mounted," "The Bowery Boys"), comedies (*Hillbilly Blitzkrieg*, 1942; *Leave It to the Irish*, 1944; *She's in the Army*, 1942) and mysteries (*The Mystery of the Thirteenth Guest*, 1932; *Murder by Invitation*, 1941; *There Goes Kelly*, 1945). Jean Parker, Duncan Renaldo, Sidney Toler, Leo Gorcey and Huntz Hall were its most famous actors. While never known for the quality of its productions, Monogram could match almost any other company in terms of quantity; it released 53 features in 1940, for example.

Unlike Monogram, Mascot was never resurrected after it became part of Republic in 1935. Before that it had mainly existed as a supplier of serials ("The Vanishing Legion," "The Lost Jungle," "The Phantom Empire," "The Fighting Marines"). It did produce a few features, including literary adaptations (*Little Men*, 1934), war films (*Crimson Romance*, 1934) and, of course, westerns (*In Old Santa Fe*, 1934). John Wayne appeared in some of the company's serials ("Shadow of the Eagle," "The Hurricane Express," "The Three Musketeers"), and Tom Mix ended his career in one ("The Miracle Rider"). Other Mascot actors included Harry Carey, legendary stuntman Yakima Canutt, Joe Bonomo and animal stars Rin-Tin-Tin Jr. and Rex the Horse. Nat Levine was Mascot's chief executive.

Producers Releasing Corporation (PRC), formed in 1940, made cheap pictures of generally inferior quality. Once again, westerns (*Along the Sundown Trail*, 1942; *Thundering Gun Slingers*, 1944; *Rustler's Hideout*, 1945) were its staple, but it also offered comedies, various types of melodrama and western series ("Billy the Kid," "Frontier Marshal," "The Lone Rider"). Occasionally,

PRC would make a film with "A" pretensions, such as *Minstrel Man* (1944) or *Enchanted Forest* (1945). The studio's head was Ben Judell, its production chief George Batcheller.

Majestic Productions existed from 1932 to 1935. Its production head, Larry Darmour, promised high-class entertainments based on literary properties, but he mostly delivered standard low-budget product (e.g., *The World Gone Mad*, 1932; *The Vampire Bat*, 1933; *Gun Law*, 1933).

Active from 1936 to 1940, Grand National Pictures produced westerns starring aspiring cowboy star Tex Ritter and aging hero Ken Maynard. It also signed James Cagney while he was involved in a contract dispute with Warner Bros. Cagney made *Great Guy* (1936) and *Something to Sing About* (1937) for Grand National, but the company was unable to carve out even a small corner of the business. Its two presidents were Edward L. Alperson (1936–38) and E.W. Hammons (1938–40).

Independent producers

Except for United Artists and, to a lesser extent, RKO, the major studios did not support or encourage production by independent companies. And without direct access to a well-dispersed distribution network and/or theater chain, the independent producer had a difficult time raising money to underwrite the costs of filming. He also had problems lining up professionals to work on his pictures. Despite the obstacles, many attempted to succeed at the independent game and a few managed it very well indeed.

Samuel Goldwyn was one example. His name notwithstanding, Goldwyn never had anything to do with Metro-Goldwyn-Mayer, remaining independent throughout the Classical Period. He occupied his own studio and built a formidable roster of contract talent that included, at one time or other, Ronald Colman, Eddie Cantor, Gary Cooper, Merle Oberon, David Niven, Danny Kaye, Dana Andrews, director William Wyler, writer Lillian Hellman and cinematographer Gregg Toland. Goldwyn supplied United Artists with a number of respected and successful pictures until 1941 when he struck a deal with RKO to distribute his productions. His most famous film was *The Best Years of Our Lives*, which captured seven Academy Awards in 1946.

Goldwyn's chief rival in the independent ranks was David O. Selznick. After working in various executive capacities at Paramount, RKO and MGM, Selznick established his own company in 1935 and immediately became a major force in the industry. He also had his own studio and developed a strong talent pool. Selznick brought director Alfred Hitchcock to America and placed

Ingrid Bergman, Joseph Cotten, Joan Fontaine, Jennifer Jones and Dorothy McGuire under contract. *Gone with the Wind*, by far the most successful film of the era, was his crowning achievement. In order to cast Clark Gable in the role of Rhett Butler, he was forced to give MGM partial ownership in and distribution rights to the film. Otherwise, his pictures were released by United Artists. Selznick's output lessened noticeably after *Gone with the Wind*; indeed, he produced only three films between 1940 and 1945. His filmmaking activities would increase slightly after the war.

Walt Disney was the unchallenged industry leader in animation. His short cartoons, featuring Mickey Mouse, Donald Duck, Pluto and Goofy, won awards and great popularity, and his first feature-length effort, *Snow White and the Seven Dwarfs*, was a blockbuster hit in 1938. He followed it with *Pinocchio* (1940), *Fantasia* (1940), *Dumbo* (1941), *Bambi* (1942) and other famous children's stories. Disney cooperated closely with the government during World War II, producing animated sequences for the "Why We Fight" series of documentaries, as well as films that supported the war effort (*Victory Through Air Power*, 1943). The Disney studio also helped to cement relations with the country's South American neighbors (*Saludos Amigos*, 1943; *The Three Caballeros*, 1945). Disney released through Columbia from 1930 to 1932, then moved to United Artists until 1936 and finally forged an alliance with RKO which marketed his films into the 1950s.

Other notable Hollywood-based independents included Walter Wanger (*Algiers*, 1938; *Stagecoach*; *Foreign Correspondent*), Hal Roach (*Topper*, 1937; *One Million B.C.*, 1939; *Of Mice and Men*, 1939), Sol Lesser (the "Tarzan" films; *Our Town*, 1940; *Stage Door Canteen*, 1943) and Edward Small (*The Man in the Iron Mask*, 1939; *The Son of Monte Cristo*, 1940; *Brewster's Millions*, 1945).

In order to help fund the war effort, the US government raised income tax rates significantly during the war years. By 1945, those earning more than $1 million per year were turning over 94 percent of their taxable income to Uncle Sam. Even before the end of the war, Los Angeles accountants began to advise their highly paid clients that there were significant advantages to be gained from forming their own independent companies and earning money as a company executive rather than picking up a regular paycheck from one of the big studios. Soon enough, "indies" were popping up all over Hollywood. Among the producers who created their own independent operations in the first half of the 1940s were Hunt Stromberg (*Lady of Burlesque*, United Artists, 1943), Arnold Pressburger (*Hangmen Also Die!*, United Artists, 1943), Benedict Bogeaus (*The Bridge of San Luis Rey*, United Artists, 1944), Samuel Bronston (*Jack London*, United Artists, 1944) and Leo McCarey (*The Bells of*

St. Mary's, RKO, 1945). International Pictures (*Casanova Brown*, RKO, 1944; *The Woman in the Window*, RKO, 1944; *Along Came Jones*, RKO, 1945), an independent founded by Leo Spitz and William Goetz in 1944, would merge with Universal in 1946 to create Universal-International. The formation of independent production entities continued to gain momentum after the end of the war and into the post-Classical Period.

Production

Hollywood in the Classical Period manufactured hundreds of new films every year. In order to make its product in the most efficient way, at the lowest cost, plants (or studios) were set up and staffed. Within these plants, there was clear division of labor. A strict hierarchical system made clear each employee's responsibilities and to whom he or she reported for supervision.

And yet motion picture studios never functioned like other manufacturing plants. The assembly-line methods conceived and innovated by Henry Ford for his automobile factories did not work for movie production because each new product had to be different from the others. The public demanded a certain amount of freshness, of innovation, of novelty in the films it watched. Thus, the studio system of production could be standardized only to a limited extent. It had to combine some standardization in order to function smoothly and cut costs with a level of flexibility and differentiation that would result in motion pictures featuring at least a modicum of novelty and distinctiveness. The system collapsed if it was unable to cope with the unique requirements, challenges and problems presented by every filmmaking venture.

Studio production methods

Most production was accomplished in the California studios. Each company's production year generally began in late spring or early summer to accommodate the release year which commenced in September (see Distribution). Earlier, often in January, top studio executives would meet to map out production plans. A target number of films would be agreed upon with an approximate overall budget for the year's production activities. Other topics which the executives might discuss included the studio's major talent and how best to utilize it, the literary properties owned by the company and their suitability for filming and the number of big-budget pictures to be produced compared to less-expensive efforts.

Each company's *head of production* would then assume responsibility for implementing the overall plan. With the exception of United Artists and some of the minor companies, each studio had a diversified cadre of workers, organized along departmental lines, to help the production chief bring films to completion (see Figure 2.3). Perhaps the easiest way to understand how the system worked is to follow a mythical film from beginning to end.

The starting point usually was the *story department*. There, *readers* would synopsize and critically evaluate the full range of narrative material (novels, plays, nonfiction books, short stories, magazine articles, original scripts, etc.). Their recommendations were then forwarded to the head of production who would read the material that seemed most interesting. If he liked something, the company would attempt to purchase the rights.

Once the studio acquired rights to a piece of material, it was assigned to a *contract producer*. This individual would supervise one or more of the company's *contract writers* on the development of the screenplay. When the script began to take shape, the producer and production head decided upon a *contract director* to oversee the actual filming. Producer, director and production head then began to make casting decisions, relying initially on the studio's roster of *contract actors* before thinking of free-lance or borrowed talent. (In many cases, the star or stars were decided upon even before the company acquired the property.)

Around the time that first drafts of the screenplay became available, other departments began to contribute. The *production department* prepared a preliminary budget. The *art department* assigned an *art director* and/or *production designer* who produced sketches and drawings ofdthe sets. Members of the *costume department* started to design the outfits that the various actors would wear. The *wardrobe department* pulled out and altered any costumes from previous pictures that could be reused. Likewise, the *property department* assigned a *property master* who scoured the studio's inventory, then made arrangements to purchase or rent any necessary props that the studio did not already own.

When the script was rounding into shape, and everyone was basically satisfied with it, a production start date was announced. Set construction then commenced with *carpenters, plasterers, painters* and other *building experts* assigned by the *construction department*. In addition, other key members of the team were assembled. The *director of photography* and his *camera crew* (including *grips* and *gaffers*) came from the *camera department*, the *editor* and his or her assistants from the *editorial department*, the *sound recordist* and *mixer* from the *sound department*. If special effects were needed, members of

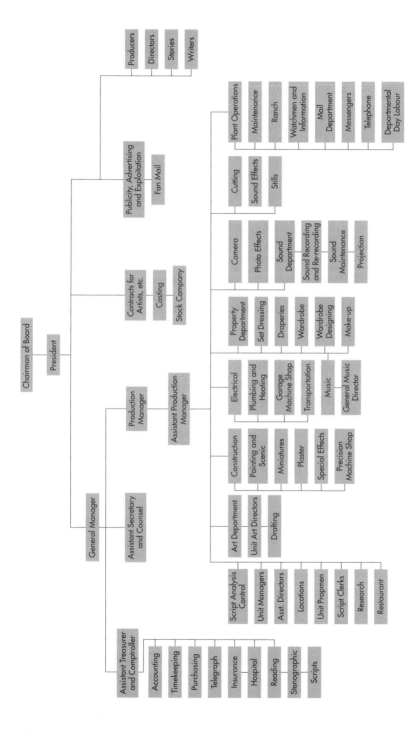

Figure 2.3 RKO Studio Organizational Chart from 1934. Courtesy of the RKO Radio Pictures Archive.

the *special effects department* were given the job. The *unit production manager, assistant director, script supervisor, make-up artists, hair dressers* and other *specialists*, as needed, were provided by the production department. Thus, every necessary function would be covered on the day that principal photography began.

On that day, the producer backed away, leaving the film in the hands of the director. As long as the dailies looked good and filming proceeded on schedule and within budget, the producer and production chief would concentrate on other projects. Problems sometimes arose, however, prompting the men in power to replace a crew or cast member or even a director. On rare occasions, an entire production would be shut down and written off.

When photography was complete, the producer once again took control. A few directors were allowed to supervise the first cut of the picture, but most were either sent on vacation or assigned to another picture once the shooting was finished. Thereafter, the producer handled post-production, working closely with the editor and the sound department which put together sound effects and prepared the final mix. This mix would usually include a musical score composed by someone from the *music department*. The head of the music department was also responsible for the acquisition of rights to any incidental music in the picture and for hiring the *musicians* who played the score.

Once the film was finished it was usually previewed before an audience of "civilians" at a theater in the southern California area. Typically, such previews would be held in such cities as Glendale, San Bernardino or Santa Ana – as far away as possible, that is, from industry-savvy Hollywood and Beverly Hills. Though the studios were interested in the reactions of a diverse crowd, their audience selection process was largely unscientific. The audience's reaction would often suggest that some corrective surgery was needed; this ran the gamut from minor editing changes to major re-shooting. One of the advantages of the system was the relative ease with which cast, crew, sets and costumes could be reassembled for additional filming. The revised version would usually also be tested before one or more preview audiences. When the producer and head of production were finally satisfied, the negative was cut in the editorial department and shipped to New York where prints were made for dissemination by the company's distribution arm.

A film studio also required the services of many people who were never directly involved in the filmmaking process. The *legal department*, for example, was staffed by lawyers who prepared the personnel contracts and defended the company against the cascade of lawsuits that its business attracted. The *accounting department* kept time sheets, prepared paychecks and constantly monitored the fiscal well-being of the overall operation. The *publicity department* made sure the studio, its films and its personalities were continually seen by the public in a favorable light. The *talent department* scouted for promising young actors and actresses, while also keeping a lookout for individuals with producing, directing, writing or other creative abilities. The *research department* provided information to writers, art directors, costume designers and other members of the production team who wanted their contributions to be as detailed and accurate as possible.

Naturally, costs varied from film to film, but the most expensive elements were nearly always cast, direction, story and/or script preparation, set design and construction. The studio system was especially successful in keeping technical costs under control. Rarely would the camera crew, editors, sound specialists and special effects experts represent more than 10 percent of a film's total budget. In order to account for the expense of running its filmmaking plant, each studio added an overhead charge to the negative cost of every film. This indirect charge, which was usually around 30 percent, reflected the salaries of the executives and other workers not directly involved with production activities, as well as the costs of studio real estate, security, insurance, maintenance and other miscellaneous items.

The studio actually functioned as a small, self-contained city. As such, it had its own private electrical and water systems, its own telephone exchange, its own medical and dental clinics, its own firefighting unit. There was also a commissary, drugstore, plant nursery, barbershop, custodial staff and a security force to guard against theft and unauthorized visitors. In addition to the many individuals who worked in these units, studio operations required numerous secretaries, stenographers, projectionists, repairmen, laborers and assistants of all kinds in order to maximize output.

"A" vs. "B" productions

In Hollywood, production was conceptualized in terms of "A" and "B" films. "A" films had substantial budgets and generous shooting schedules, featured recognizable stars in key roles, and relied upon top producers, directors, writers, cinematographers, composers and other experienced personnel to bring the projects to fruition. When finished, the "A" film typically ran 85 minutes or longer. "B" films were made inexpensively on abbreviated shooting schedules, contained casts lacking in stars and represented the handiwork of the company's second echelon of production talent. Their usual running time was between 55 and 70 minutes.

In reality, the "A" vs. "B" dichotomy was a misleading oversimplification. Most major studios released three distinct types of pictures, and some four. All the big companies produced "A" films with budgets of $400,000 and up in the 1930s. Between the typical "B," costing around $100,000 in the 30s, and the typical "A" was another category: the film that was more expensive than a "B" because of cast, story, production values, etc., but did not have all the elements that one expected to find in a true "A" picture. While these films had no official designation, they were informally known throughout the industry as "in-betweeners." Additionally, several of the studios (RKO, Columbia and Universal, among others) turned out westerns that cost less than $50,000 to produce. These pictures were usually tailored to the personalities of their leading actors (e.g., Tom Keene, Buck Jones, Hoot Gibson) and filmed on very short shooting schedules. The majority of films made by such studios as Monogram, Republic and PRC fell into this category. It should be noted that budgets did not remain steady throughout the Classical Period. Because of the extraordinary commercial success of their releases during the war years, studio heads allowed the costs of their pictures to rise significantly. By 1945 an "A" film that cost under $1 million was a rarity, while the budgets of films in the other categories had also escalated.

The "A" vs. "B" differentiation operated at the distribution level as well. Companies expected theaters to lease their "A" films (in first and second run, at the least) for a percentage of the box office intake. This figure was generally 25 to 30 percent. "B" films, on the other hand, were rented for a flat fee, without consideration of admission price or the number of people who watched them. The "in-betweeners" caused significant friction between distributors, who usually demanded that exhibitors pay "A" terms for them, and theater owners who looked at them as "Bs" and insisted that they be priced accordingly. The low-budget westerns did not spark similar disputes; they were always placed in a special "B" niche whose fixed cost was less than most other features.

All the studios made "B" films (even MGM, though it tried to convince the world it did not). While one occasionally reads that "B" pictures were introduced because of the Depression-era practice of double features, the "B" film was a well-established genus in the silent period. Though it was impossible for a "B" film to become a blockbuster hit, these productions did not involve significant risk; indeed, most "B" films made money. In addition, the studios' "B" features and shorts were an excellent training ground for new talent. Many actors, directors, producers, writers and technical artists learned their crafts working on inexpensive productions. And while "B" films were generally looked down upon aesthetically (most American newspapers did not even review them), a number of interesting and provocative "Bs" were made, just as many poor "A" films were made.

The star system

The movie star was a key element in the business strategies of most film companies. Audiences came to treasure certain actors and flocked to films in which these stars appeared. Studios recognized their value and exploited the dynamic relationship between actor and audience to the fullest extent possible. While no star could guarantee success for his/her pictures, the injection of stars became the best insurance for "A" films, which cost the most and had the potential to generate large profits or post substantial losses. Therefore, studios depended on stars to sell their major pictures through advertising that would emphasize their image and screen persona.

For the most powerful studios, an assemblage of star talent, exclusively obligated to make movies for the company, was a clear necessity. These studios were expected to produce at least 20 "A"-level productions during each release year. In order to cast their films with stars, the companies placed great emphasis on the development of "personalities" and used the long-term contract to stabilize the talent equation (see chapter 7 for further details).

Labor developments in Hollywood

"Hollywood is a union town. From the highest-paid directors to the lowly electricians, every group is organized," wrote Murray Ross in 1941. The motion picture industry had, indeed, become unionized by the early 40s, but the victories of the workers were difficult, hard-fought and not without casualties.

Union activities in the 1930s were dominated by the International Alliance of Theatrical Stage Employees (IATSE), a powerful organization that represented diverse groups of amusement workers, including theater projectionists. Determined to bring various studio craft workers into the fold, IATSE had succeeded by 1927 in unionizing stagehands, carpenters, painters, electricians, musicians, cameramen, laboratory technicians and other studio workers. It had also become the first labor organization to gain recognition from the major production companies, which had been stubbornly committed to the open shop up to that point.

In May 1927, the Academy of Motion Picture Arts and Sciences was founded. In addition to promoting technical achievement and recognizing screen excellence through the handing out of awards, the Academy intended to represent the interests of members of its five branches: Actors, Directors, Writers, Producers and Technicians. For the next 10 years, the Academy would be arguably the most controversial organization in Hollywood, mainly because of its labor union aspirations. To some, it would come to represent a noble attempt to foster harmony between studios and their employees. To others, it would seem a baldfaced company union designed to protect the interests of studio management at any cost.

Except for a few minor flare-ups, there was no serious trouble between film labor and the employers until 1933. Nor had there been any success, to that point, in convincing the industry's most highly paid workers – its actors, directors and writers – to organize. But in March 1933, just after Franklin D. Roosevelt became President and ordered the national bank holiday, the Academy recommended that studio employees take substantial pay cuts to help their companies weather the difficult times and prevent a threatened shutdown of all Hollywood production. After considerable wrangling, workers who made over $100 per week were required to accept a 50 percent cut for eight weeks (perhaps less), with lower-salaried employees enduring smaller percentage reductions. The obligatory salary waivers upset the entire industry; they especially infuriated the workforce at Warner Bros. and Samuel Goldwyn, two companies that refused to reinstate full salaries, as promised, after the eight weeks had passed. The gambit cost Warner Bros. the services of production expert Darryl F. Zanuck, who was so outraged by the breach of faith that he quit. It also meant the beginning of the end of the Academy as a representative of motion picture labor.

Convinced by the salary waiver episode that the Academy was a company union, a group of scriptwriters began to meet with the intention of reviving an earlier, failed attempt at labor organization: the Screen Writers Guild (SWG). In March 1933, 20 writers resigned from the Academy and announced that the SWG would henceforth represent their collective interests. A group of similarly inclined actors created the Screen Actors Guild (SAG) in July 1933. Referring to themselves as "guilds," incidentally, reinforced the groups' self-perceived status as talented craftsmen, or artisans, and downplayed their similarities to unions. These two groups would oppose the Academy most vociferously, but it would take four years of bitter struggle before the studios finally began to accede to their demands.

The next major altercation involved the drafting of the Motion Picture Code of the National Recovery Administration. The film business, along with many other American industries, was required to develop a code that would govern its activities and the ongoing relationship between labor and management. Attempting to rebuild its faltering reputation, the Academy took an active hand in framing the NRA Code. When completed, the Code contained three provisions that infuriated the newly organized writers and actors. One provision would have prevented producers from "raiding" talent from their competitors by offering them more generous salaries. A second would have required agents to be licensed, giving producers more control over them and their practices. A third called for the creation of an industry board to limit the salaries of the highest-paid creative talent.

The Code, as released in late November 1933, contained the offensive provisions, but they were suspended after a meeting between SAG president Eddie Cantor and President Roosevelt, held over the 1933 Thanksgiving holiday. Even though the controversial provisions were never implemented and the NRA itself was declared unconstitutional in 1935, the episode further tarnished the Academy's reputation. Scores of members resigned, while others found more dramatic ways to protest the organization's labor union pretensions. Dudley Nichols, for example, became the first person to refuse an Academy Award, which he had won for writing the screenplay of *The Informer* (RKO, 1935). To accept the honor, he reasoned, would undermine the cause of his own union, the Screen Writers Guild. In 1936, film directors joined the movement, establishing the Screen Directors Guild (SDG) which included assistant directors and, in an allied guild, studio production managers.

Although the Academy wisely dropped its labor aspirations in the last half of the 30s, choosing to concentrate on its other activities (especially the awards), this continued to be a difficult, contentious period in management–worker relations. A coterie of writers who were not in sympathy with the goals of the SWG formed the Screen Playwrights in May 1936; this group was eventually accepted by the producers who had refused to recognize the Screen Writers Guild. Believing that the studios had created another company union, many members of the SWG fought the new union bitterly. But others feared for their jobs and dropped their memberships in the Guild. The National Labor Relations Act of 1935 (the Wagner Act) saved the organization, enabling it to force an election in August 1938 that established the SWG as the sole bargaining agent for writers in Hollywood. Nevertheless, studio heads continued to resist, but they were finally forced to recognize the Guild in 1941. In 1937, they had given in and approved a guild shop with the Screen Actors Guild after a poll revealed that 99 percent of the performers were prepared to strike if producers continued to treat their union as the enemy.

Other groups to unionize in the 1930s included the film editors, art directors, set designers, script clerks, cartoonists and screen publicists. Studio white-collar workers, including stenographers, switchboard operators and bookkeepers, were among the last to organize. They formed the Screen Office Employees Guild in December 1939. Like the majority of other Hollywood unions, it became affiliated with the American Federation of Labor.

The most deplorable chapter in Hollywood labor history involved IATSE. Moribund from August 1933 through December 1935 following a disastrous jurisdictional dispute over soundmen, the Alliance returned to prominence after George E. Browne, who was connected to Chicago mobsters, became the organization's president. Fearing that Browne would call a widespread projectionists' strike, the studios agreed to his closed-shop demand. Craft workers were informed that they had to join IATSE to keep their jobs, causing membership to explode from approximately 100 to over 12,000.

Browne placed William Bioff, a former pimp from Chicago, in charge of the Hollywood locals. Browne, Bioff and their henchmen then proceeded to siphon off most of the members' union dues and special assessments while, at the same time, extorting hundreds of thousands of dollars from the producers by promising to keep their workers docile and undemanding. Browne and Bioff were finally exposed by lawyer Carey McWilliams and journalist Westbrook Pegler, convicted of extortion and tax evasion and sent to prison in the early 1940s. Also sentenced to one year in jail was Twentieth Century-Fox chairman Joseph Schenck who made an illegal payoff of $100,000 to Bioff and was found guilty of perjury and income tax irregularities.

The labor–management arena was relatively calm during most of World War II when salaries were controlled by government edict. However, the Browne–Bioff scandal left the IATSE in disgrace, enabling a new organization, the Conference of Studio Unions (CSU), to gain a foothold in the industry. This band of craft workers, led by Herbert Sorrell who had been deeply involved in a strike against the Disney Studios in 1941, would pursue benefits much more forcefully than the Alliance ever had. Conflict was inevitable; it broke out in March 1945, with the studios and IATSE on one side and the CSU on the other. A CSU strike was called and before it ended eight months later, Sorrell and his associates had been branded Communists and Warner Bros. had employed goon squads to attack picketers outside its studio. This episode turned out to be a prelude to an even more turbulent period of strikes and dirty tactics that would contaminate the working environment in post-war Hollywood.

Distribution

Each company's distribution arm was charged with marketing the studio's product. It took responsibility, therefore, for "sales" (actually leasing), collections, promotion and advertising, the physical movement of films to the company's exchange offices and then from the exchanges to theaters and back, print quality and control and other related matters. The distribution headquarters for all major studios were located in New York.

The exchanges represented key points in the distribution chain. Each exchange handled the company business in a specific territory and was generally located in the largest city in the territory (see Figure 2.4). The major studios maintained exchange offices in more than 30 cities. These key cities included: Albany, Atlanta, Boston, Buffalo, Charlotte, Chicago, Cincinnati, Cleveland, Dallas, Denver, Des Moines, Detroit, Indianapolis, Kansas City, Los Angeles, Memphis, Milwaukee, Minneapolis, New Haven, New Orleans, New York, Oklahoma City, Omaha, Philadelphia, Pittsburgh, Portland, St. Louis, Salt Lake City, San Francisco, Seattle and Washington, DC. It was estimated that the cost of maintaining a nationwide distribution arm was between $80,000 and $125,000 per week in 1945.

Employed in the exchanges were print inspectors and shipping clerks, secretaries, accountants and, most importantly, managers and sales people who labored to convince theater owners to book the studio's pictures. These individuals were crucial members of every organization, the five vertically integrated majors as well as the other companies that owned no theaters and, thus, had no guaranteed outlet for their productions. In reality, the studio-owned or -controlled theaters represented only 17 percent of the screens in America; clearly, it was imperative that each company have a persuasive sales force that could convince independent exhibitors to play their films. The studios did not exert an absolute monopoly over their own theaters, either. Each knew its chains could fail if they were required only to show their parent company's product; to maintain profitability, the Big Five's chains would often scramble for the most popular films, regardless of studio origin.

The mechanics of distribution

Each studio's release year began in September and lasted until the following August. Three or four months before the beginning of the release year, the companies would hold their annual sales conventions, usually in Chicago

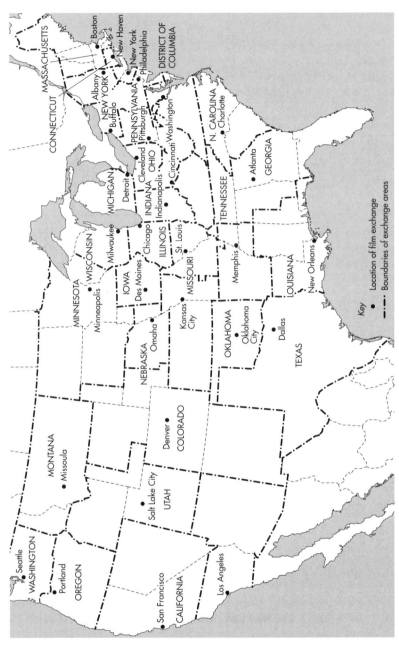

Figure 2.4   Film distribution map showing the locations of the studios' exchange cities and the territories they serviced. Courtesy of the RKO Radio Pictures Archive.

because of its central location. Invited to these events would be branch managers, top sales people, important exhibitors and often a contingent of actors, producers and executives from Hollywood. The purpose of the convention was to generate enthusiasm for the coming year's product (most of which was still in the preparatory stage). Announcements concerning recently acquired literary properties, casts of forthcoming pictures, continuations of successful series, new stars, promotional gimmicks, sales materials, etc. were supposed to inspire confidence in employees and exhibitors alike concerning the quality and commercial viability of the coming productions.

After the branch managers and sales people returned home, they would begin to call on theater owners in their territories. Communicating the information and enthusiasm they had picked up at the convention, they would attempt to convince these exhibitors to commit to a *Block* of the company's films. Until 1941, films were sold in large blocks that often included shorts, newsreels and cartoons as well. A full block represented the entire output of a studio for the release year. Although smaller blocks could be purchased (the smallest would be about 12 features), the overwhelming desire was to sell full blocks and various incentives were offered to those who booked them. Assurances of quality were voiced but, in fact, there was no guarantee that the films that would begin to arrive in early September would please the paying customers. This practice was so prevalent that it earned the nickname *Blind bidding*, because theater owners were forced to commit, without an opportunity to examine the merchandise. In fact, production had not yet begun on most of the coming year's films when theater owners were asked to book them.

Sales pitches continued throughout the summer and escalated toward the end of August. Studios liked to premiere an exciting picture at the beginning of each release year, a time when exhibitors would often buy a substantial block in order to acquire the apparent hit. RKO, for example, offered two Astaire–Rogers musicals, *Top Hat* and *Swing Time*, as its Labor Day releases in 1935 and 1936 for this reason. The selling period did not end in September. It continued, in less intense fashion, until it was time to start thinking about the next year's releases.

Controversial distribution practices

The relationship between motion picture companies and the independent theaters they supplied was always antagonistic and vexing. Distributors complained about incompetent projectionists, print damage, the difficulty of collecting rentals in a timely fashion and the tendency of some theater owners to underreport ticket sales and, thus, underpay the supplier for films leased on a percentage basis. Many exhibitors were so distrusted that distributors paid individuals (called checkers) to stand nearby and count the number of patrons who paid for specific showings. If a checker's tally differed markedly from the exhibitor's report, a showdown would quickly occur.

Still, distributor complaints about exhibitors were minor compared to the howls of protest that continually issued from independent theater owners, particularly the smaller outfits that had very little leverage. Beginning in the silent era, these exhibitors importuned the government to scrutinize the distribution practices of the big companies, which they felt were highly unfair to them and, in fact, monopolistic. *Block booking* and blind bidding represented only two of several strategies they found objectionable. To understand the others it is necessary to pause and discuss a subject that might otherwise be reserved for the next section: the theater chains of the Big Five companies.

While the theaters that were part of the MGM, Paramount, Warner Bros., Twentieth Century-Fox and RKO empires represented less than one-fifth of American motion picture venues, they were among the largest and best facilities in the nation. Most were spacious (2,000 seats, on average), plush, comfortable, located in the downtown sections of major cities and designated first-run, which meant that new films opened in them. Since filmgoers paid the highest admission prices to attend these palaces, company distribution arms developed a modus operandi that would encourage people to patronize the first-run theaters, rather than wait for movies to trickle down to the independently owned houses where they could see them for a lesser cost.

The *Clearance Period* was one element in the overall strategy. It referred to the number of days that had to pass before a film, having completed one run, would be available to certain theaters for its next run. This clearance or "dead" time always existed between the first and second run, meaning an "A" film would be unavailable for viewing after it closed its initial engagement. Realizing that they might have to wait a long time to see a new, enticing picture if they missed the first run, many spectators paid the premium price. When the film finally arrived at a subsequent-run house, often four weeks or longer after it had ended its first run, it was naturally not as exciting to moviegoers who were then being wooed, by advertising and promotion, to see the latest first-run attraction. Clearances also applied to third-, fourth- and fifth-run theaters which usually had to wait months to offer a film. *Zoning* contributed to the independents' frustration. Theaters were organized into geographical zones that were sometimes quite large. Any film playing in a specific zone was generally unavailable to another theater in that zone until it closed and the requisite clearance period expired.

In addition, studios that were theoretically in competition with one another routinely played each other's films in their theaters. Since each of the Big Five had exhibition strengths in different sections of the country, this *Pooling* arrangement enabled them to showcase their product in the best theaters throughout America's largest cities. It also meant that independents, some of whom operated very good houses in these cities, were generally unable to procure first-runs from studios that controlled no theaters in the area.

There was apparent collusion in the *Fixing of Admission Prices* as well, since distribution contracts routinely (and uniformly) stipulated the minimum price that a theater could charge its patrons. This eliminated any significant price wars among rival exhibitors and protected the first-runs by making sure that their prices were not undercut substantially. Finally, exhibitors claimed that certain independent theater owners – especially the owners of chains who were in a position to generate a large volume of business – were accorded preferential treatment regarding specific bookings, as well as runs, clearances and minimum admission prices.

The combined weight of all these distribution practices, argued the independents, was in restraint of trade and, therefore, monopolistic. It left the small exhibitors in an untenable negotiating position; they either accepted the dictated terms or abandoned the business. The independents contended that the only way to rectify the situation was to eliminate block booking and force the Big Five to sell their exhibition outlets. Each theater could then compete for specific pictures on its own merits. After years of investigation and preliminary legal skirmishes, the Department of Justice finally took up the exhibitors' cause, filing suit in 1938 against all the majors. This action, known informally as the "Paramount Case," included the Little Three, even though those studios owned no theaters. Charging that their distribution methods did not differ markedly from those of the Big Five, it was alleged that they, too, engaged in forced clearances, zoning, price fixing and preferential treatment for certain exhibitors.

The compromise of 1940

In late 1940, the Big Five resolved the matter by entering into a consent decree with the government. In order to stave off the divorcement of their theater chains, they agreed to:

1. limit blocks to no more than five films
2. eliminate blind bidding by offering exhibitors a chance to view films before they bid on them

3. stop requiring theater owners to take shorts, westerns, reissues, newsreels, cartoons, etc. in order to obtain desirable feature films
4. submit disputes over distribution practices to arbitration
5. stop acquiring theaters, except in extraordinary circumstances.

These remedies, which took effect in 1941, pleased neither side. The studios grumbled about having to wait until they had completed five appropriate pictures for "trade showing," thus disrupting normal release patterns and affecting cash flow and interest payments on their bank debt. Exhibitors complained about the arbitration system which was costly and, lacking definite standards, subject to the whim of the arbitrator. They pointed out that the blocks of five generally contained only one or two desirable films; thus, they still had to accept more unwanted pictures than they would have liked. Additionally, since the trade screenings took place only in exchange cities, theater owners in distant sections of the territory found it very difficult to attend. After a while, a number of disgruntled exhibitors who lived close to the exchanges also stopped going, believing the whole process to be a waste of time. Like the exhibitors who lived far from the key cities, they tended to rely on trade-paper reviews to guide their bookings.

For these and other reasons, the consent decree collapsed in 1942. The United Motion Picture Industry Council (UMPIC) was then created by the Big Five and offered exhibitors the "Unity Plan." Henceforth, blocks of 12 films would be available for booking, with five completed and screened for the trade. Enraged theater owners, offered no significant concessions by their suppliers, once again clamored for government intervention. But the Roosevelt administration, concentrating its energies on the war effort and fully aware of the value of Hollywood's propaganda films and other contributions, was not in a trust-busting mood. When it became clear that the Allies would be victorious, however, the government decided to reopen the case. The fact that most of the major studios were earning unprecedented profits at the time and that the recently formed Society of Independent Motion Picture Producers had decided to back the cause of the theater owners also factored into the decision. In August 1944, the Department of Justice announced that it would file antitrust charges with the principal goal of forcing the Big Five to get out of the exhibition business. Although several more years would pass before a final consent decree was accepted in the "Paramount Case," this time the outcome would be different and substantially alter the business of motion pictures in the post-war years.

Foreign distribution

The major studios maintained distribution offices in many foreign countries, deriving an estimated 33 percent of their revenues from abroad during the Classical Period. Language and cultural barriers notwithstanding, the American cinema was popular in nations as diverse as Bulgaria, Turkey, India, New Zealand and Argentina. With Canada considered part of the domestic market, Great Britain proved to be the most lucrative territory, accounting for about 35 percent of all foreign earnings.

International distribution was unstable throughout most of the Classical Period. While neither the USSR nor Japan was a heavy importer of American films, Germany was an active customer until the Nazis took control in 1933. Thereafter, the marketing of American films in Germany declined steadily; it also became problematic in Mussolini's Italy in the late 30s. World War II cut off distribution to most of Europe. As soon as Czechoslovakia, Austria, Poland, France, Norway, Denmark, Belgium, Greece, etc. fell to the Axis, these countries stopped importing American movies. Even Great Britain became something of a problem. Facing a financial crisis brought on by the costs of waging war, the British froze the earnings of foreign companies within the British Isles. Several studios established production units in the besieged country in order to make films with their "frozen funds."

The wartime loss of so many foreign outlets caused the industry to concentrate a considerable amount of energy on the exploitation of Central and South America. Films such as *Moonlight in Havana* (Universal, 1942), *You Were Never Lovelier* (Columbia, 1942), *Saludos Amigos* (Disney/RKO, 1943), *The Gang's All Here* (Twentieth Century-Fox, 1943), *Brazil* (Republic, 1944) and *Pan-Americana* (RKO, 1945) were tailored to please the Latin American market. This strategy was encouraged by US government officials whose aggressive "Good Neighbor" policy was designed to assure that none of the countries to the south became allied with the Axis powers. Business did improve in the Central and South American countries, enabling the studios to maintain their foreign earnings just below the level that they had managed throughout the 1920s. The main source of film company prosperity during the war years was the vital domestic market, but overseas distribution still contributed more than anyone had a right to expect.

Conducting business in foreign countries was a complicated adventure. The problems of dubbing or subtitling films, dealing with local censors, negotiating and enforcing contracts, shipping and protecting prints and handling political and cultural changes were a formidable challenge. In economic terms,

American movie companies were equal to it; they dominated world film business throughout the Classical Period.

The costs of distribution

Marketing films was an expensive process. Like production, its costs were broken down into two categories: direct and indirect. Direct charges for each film included the expenses of making approximately 200 prints, transporting those prints to and from theaters, insuring the negative and prints, copyright and censorship fees, payments to checkers, the costs of advertising and promotion including preparation and production of press books and posters, advertisements in trade papers and magazines, plus miscellaneous costs, such as the costs of making foreign versions.

The indirect charge paid for the maintenance of the worldwide distribution network. The salaries of all the managers, sales people and other workers in the domestic exchanges and foreign offices, as well as the expenses attendant to the maintenance of these branches, had to be apportioned in some fashion, so they were parceled out to each picture as an indirect, or overhead, charge. Also known as the distribution fee, this charge was collected as a percentage of the gross receipts (rentals) that a film generated. Depending on the particular release year the distribution fee would range between 20 and 30 percent.

To understand the way in which distribution fees figured in company accounting, it is necessary to study the profits and losses of one year's worth of product (see Figure 2.5 on pp. 84–85). Because we do not know the distribution fee for this release year, it is not possible to determine the precise direct and indirect costs of distribution. But we can figure the total distribution costs for a profitable film by: i) Taking the total amount the film *made* (*income*); ii) Subtracting its *cost of production*; and iii) Subtracting the amount reported as *profit*. We then infer the remainder to be its *distribution* cost. For example:

King Kong
$1,856,000	world gross film *income*
– 672,000	studio production *cost*
– 650,000	*profit*
= $534,000	total direct and indirect costs of distribution

To determine the distribution costs of an unprofitable film, i) Take the total amount the film *made* (*income*); ii) *Add* the amount reported as *loss*; and

iii) Subtract its *cost of production*. We then infer the remainder to be the total direct and indirect costs of distribution.

Our Betters

$395,000	world gross film *income*
+ 100,000	reported *loss*
− 356,000	studio production *cost*
= $139,000	total direct and indirect costs of distribution

In order to figure the distribution costs of a movie that did not generate as much income as it cost, i) Take the *cost of production*; ii) Subtract the total amount the film *generated* (*income*); and iii) Add the amount reported as *loss*. We then infer the remainder to be the specific amount spent on *distribution*.

The Conquerors

$619,000	studio production *cost*
− 586,000	world gross film *income*
+ 230,000	*reported loss*
= $263,000	total direct and indirect costs of distribution

The distribution fee would remain steady for all films, though one that brought in lots of money (such as *King Kong*) would obviously have a larger amount subtracted than one that did not. Direct charges were also roughly proportional. Much more would be spent on the advertising and exploitation of an expensive film that might generate substantial rentals than on an inexpensive film. However, these charges were kept in check by requiring theater owners to carry part of the burden. They usually paid for local newspaper ads, as well as posters, lobby cards, stills and trailers that the companies provided to help promote their pictures.

Exhibition

Motion picture theaters during the Classical Period ran the gamut from small houses in rural areas (some with fewer than 100 seats) to New York's Radio City Music Hall, a show business Taj Mahal that could accommodate 6,200 people per performance. Movie palaces with capacities of 1,500 plus, such as the Music Hall, often featured live performers as well as celluloid programs. Although they represented only a small percentage of the nation's theaters, they

No.	Amort. Release Date W.E.	Title	Director	Cast	Studio Prod. Cost	Estimated Eventual World Gross Film Income			Profit (Loss)
						Domestic	Foreign	Total	
					(Stated in Thousands of Dollars)				
1	4/ 1/33	King Kong	Cooper-Schoedsack	Wray-Armstrong-Cabot	672	745	1,111	1,856	650
2	8/19/32	Bring 'Em Back Alive	Elliott	Frank Buck	Buren	692	352	1,044	155
3	10/22/32	Phantom Of Crestwood	Ruben	Cortez-Morley-Louise	187	348	88	436	100
4	3/18/33	Our Betters	Cukor	C. Bennett-Roland	356	277	118	395	(100)
5	7/22/33	Bed Of Roses	La Cava	C. Bennett-McCrea	313	330	63	393	(50)
6	11/18/33	After Tonight	Archainbaud	C. Bennett-Roland-Ellis	355	250	130	380	(100)
7	12/24/32	Secrets Of The French Police	Sutherland	Andre-Ratoff-Morgan	196	173	65	238	(50)
8	6/24/33	Professional Sweethearts	Seiter	Rogers-Foster-McHugh	122	225	49	274	50
9	1/ 7/33	Penguin Pool Murder	Archainbaud	Oliver-Gleason-Clark	146	221	99	320	60
10	7/ 1/33	Melody Cruise	Sandrich	Ruggles-Phil Harris	163	316	169	485	150
11	3/ 4/33	Topaze	D'Arrast	Barrymore-Loy-Alberni	313	310	95	405	(50)
12	9/ 9/33	Blind Adventure	Schoedsack	Armstrong-Mack-Young	110	110	40	150	(25)
13	9/15/33	Deluge	Feist	Shannon-Wilson-Blackmer	Admiral	135	116	251	30
14	12/31/32	Half Naked Truth	La Cava	Velez-L. Tracy-Morgan	199	311	71	382	50
15	2/11/33	Past Of Mary Holmes	Thompson	Linden-Mackellar-Arthur	111	136	78	214	25
16	6/16/33	Big Brain	Archainbaud	Holmes-Wray-Stone	Admiral	138	52	190	20
17	10/ 8/32	Come On Danger	Hill	Keene-Haydon-Ates	31	79	27	106	30
18	12/ 3/32	Renegades Of The West	Robinson	Keene-Furness-Ates	34	81	31	112	30
19	2/ 4/33	Cheyenne Kid	Hill	Keene-Mason	35	78	30	108	25
20	3/25/33	Scarlet River	Browner	Keene-Wilson-Ates	36	86	31	117	35
21	5/13/33	Son Of The Border	Nosler	Keene-Haydon-Chaney	31	74	27	101	25
22	7/ 1/33	Cross Fire	Browner	Keene-Furness-Kennedy	26	74	24	98	20
23	4/22/33	Sweepings	Cromwell	Barrymore-Dinehart	335	312	117	429	(25)
24	9/30/32	Bill Of Divorcement	Cukor	Hepburn-Barrymore-Burke	250	383	148	531	110
25	5/20/33	Silver Cord	Cromwell	Dunne-McCrea-Dee	153	244	75	319	50
26	8/26/33	Before Dawn	Pichel	Erwin-Wilson-Oland	78	118	56	174	30
27	2/ 4/33	Monkey's Paw	Ruggles	Smith-Simpson-Lawford	153	54	67	121	(85)
28	8/12/33	Headline Shooter	Browner	Bellamy-Gargan-Dee	109	167	51	218	30
29	9/17/32	Hold 'Em Jail	Taurog	Gracie-Wheeler-Woolsey	408	416	95	511	(55)
30	9/10/32	Age Of Consent	La Cava	Wilson-Cromwell-Linden	99	206	25	231	50
31	11/19/32	Little Orphan Annie	Robertson	M. Green-Robson-Kennedy	128	246	38	284	50
32	10/ 8/32	Hell's Highway	Brown	Dix-Brown-Hudson	272	279	59	338	(50)
33	11/11/33	Great Jasper	Ruben	Dix-Engles-Oliver	261	277	83	360	(30)
34	8/19/33	No Marriage Ties	Ruben	Dix-Allen-Kenyon	215	247	60	307	(15)
35	1/21/33	Animal Kingdom	Griffith	Harding-Howard-Loy	458	439	89	528	50
36	12/10/32	Conquerors	Wellman	Dix-Harding-Oliver	619	462	124	586	(230)
37	8/ 5/33	Double Harness	Cromwell	Harding-Powell	329	379	114	493	10
38	1/28/33	No Other Woman	Ruben	Dunne-Bickford-Andre	207	216	68	284	(20)
39	10/ 1/32	Most Dangerous Game	Pichel	McCrea-Wray-Banks	219	263	180	443	75
40	4/ 1/33	Christopher Strong	Arzner	Hepburn-Clive-Burke	284	232	154	386	(35)

No.	Amort. Release Date W.E.	Title	Director	Cast	Studio Prod. Cost	Estimated Eventual			
						World Gross Film Income			Profit (Loss)
						Domestic	Foreign	Total	
					(Stated in Thousands of Dollars)				
41	12/24/32	Men Of America	Ince	Boyd-Wilson-Ince	88	147	41	188	30
42	2/11/33	Lucky Devils	Ince	Boyd-Wilson-Gargan	117	179	106	285	65
43	6/10/33	Emergency Call	Cahn	Boyd-Gibson-Gargan	91	157	60	217	45
44	10/14/33	Flaming Gold	Ince	Boyd-Clarke-O'Brian	127	138	46	184	(10)
45	7/29/33	Flying Devils	Birdwell	Bellamy-Judge-Cabot	108	169	68	237	40
46	11/26/32	Sport Parade	Murphy	McCrea-Marsh-Gargan	127	185	46	231	20
47	10/22/32	Thirteen Women	Archainbaud	Dunne-Cortez-Loy	200	230	58	288	(10)
48	4/28/33	India Speaks	Halleburton		Futter	67	8	75	7
49	5/20/33	Diplomaniacs	Seitzer	Wheeler-Woolsey-White	242	323	138	461	65
50	1/27/33	Goldie Gets Along	St. Clair	Damita-Morton-Page	King	106	26	132	(8)
51	11/10/33	Goodbye Love	Humberstone	Ruggles-Teasdale-Methot	Joma	107	40	147	14
52	3/24/33	Man Hunt	Cummings	Durkin-Hervey-Reid	King	75	25	100	(11)
53	11/18/32	Men Are Such Fools	Nieh	Osborne-Carrello-Merkel	Joma	102	35	137	Nil
54	2/10/33	Sailor Be Good	Cruze	Oakie-Osborne-Stone	Joma	165	46	211	33
55	10/ 7/32	Strange Justice	Schertzinger	Marsh-Denny-Bennett	King	101	40	141	4
56	10/21/32	Theft Of The Mona Lisa	Von Bolvary	Forst-Von Mold	Tobis	17	-	17	(8)
57	6/ 2/33	Tomorrow At Seven	Enright	Morris-Osborne-Jenkins	Joma	142	56	198	27
					Total	12,539	5,308	17,847	1,143

Figure 2.5   RKO profit/loss table for the 1932–33 release year. Source: The C.J. Tevlin Ledger ("Statistics on Feature Releases," June 1952. Courtesy of the RKO Radio Pictures Archive.

Figure 2.6   One of the motion picture palaces of the 1930s – the Paramount Theater in Aurora, Illinois. Courtesy of the Academy of Motion Picture Arts and Sciences Library.

contained more than 21 percent of the available seats. And because of their first-run status, they generated approximately 50 percent of the total domestic rentals of "A" films. Thus, one can readily understand why these theaters were crucial to the business strategies of the Big Five, who owned or controlled a majority of them. (Figure 2.6)

Theater operations slumped during the early 30s, forcing many owners to close their houses. It was estimated that more than 5,000 were shuttered during the darkest days of the Depression. But when the crisis began to ease, a number of these theaters returned to life. Near the peak of Hollywood's most successful era in 1945, there were 18,076 movie theaters in the US, of which 3,137 were owned or controlled by members of the Big Five. Approximately 70 percent of the first-run houses in cities of more than 100,000 were allied with Big Five companies. Paramount held sway over 1,395 theaters, then came Twentieth Century-Fox (636) and Warner Bros. (501), while Loews/MGM (135) and RKO

Figure 2.7 The exterior of the Warner Bros. Theater in Beverly Hills, California, photographed in 1938. Courtesy of the Academy of Motion Picture Arts and Sciences Library.

(109) controlled smaller, but well positioned, chains. In addition, various combinations of the Big Five companies owned 361 theaters jointly. (Figure 2.7)

Each organization had strengths in different sections of the country. Twentieth Century-Fox dominated west coast and mountain time-zone exhibition; Paramount was strong in New England, the midwest and south; Warner Bros. in the mid-Atlantic region; Loews in the New York area and parts of the midwest; and RKO in New York City, New England and other portions of the midwest. Some of the majors, such as Paramount, Fox and Loews/MGM, owned or controlled theaters in Canada, the United Kingdom, France, South Africa, Australia and other countries as well. There were also powerful independent chains, such as Griffith in the southwestern US and Crescent in the southern states, as well as thousands of individually owned theaters scattered throughout the nation.

Admission prices varied with the theater's location, the film's run (spectators attending first-runs paid a premium price) and time of day (matinees were less expensive than evening shows). However, it is possible to track general price trends during the period.

Year   *Average admission price*
1935   25 cents
1939   27 cents
1940   29 cents
1945   40 cents

It is clear that after an initial period of price-slashing to help lure Depression audiences back, prices stabilized during the 1930s, then began to climb significantly during the war years. They would top out in the late 1940s and then begin to slide backward as television and other factors put pressure on the box office.

First-run engagements generally lasted a week or more, with popular films usually "held over" for several weeks. Subsequent runs were shorter. In fact, during the Depression most of America's theaters changed their programs two or three times a week. Since the majority of these theaters played double features, their owners had to deal with several distributors to supply their total requirements. For example, consider the following programs offered by the Glassell Theater, a subsequent-run house in the northeast section of Los Angeles, in late October 1935:

Wednesday, October 23
Calm Yourself (MGM)
Chasing Yesterday (RKO)

Thursday, October 24
Paris in Spring (Paramount)
Stone of Silver Creek (Universal)

Saturday, October 26
Broadway Gondolier (Warner Bros.)
Old Man Rhythm (RKO)

Wednesday, October 30
Love Me Forever (Columbia)
She (RKO)

In little more than a week, the Glassell ran films from six of the major studios. And while the typical program contained one "A" film and one "B," the October 30 double bill presented two films that were initially intended by their respective studios to be "A" pictures: *Love Me Forever*, a musical starring Grace Moore, and *She*, a fantasy/adventure starring Helen Gahagan and Randolph Scott. It was also not unusual to find smaller theaters showing two or three "B" productions, plus assorted cartoons, shorts and newsreels. Finally, while some theaters maintained an orderly schedule of program changes, others were more flexible. The Glassell changed its double features 12 times in October 1935 – four times on Wednesdays, four times on Thursdays, three times on Saturdays and once on a Sunday.

Average attendance for a week shaped up this way:

Monday	10 percent
Tuesday	10 percent
Wednesday	10 percent
Thursday	10 percent
Friday	15 percent
Saturday	20 percent
Sunday	25 percent

For obvious reasons, theater owners attempted to book the most attractive pictures on weekends. They offered the lion's share of promotional gimmicks, such as games, contests and giveaways, on the slow nights, mainly Mondays and Tuesdays. Most patrons attended evening shows; it was estimated that 75 to 85 percent of a day's receipts were taken in between 7:30 and 8:30 p.m.

The optimum times to open major films in first-run houses were just before the following holidays: Christmas (December), New Year's (December/January), Washington's Birthday (February), Easter (March or April), Decoration Day (May), Labor Day (September), Columbus Day (October), Armistice Day (November) and Thanksgiving (November). Interestingly, in contrast to the present-day emphasis on summer releases, Independence Day was not considered a propitious time to open a big film for two reasons. First, many people scheduled vacations around July 4, taking them away from the cities and, therefore, away from the key first-run theaters. Second, many American theaters were not air-conditioned, causing patrons to shun them during the hottest months. This situation began to change as the Depression eased and more and more owners installed "air cooling," but it still affected distribution and exhibition practices into the 1940s.

3

Technology

In the mid-1920s, problems involving the precise synchronization of picture and sound source, as well as the necessary amplification to produce acoustically acceptable levels of sound in even the largest movie theaters, were overcome, setting the stage for what to date remains the most significant technological advance in motion picture history: the transition from silent to sound films. This evolution reverberated throughout the industry: it required millions of dollars in re-equipping costs, caused many workers who had earned their livelihoods from silent films to lose their jobs, and opened up opportunities for technical experts, actors, writers and others whose skills were needed by the new medium. In fact, the Classical Period in American film history dawned largely because of the impact of the coming of sound to celluloid entertainment.

While there were many other technological developments during this period, none of them sent tremors rumbling through the entire structure of the industry as the arrival of the "talkies" did. Most were refinements that enabled films to look and sound better, broadened the creative possibilities of film artists and made the always-difficult production process less intimidating and expensive. The only other potentially revolutionary technological breakthrough was the introduction of a "perfected" Technicolor process in 1932. However, this innovation did not lead to an immediate abandonment of black-and-white filmmaking. Even after feature films began to be made in "three-strip" Technicolor in the mid-30s, the studios continued to produce more than 90 percent of their output in monochrome. Color was saved for "special" productions in which its extra cost could be justified both aesthetically and financially.

The changes that occurred in cinema technology came from a variety of sources. Some were developed by giant corporations (e.g., American Telephone and Telegraph, Radio Corporation of America) whose principal business objectives lay apart from motion pictures. Others originated with notable companies

(Kodak, Technicolor) more directly involved with the film industry. Important contributions were also made by small concerns (Mole-Richardson, Mitchell Camera) that were umbilically joined, in a business sense, to Hollywood. Finally, the various technical departments within the studios, particularly Camera, Sound and Special Effects, gave employees enough research and development time to discover new processes, fashion new pieces of equipment and reformulate approaches to production that turned out to be cinematic advancements.

Most developments were willingly shared by all members of the industry. One of the beneficial functions of the fledging Academy of Motion Picture Arts and Sciences was its activity as a clearinghouse for new technological information and its encouragement of experimentation through awards given from 1931 onward to companies and individuals who made significant contributions. The Hollywood film industry could never be accused of being a collegial enterprise, but in the technological arena a high level of cooperation did prevail. As a consequence, no studio's films were ever significantly more advanced from a technical standpoint than its competitors' products. In fact, the films that came from Hollywood during the Classical Period were remarkably homogeneous in both style and technical polish.

The Sound Revolution

Perhaps the most fascinating aspect of the passage from silent to sound pictures was that none of the true pioneers foresaw how their efforts would turn out. Neither Dr. Lee DeForest, whose inventions helped surmount the technical barriers to true sound movies, nor the Warner brothers, the movie moguls who would profit most handsomely from taking a leadership position with respect to sound, nor William Fox, another entrepreneur who had the good sense to steer the industry toward the sound-on-film option, realized the extent to which audiences would fall in love with motion pictures containing the sound of human voices. They believed in the advantages of marrying music and sound effects to film, even to giving voice to musical performers and newsreel subjects, but they did not envision the commercial power of feature films with dialogue.

The conversion to "talkies" required several years to complete. It began to take shape when Warner Bros. and Western Electric (the manufacturing subsidiary of American Telephone and Telegraph) formed an alliance in 1926. The Warners believed that the advantages of films with sound, which included the possible elimination of vaudeville acts and live musical accompaniment in theaters, plus the opportunity for spectators to experience the same high level of entertainment in the smallest as well as largest houses, would translate into higher film rentals for their company. Therefore, the studio and its new partner took the financial gamble of re-tooling production facilities to produce sound films and, most importantly, of installing the necessary apparatus in key theaters of the Warners' growing exhibition chain. The Warner Bros.–Western Electric joint venture was named Vitaphone.

In early 1926, Vitaphone presented its first program in New York City. Composed of a series of shorts (most featuring classical music) followed by *Don Juan*, a feature film starring John Barrymore and Mary Astor which contained a synchronized musical score and sound effects, the package was a success with both reviewers and audiences. Warner Bros. quickly moved forward, producing more musical shorts, the majority starring leading vaudeville performers. Meanwhile, Western Electric engineers worked overtime to install sound reproduction equipment in as many theaters as possible. By the end of 1926, more than 100 houses could show the Warner programs.

Although Western Electric had developed both sound-on-film (optical sound) and sound-on-disc systems, the initial Vitaphone offerings were all sound-on-disc, primarily because the sound quality was superior in the disc system. But sound-on-disc had many drawbacks that affected both production and exhibition. In order to edit the early disc films, multiple cameras had to be used in shooting. If an actor made a mistake during a take, the entire scene would be scrapped and the production team would have to begin again. Many things could (and did) go wrong in the projection booth as well, including the breakage of discs and other accidents (some as simple as bumping into the turntable) that could destroy synchronization. Not the least of the drawbacks was economic; the disc system required two operators, one for the projector and one for the turntable, thus increasing the projection costs for each theater substantially.

William Fox, of the Fox Film Corporation, recognized these liabilities and opted for sound-on-film. Choosing a system developed by Theodore W. Case and Earl I. Sponable, Fox formed the Fox-Case Corporation in 1926 with the initial idea of producing shorts featuring vaudeville acts. But he soon discovered that Warner Bros. had signed up most of the important variety stars, so he accepted the advice of Courtland Smith, president of the Fox newsreel company, and set about introducing the sound newsreel. After wiring several of the theaters in his chain, Fox began to present the Fox Movietone News. Among the earliest offerings were the departure of Charles Lindbergh on his historic solo flight across the Atlantic in May 1927 and his triumphant return to the US one month later. When audiences responded boisterously to Movietone's visual and audible coverage of the Lindbergh heroics, William Fox accelerated his commitment to sound, expanding production of the newsreels and arranging for more theater installations.

In October 1927, Warner Bros. premiered *The Jazz Singer*. The film maintained the trappings of a silent feature except for its musical sequences and brief segments of apparently improvised dialogue that issued from the mouth of star Al Jolson. Audiences were especially stirred by Jolson's singing and speaking. After *The Jazz Singer* played to record crowds in St. Louis, Detroit, Los Angeles, Baltimore, Washington, DC, Columbus and other cities, the Warner executives were forced to rethink their negative assessments of true "talking" pictures. Within three months of the opening of *The Jazz Singer*, Warners had produced an "all-talking" comedy short entitled *My Wife's Gone Away*. Again, the customers embraced the film, and the death rattle of the silent cinema began to resonate.

Nevertheless, some important members of the industry refused to hear it. In 1928, Harold Franklin, president of West Coast Theaters, stated, "The silent motion picture is too well established to vanish because of this new development." Joseph Schenck, then president of United Artists, took an even stronger stand. He announced in August 1928 that his company would not make "talkies":

> I do not believe that the present talking picture craze is more than a public curiosity in a novelty. It is a novelty and a badly done one. I prophesy they [*sic*] will not last more than four or five months.

What did not last was Mr. Schenck's resolve to sidestep the mushrooming "novelty." Following the giant success of Warner Bros.' first all-talking feature *The Lights of New York* in 1928 and William Fox's enthusiastic move in the same year to Movietone feature films, the other major companies began the expensive conversion process. The major beneficiary of all the activity was Western Electric, which signed agreements with Loews/MGM, Paramount, Universal, United Artists, First National and other companies for the installation of sound equipment in their studios. Western Electric managed to sew up the lion's share of theater wirings as well.

This did not sit well with David Sarnoff and other executives of the Radio Corporation of America, which had begun offering its Photophone sound equipment to the industry in 1927. A handful of the smaller concerns – such as Pathé, Mack Sennett, FBO, Tiffany Stahl and Educational – signed up with

RCA, but these commitments from second-ranked companies did not satisfy Sarnoff. He decided to create his own major studio which would utilize Photophone and become a launching pad for his legal assault on the near monopoly held by Western Electric and its recently formed Electrical Research Products Incorporated (ERPI) division, set up to handle the non-telephone aspects of its business. The new studio was Radio-Keith-Orpheum (see chapter 2), and the Sarnoff strategy ultimately paid dividends. By the mid-1930s, RCA and ERPI would hold nearly equal shares of the sound film equipment market.

The key transitional year was 1929. At the beginning of that year, most of the studios were still releasing silent and/or partial-talkie films. By the end, the majors were committed to a full slate of talking pictures. The transformation of the theaters, however, took longer. While some 13,500 houses could present sound films at the end of 1930, approximately 8,200 others still had not installed the necessary equipment, forcing the studios to release silent versions of their sound films. Many of the unwired theaters would never show a talkie; faced with the expense of installation at a time when their Depression-battered audience members were in decline, numerous owners simply abandoned the business.

Nearly all of the first theaters to convert opted for systems that could play both sound-on-disc and sound-on-film. The engineers at Western Electric determined that a projection speed of 90 feet per minute (24 frames of film per second) would be ideal for both systems; the industry soon adopted this speed as its standard. Improvements in sound-on-film reproduction combined with a growing dislike for the cumbersome disc method caused the turntables to be phased out in 1930. Optical sound eliminated the need for two operators, significantly reduced the technical glitches in theater presentations and cleared the way for improvements in the production process that would soon elevate the artistic possibilities of motion pictures.

The sweeping technological transformation affected everyone whose job was related to the film industry. The most prominent "casualties" were high-profile actors; many notable Hollywood careers declined rapidly in the late 20s and early 30s. The reasons for the stars' loss of box office drawing power are generally far more complex than the usual platitudes about foreign accents, voices that didn't "match" screen personas or inability to utter dialogue convincingly. But, without question the coming of sound had a negative impact on such performers as Gloria Swanson, Mary Pickford, Theda Bara, John Gilbert, Pola Negri, Douglas Fairbanks, Buster Keaton, Clara Bow, Emil Jannings, Mae Murray and Harold Lloyd.

A number of famous directors also endured a rapid decline in the new production environment. D.W. Griffith, arguably the greatest innovator and artist of the silent cinema, made his final film (appropriately titled *The Struggle*, Griffith/United Artists) in 1932, though he lived until 1948. Herbert Brenon, who had directed the well-regarded *Peter Pan* (Paramount, 1924) and *Beau Geste* (Paramount, 1926), quickly fell on hard times in the early 1930s. And James Cruze, responsible for the hugely successful epic western *The Covered Wagon* (Paramount, 1923), was making "B" pictures such as *Prison Nurse* (1938) and *The Gangs of New York* (1938) for Republic in the late 30s.

Other studio workers, including writers of silent film scenarios and inter-titles, also encountered difficulties in the world of talkies, but the largest group to be thrown out of work was the theater musicians who earned their livings accompanying silent films. From pianists and organists who played in typical movie houses to members of good-sized orchestras who performed in the urban film palaces, these talented individuals suddenly found themselves without employment just as the Depression was engulfing America. Despite the efforts of the American Federation of Musicians to save jobs, some 18,000 were fired.

The sound revolution did create opportunities as well. A new breed of actor – generally with stage and/or vaudeville experience – arrived in Hollywood. In a relatively short time, new stars would emerge from this coterie: Mae West, James Cagney, Spencer Tracy, the Marx Brothers, Claudette Colbert, Paul Muni, Clark Gable and Bette Davis, among others. Likewise, the new medium would require writers with a flair for dialogue as well as an acute dramatic sensibility. Among the trailblazers of sound film screenwriting would be Ben Hecht, Dudley Nichols, Robert Riskin, W.R. Burnett, Joseph L. Mankiewicz, Samson Raphaelson, Charles MacArthur, Sidney Buchman, Jo Swerling, Donald Ogden Stewart and Nunnally Johnson. Although some new directors did enter the business at this time, including George Cukor, Rouben Mamoulian, James Whale, Mitchell Leisen and John Cromwell, a remarkable number of silent filmmakers were able to grasp the requirements of sound quickly and move ahead to long and impressive careers in the following decades. Some of the most famous were John Ford, Victor Fleming, Cecil B. DeMille, Howard Hawks, William Wellman, William Wyler, Ernst Lubitsch, Frank Capra, Mervyn LeRoy, Raoul Walsh, Lewis Milestone, Henry King and Clarence Brown. Silent film personalities – even those who continued to work steadily in talking pictures – had a hard time maintaining their star status. A few who remained popular (or even grew in acclaim) during the early 30s were Janet Gaynor, Joan Crawford, Will Rogers, Greta Garbo, Gary Cooper, Carole Lombard, Jean Arthur and Charles Chaplin. Finally, talking pictures brought a whole new group of specialists to Hollywood: engineers (most with radio or telephone backgrounds) to install the sound equipment in the studios and to staff sound departments, dialogue coaches, elocution experts, composers, musicians to play the scores when they were recorded, etc.

A great deal has been written about the cinematic rigor mortis that afflicted many early talking pictures, thanks to limitations imposed by the unsophisticated recording apparatus. A majority of the initial sound efforts do seem visually static, dramatically awkward and creatively uninspired. While some of the problems may be blamed on the primitive omnidirectional microphones that picked up sounds indiscriminately, the windowed sound-proofed camera booths which limited the possibilities for movement and composition, and the tyranny of the sound recordist who placed the quality of the sound above all other considerations, it is important to consider the aesthetic qualities of early sound films in a broader context.

Unquestionably, the greatest films of the late silent period, such as *Sunrise* (Fox, 1927), *The Crowd* (MGM, 1928) and *The Wind* (MGM, 1928), achieved a high level of cinematic expression with respect to camera work, editing, visual design and acting, but they stand apart from routine releases of their period almost as dramatically as they do from the early talkies. On the other hand, if we compare the typical late silent film to the typical early sound picture, the aesthetic gulf between them does not seem so large. Moreover, the evidence contained in films from the early sound era reveals that filmmakers who were concerned about the visual sophistication of their productions and had sufficient budgets to accomplish their goals were able to overcome most of the obstacles presented by the machinery of sound with surprising effectiveness. Rouben Mamoulian in *Applause* (Paramount, 1929), King Vidor in *Hallelujah!* (MGM, 1929), Lewis Milestone in *All Quiet on the Western Front* (Universal, 1930), Ernst Lubitsch in *Monte Carlo* (Paramount, 1930) and John Murray Anderson in *King of Jazz* (Universal, 1930) all managed to produce early sound pictures whose cinematic qualities were more accomplished than those of most late silents. (Figure 3.1)

Their efforts were abetted by an army of creative minds who recognized the necessity of improving the quality of sound films and set to work solving the problems. They came up with camera booths on wheels which allowed some movement, then sound-insulating "blimps" or "bungalows" which, when installed on the camera, freed it from the booth altogether. They also developed mobile "boom" microphones, eliminating the need to hide the mike(s) on the set and giving actors more freedom of movement. Better, nearly noiseless lighting systems, more acoustically acceptable set and costume materials, fine grain film stocks for high-quality sound recording, breakthroughs in the mixing of different types of sound information and other improvements reopened the

Figure 3.1   Photographed silent with the sounds of gunfire and explosions added later, the battle scenes in *All Quiet on the Western Front* (produced by Carl Laemmle Jr. for Universal, 1930) were realistic and visually dynamic. Courtesy of the USC Cinema-Television Library.

filmmaker's box of cinematic tricks in a relatively short time. Proof of this may be found in Mamoulian's *Love Me Tonight*, a witty tour de force of cinematic technique released by Paramount in 1932. The fact that few 1930s films approach the artistic level of *Love Me Tonight* or *Sunrise*, for that matter, should at least be partially blamed on a paucity of filmmaking imagination and/or production funding rather than entirely upon limitations imposed by the technology, a rather reductive interpretation of complex factors.

One of the perplexing questions that accompanied the sound revolution was how to prepare films for presentation in non-English-speaking markets. During the silent era, the solution had been both simple and inexpensive: inter-titles were translated into the designated language, filmed and spliced into the picture at the appropriate points. But dialogue movies complicated the process enormously. When the first attempts at dubbing voices and subtitling prints proved unsatisfactory, most of the studios began producing alternate versions in at least three languages (French, Spanish, German) and sometimes more. Initially, these films were made in American studios, using the same sets as the English language version, though they were often shot by different directors and usually featured different actors. For example, some critics, scholars and buffs prefer the more erotic Spanish-language version of *Dracula* (Universal, 1931) starring Carlos Villarias, to the famous Bela Lugosi version. In 1930, the executives of Paramount came up with a new solution. They decided to set up their own studio at Joinville, France, where foreign versions of Paramount movies would be produced. Other companies joined Paramount in Joinville and, for a time, the studio became extremely active.

Soon, however, distribution ledger sheets revealed that these films did not generate enough revenue to justify their costs. Thankfully, improvements in the suppression of track noise in 1931 and in mixing techniques around the same time elevated the quality of dubbing. The studios decided to try this relatively inexpensive solution once again and found foreign audiences more receptive to the dubbed pictures. Paramount subsequently transformed Joinville into a giant dubbing studio where most European versions of Hollywood movies were prepared from 1932 on.

Efforts to improve the sound component of motion pictures continued throughout the remainder of the Classical Period. The introduction of dynamic microphones in the early 1930s and unidirectional mikes in the late 30s, of nonslip printers in the mid-30s, of multiple-channel music recording and mixing in the late 30s, of progressively better fine grain film stocks for recording sound, plus refinements in cameras, recorders, lighting systems, set construction materials, etc., produced soundtracks with a greater dynamic range but less noise and distortion. The coming of sound to Hollywood motion pictures, then, is not just a narrative of jobs lost and new ones created; it is also one of directors, technicians and actors forced to adapt and innovate under turbulent circumstances. Lighting systems, for example, had to be redeveloped when their hissing, buzzing sonance was picked up by microphones. The quality of light produced by the quieter light sources in turn required new approaches to make-up, because actors suddenly looked ghoulish in the standard face paint developed for silent filmmaking. The list goes on.

The industry-wide obsession with advancements in sound may be inferred from the technical awards presented by the Academy of Motion Picture Arts and Sciences during the decade. Of the 50-plus awards handed out between 1931 and 1940, more than 75 percent were for sound-related achievements. Though ERPI, RCA and other corporations with a big investment in research captured quite a few, the majority went to the studios for their in-house resourcefulness and ingenuity. By the time Orson Welles arrived in Hollywood in 1939, there were no technical barriers standing between the creative filmmaker and cinematic art. His *Citizen Kane* (RKO, 1941) is a testament to the high level of visual and acoustic sophistication that the medium had reached before America entered the World War. Welles' extensive experience as a radio dramatist, of course, was instrumental in the creation of the film's dynamic sound track, but he also was fortunate to find both the knowledgeable personnel and the requisite technology to realize his unique vision at his home studio, RKO.

The period even witnessed some tentative experiments with stereophonic sound. In 1940, Walt Disney released *Fantasia* in "Fantasound." Requiring an interlock system because the sound elements were contained on a separate strip of film with three optical tracks (controlling speakers positioned behind the left, center and right portions of the screen), the film featured a bold, innovative use of its stereo possibilities. Critics and filmgoers who witnessed the "Fantasound" shows were highly impressed, but this represented a small percentage of the potential audience. Disney only managed to wire theaters in six cities for the stereo presentation, so most spectators saw the film with a standard monaural track when it was distributed widely by RKO in 1942. Warner Bros. tried out its "Vitasound" system on *Santa Fe Trail* (1940), which appears to have made very little impression on theater patrons or the very executives who had been largely responsible for the coming of sound in the first place. The true age of stereo and high fidelity movie sound would commence in the 1950s.

Color Film Production

The technological challenge of making movies in full color had fired the imagination of many inventors from the dawn of the cinema onward. Approximately 50 different color processes had been tried by the early 1930s, each with varying degrees of success. However, none of these processes was capable of producing the full spectrum of vivid and realistic color images.

At the beginning of the Classical Period, there was considerable interest in a "two-strip" (or "two-color") imbibition process introduced by the Technicolor Corporation in 1928. Clearly superior to any previous process, this new Technicolor was embraced by nearly all the major studios. Not wanting to be left behind if color became the next important technological breakthrough, they used it for certain short subjects and climactic sections of numerous features. Feature pictures with sequences in two-strip included *Broadway Melody* (MGM, 1929), *The Desert Song* (Warner Bros., 1929), *Glorifying the American Girl* (Paramount, 1929), *Rio Rita* (RKO, 1929), *Broadway* (Universal,

1929) and *Hell's Angels* (Caddo/United Artists, 1930). Between 1929 and 1931 more than 35 features contained sections in Technicolor, with all the major studios participating in the experiment.

On with the Show! (Warner Bros., 1929) became the first all-talking, all-color film and a big box-office success. The Warner studio followed it in the same year with *The Gold Diggers of Broadway*, which made even more money, prompting other companies to produce full features in two-strip. Among the 28 films of this kind released between 1929 and 1931 were *Redskin* (Paramount, 1929), *Loves of Casanova* (MGM, 1929), *King of Jazz*, *Leathernecking* (RKO, 1930), *The Melody Man* (Columbia, 1930) and *Whoopee* (Goldwyn/United Artists, 1930). Industry demand was so great during this period that Technicolor had to double its laboratory capacity in 1930.

Toward the end of 1931, however, the usage of two-strip in Hollywood films fell off precipitously. After the initial excitement created by this new mode dissipated, audiences and producers began to notice its flaws. While the process rendered blacks and whites and skin tones fairly well, it could not accurately produce deep blues or greens or reds and some colors were practically impossible to capture. Yellows, for example, generally came out looking pink. Other factors that affected the decline of two-strip Technicolor included a curtailment in the production of musicals (which had featured more color than any other genre) and, of course, the pernicious effects of the Depression on the movie business. During a period of stringent budget control, it was difficult to justify the added expense of Technicolor since it had not been shown to bolster significantly the revenues of films released in 1930 and 1931.

Herbert Kalmus, president of Technicolor, announced that his company had overcome all the limitations of two-strip in its "three-strip" process which he began offering to the studios in 1932. In fact, three-strip did represent a dazzling improvement; finally a process was available that could render all colors vibrantly and realistically. However, the new approach was complicated. It required a giant, noisy camera capable of exposing three reels of film at once, special filters and prisms, very powerful lighting units and exacting laboratory work to produce a release print in this "perfected" process.

Consequently, the major companies expressed little interest. The special challenges presented by filming in three-strip, plus estimates that it would add at least 30 percent to feature budgets at a time when nearly every enterprise in Hollywood was losing money, had a great deal to do with the resistance. And what if the public response to this wondrous color process duplicated the talking pictures phenomenon? Movie executives were frightened by a vision of spectators unwilling to watch black-and-white films after being exposed to the prismatic glories of the new Technicolor. The monetary investment required to shift to a full slate of color productions was daunting, especially when one considered contemporary economic realities.

Thus, none of the major studios was initially willing to make a three-strip feature. Instead, independent Walt Disney began a long-lasting relationship with Technicolor in 1932. He would employ three-strip in his highly successful cartoons, beginning with "Flowers and Trees," a Silly Symphony which represented the first commercial use of the process. Two years later, *The House of Rothschild* (Twentieth Century/United Artists) and *Kid Millions* (Goldwyn/ United Artists) contained three-strip sequences, but still no company would undertake a full feature.

That task ultimately fell to an independent enterprise formed by two wealthy investors in Technicolor, John Hay Whitney and Cornelius Vanderbilt Whitney. At the suggestion of their friend Merian C. Cooper, then production chief at RKO, the two cousins set up Pioneer Pictures in 1933. Before embarking on a full-length film, they decided to make a short demonstrating the quality and range of color possibilities offered by the process. Renowned set and costume designer Robert Edmund Jones was hired, and he and director Lloyd Corrigan turned out *La Cucaracha*, a flimsy tale about a Mexican girl (Steffi Duna) whose perseverance enables her to capture the affections of a handsome dancer. Despite its dramatic and comedic shortcomings, the film was formally beautiful and received an enthusiastic welcome from critics and audiences. The Academy named it Best Short Subject (Comedy) of 1934.

Convinced that the first three-strip feature had to be outstanding in every way, the Pioneer executives and producer Kenneth Macgowan spent time choosing a property that would carry more literary cachet than *La Cucaracha*. *Hamlet, Joan of Arc, Tristan and Isolde, The Three Musketeers* and other famous stories received consideration before *Becky Sharp* was selected. The film would be based on Langdon Mitchell's eponymous play which had been adapted from William Makepeace Thackeray's famous novel *Vanity Fair*.

The production of *Becky Sharp*, which began in December 1934, proved to be cursed. Lowell Sherman, the original director, contracted pneumonia and died less than a month into filming. His replacement, Rouben Mamoulian, had to cope with unending difficulties that included illness among cast and crew, the damaging effects of the intense lights on the eyes of the actors (especially star Miriam Hopkins) and a plethora of unexpected sound problems. When finished, *Becky Sharp* had gone well over schedule and budget, costing close to $1.1 million. (Figure 3.2)

The premiere of *Becky Sharp* in June 1935 was the most anxiously awaited

Figure 3.2   The massive three-strip Technicolor camera dwarfs Rouben
Mamoulian (*center*, with glasses) as he directs Miriam Hopkins in *Becky Sharp*
(produced by Kenneth Macgowan for Pioneer Pictures/RKO, 1935). Courtesy of
the Academy of Motion Picture Arts and Sciences Library.

Hollywood event in years. The general response and subsequent box office
performance of the film (distributed by RKO) proved reassuring to those
who feared another expensive industry revolution. While critics and spectators marveled at the orchestration of color, which had been carefully planned
by art director Robert Edmund Jones and director Mamoulian to underscore
the varying moods of the drama, they were less than enthusiastic about other
aspects of the film. The story did not absorb, nor did the performances of
Miriam Hopkins and other cast members enthrall. As a consequence, *Becky
Sharp* turned out to be a financial disappointment for Pioneer Pictures, which
made one more Technicolor feature (the lackluster *Dancing Pirate* in 1936),
then went out of business. Clearly, there would be no public mandate for an
all-Technicolor program of releases.

Now able to relax about the color issue and feeling more optimistic about
the future of their businesses, Hollywood executives began to consider the

occasional use of Technicolor for "special" productions. The bulky cameras, the excessive lighting requirements (and their attendant liabilities, including heat on the set and potential eye damage to the actors), such technical limitations as the absence of wide-angle and long focal-length lenses and, of course, the additional expense of making a film in three-strip meant that a careful justification process would take place before a commitment was made. Nevertheless, several studios did begin to produce occasional Technicolor features. The newly formed independent company Selznick International (which included the Whitneys among its investors) took a leadership role, completing *The Garden of Allah, A Star Is Born, Nothing Sacred* and *The Adventures of Tom Sawyer* for release by United Artists between 1936 and 1938. Paramount (*Trail of the Lonesome Pine*, 1936) and Twentieth Century-Fox (*Ramona*, 1936) also started making Technicolor films, with Warner Bros. (*The Adventures of Robin Hood*, 1937) and MGM (*Sweethearts*, 1938) soon joining the ranks.

The fact that *Snow White and the Seven Dwarfs* (Disney/RKO, 1937) and *Gone with the Wind* (Selznick/MGM, 1939) became the most financially successful films of the decade raised the status of Technicolor enormously. *Gone with the Wind*, winner of the first Academy Award given for Color Cinematography, was especially important. It demonstrated the quality of Technicolor's new, faster film which required much less light, produced sharper, less grainy images and made greater depth of field possible. A 25 mm (wide-angle) lens was also put into service for the first time during the picture's shooting; although limited to specific kinds of shots, the lens did expand the pictorial possibilities of color filmmaking. As a result of the technical breakthroughs and of the heady box office performances of such films as *Snow White* and *Gone with the Wind*, Technicolor suddenly had plenty of business. It enlarged its plant, ordered the production of more cameras and added a research laboratory to its complex.

Twentieth Century-Fox eventually became the company's biggest customer. The studio averaged more than six Technicolor films per year from 1939 to 1945. Filmgoers could count on color musicals from Fox, especially those starring Betty Grable (e.g., *Down Argentine Way*, 1940; *Springtime in the Rockies*, 1942; *The Dolly Sisters*, 1945), as well as occasional westerns (*Western Union*, 1941), adventure films (*The Black Swan*, 1942) and biographies (*Wilson*, 1944). Paramount called upon Technicolor regularly, making several of the Cecil B. DeMille spectaculars (*Northwest Mounted Police*, 1939; *Reap the Wild Wind*, 1942; *The Story of Dr. Wassell*, 1944) in color, plus musicals (*Riding High*, 1943; *Lady in the Dark*, 1944; *Bring on the Girls*, 1945) and other types of pictures. MGM became an active patron during the war years; the studio was especially partial to Technicolor musicals (*Thousands Cheer*, 1943; *Meet Me in St. Louis*, 1944; *Anchors Aweigh*, 1945) and children's films (*Lassie Come Home*, 1943; *Son of Lassie*, 1945; *National Velvet*, 1945). Universal also developed into an important producer of color films during the war, using Technicolor principally for its exotic Maria Montez–Jon Hall pictures (*Arabian Nights*, 1942; *Cobra Woman*, 1943; *Ali Baba and the Forty Thieves*, 1944). Walt Disney continued his long relationship with the company, making all his cartoons and features in Technicolor (e.g., *Pinocchio*, 1940; *Dumbo*, 1941; *Saludos Amigos*, 1943). Other independents like Sam Goldwyn, who adopted Technicolor for musicals made near the war's end (*Up in Arms*, 1944; *The Princess and the Pirate*, 1944; *Wonder Man*, 1945), were added to the company's client list. Studios that remained aloof included Warner Bros., which had produced several three-strip films in the late 30s but released only six from 1940 to 1945, plus Columbia and RKO, which finally stepped up Technicolor filming in 1945.

Technicolor had rigid requirements designed to maintain quality control over its product. In order to make a film in Technicolor, a studio had to rent the cameras, employ a cinematographer supplied by Technicolor (who usually worked in tandem with a director of photography assigned by the studio), hire a Technicolor "color director" who would advise on the most appropriate color schemes for each scene in the film, use Technicolor make-up and, finally, develop and print the film in the Technicolor lab. Many studio professionals resented the detailed advice of the "color director" (who was usually Herbert Kalmus' ex-wife Natalie), as well as other members of the Technicolor team, but little could be done. The company held a virtual monopoly on color film-making in Hollywood throughout the Classical Period.

The Technicolor brand name quickly developed a specific meaning to theater owners and audiences. Even if a picture did not boast top stars, Techni-color automatically elevated it into the "A" category. In terms of content and approach, a Technicolor film was expected to be lighthearted and upbeat. With notable exceptions, such as *The Phantom of the Opera* (Universal, 1943) and *Leave Her to Heaven* (Twentieth Century-Fox, 1945), one did not expect horror films or disturbing melodramas to be made in color. Nor was one likely to encounter a Technicolor gangster film, thriller, social problem picture or realistic war movie; black-and-white was de rigueur for those genres. The ani-mated cartoon and the musical were the preferred Technicolor genres, with westerns, comedies, adventure films, children's films and other types of stories sometimes given color treatment.

Although extremely proud of three-strip, Herbert Kalmus recognized that a "monopak" system with all the color elements contained on a single strip of film capable of exposure in a conventional 35 mm motion picture camera would ultimately replace it. Such a system would save time and money, as well as give filmmakers greater flexibility in shooting. In the early 1940s, a Technicolor monopak emerged from the Kalmus laboratory and was soon being used for sequences in three-strip films: *Dive Bomber* (Warner Bros., 1941), *The Forest Rangers* (Paramount, 1942), *Captains of the Clouds* (Warner Bros., 1942), *Lassie Come Home*. Twentieth Century-Fox shot the entirety of *Thunderhead, Son of Flicka* (1944) in the new system, but the overall quality was not comparable to three-strip and Technicolor's initial monopak soon disappeared from the Hollywood scene. Despite the disappointment, Kalmus still believed that a superior monopak would soon become available, if not from Technicolor then from one of its competitors. Consequently, he instructed his workers to cease production of the three-strip cameras. This would prove to be a definite hardship for the industry after World War II when the demand for color films picked up substantially.

A few other color systems were in evidence during the Classical Period. Magnacolor, a two-color subtractive process developed by Consolidated Film Industries (CFI), was used for some early-30s shorts and later for a few Republic westerns (*Rough Riders of Cheyenne*, 1945; *Home on the Range*, 1946, etc.) produced in the mid- to late 40s. Multicolor, another two-color subtractive process, was seen in shorts and sections of such black-and-white features as *The Great Gabbo* (James Cruze Productions/Sono Art–World Wide, 1929), *The Fox Movietone Follies of 1929* and *Good News* (MGM, 1930), but the company that offered it went bankrupt in 1932. Small studios like Monogram and PRC sometimes used Cinecolor, a two-color subtractive process dating from the early 30s. It would gain wider acceptance after the end of the war. However, none of these processes represented a threat to the dominance of Technicolor during the Classical Period.

Wide-Screen Experiments of 1929–31

At the time when sound systems were being feverishly installed in theaters and two-strip Technicolor was enjoying its vogue, a new technological development began to excite certain film producers. Believing audiences would be enthralled by larger, more imposing and monumental cinematic presentations, William Fox entered into a relationship with the Mitchell Camera Company and Eastman Kodak to make 70-mm wide-screen films featuring a horizontal to vertical aspect ratio of 2.13×1 (the industry standard was 1.33×1).

The first feature in Fox's "Grandeur" process was *The Fox Movietone Follies of 1929*. With superior sound, thanks to its oversized optical soundtrack, and clear, sharp image quality, the film was well received by audiences who saw it in the few theaters equipped to show it properly. Even when reduced to 35 mm for regular distribution, it could still be presented in a wide-screen format by houses that owned "Magnascope" projector lenses. These lenses magnified 35-mm film and could adapt it to several screen configurations, including 1.85×1 and 2×1.

Fox's commitment to "Grandeur" films continued in 1930. *Happy Days*, *Song of My Heart* and *The Big Trail* were produced and partially distributed in 70 mm, promoting other companies to enter the field. MGM tried out the same process (which it tradenamed "Realife") on *Billy the Kid*, released in fall 1930, and then *The Great Meadow*, which came out in spring 1931. RKO employed "Natural Vision," a 63-mm process, on *Danger Lights* (1930), but only one US theater (in Chicago) was equipped to show it in true "Natural Vision." Warner Bros. entered the arena with *The Lash* (1930) and *Kismet* (1931), both made in a 65-mm process called "Vitascope." Paramount also experimented with a 56-mm system named "Magnafilm" but apparently did not produce a full feature in the process.

By summer 1931, the movement to wide-screen had fizzled. The biggest naysayers were theater owners who had only recently invested thousands of dollars to equip their houses for sound film presentations. Most were uninterested in reconfiguring their screens and seating arrangements to accommodate wide-screen presentations or in acquiring the necessary projection equipment, especially with the Depression worsening. The fact that no discernible industry standard for wide-screen had emerged from the various film widths and aspect ratios proffered by the different releasing companies did not help either. Wide-screen entered a state of suspended animation; it would be reborn and thrive, like stereophonic sound, in the 1950s.

Special Effects

While special effects have generally been associated with specific film genres, such as fantasy, horror and science fiction, they were used to facilitate the production of nearly all Hollywood films made during the Classical Period. Special effects could transport audiences to exotic locations, create situations and characters far removed from everyday reality and conjure forth a magical array of cinematic techniques. They could also accomplish a wide variety of more mundane, but important, tasks as well. Most crucially for the production companies they could save an incalculable amount of money. The evolution of special effects techniques played a key role in keeping theatrical film costs under control during the Depression years.

The term "special effects" encompassed a broad range of techniques, and it was rare for one person to be proficient in all of them. Studios employed experts in rear projection, glass shots, mattes and traveling mattes, optical printer work, miniatures and models, pyrotechnics and physical and mechanical effects. Among the acknowledged masters were John Fulton of the Universal Special Effects Department, Vernon Walker and Linwood Dunn of RKO, Gordon Jennings and Farciot Edouart of Paramount, first James Basevi and then A. Arnold Gillespie of MGM, Fred Sersen of Twentieth Century-Fox, Roy Davidson of Columbia, Fred Jackson and then Byron Haskin of Warner Bros., and Howard and Theodore Lydecker of Republic.

Though well known within the technical circles of the industry, these men rarely received exposure or publicity outside Hollywood. Most studio executives believed that the mechanics of professional filmmaking should be kept from the public at large; indeed, they were most gratified when special effects work went unnoticed. After all, they reasoned, if the spectator found out how things "were done," the illusion would be shattered and, with it, the magic of the entertainment experience.

Rear projection

The coming of sound made it especially desirable to shoot pictures under controlled conditions. This meant, whenever possible, using a stage where extraneous noise could be effectively eliminated. But how was this possible when the script called for a scene in a moving car, a train, a ship or some similar location?

The solution was to remain in the studio, projecting the necessary background onto a translucent screen and then photographing the important action in front of the screen. Although this technique, also known as process photography, had been used as early as 1913 by Norman O. Dawn, it was refined and became standard practice during the early 1930s. Farciot Edouart of Paramount was one of the acknowledged masters of the technique, which required that the projector and camera be run synchronously by interlocked motors. Most of the medium and close shots in *For Whom the Bell Tolls* (Paramount, 1943) were made by Edouart's crew. They shot almost 300 setups, the majority of which were used in the picture. Audiences were apparently not bothered by the artificiality of the technique, for it is rare to find a feature made from the early 1930s on that does not contain some examples of process photography. The Alfred Hitchcock-directed *Lifeboat* (Twentieth Century-Fox, 1944), which was largely photographed in a studio tank, utilized a rear projected background for most of its running time. Though the technique is easy to spot, even laughably so when watching these films today, its heavy usage during the Classical Period speaks volumes about its acceptance by contemporary audiences as a cinematic convention, as well as their willingness to suspend disbelief while caught up in an enjoyable story. Digital effects have become the present-day equivalent; we can perhaps spot their usage in such films as the *Lord of the Rings* trilogy (New Line/Warner Bros., 2001, 2002, 2003), but the power of narrative, as it did in the Classical Period, ensures our dramatic interest.

Glass shots, mattes and traveling mattes

Often used to create spectacular effects, always used to save money, glass shots, mattes and traveling mattes were methods of combining different elements within a single frame of film. The simplest technique was the glass shot, wherein portions of a scene would be painted onto a pane of glass. The camera would then shoot through the glass, giving the illusion that the live elements were occurring within a setting that looked real but was actually a painting.

Matte work, another way of compositing, also often involved painted settings. In this case, portions of the frame would be masked during the initial filming. Later all the elements would be added in their proper positions, and a final image would be produced, either in the camera or later in the laboratory or optical printer. Approximately 100 matte shots were required for *Gone with the Wind*.

While mattes had been employed since the earliest days of the medium, traveling mattes were a later development. By changing the shape of the matted elements from frame to frame, traveling mattes enabled moving action to be composited with the other portions of a scene. One of the most brilliant uses of the technique was by John Fulton of Universal for *The Invisible Man* (1933). The same approach would be employed in later Universal films with invisible protagonists (*The Invisible Man Returns*, 1939; *The Invisible Woman*, 1941; *The Invisible Agent*, 1942; etc.), as well as some films that contained ghostly apparitions such as *Topper* (Roach/MGM, 1937) and *Topper Takes a Trip* (Roach/United Artists, 1939). (Figure 3.3)

Figure 3.3 Claude Rains and Gloria Stuart in *The Invisible Man* (produced by Carl Laemmle Jr. for Universal, 1933). The technicians in the Special Effects Department at Universal Pictures were crucial to the film's success. Courtesy of the USC Cinema-Television Library.

Optical printing

Originally designed to make exact celluloid copies of films, an optical printer is essentially an interlocked projector and camera in which negative film is exposed by the projected images and duplicates those images. Specialists like Linwood Dunn at RKO soon discovered, however, that with certain attachments the optical printer could produce a cornucopia of effects: dissolves, freeze frames, wipes, fades, superimpositions, multiple images, split screens, fast motion, slow motion, enlargements of parts of the frame to create close-ups, etc.

Although many of these techniques could be done in other ways, the optical printer simplified their production, enabling them to be made faster, less expensively and, often, more effectively. Such films as *Melody Cruise* (RKO, 1933) and *Flying Down to Rio* (RKO, 1933) contain multiple examples of Dunn's amazing work, as does *Citizen Kane*. A number of important scenes in Welles' famous film, originally thought to be examples of cinematographer Gregg Toland's "deep focus" photography, were actually "in camera" mattes or composites of different shots put together by Dunn in the optical printer. Dunn claimed that up to 80 percent of some reels was optically printed.

Miniatures and models

Miniatures are scaled-down replicas which, when photographed properly, appear to be life-size (and sometimes lifelike). Most models used in films from the 1930s and 40s were miniatures, but occasionally larger-than-life models were constructed for special purposes. In *King Kong* (RKO, 1933), for example, the mighty ape was usually portrayed by an 18-*inch* miniature which had to be painstakingly animated, but Willis O'Brien, head of the special effects team on the picture, also built an 18-*foot*-tall model of Kong's head, shoulders and chest for closer shots. The torso required three men, operating various levers from the inside, to move the mouth, neck and other body parts. *Dr. Cyclops* (Paramount, 1940) utilized oversized models even more extensively than *Kong*, as well as a wide range of other special effects accomplished in three-strip Technicolor. (Figure 3.4)

Miniatures and models were by no means confined to "trick" pictures like *King Kong* and *Dr. Cyclops*. They ran the gamut from the shoddy and laughably cheap (e.g., the space ships and interplanetary cities of Universal's "Flash Gordon" serials) to the intricately detailed and expensive. Designed for many different films, these models often saved huge sums of money, as in the high seas battle sequences of *Cleopatra* (Paramount, 1934), *The Sea Hawk* (Warner Bros., 1940) and *The Black Swan* (Twentieth Century-Fox, 1942). The multitude of combat movies produced during the war years required miniature battleships, aircraft, submarines, etc., and the studios, flush with cash from their booming businesses, made them larger, more detailed, more realistic. Such films as *Flying Tigers* (Republic, 1942), *Bombardier* (RKO, 1943), *Air Force* (Warner Bros., 1943) and *Thirty Seconds over Tokyo* (MGM, 1944), despite their use of newsreel footage and extensive military cooperation, could not have been made without miniatures.

Pyrotechnics and physical and mechancial effects

Studios also found work for people who knew how to blow things up, burn them down and create, in relative safety, other sorts of spectacular moments for the cameras. In some cases, their work was so sensational that it over-

Figure 3.4 King Kong (produced by Merian C. Cooper and Ernest B. Schoedsack for RKO, 1933), the trailblazing special effects film of the Classical Period. Courtesy of the USC Cinema-Television Library.

shadowed the picture itself. The earthquake sequence in *San Francisco* (MGM, 1936), created by A. Arnold ("Buddy") Gillespie and the studio effects team, was the most unforgettable part of a movie that boasted an impressive roster of stars (Clark Gable, Jeanette MacDonald, Spencer Tracy). Likewise, Jim Basevi supervised the building of a very large Polynesian village in miniature for *The Hurricane* (Goldwyn/United Artists, 1937), then destroyed it in the simulated storm. The rest of the drama seemed rather limp compared to the fury unleashed by Basevi and his colleagues. And the burning of Atlanta was one of the high points of *Gone with the Wind*, a film that contained many fondly remembered scenes. Lee Zavita orchestrated the fiery destruction which consumed sets from a number of earlier films including *The King of Kings* (Pathé, 1927).

Without question, *King Kong* was the greatest special effects achievement produced during the Classical Period. Working with co-directors Merian C.

Cooper and Ernest B. Schoedsack, effects coordinator Willis O'Brien utilized every technique at his disposal to vivify this "beauty and the beast" fantasy updated to the modernist world of the 1930s. During the protracted production and post-production phases, *King Kong* required many miniatures and models, stop-motion animation of the miniatures, glass shots, traveling mattes, optical printing, rear projection, miniature rear projection, etc. The technical virtuosity of this complex picture (which included its dynamic use of sound) is evidence that the technological wizardry available to the Hollywood studios in the early 1930s was highly advanced and, in fact, capable of visualizing almost anything that the industry's most fertile creative minds could imagine.

4

Censorship

The impact that films have on the people who watch them has been a matter of concerned debate since the earliest days of motion pictures. While the power of movies to "seduce" people into behavior that they would not otherwise exhibit has never been proven scientifically, social, political and religious reformers have continuously asserted the corruptive powers of the medium and never ceased calling for its control. The advocates of censorship won an important victory in 1934 when the Hollywood industry instituted the Production Code Administration (PCA), charged with the enforcement of a prescriptive document of "morally responsible" screen entertainment and sufficiently powerful to make its pronouncements stick. Although the PCA did clearly affect the kind of screen stories the studios could offer and the ways creative talents could present them throughout the remainder of the Classical Period, it was not a monolithic, inflexible organization that pasteurized all manner of narrative potentialities into bland gruel. Before proceeding to a detailed discussion of the Production Code, its enforcement and the consequent influence on studio filmmaking, however, it is necessary to sketch in key silent era developments in censorship and then examine the factors that led to the creation of the PCA.

Silent Era Background

Several important events set the stage for the imposition of industry-mandated censorship. By 1915, a number of states and municipalities had established offices to inspect and license films for presentation in their areas. These offices could reject films that were deemed objectionable or mandate changes which the distribution company would be required to make in order to secure a license. While the legality of state and local censor boards had been occasionally tested in court before 1915, the most important case reached the United States Supreme Court in that year. The outcome of Mutual Film Corporation vs. the State of Ohio would have ramifications for decades to come.

Mutual, a distribution company that operated in Ohio and other states, sought to overturn the Ohio state system of censorship on several grounds, including the belief that it violated the free speech guarantees of the Ohio Constitution and of the First Amendment of the United States Constitution. In a unanimous decision, the Court rejected the claims of Mutual, thereby upholding the right of Ohio to censor motion pictures.

Two parts of the decision were especially noteworthy. First, the Court set forth its belief that the "exhibition of motion pictures is a business pure and simple, originated and conducted for profit . . . not to be regarded . . . as part of the press of the country or as a means of public opinion." Therefore, since the Court deemed the movies to be a business and not a vehicle for speech or public opinion, the US Constitution offered the medium no special protection and all manner of censorship was permissible. Second, the decision described films as "mere representations of events, of ideas and sentiments, published or known, vivid, useful and entertaining, no doubt, but . . . capable of evil, having power for it, the greater because of their attractiveness and manner of exhibition." In expressing the idea that films were, in fact, "capable of evil," the Supreme Court justices validated the position of many censorship-minded critics whose goal was to prevent irresponsible producers from contaminating the country and, in fact, the world, with this "evil."

The Mutual Case created a landscape for film censorship in which anything was possible. Though film companies in the coming years would be bedeviled by a growing number of state and local agencies with non-uniform criteria and methods of operation, the greatest fear of studio executives was national censorship, imposed and enforced by the US government. The very notion of government control of their expanding industry was anathema; industry leaders pledged to do whatever was necessary to keep national censorship at arm's length.

A decisive gambit to this end occurred in 1922 when the Motion Picture Producers and Distributors of America (MPPDA), a trade organization, was established and Will H. Hays hired as its first president. The MPPDA would represent the industry in a variety of arenas, including political lobbying and international trade negotiations, but its immediate objective was to keep the reformers in check and, most importantly, to forestall any movement toward government censorship.

Will Hays turned out to be an astute choice to guide the new organization.

A midwestern ascetic and elder in the Presbyterian Church, he had strong connections in Washington where he had served as chairman of the Republican Party and Postmaster General in the Harding administration. He would need his connections and his considerable flair for public relations, for he took charge at a time when movies featuring more liberal attitudes toward sex, divorce, smoking and drinking (despite Prohibition) had provoked outrage from women's clubs, educators, clergymen, literary societies, newspapers, magazines and other sources. Compounding Hays' difficulties were a series of scandals involving such film personalities as Roscoe "Fatty" Arbuckle, Wallace Reid, Mary Miles Minter and Mabel Normand. Hays had to counter the perception that Hollywood was rotten – both on- and off-screen.

Hays promised "moral" entertainment, then had the studios include "morality clauses" in personnel contracts, giving them the right to suspend or dismiss employees who committed criminal or offensive acts. He also set up the Committee on Public Relations, a body composed of representatives from more than 70 national organizations concerned about the effects of screen content. The Boy Scouts of America, the YMCA, the International Association of Catholic Alumnae and the Daughters of the American Revolution were some of the groups that agreed to participate. Perhaps his greatest coup was a campaign designed to defeat a censorship referendum in Massachusetts. Hays' publicity experts succeeded in convincing state voters that censorship was autocratic, unconstitutional and un-American, and the referendum went down to defeat by more than 300,000 votes. No major state censorship laws were passed after this.

Will Hays, whose tenure as president of the MPPDA lasted until 1945, has often been characterized as the first important censor of American movies. In fact, he was not a censor at all and probably felt least comfortable dealing with the prickly matters of controversial screen content. He was most at home playing games of political give and take on the international as well as domestic levels; he did not enjoy the endless debates about movie morality and involved himself in specific censorship cases reluctantly when there seemed little alternative. Nevertheless, the MPPDA (or "Hays Office" as it was known familiarly) soon became synonymous with internal industry censorship.

Its first attempt to regulate motion picture content was instituted in 1924 and dealt exclusively with adaptations of literary works. "The Formula" discouraged studios from purchasing books that contained "salacious or otherwise harmful" subject matter which might have "a deleterious effect on the industry in general." It singled out popular works, such as *Black Oxen*, *Flaming Youth* and *Three Weeks* and attempted to prevent them from being transformed into motion pictures. Hays could not stop the march of the aforementioned stories from page to screen, but he claimed in 1925 that "The Formula" had blocked production of more than 150 important books and plays whose screen rights were worth in excess of $2 million.

By 1927, the Association had expanded its methods of regulation, compiling a code to govern production. Familiarly called the "Don'ts and Be Carefuls," this document was essentially a synthesis of all the sensitive areas that provoked eliminations by municipal, state and foreign censors. The "Don'ts and Be Carefuls" would be administered by a Hays Office department called the Studio Relations Committee (SRC), which was headed by Colonel Jason Joy. The weakness of both "The Formula" and the "Don'ts and Be Carefuls" was their advisory status. Initially, studios were not even required to submit scripts to the SRC. In 1928, it became mandatory for producers to forward script materials for SRC critique, but there was still no effective way to force a studio to follow its recommendations.

Colonel Joy did his best to convince filmmakers that his office could be of significant benefit to them. If they would make the changes suggested by the SRC, they would save themselves considerable trouble with the various censor boards later on. In 1929, he produced statistics to show that substantially fewer deletions had been required from SRC "approved" films than from those whose creators paid no attention to SRC recommendations. A case could be made that with the sound revolution sweeping the industry, the SRC's services were even more vital. Elimination of dialogue sequences for censorship reasons could be devastating to the coherence and intelligibilty of a "talkie."

Yet, despite the certain knowledge that their films would encounter censorship difficulties, some producers continued to operate as if the SRC did not exist. They made movies that captured the enthusiastic abandonment of Victorian restraint so characteristic of urban life during the "Jazz Age." Pictures like *It* (Paramount, 1927), *Our Dancing Daughters* (MGM, 1928) and *Charming Sinners* (Paramount, 1929) helped make stars of Clara Bow, Joan Crawford and Ruth Chatterton while, at the same time, convincing the reform-minded that Will Hays had had little effect on the visual pollution that continued to spew forth from Hollywood.

The Production Code

One industry insider, profoundly dismayed by the MPPDA's ineffective censorship policies in the late 1920s, offered to help. Martin Quigley was editor and publisher of the *Motion Picture Daily* and *Motion Picture Herald*. His commitment to fostering more wholesome and beneficial screen entertainment stemmed from his Catholic religious beliefs and his thoroughgoing opposition to government censorship, which he feared was inevitable if the industry did not quickly sanitize its product. With the assistance of Father Daniel Lord, a Jesuit priest and professor at St. Louis University, Quigley set about drafting a code of cinematic right and wrong based on an enunciated philosophy of morally responsible entertainment. The idea of a formal code appealed to Will Hays for many reasons, including its public relations value and the likelihood that it would defuse criticism from one of the industry's largest and most organized pressure groups: the Catholic Church.

The final version of the Motion Picture Production Code, adopted by the studios on March 31, 1930, was the work of many hands. Besides Quigley and Lord, Will Hays, Colonel Jason Joy and several industry executives had input, and part of the document was clearly based on the "Don'ts and Be Carefuls." It superseded the latter and would be administered by Joy's Studio Relations Committee.

The Code began with a preamble acknowledging that motion pictures are "important influences in the life of a nation" and "may be directly responsible for spiritual or moral progress, for higher types of social life, and for much correct thinking." Therefore, because of this important responsibility, the movie industry had decided to subscribe to this Code; it asked for understanding and a "spirit of cooperation" from the public and its leaders in order "to bring the motion picture to a still higher level of wholesome entertainment for all the people." As printed in the trade papers and other publications, the "General Principles" and "Particular Applications" of the Code which followed were straightforward and seemingly comprehensive:

General Principles
1. No picture shall be produced which will lower the moral standards of those who see it. Hence the sympathy of the audience should never be thrown to the side of crime, wrongdoing or sin.
2. Correct standards of life, subject only to the requirements of drama and entertainment, shall be presented.
3. Law, natural and human, shall not be ridiculed, nor shall sympathy be created for its violation.

Particular Applications
I – Crimes against the law
These shall never be presented in such a way as to throw sympathy with the crime as against law and justice or to inspire others with a desire for imitation.

1. Murder
a. The technique of murder must be presented in a way that will not inspire imitation.
b. Brutal killings are not to be presented in detail.
c. Revenge in modern times shall not be justified.
2. Methods of Crime should not be explicitly presented.
a. Theft, robbery, safe-cracking, and dynamiting of trains, mines, buildings, etc., should not be detailed in method.
b. Arson must be subject to the same safeguards.
c. The use of firearms should be restricted to essentials.
d. Methods of smuggling should not be presented.
3. Illegal drug traffic must never be presented.
4. The use of liquor in American life, when not required by the plot or for proper characterization, will not be shown.

II – Sex
The sanctity of the institution of marriage and the home shall be upheld. Pictures shall not infer that low forms of sex relationship are the accepted or common thing.
1. Adultery, sometimes necessary plot material, must not be explicitly treated, or justified or presented attractively.
2 Scenes of passion
a. They should not be introduced when not essential to the plot.
b. Excessive and lustful kissing, lustful embraces, suggestive postures and gestures, are not to be shown.
c. In general passion should so be treated that these scenes do not stimulate the lower and baser element.
3. Seduction or rape
a. They should never be more than suggested, and only when essential for the plot, and even then never shown by explicit method.
b. They are never the proper subject for comedy.
4. Sex perversion or any inference to it is forbidden.
5. White-slavery shall not be treated.
6. Miscegenation (sex relationships between the white and black races) is forbidden.
7. Sex hygiene and venereal diseases are not subjects for motion pictures.
8. Scenes of actual child birth, in fact or in silhouette, are never to be presented.
9. Children's sex organs are never to be exposed.

III – Vulgarity
The treatment of low, disgusting, unpleasant, though not necessarily evil, subjects should be subject always to the dictates of good taste and a regard for the sensibilities of the audience.

IV – Obscenity

Obscenity in word, gesture, reference, song, joke, or by suggestion (even when likely to be understood only by part of the audience) is forbidden.

V – Profanity

Pointed profanity (this includes the words, God, Lord, Jesus, Christ – unless used reverently – Hell, S.O.B., damn, Gawd), or every other profane or vulgar expression however used, is forbidden.

VI – Costume

1. Complete nudity is never permitted. This includes nudity in fact or in silhouette, or any lecherous or licentious notice thereof by other characters in the picture.
2. Undressing scenes should be avoided, and never used save where essential to the plot.
3. Indecent or undue exposure is forbidden.
4. Dancing costumes intended to permit undue exposure or indecent movements in the dance are forbidden.

VII – Dances

1. Dances suggesting or representing sexual actions or indecent passion are forbidden.
2. Dances which emphasize indecent movements are to be regarded as obscene.

VIII – Religion

1. No film or episode may throw ridicule on any religious faith.
2. Ministers of religion in their character as ministers of religion should not be used as comic characters or villains.
3. Ceremonies of any definite religion should be carefully and respectfully handled.

IX – Locations

The treatment of bedrooms must be governed by good taste and delicacy.

X – National Feelings

1. The use of the Flag shall be consistently respectful.
2. The history, institutions, prominent people and citizenry of other nations shall be presented fairly.

XI – Titles

Salacious, indecent, or obscene titles shall not be used.

XII – Repellent Subjects

The following subjects must be treated within the careful limits of good taste:

1. Actual hangings or electrocutions as legal punishments for crime.
2. Third Degree methods.
3. Brutality and possible gruesomeness.
4. Branding of people or animals.
5. Apparent cruelty to children or animals.
6. The sale of women, or a woman selling her virtue.
7. Surgical operations.

Appended to the "General Principles" and "Particular Applications" were several pages of supplementary material. This information was supposed to explain the philosophical basis of the Code and to clarify the reasons that certain screen presentations had to be handled as the Code prescribed. Although a good deal of it was redundant, the "Reasons Supporting Preamble of Code," "Reasons Underlying the General Principles" and "Reasons Underlying Particular Applications" did offer some additional insights.

The "Reasons Supporting Preamble of Code" contained the following suppositions:

1. That the movies are primarily entertainment and that entertainment has the power either to improve or to degrade the human race. Thus, movies are of "moral importance."
2. That the movies are also an art form, specifically "the art for the multitudes." Because of the widespread popularity of motion pictures, their effects upon the lives of men, women and children are profound.
3. That the movies have "special moral obligations." Because they are, by nature, different from books, newspapers and plays, motion pictures attract all classes of people in small communities as well as large cities. Therefore, "the mobility, popularity, accessibility, emotional appeal, vividness, straightforward presentation of fact in the film make for more intimate contact with a larger audience and for greater emotional appeal. Hence the larger moral responsibilities of the motion pictures."

The "Reasons Underlying the General Principles" reiterated much of the content already included in the earlier section. It did argue, rather extravagantly, that the presentation of positive role models and behaviors in films could be highly beneficial to the human species: "If motion pictures consistently hold up for admiration high types of characters and present stories that will affect lives for the better, they can become the most powerful natural force for the improvement of mankind." It also defined what the Code meant by natural law ("the law which is written in the hearts of all mankind, the great undying principles of right and justice dictated by conscience"), as opposed to human law ("the law written by civilized nations"). The "Reasons Underlying the Particular Applications" belabored, in tedious fashion, the 12 categories of "Particular Applications" without providing any significant additional information.

Without question, Martin Quigley, Father Daniel Lord, Will Hays, Colonel Jason Joy and the industry executives who worked on the Code had spent a great deal of time and thought hammering out the document. And yet they overlooked the crucial ingredient to its success – a penalty system for those who chose to ignore it. Because the Code contained no effective means of enforcement, the Studio Relations Committee was placed in an untenable position. Studios could accept the SRC's recommendations . . . or ignore them. Most chose the latter course of action proving, once again, that voluntary compliance won't work, at least not in Hollywood. Despite the hosannas which issued forth from industry publicists hailing the arrival of the Production Code era, the antagonists of the motion picture industry would soon grow in number. Their outrage would also grow, soon reaching the boiling point.

"Pre-Code" Hollywood

The period from 1930 until mid-1934 is often referred to as the "Pre-Code" era in Hollywood censorship history. The appellation is, of course, a misnomer for the Production Code was in place during this time, having been embraced by the MPPDA member companies in early spring 1930. In another sense, however, the Pre-Code description seems appropriate because many studios paid scant attention to its strictures and requirements. This was, in essence, a time of "pre-enforcement"; the SRC did have certain powers and it was able to strong-arm some producers into making changes in their works. Yet, the era is recalled more for its flagrant disavowal of both the spirit and letter of the Production Code than for any significant infringement on the creative efforts of Hollywood moviemakers. Indeed, the liberalization in screen content and treatment, especially with respect to sex and violence, was shocking to many viewers in the early 1930s.

The violations to the Code were not as cynical or hypocritical as they might seem. Decisions to offer movie customers more sensational and titillating fare were mainly a pragmatic response to the Depression and the devastating impact that it was having on motion picture business. Production executives believed urban filmgoers, strapped for cash and worried about their futures, would spend money on a non-necessity like the movies if, and only if, they were offered something fresh and more stimulating than they were used to seeing. Extant financial information suggests that the studio chiefs were right; a number of these controversial films appear to have been successful profitmakers. But they also provided the pro-censorship factions with ample ammunition in their anti-Hollywood campaigns.

It is important to emphasize the near-impossible job that Colonel Joy and the other employees of the Studio Relations Committee were asked to perform. As members of the Hays Office team, they were expected to safeguard the interests of the entire industry. This meant representing the studios in negotiations with the multitude of state, local and international censor boards. Of course, the job was easier if they could convince producers to fashion their films in conformity to the Production Code. However, many writers, directors, producers and studio heads viewed the Code as just another list of recommendations, to be brushed aside if they seemed detrimental to the artistic or commercial possibilities of the story they were trying to present. In fact, the SRC did have the power to force changes on producers by withholding MPPDA approval of the final film. But faced with the reality that jobs were riding on the success of each film, they were, in the main, quite lenient in their guardianship of the Code. Also, when they did say "No" to a film that they believed to represent a danger to the industry, its studio could appeal the decision to a "Hollywood jury" composed of producers and executives from other companies. In most cases, these three men would overturn the SRC decision, perhaps because they hoped for similar treatment when one of their films came forward on appeal. Members of the SRC also found themselves beset by a wide range of religious, civic, and other special interest groups aligned against the industry in the censorship debate. They were the focal point of many zealots, all of them fractious, convinced of their rightness and determined to have their way.

One clear area of Production Code violation was nudity, which found its way into several films during the period. Both *Bird of Paradise* (RKO, 1932) and *Tarzan and His Mate* (MGM, 1934) contained nude swimming scenes featuring Delores Del Rio and Maureen O'Sullivan (or, more likely, their "body doubles"), though the initial release prints of *Tarzan and His Mate* were recalled and the offending scene replaced. A brief glimpse of the breasts of Jean Harlow was offered in *Red Headed Woman* (MGM, 1932), while *Gold Diggers of 1933* (Warner Bros., 1933) contained the shadowed silhouettes of nude women in one of the Busby Berkeley-choreographed dance numbers. *Blonde Venus* (Paramount, 1932) opened with a scene of nude women frolicking at a swimming hole and Cecil B. DeMille's *The Sign of the Cross* (Paramount, 1933) and *Cleopatra* (Paramount, 1934) both featured milk bath scenes that revealed a bit too much of star Claudette Colbert.

Paramount, the studio that released *Blonde Venus* and the DeMille pictures, presented more problems for the SRC than any other studio. Faced with staggering losses and headed for receivership (see chapter 2), Paramount pushed the outer limits of cultural taste and public acceptability during the period. A sophisticated comedy like *Trouble in Paradise* (1932) fractured the Code in any number of ways. It dealt with a pair of appealing thieves (Herbert Marshall and Miriam Hopkins) who live together openly without benefit of marriage. Marshall becomes involved in an affair with a wealthy Parisian widow (Kay Francis) from whom he expects to steal a considerable sum of money and jewels. At the end, the charming rogues escape, looking forward to more larcenous adventures and to the rekindling of their romance which had been temporarily threatened by Marshall's liaison with Francis. Even though the film treated seduction comedically, made "illicit" relationships seem not only "permissible" but "delightful" and "daring," spotlighted criminals who were the heroes and with whom the audience was supposed to sympathize, despite their crimes, the SRC apparently passed the film with nary a grumble because of the "light touch" of its famous director, Ernst Lubitsch.

Other Paramount films caused more tribulation. *A Farewell to Arms* (1932), *Blonde Venus*, *The Song of Songs* (1933), *Design for Living* (1933) and *Bolero* (1934) required extensive negotiations between the studio and the SRC before they were approved. *The Story of Temple Drake* (1933), an adaptation of William Faulkner's novel *Sanctuary*, was especially problematic. Initially, the MPPDA had told studios that no motion picture based on this notorious book would be approved. Nevertheless, Paramount pressed ahead. A number of concessions, including the title change, were wrested from the studio, and it agreed not to make reference to *Sanctuary* in the advertising or promotion of the picture. However, the most controversial event in the book – the rape of Temple by a gangster using a corncob – was strongly suggested. Despite SRC objections, the scene was conveyed by having the gangster (Jack La Rue) advance on Temple (Miriam Hopkins) in a barn with abundant corncobs lying about, then cutting as her scream filled the soundtrack. Paramount also declined to shoot an SRC-recommended epilogue in which the fallen heroine is shown rebuilding her character by performing welfare work in China.

Mae West and her films for Paramount probably caused the SRC the most turmoil. Ms. West's lascivious walk, her openness about sexual matters, her fondness for jewels and racy double entendres, and her unrelenting gusto for men set off a tidal wave of protest in the early 1930s. Part of the problem was the popularity of her films; audiences flocked to *She Done Him Wrong* (1933), *I'm No Angel* (1933) and *Belle of the Nineties* (1934), helping Paramount move back in the direction of financial stability while, at the same time, strengthening the cries of the reproachful who were convinced that the Production Code was a sham and that stronger censorship measures were required.

Mae West was notorious before she ever appeared in a motion picture. Her stage shows had generated widespread controversy, prompting Will Hays to forbid the production of *She Done Him Wrong*, based on her play *Diamond Lil*. However, the executive board of the MPPDA allowed Paramount to proceed with the film. Director Lowell Sherman and producer William LeBaron, as well as the star, made a number of concessions to the SRC, but still managed to complete a film that presented the West persona everyone was expecting – a connoisseur of men and diamonds who uses her sexual allure to seize what she desires from life. Arguably the most outrageous elements in the film were its risqué songs, particularly "I Wonder Where My Easy Rider's Gone" and "A Guy What Takes His Time," sung by West. And, despite a rather forced ending in which an undercover cop (Cary Grant) slips a diamond ring on her finger and announces his intention "to be [her] jailer for a long, long time," the film ran roughshod over the Production Code, leaving it in tatters. So did *I'm No Angel*, which again featured Cary Grant as the only man with a chance to make this highly experienced woman settle down. (Figure 4.1)

Paramount was hardly alone in its casual attitude toward the Production Code. All the studios made films that featured seduction, infidelity, prostitution, illegitimate children, violence, criminal activities and other questionable elements. MGM, for example, titillated audiences with Joan Crawford portraying Clark Gable's "kept woman" in *Possessed* (1931), Norma Shearer as a "high class harlot" (so described by a publicity staff member of the MPPDA) in *Strangers May Kiss* (1931), Helen Hayes playing a rich man's mistress who later becomes a prostitute in order to send her son to medical school in *The Sin of Madelon Claudet* (1931), Greta Garbo cast as an adulteress in *Inspiration* (1931) and a woman, born out of wedlock, who has sexual relationships with several men before finally convincing her true love (Clark Gable) to give her another chance in *Susan Lenox (Her Fall and Rise)* (1931). Jean Harlow, whose ripe sensuality and aggressive attitude toward men rivaled Mae West's, starred in several MGM films that the studio managed to maneuver through the SRC. Perhaps the most controversial was *Red Headed Woman* (1932), a comedy about a clever gold digger who sleeps her way to the top, wreaking considerable havoc on "respectable" relationships along the way. It appears that she will

Figure 4.1 Mae West, the sexiest star of her day, in *I'm No Angel* (produced by William LeBaron for Paramount, 1933). Courtesy of the USC Cinema-Television Library.

finally get her comeuppance at the end of the film when her dalliance with her rich lover's chauffeur is discovered and she is banished without a cent. But a short epilogue which takes place one year later reveals that she has transplanted her unbridled approach (and the chauffeur) to France, where she has become the toast of the Parisian beau monde.

A similar tale of a woman's willingness to use her body to achieve wealth and social status was the Warner Bros. film *Baby Face* (1933), starring Barbara Stanwyck. Though comedic in spots, *Baby Face* was more disturbing to the SRC and to film audiences because its overall tone was more realistic. Shortly after release, the film was pulled out of circulation and extensive changes were negotiated between the studio and the SRC in order to make *Baby Face* more palatable to censor boards. The reconstructed movie still showed Stanwyck's character advancing up the hierarchy of a bank by seducing various employees, but it changed one character from an exponent of Nietzschean philosophy who encourages her behavior to a moral mouthpiece who condemns her, excised some of the more explicit examples of her seductions and imposed an ending that returned her to her humble origins, thus emphasizing that her gold digging had been in vain. Despite the overhaul, *Baby Face* was still rejected by the Virginia censor board.

Warner Bros. made other films that contained plenty of sexual hanky-panky. *Female* (1933) offered Ruth Chatterton espousing "free love" and seducing several men who work for her automobile company; *Illicit* (1931) and its remake *Ex-Lady* (1933) contained liberated young women (Barbara Stanwyck and Bette Davis) whose relationships are spoiled after they are forced, by societal pressure, to marry their lovers; *The Strange Love of Molly Louvain* (1932) concerned the multiple affairs and illegitimate daughter of Ann Dvorak; *Scarlet Dawn* (1932) included a scene in which Douglas Fairbanks Jr. takes part in an orgy with his mistress Lilyan Tashman; and *Employee's Entrance* (1933) presented a tangled web of sexual relationships among workers in a department store.

Although they received less initial attention from the SRC and censor boards than the sexually-themed films, the gangster films produced by Warner Bros. would eventually generate a good deal of heated debate. *Doorway to Hell* (1930), *Little Caesar* (1931) and *The Public Enemy* (1931) contained criminal protagonists who pay for their violence and rapaciousness by dying violently at the end. But the gangster figures in these films were certainly the most central and exciting characters in the stories, provoking the fear that audience members would empathize with them and their antisocial behavior. To many concerned viewers, these films seemed flagrantly to violate Code prohibitions against movies that "teach methods of crime," "inspire potential criminals with a desire for imitation" and "make criminals seem heroic and justified."

Other mob pictures, such as *Bad Company* (RKO, 1930), *The Secret Six* (MGM, 1931), *Quick Millions* (Fox, 1931) and *City Streets* (Paramount, 1931) also disturbed certain reform-minded individuals and groups, but the arguments that attended their release paled in comparison to the wrangling that affected *Scarface* (Caddo/United Artists, 1932). This picture, based loosely on the career of Al Capone, appeared so dangerous to the interests of the industry that Will Hays himself became enmeshed in the contentious negotiations.

Even before Hays' involvement, SRC-suggested cuts had been made to reduce the glorification of the film's protagonist Tony Camonte (Paul Muni), to mask inferences of an incestuous relationship between Camonte and his sister (Ann Dvorak) and to emphasize that Camonte, left without his henchmen and defenses at the end, was really a coward at heart. In addition, a preamble announcing that the film was an "indictment of gang rule in America" and calling upon the populace to take action against the crime lords had been inserted and a new ending, in which Camonte is captured, tried and hanged for his crimes, had been shot for the all-important New York territory whose censors refused to allow the presentation of the film with its original ending, wherein Camonte is shot down by the police while attempting to escape.

Hays, however, was still uncomfortable with *Scarface*. He wanted all sympathy for Camonte removed, a more emphatic "anti-gun purchase" message included and the title changed. More cuts were made, including one scene in which Tony is shown buying a present for his mother; nevertheless, the negotiations between Hays and producer Howard Hughes dragged on, with Hughes growing more angry and recalcitrant, especially when the New York censor board rejected the film even though he had made the changes they demanded. Will Hays and Howard Hughes finally reached an agreement and the New York censor board reversed its decision, perhaps because Hughes threatened to sue them. The film, now called *Scarface, the Shame of a Nation* for New York theater presentations, opened in May 1932. The controversy may have helped it at the box office; the picture did well financially, and the National Board of Review, a New York-based organization, singled it out as one of the best films of the year. (Figure 4.2)

It appears that Hughes' status as an independent producer limited his ability to stand firm against the SRC and Hays. They also forced him to take so much out of *Cock of the Air* (Caddo/United Artists, 1932), the story of a pilot/seducer (Chester Morris), that Hughes was convinced the cuts had ruined his film. The major studios seem to have been given more leeway; still, the issue

Figure 4.2 Paul Muni in the ultra-violent *Scarface* (produced by Howard Hughes for Caddo/United Artists, 1932). Courtesy of the USC Cinema-Television Library.

of preferential censorship treatment for certain studios was constantly voiced. Carl Laemmle Jr., for example, was outraged when Paramount was allowed to proceed with Mae West's *Diamond Lil* (released as *She Done Him Wrong*) after Laemmle had been told that Universal could not make it. Jack Warner complained that MGM was able to "get away" with material in such films as *Possessed* that the other studios could not. Columbia also thought MGM received special treatment, especially after the studio filmed *The Easiest Way* (1931) with Constance Bennett, Adolph Menjou and Robert Montgomery. The Hays Office had prevented Columbia, as well as the other companies, from producing it.

By 1933, working for the SRC must have been a nightmare. The industry itself was imperiled by the growing economic calamity, outside agitation against movie content was reaching a crescendo and MPPDA member companies were attacking each other and the mechanism of industry self-censorship over allegations of favoritism. Colonel Jason Joy had abandoned the SRC for a position at Fox in 1932, and the office was now being run by Dr. James Wingate, former director of the New York censorship board. Tough and inflexible at first, Wingate soon became more accommodating as the financial condition of the movie business worsened. Too accommodating, perhaps, for in the fall of 1933 he was demoted in favor of Joseph I. Breen, a former journalist and Irish-American Catholic who had been working for the MPPDA since 1931. Though given the vague title of "Assistant to the President," Breen began functioning as head of the SRC that fall and was placed in charge of West Coast operations of the MPPDA in December 1933. Breen soon proved tougher and more determined than his predecessors; now, things would begin to change.

The Payne Fund studies

In the year of Breen's ascendence, the ammunition that many censorship-minded antagonists of the industry had been seeking presented itself. A series of scientific investigations concerning the influence that movies have on young people had been first undertaken in 1929, funded by a $200,000 grant from the Payne Fund. They were carried out by a group of social scientists headed by Dr. W.W. Charters of Ohio State University, with initial findings published in 1933. Though naive in methodology and by no means consistent in their conclusions, the studies did suggest that Hollywood movies exerted a strong influence on American youth, an influence that could come into conflict with the teachings of parents, schools and churches.

It is probable that the Payne Fund studies themselves would have drawn scant general notice if a popularized version of the research findings, entitled *Our Movie Made Children*, had not been published by Macmillan in 1933. Author Henry James Forman culled through the studies, picking out data and examples that cast the film industry and its influence in the most alarming light. While the Payne Fund studies were, on the whole, tempered and objective, Forman's book suggested hyperbolically that the emphasis on sexual and criminal behavior in movies was destroying the moral fiber of the country's youth. Reading Forman, one could only conclude that Hollywood was a national menace and that strong governmental measures were needed to control its contaminating effects.

Forman's work was challenged by philosopher Mortimer Adler and sociologist Kimball Young, among others, but the impact of *Our Movie Made Children* far outweighed the counter-arguments of Forman's critics. Soon, the Payne Fund material was being used as the basis for articles in newspapers, popular magazines and academic journals bearing such titles as "Minds Made by the Movies" and "What's Wrong with Hollywood?". Will Hays attempted to calm the groundswell of bad publicity by circulating "Authoritative Statements Concerning the Screen and Behavior," a pamphlet filled with testimony that refuted most of the allegations in the Forman volume. Like the efforts of Adler and Young, the pamphlet did little to retard the juggernaut of adverse public opinion bearing down on the MPPDA and its member companies.

The Legion of Decency

An even more worrisome element entered the censorship equation in 1933. In an October speech delivered to the annual convention of Catholic Charities in New York, Archbishop Amleto Giovanni Cicognani, the Papal Secretary of State, called for a crusade against the movies:

> What a massacre of innocence of youth is taking place hour by hour! How shall the crimes that have their direct source in immoral motion pictures be measured? Catholics are called by God, the Pope, the Bishops and the priests to a united and vigorous campaign for the purification of the cinema, which has become a deadly menace to morals.

Cicognani's call to arms gained momentum in November during a general meeting of US Catholic Bishops in Washington, DC. The "problem" of Hollywood pictures was an important agenda item, with Father Daniel Lord on hand to express his growing belief that the industry was incapable of cleaning up its own house, despite his beloved Production Code. Following the suggestion of Bishop Cantwell of Los Angeles that the Church form a legion of decency for motion pictures, a four-man Episcopal Committee on Motion Pictures was organized to plan and direct a national campaign to improve the "moral quality of films."

The Committee evidently fancied Bishop Cantwell's title for, in April 1934, it announced that a National Legion of Decency would be formed to combat immoral motion pictures. Most Reverend John McNicholas, the chairman of the Episcopal Committee, explained:

> It is not our purpose to destroy any industry or business. It is our purpose to protect the souls of the children committed to our keeping. Legitimate recreation is necessary almost as much as the bread we eat and the air we breathe, but it must be good and wholesome. We must array ourselves against that which is detrimental to the mind, heart and soul of our children.

Methods for recruiting members into the Legion varied, but most individuals were enlisted through their local churches. New members would sign a pledge announcing their opposition to "vile and unwholesome motion pictures," promising to speak out and "arouse public sentiment against the portrayal of vice [in movies] as a normal condition of affairs" and agreeing "to secure as many members as possible for the Legion of Decency." While the most popular early version of the pledge did not specifically forbid a member from attending any film, it was implied that he/she would be called upon to boycott pictures which the Church decided were not "clean entertainment and educational features." Later versions of the pledge clearly stated that a member should "remain away" from "pictures that are dangerous to my moral life."

Considerable pressure was applied to US Catholics to join the Legion, and the swelling ranks of the organization were then used to force theater owners to stop presenting the wrong sorts of films. In late May 1934, the Archbishop of Philadelphia ordered his Legion members to boycott all films showing in the city; reports suggest that movie business fell 40 percent as a result. Soon, other dioceses were threatening similar action. In most areas, however, a boycott of specific films was adopted as the proper approach. In Chicago, for example, Cardinal Mundelein issued a list of 124 films: 52 deemed suitable for Catholic filmgoers; 41 that were "offensive in spots"; and 31 considered "immoral and indecent." The last group, to be shunned by members of the Chicago Legion, included *Manhattan Melodrama* (MGM, 1934), *The Life of Vergie Winters* (RKO, 1934), *Fog over Frisco* (Warner Bros., 1934), *Little Man, What Now?* (Universal, 1934) and *Sisters Under the Skin* (Columbia, 1934).

By summer of 1934, millions had signed the Legion pledge and other religious sects were lending their support to the Catholic offensive. Both Protestant and Jewish groups encouraged their congregations to become involved in the crusade; surprisingly, many non-Catholics were urged to become members of the Legion itself. In July a meeting took place in New York to coordinate the efforts of the different religious factions. It was decided to organize an interfaith pressure group that would focus on all matters that affected public morals, most specifically motion pictures. The group even proposed that the Hays Office be disbanded, to be replaced by a new board of oversight composed of representatives from the "ministries of America, the public, and the industry."

Given support by the Pope, who offered his "special blessing and the strongest encouragement" to its war on immoral films, the Legion of Decency continued to move forward aggressively. By the end of 1934, the Chicago rating of films had become known as the "Motion Picture Guide" and been widely accepted as the authoritative voice on movie suitability. Displayed in Catholic Churches throughout the country, this publication offered the information that Legion members required before making their moviegoing decisions. It grouped films into three categories: "Class A – unobjectionable and suitable for public entertainment"; "Class B – more or less objectionable because of their possible suggestiveness or vulgarity or sophistication or lack of modesty. Neither approved nor forbidden but for adults only"; "Class C – indecent and immoral and unfit for public entertainment." The initial "Motion Picture Guide," which appeared in December 1934, placed 37 films in "Class A," 32 films in "Class B" and 36 films in "Class C." Among the titles in the "C" group were *The Affairs of Cellini* (Twentieth Century/United Artists, 1934), *Nana* (Goldwyn/United Artists, 1934), *Of Human Bondage* (RKO, 1934), *Madame Du Barry* (Warner Bros., 1934), *The Girl from Missouri* (MGM, 1934), *One More River* (Universal, 1934) and *The Scarlet Empress* (Paramount, 1934).

The "Motion Picture Guide" offered the last word for Legion of Decency members until February 1936 when the International Federation of Catholic Alumni (IFCA), which had been reviewing films even longer than the Chicago group, was recognized as the official ratings body of the Legion. Composed of women who had graduated from Catholic convent schools and Catholic colleges, the IFCA movie reviewers were supplemented by laymen and priests who became involved whenever a disagreement arose over a particular film's rating. The IFCA broadened the rating categories: "A-1 – morally unobjectionable for general patronage"; "A-2 – morally unobjectionable in part for all"; "B – morally objectionable in part for all"; and "C – condemned, positively bad." The work of the IFCA reviewers would continue for many years to come.

The Production Code Administration

Stung by the inflammatory charges that grew out of the Payne Fund Studies and by the rapidly increasing influence of the Legion of Decency, the MPPDA began to reassess its position. A halfhearted attempt to counter industry critics was made through radio broadcasts in May 1934, but Will Hays and the studio executives quickly realized that more dramatic measures would be necessary. In fact, Joseph Breen had been much tougher in his application of the Code to movies than his predecessors, but the system was still stacked against him. A "Hollywood jury" reversed his rejection of *Queen Christina* (MGM, 1934), for example, and it was reported that similar reversals had taken place on four other films that Breen refused to certify.

In late June, Martin Quigley and Breen, at Hays' request, met with the Episcopal Committee of the Catholic Church. Even though Breen offered evidence of the ways that the MPPDA was working to improve film content, the Bishops expressed the opinion that there were still too many immoral films and vowed to continue their fight against them. Quigley stated that the problem pictures could be quickly eliminated if the Production Code was firmly enforced. Impressed by this argument, the Bishops agreed that the Legion would relax its campaign when the Hays Office began to force filmmakers to abide by the Code.

On July 1, 1934, the beleaguered directors of the MPPDA voted to abolish the Studio Relations Committee and replace it with the Production Code Administration (PCA), which would be run by Joseph Breen. As before, the office would read synopses, treatments and script materials before a film went into production, offering lists of problems and suggestions for changes. Following production, PCA officials would view the final release version to determine if it conformed to the Code. If it did, the film would receive the Code's Seal of Approval which it could display in the credits. If not, a list of specific changes would be presented; these changes would have to be made before a Code Seal could be affixed. MPPDA member companies agreed that they would not release, distribute or exhibit a film without a Code Seal and that any company which breached the agreement would have to pay a fine of $25,000. However, the principal discouragement was not the fine, but the prohibition against exhibiting a film without a Code Seal in Big Five theaters. Without access to these primarily urban, primarily first-run theaters, a film with a significant budget could not possibly recoup its costs; thus, economic suicide would likely result from any attempt to evade the PCA's decision. Equally important, from Breen's perspective, was the elimination of the "Hollywood jury." Now appeals would be heard by the MPPDA board in New York, presided over by Will Hays. (Figure 4.3)

The public relations arm of the industry embraced the new machinery of self-censorship. Warner Bros. promised to begin producing pictures for "family audiences," Fox writers were warned that they would be held responsible for

Figure 4.3   Joseph I. Breen (*center*), head of the Production Code Administration, visits the set of *Three Smart Girls* (Universal, 1936). Seated to the left of Breen is actress Deanna Durbin and peering over his shoulders are producer Joe Pasternak (*left*) and director Henry Koster (*right*). Courtesy of the USC Cinema-Television Library.

moral criticisms leveled at films they had scripted, Paramount and Universal both announced their commitment to "clean" pictures, and B.B. Kahane of RKO summed up the basic industry position:

> There is no need and no excuse whatsoever for productions which scoff at chastity and the sanctity of marriage, present criminals and wrong doers as heroes or heroines, or in which smut and salaciousness are deliberately injected for the appeal they may have to coarse and unrefined minds.

The Catholic Church adopted a wait-and-see attitude. The campaign of the Legion of Decency would continue, at least until significant positive change was evident in the content of Hollywood productions.

The newly-constituted PCA went to work on July 15, 1934. Recognizing the importance of adopting a determined, no-nonsense posture, Breen and his staff were extremely tough in their initial enforcement of the Code. In short order, nudity, free love, prostitution and rape practically disappeared from films, while instances of infidelity, seduction and illegitimacy fell off precipitously. Genres were affected: sex comedies and "fallen woman" melodramas faded away, and gangster films featuring sympathetic criminals became unproducible. Breen even informed the studios that they would not be allowed to make a film about notorious criminal John Dillinger, shot to death by FBI agents in 1934.

Some stars felt the sting of the PCA, none more than Mae West. She came across as an uncomfortable imitation of herself in *Klondike Annie* (Paramount, 1936). Following a thorough overhaul of the script by the PCA, Ms. West played a character who "gets religion," raises money for a missionary organization in Alaska, then voluntarily returns to San Francisco to face a murder charge. Despite the efforts of Breen and Co., the picture was still attacked by various newspaper writers, denounced by the Legion of Decency and subjected to further cuts by local and state censor boards. Straitjacketed by her reputation, as well as by the PCA, Mae West's film career would last only a few more years.

The transition to PCA authority did not proceed with uniform smoothness. In April 1935, for example, a PCA official granted a Code Seal to *The Devil Is a Woman* (Paramount) without viewing the finished film. The story of a Spanish femme fatale (Marlene Dietrich) and her devastating impact on several men caused Will Hays significant discomfort when he saw it shortly before its scheduled release. To Hays, the main character appeared to be a high-class prostitute whose actions made "adultery appear profitable." Breen was similarly upset with the picture, most especially because the Dietrich character was not punished for her sins. He suggested that Paramount make several changes, including filming a new ending in which she is killed while begging for forgiveness, in order to "clearly and unmistakably establish the fact that she cannot get off scott-free (*sic*) after years of despicable conduct." A few minor alterations were made but the Paramount executives, Code Seal in hand, held firm to the basic story line and ending in which no punishment is exacted. Breen would be vigilant in the future to make sure that final approval was withheld until a definite release print had been scrutinized by himself and/or other PCA workers he trusted.

One of the most telling signs of the "new censorship order" in Hollywood was the large number of pre-1934 films which Breen refused to certify when they were submitted to the PCA for re-release. Among the titles forced out of circulation by this mechanism were *The Sin of Madelon Claudet*, *The Public Enemy*, *Blonde Venus*, *Trouble in Paradise*, *Back Street* (Universal, 1932), *The Painted Woman* (Fox, 1932), *Call Her Savage* (Fox, 1932), *Scarface*, *Cock of the Air*, *The Greeks Had a Word for Them* (Goldwyn/United Artists, 1932), *The Animal Kingdom* (RKO, 1932), *Topaze* (RKO, 1933), *Ann Vickers* (RKO, 1933), *The Song of Songs*, *She Done Him Wrong*, *I'm No Angel* and *Design for Living*. Occasionally, studios would agree to make PCA-mandated cuts in order to gain permission to re-issue a film. RKO, for example, excised certain "gruesome" moments from *King Kong* (1933), as well as part of a scene in which the giant ape plucks off some of Fay Wray's clothing. Likewise, Paramount, in order to redistribute *Dr. Jekyll. and Mr. Hyde* (1932), eliminated Ivy's undressing scene and a line of dialogue in which Jekyll (Fredric March) tells Ivy (Miriam Hopkins) that he "wants her."

The emphatic methods of Joseph Breen and his PCA had the desired effect on industry critics. Cuts required by municipal and state censor boards declined markedly and, for the most part, calls for government censorship of the movies were stilled. Since the PCA was well-schooled in the vicissitudes of foreign censorship, studios received plentiful warnings about segments of their pictures that would prove problematic abroad. It was then up to them to fashion their pictures so as to encounter as few international problems as possible. For example, the ubiquitous twin beds in post-1934 Hollywood films were evidently an accommodation to British censors. Since Great Britain represented the industry's chief overseas market, the requirements of English censors would naturally be taken more seriously than those of other foreign censoring bodies.

With a Catholic in charge, enforcing a document conceived and prepared, for the most part, by two Catholics, the PCA also slowed the momentum of the Legion of Decency. However, the Legion refused to disappear and, on occasion, came into conflict with Breen's decisions. The head of the PCA was particularly exasperated by the Legion's disapproval of *One More River*. After wrestling mightily with the studio over their adaptation of John Galsworthy's novel and forcing the removal of several examples of "sadism," as well as other questionable elements, the PCA awarded the film a Code Seal. The Legion, however, found the film's presentation of divorce not to its liking and placed it in the dreaded "C" category. Breen seemed almost embarrassed about the tenets of his own religion in an August 1934 letter to Universal studio chief Carl Laemmle Jr. concerning the film: "this is the first picture passed under the recently set-up machinery to be so condemned. I suppose it is the divorce angle which brings down condemnation of the Catholics; and I suppose that in the face of their very definite viewpoint on the subject of divorce, we are help-less under the circumstances."

"Compensating moral values"

After the initial crackdown, Breen and his staff became more flexible and their interpretation of the Code more liberal. Once again, the relationship between industry self-censorship and creative filmmaking became one of bi-directional negotiation rather than uni-directional enforcement. Prostitutes, initially camouflaged as bar girls or hostesses in such films as *Marked Woman* (Warner Bros., 1937), returned to the screen in *Dead End* (Goldwyn/United Artists, 1937), *Stagecoach* (Wanger/United Artists, 1939), *Primrose Path* (RKO, 1940) and *Waterloo Bridge* (MGM, 1940). Likewise, sympathetic gangsters were reintroduced by Warner Bros. in *Angels with Dirty Faces* (1938), *The Roaring Twenties* (1939) and *High Sierra* (1941). Although a veritable war was fought between Breen and David Selznick over questionable material in Selznick's adaptation of *Gone with the Wind* (Selznick/MGM, 1939), the producer won most of the battles, including the right to have Rhett Butler (Clark Gable) tell Scarlett O'Hara (Vivien Leigh), "Frankly, my dear, I don't give a damn" near the end of the film. Breen would have preferred, "Frankly, my dear, I don't care."

One of the reasons the PCA grew more cooperative over time was declin-ing pressure from industry foes. Another was sensitivity to protests from professors, artists, advocates of free speech and filmmakers who charged that Breen and his acolytes were anti-intellectual philistines impeding the develop-ment of the cinema as a mature art form. Consequently, the PCA watchdogs were particularly lenient with films adapted from literary classics such as *Anna Karenina* (MGM, 1935), *Dodsworth* (Goldwyn/United Artists, 1936) and *Camille* (MGM, 1937). They also seemed more willing to compromise on expensive productions that represented a significant financial risk to their studios than on the less costly "B" and "in-between" pictures.

Oddly, the loophole which enabled Breen to justify worrisome plot elements in PCA-approved pictures was not mentioned in the Production Code. The concept of "compensating moral values" had been occasionally employed in the SRC days; under Breen, however, it would become ubiquitous and function as the cornerstone of adjudication of the Code. In essence, a film with proper compensating moral values might contain evil acts such as adultery or murder as long as those acts were counterbalanced in the narrative, preferably by punishment of the offending parties or other forms of suffering, moral regen-eration, penance, etc. Thus, according to PCA thinking, compensating moral values would make audiences clearly aware of the "wages of sin" and discourage imitation of immoral behavior.

PCA employees were trained to use the concept to defend their decisions and fend off critics who believed the office was too lax and open-minded. Testifying before a Congressional Committee in 1940, Francis Harmon of the PCA cited *Conquest* (MGM, 1937) as an example of how compensating moral values had been injected to neutralize the story's objectionable elements. The historical drama concerned Marie Walewska (Greta Garbo) who became the mistress of Napoleon and bore him a son out of wedlock. Marie is married to a Polish count when the first assignation occurs and, while initially motivated by the potential benefits to Poland if she gives herself to the powerful emperor, she falls in love with him and is deeply hurt when he decides to marry another woman. Harmon listed seven different examples of compensating moral values in the film, including the use of Marie's husband as a "voice of morality" who challenges the idea that his wife's adultery can "be justified on patriotic grounds," a scene in which it is suggested that Marie "made a serious effort to secure concessions [for her country from Napoleon] and at the same time protect her virtue," a scene in which Marie's beloved brother, upon discovering the truth about his sister's affair, "upbraids her severely, expresses humiliation, and leaves in a fury," the pain which Marie feels when Napoleon announces his forthcoming marriage to Marie Louise of Austria and a scene near the end when Napoleon is forced to recognize the sad position of his illegitimate son who has never been told his father's name. Harmon argued, "Thus, through constructive collaboration during production the historical fact of this illicit love was not altered but the surrounding details were so handled as to indicate clearly to theater audiences that such conduct was wrong, that it brought tragedy in its wake, and that innocent persons suffered as a result."

What Harmon did not tell the Congressmen was that the PCA wanted even more concessions. During the negotiations, Breen suggested that a final scene which took place at the time of Marie's death be rewritten "to indicate that she is a repentant soul, who foolishly bartered away her body for what she thought was a worthy cause, only to learn in the end that it was futile . . . ." MGM declined to end the film in this fashion, deciding instead to use the death of Napoleon as the finale.

Another example of Breen's failure to force a studio to accept his proposals took place on *Kitty Foyle* (RKO, 1940). Breen objected to a scene in which Kitty (Ginger Rogers) and her future husband Wyn (Dennis Morgan) spend the night together in a mountain cabin. Ultimately, he allowed the scene because the studio eliminated even more disturbing elements from its adaptation of

Christopher Morley's novel, including an abortion. Most importantly, Breen was satisfied that the heroine's trials and tragedies, including the death of her child, the shabby way she is treated by Wyn's wealthy family who look down on Kitty because of her working-class origins, and Wyn's ultimate decision, after securing a divorce from Kitty, to marry someone from his own social set, represented the sort of "punishment" necessary to show that her affair was unquestionably wrong. Appropriate compensating moral values had been injected into the story.

"Exploitation" Films and Foreign Imports

For years a small group of renegade filmmakers had been producing and distributing pictures containing content that major studio executives considered taboo, even during the liberal Pre-Code period. Made inexpensively and sold to individual theater owners in a "states' rights" (territory-by-territory) fashion, these films dealt with such topics as nudism, drug use, white slavery, psychotic behavior, vice, venereal disease and other "sex hygiene" subjects. Though sometimes characterized as "travelogues" or "exposes," they were usually promoted as "educational" productions and often accompanied in theaters by an "expert" lecturer who emphasized the importance of bringing information about the particular topic to the community's attention before it was too late. In fact, the education argument was an excuse to include scenes of sexual activity, nudity, and various kinds of human atrocity that could be "exploited" in lurid advertising and would attract enough curious patrons to generate a heady profit. Furthermore, the "educational" nature of the presentations proved useful in dealing with state and local censor boards which typically resisted their requests for exhibition licenses and with courts of law whenever the makers were arrested on obscenity charges. Among the representative titles from the 1930s: *The Seventh Commandment* (1932), *Guilty Parents* (1933), *Narcotic* (1933), *Maniac* (1934), *Marihuana* (1936), *Hell-A-Vision* (1936), *Slaves in Bondage* (1937), *Damaged Goods* (1937) and *Human Wreckage* (1938).

The Hollywood establishment deplored these films, both before and after the creation of the PCA. They hated the fact that fly-by-night "exploitation" producers played by a different set of censorship rules than they did. But they were particularly outraged that these shabby, amateurish, often incoherent movies were regularly mistaken for their own product, and that they were often blamed for making them. The fact that theater owners sometimes put together double bills featuring a major studio release and an "exploitation" picture deepened the confusion. In addition, since any producer willing to pay a fee could submit a feature film to the PCA for its stamp of approval, Joseph Breen occasionally found himself in the uncomfortable position of awarding a Code Seal to an edited version of one of these pictures. The Seal generally enabled the producer to gain bookings in higher-class theaters where, in many instances, the original "uncut" version would be projected. Breen, of course, would react angrily when he learned of the ruse and immediately revoke the Seal. But the wily producer chuckled all the way to the bank.

Nothing would have pleased the moguls more than the banning of all "exploitation" pictures. But they knew they could not lobby for this remedy because it might ultimately lead to outside censorship of their own product. They were also displeased by the importation of foreign films that were a good deal racier than their own productions. The most famous of these was a 1933 film made in Czechoslovakia entitled *Ecstasy*. In addition to a nude swimming scene, this story of adultery included a scene of sexual activity containing an extended close-up of the face of the female lead as she experiences orgasm. Efforts to import *Ecstasy* into the US, beginning in 1935, summoned forth an unprecedented amount of government obstruction and a concomitant mountain of publicity. By the time the producers' persistence paid off and *Ecstasy* began to penetrate American screens in the late 30s, often in severely truncated versions, the film had become a cause célèbre. Though Joe Breen declared he would never award *Ecstasy* a Code Seal when it was submitted to the PCA, it didn't much matter. He and his industry brethren could do nothing to stem its fulsome box office returns. In fact, one studio did profit from the movie and its attendant publicity; Louis B. Mayer signed the principal actress, changed her name to Hedy Lamarr and watched contentedly as she developed into another popular member of the MGM star contingent.

Politics and the PCA

Although the PCA became more relaxed in the late 1930s with respect to most of the Code-sensitive areas, its attitude toward political commentary in films grew increasingly cautious and restrictive. This was primarily a response to growing world instability during the period. With Europe moving toward another war and most Americans determined that their nation remain neutral, Breen and his staff took it upon themselves to safeguard movie customers from material they deemed politically volatile and propagandistic.

Protection of the studios' business interests provided the major rationale.

On several occasions, countries had threatened to ban the importation of a particular company's product, and sometimes all American motion pictures, because their leaders had been offended by depictions of their land and/or people in a specific film. Thus, it was felt that any broadside against the highly sensitive Nazis in Germany or Fascists in Italy would surely result in a foreign boycott with considerable loss of revenue. Consequently, concerned film-makers who wished to use the medium as a weapon against the burgeoning totalitarian menace generally found their efforts blocked or blunted.

MGM, for example, paid $50,000 for the rights to Sinclair Lewis' *It Can't Happen Here*, a play based on his novel about a Fascist movement that takes root in the United States. Joseph Breen eventually convinced Louis B. Mayer to abandon the project because of the controversial subject matter and its pos-sible international repercussions. Walter Wanger managed to bring *Blockade* (Wanger/United Artists, 1937) to the screen, but the PCA worked over the Spanish Civil War story so thoroughly that there was no indication (through dialogue, uniforms, etc.) of who the combatants were. An impassioned anti-war statement did manage to break through, but only those thoroughly acquainted with world affairs recognized that the sympathies of the filmmakers lay with the Loyalists in their losing struggle with the Fascists. Even though most spectators probably left theaters showing *Blockade* in a state of substantial perplexity, the Knights of Columbus and other Catholic groups protested the film throughout the US. The Catholic Church had sided with the Fascists in the war.

Whenever Joseph Breen spotted political trouble in a script, he invoked the "National Feelings" section of the Code and insisted that creative talent refrain from pointed ideological commentary. After spending $125,000 to secure the rights to Robert Sherwood's Pulitzer Prize-winning play, *Idiot's Delight*, MGM was forced to hire the author to strip away much of his story's anti-Fascist intent. The drama originally took place in an Italian hotel near the Swiss border, but the film (1939) was set in an unnamed European country with foreign phrases delivered in Esperanto (an artificial language) in hopes that no one would take offense. As with *Blockade*, some of the play's anti-war message filtered through, but the brutal Italian ideology and political leadership which Sherwood had attacked in his stage piece were totally masked. Ironically, the film never played in Italy anyway because of commercial limitations and was banned in several other countries because of the play's reputation. Some American critics, familiar with the original material, savaged the filmmakers for their spineless timidity.

The first forceful motion picture to break through the PCA's artificial barriers was *Confessions of a Nazi Spy* (Warner Bros., 1939). The PCA did everything it

Figure 4.4   Paul Lukas salutes a group of young Americans being indoctrinated in the ways of the Nazi Party in *Confessions of a Nazi Spy* (produced by Robert Lord for Warner Bros., 1939). Courtesy of the USC Cinema-Television Library.

could to discourage its production and water down its content, but the story, based on the actual capture and conviction of four German spies operating in the northeastern United States, provided the studio with "factual" leverage to justify an anti-Nazi diatribe without significant compromises. (Figure 4.4)

While no one at the PCA seemed in favor of the film's production, there was apparent disagreement about the types and amount of damage it might cause. After inspecting the first draft of the script, the PCA sent Warner Bros. a report indicating that the story appeared "technically" to conform to the Production Code but could be rejected by censor boards concerned that it might cause public disorder or incite riots. PCA employee Karl Lischka found it even more dangerous. In an internal memo, he expressed the opinion that the story did violate the Code because "Hitler and his government are unfairly represented." Lischka then proceeded to list a number of problematic story elements and concluded that release of the film would be "one of the most lamentable mistakes ever made by the industry." In addition, a Paramount executive warned that if Warner Bros.

made *Confessions*, the Warners would have "on their hands the blood of a great many Jews in Germany." The German Consulate in Los Angeles also petitioned the PCA to stop its production. However, the PCA was basically powerless to do this because of the factual basis of the story and the semi-documentary style employed in its telling. No one could say that the Nazi espionage was "made up" or "never happened." Evidence presented in the court trial and dramatized in the picture contradicted charges of fabrication and sensationalism.

The German response to the release of *Confessions of a Nazi Spy* was predictable; the Nazis threatened to ban all future films that employed anyone connected with the picture. By that time it didn't much matter since the studios were doing little business with Germany anyway. Although nearly 20 other nations refused to allow *Confessions* to be shown, the picture performed well financially, thanks to a generally enthusiastic domestic reception. Warner Bros. reported instances of vandalism in some of the theaters that showed it, but there were no riots or significant uproar in any American city.

Despite the box office success of *Confessions of a Nazi Spy*, there was no rush by the other studios to produce anti-Nazi movies. This appears to have resulted from the continuing strength of isolationism in the US, rather than because of attempts to stifle activist filmmaking by the PCA. At the end of 1940, the battle-field victories of the Nazis in Europe had made most of the continent off-limits to American feature films, so protection of that portion of the foreign market had become a moot point. Certain companies did ruffle isolationist feathers by making films with anti-Nazi themes. They included: *Arise, My Love* (Paramount, 1940), *The Great Dictator* (Chaplin/United Artists, 1940), *Foreign Correspondent* (Wanger/United Artists, 1940), *The Mortal Storm* (MGM, 1940), *Escape* (MGM, 1940), *Four Sons* (Twentieth Century-Fox, 1940), *The Man I Married* (Twentieth Century-Fox, 1940), *Man Hunt* (Twentieth Century-Fox, 1941) and *Underground* (Warner Bros., 1941).

The Outlaw

The first producer to rebel against the authority of the Production Code Administration was independent Howard Hughes. After abandoning the film industry in the early 1930s, Hughes returned to Hollywood in 1940 to make a western about legendary figures Billy the Kid (Jack Beutel), Doc Holiday (Walter Huston) and Pat Garrett (Thomas Mitchell). Howard Hawks, who had directed *Scarface* for Hughes, was the original director but Hughes fired him after a short time and took over the film himself.

PCA officials spotted a number of problems in the script of *The Outlaw*, pointed them out in letters to Hughes and discussed them with screenwriter Jules Furthman, who agreed to take care of the dubious elements. They also consulted with Furthman and, to a lesser extent, Hughes during the filming. Thus, they were unprepared for the cut version that was screened for them in March 1941. The difficulties mostly concerned the character of Rio (Jane Russell) who becomes involved in sexual relationships with both Billy and Doc (without compensating moral values) and whose breasts, according to a letter from Joseph Breen to Hughes, were "not fully covered" in many of the film's scenes. Sensing trouble, Breen sent a copy of the Hughes letter, informing him that *The Outlaw* was in violation of the Code, to Will Hays and added, in a cover letter:

> In my more than ten years of critical examination of motion pictures, I have never seen anything quite so unacceptable as the shots of the breasts of Rio ... throughout almost half of the picture, the girl's breasts, which are quite large and prominent, are shockingly emphasized and, in almost every instance, are very substantially uncovered.

In May 1941, Howard Hughes appealed Breen's decision to the MPPDA executive board. They voted to uphold the PCA verdict. At this point, a list of specific deletions necessary to receive a Code Seal was presented to the producer, who argued some more but ultimately complied with the censors' demands. However, even though *The Outlaw* now boasted a Seal, Hughes decided not to release it.

More than a year and a half later, the film opened at the Geary Theater in San Francisco. Accompanying the debut was a sexy stage show featuring Russell and Beutel and a sensational advertising campaign that had not been approved by the Advertising Code Administration, a parallel office to the PCA which examined and approved all advertising materials used to promote motion pictures. Releasing a film with unapproved advertising could result in the revocation of a Code Seal.

The San Francisco run of *The Outlaw* proved highly contentious. In short order, the film was condemned by the Legion of Decency, attacked by a number of civic and religious groups and assailed by critics who found it overly long and dramatically uninspired. Perhaps because of the harsh critical reception, Hughes again pulled back and began tinkering with the film. He would not release it widely until 1946 when the controversy would grow even more intense.

The Office of War Information Bureau of Motion Pictures

Some six months after America entered World War II, the PCA was joined by another agency that also started reviewing scripts, offering critical suggestions and attempting to steer Hollywood filmmakers in certain specific directions. The Office of War Information (OWI) Bureau of Motion Pictures (BMP) asked writers, producers and studio chiefs to consider several questions before they made a film:

1. Will this picture help win the war?
2. What war information problem does it seek to clarify, dramatize or interpret?
3. If it is an "escape" picture, will it harm the war effort by creating a false picture of America, her allies, or the world we live in?
4. Does it merely use the war as the basis for a profitable picture, contributing nothing of real significance to the war effort and possibly lessening the effect of other pictures of more importance?
5. Does it contribute something new to our understanding of the world conflict and the various forces involved, or has the subject already been adequately covered?
6. When the picture reaches its maximum circulation on the screen, will it reflect conditions as they are and fill a need current at that time, or will it be out-dated?
7. Does the picture tell the truth or will the young people of today have reason to say they were misled by propaganda?

Even though the creative talent in Hollywood were now confronted with two offices that had the potential to restrict their freedom of expression, there were few complaints. The movie industry was filled with patriotic filmmakers happy to use the medium to assist the war effort. In addition, propaganda movies made money; the public, hungry for films that emphasized the righteousness of the Allied cause and the inevitability of final victory, flocked to theaters for a full dosage of cinematic reassurance.

The OWI BMP, headed by Lowell Mellett, did become exercised about some aspects of the patriotic entertainments. It cautioned filmmakers not to stereo-type all Japanese as barbarians who should be exterminated or to use such epithets as "monkeys" or "apes" to describe them. Few producers paid much attention, however. They rarely attempted to balance "evil" Japanese charac-ters with more kindly or reasonable members of the race, and they encouraged screenwriters to come up with the most ugly epithets for characters to call the

Japanese. The portrayals in *Little Tokyo, USA* (Twentieth Century-Fox, 1942) and *Air Force* (Warner Bros., 1943) were particularly disturbing to Mellett and his staff.

Sober-minded OWI officials were equally disturbed by a screwball farce like *The Palm Beach Story* (Paramount, 1942). They objected to the film's emphasis on the frivolous behavior of the idle rich and one particular scene in which the drunken members of the "Ale and Quail Club" shoot up a private railroad car. Railroad cars were deemed essential to the war effort in 1942; therefore, according to the OWI, the cinematic destruction sent precisely the wrong message to theater patrons. OWI also found much to condemn in another comedy, *Princess O'Rourke* (Warner Bros., 1943). A Red Cross training session that was all wrong, from the phony ranks of the women to the way in which newcomers were taught first aid, represented one serious mistake, but the worst offense was a scene in which a high-ranking government official pulled strings to keep the hero (Robert Cummings) from having to serve in the military.

The OWI BMP did have some effect on the shaping of films. Changes were made in *Pittsburgh* (Universal, 1942), *Keeper of the Flame* (MGM, 1942) and *So Proudly We Hail* (Paramount, 1943), as well as other pictures, at the behest of Mellett and his staff. Nonetheless, the organization existed in a position roughly analogous to that of the Studio Relations Committee in the 1930–33 period. Though most studios were cooperative, forwarding drafts of scripts to the OWI for their comments and allowing reviewers to watch "rough cut" screenings and make suggestions, the system was voluntary. The OWI staff could cajole, wheedle, plead, complain and threaten, but it was not in a position to force studios to accept its recommendations.

The office was strengthened somewhat in 1943 when Mellett was replaced by Stanton Griffis, an industry insider, as head of the OWI Domestic Branch. Reviewing of films was turned over to the Overseas Branch, headed by Ulric Bell. Since the Overseas Branch of the OWI could deny an export license to any film that reviewers felt might harm the war effort abroad, studios became more mindful of the agency's guidelines. Industry executives certainly did not want their films restricted to the domestic market, thus limiting their earning potential.

In addition to the OWI, studios had to negotiate with other branches of the government when they wished to make certain types of pictures. In order to gain the cooperation of the Army or Navy for a combat film, a studio was expected to have its script okayed by the specific branch and allow military advisors to monitor the production. These men were, naturally, determined to ensure that the cinematic presentation of their units was accurate with respect to uniforms, behavior, etc., and flattering with respect to the men's actions, but did not breach security by including information that could be useful to the enemy.

On the one hand, it seems clear that the relationship between the various government agencies and the motion picture industry was, in the main, cooperative and supportive throughout the war. On the other hand, it also seems certain that the injection of these offices into the censorship equation resulted in motion pictures with more intrusive propaganda than might otherwise have been the case. Their presence also had a lot to do with a sharp decline in the production of films that dealt with America's own social problems or with characters, such as the criminal, the poor and the dissident, who might be considered weak links in the national chain of strength and unity. Indeed, any cinematic moment that could compromise the vision of an all-powerful, utopian United States, from realistically gruesome battle scenes abroad to black market activity at home, was forcefully discouraged. At no other time in the history of American films has their content been so carefully sculpted to offer a unified, ideologically consistent and idealized vision of the nation and its people.

The PCA during the War

The slow process of PCA liberalization continued during the war years. Filmmakers were given the freedom to present certain scenes that would have been blocked as "repellent" or "in bad taste" before the war because they demonstrated the consummate evil of America's foes. *Hitler's Children* (RKO, 1943), for example, offered the compulsory sterilization of women considered unfit to bear children for the Reich, as well as the whipping of "fit" females who refused to produce baby Nazis. *Behind the Rising Sun* (RKO, 1943) and *Women in Bondage* (Monogram, 1943) also took liberties with the Code which were justified by their propagandistic onslaught against the enemy. Joseph Breen, however, balked when the initial script of *The Hitler Gang* (Paramount, 1944) presented several high-ranking Nazis as homosexuals, suggested that Hitler, though impotent, was attracted to young girls and contained a speech stating that the Führer had replaced both God and Jesus Christ in the Nazi brand of worship. Though executive producer B.G. DeSylva fought to retain the controversial elements, Breen stood firm and the script was altered substantially before shooting began.

Comedies set on the home front also showed evidence of a relaxing PCA.

A number of films that dealt with the housing crisis in Washington, DC, such as *The More the Merrier* (Columbia, 1943), *Government Girl* (RKO, 1943) and *The Doughgirls* (Warner Bros., 1944), contained moments that bordered on the formerly forbidden bedroom farce, but Breen let them go. He also passed Preston Sturges' outrageous satire *The Miracle of Morgan's Creek* (Paramount, 1944) which concerned one Trudy Kockenlocker (Betty Hutton). In a state of drunkenness, Trudy marries a soldier whose name she cannot remember, then produces sextuplets nine months later. The PCA even abided *Lady of Burlesque* (Stromberg/United Artists, 1943), based on a story by Gypsy Rose Lee in which two strippers are strangled to death with their own G-strings.

One of the most significant changes was the sudden willingness to allow the production of films based on material that had formerly been banned. The movement or style that would later be called "film noir," its development stunted by the PCA's aversion to certain stories by such "hard-boiled" writers as James M. Cain, became established during the war years when Breen began to countenance their screen adaptation.

Double Indemnity was the watershed picture. Published as a short novel in 1935, the year that Breen was busy "restoring order," the Cain original contained a number of "sordid" elements. They included a brutal murder for money committed by the victim's adulterous wife and her lover. In a long 1935 letter outlining the story's multitudinous offenses, Breen characterized the tale as a "gross miscarriage of justice" and informed all studios that *Double Indemnity* could not be made. When Paramount decided to buy the Cain story in 1943, Breen's response was to send the studio a copy of his original "forget it" letter. The studio, however, paid little attention. It began submitting scripts, on which Breen, surprisingly, made his usual suggestions, eventually admitting that "the basic story seems to meet the requirements of the Production Code." The PCA approved the film in 1944. (Figure 4.5)

Once again, the principle of compensating moral values enabled Joseph Breen to justify the screen presentation of such "low tone" material. The film version of the murder is brilliantly planned and executed, but the relationship between the two lovers (Barbara Stanwyck and Fred MacMurray) soon begins to unravel and they end up killing each other. Crime doesn't pay, justice is served, providential order is restored. And yet . . . this was not business as usual, Hollywood style. The exceptional film, directed by Billy Wilder from a script by Wilder and Raymond Chandler, zeroed in on both the banality and eroticism of evil. It probed disturbing aspects of human psychology that few PCA-era films had even touched upon.

Thrilled and inspired by *Double Indemnity*, filmmakers rushed to explore

Figure 4.5 Venetian blinds cast ominous shadows in the prototypical film noir, *Double Indemnity* (produced by Joseph Sistrom for Paramount, 1944). The actors are (*left to right*) Richard Gaines, Fred MacMurray and Edward G. Robinson. Courtesy of the USC Cinema-Television Library.

similar terrain in such works as *The Woman in the Window* (International/RKO, 1944), *Murder, My Sweet* (RKO, 1945), *Scarlet Street* (Universal, 1945), *Mildred Pierce* (Warner Bros., 1945) and *The Postman Always Rings Twice* (MGM, 1946), another Cain story which had been banned even longer than *Double Indemnity*.

In sanctioning the production of *Double Indemnity*, Breen opened the gates to a flood of noir pictures. By 1946, he appeared to regret the decision. In remarks made to the producers at RKO, he bemoaned the proliferation of films "about unpleasant people, set down in squalid or sordid surroundings and engaged not only in criminal but in brutal activity." While admitting that the "sin is shown to be wrong, not condoned or made to appear right" in these pictures, he also recounted the strongly negative reactions of censor boards toward them, as well as the elevated level of criticism directed against the industry in general and the PCA in particular because of their release.

But Mr. Joseph Breen would prove powerless to stop the development of film noir, just as he would be unable to prevent the erosion of his beloved Production Code in the post-war years. The period of PCA hegemony in Hollywood was drawing to an end.

5

Narrative and Style

When moviegoers settled into theater seats during the Classical Period, the lights would dim and a company logo would flash up on the screen. It is doubtful these spectators paid much attention to the fact that the roaring lion meant they were about to see an MGM film or the beeping radio tower revealed the movie came from RKO or a stylized depiction of the Statue of Liberty indicated it was a Columbia product. Rather, these logos, plus the music or sound effects that accompanied them, subtly announced that the patrons were about to be transported to a very special world where a cinematic story would unfold before them. The logo prepared them to be entertained, possibly even enthralled, by a screen story.

Hollywood movies are vehicles for the presentation of stories. In the earliest days of the cinema as a commercial enterprise, producers came to realize that audiences preferred films that contained a story, not just pleasing images, and they set about developing the most effective techniques to tell stories in a visual fashion. Through trial-and-error methods, they created a cinematic "language" which conveyed narrative events effectively and could be readily understood by the full range of audience members. Although this "language" was, in fact, quite varied and complex, it functioned both to deliver narrative information in a clear, concise and dramatically effective fashion and to engage viewers actively in the on-screen happenings. Indeed, studio executives and their creative employees were convinced that good screen storytelling would immerse spectators so completely in the plot of the movie that they would never think about the totally constructed and artificial nature of the experience.

The storytelling principles mobilized to create screen entertainments were distilled from centuries of drama and literature and then reformulated to meet the requirements of the feature film. This meant that each story had to be told completely in a time frame that usually lasted between 60 and 125 minutes. Because of the necessity of fitting tales that often covered much longer periods of time into such a compact temporal "box," the members of the production team would take scripts crafted by studio screenwriters and translate them into stylistic techniques that, they hoped, would transfer the story to the screen in a captivating manner. A good movie meant a good story told in seamless fashion.

This chapter will investigate the narrative strategies and stylistic techniques employed to fashion the Hollywood movies of the period – strategies and techniques developed during the silent era and then modified and augmented during the early years of sound. Following this discussion, the film *Stagecoach* (Wanger/United Artists, 1939) will be analyzed from both perspectives in order to illustrate and further elucidate the storytelling principles and stylistic elements of the Classical Period.

Narrative Strategies

The "world" of the film

One useful way to think about the narrative strategies employed by producers, directors and screenwriters is to recognize that their principal function is to create special "worlds" in which interesting stories could be told. These worlds might bear a strong resemblance to the real world that human beings inhabit on Planet Earth. In fact, the makers of many films worked hard to convince customers that their stories were realistic depictions of human experience. But despite this veneer of authenticity, all films produced in Hollywood were totally fabricated and fictional. They imposed artificial dramatic or comedic structures on their stories, employed actors to impersonate characters who were often very different from themselves, manipulated time and space in ways that defied the laws of physics, usually relied on extramundane music to heighten the impact of their narratives and featured individuals who communicated in the English language whether they were supposed to live in ancient Rome, eighteenth-century France or contemporary China. Thus, the world of each movie had its own special qualities and internal logic which its makers fashioned so that audience members not only could comprehend it readily, but also would embrace its elements, especially its characters.

The quest for order

Most Classical narratives were tales of providential order. Either before or near the beginning, one or more events transpire that throws the world of the film into disorder. In gangster films like *Little Caesar* (Warner Bros, 1931), a dangerous criminal is on the loose, menacing society which cannot be safe until he is brought to justice or killed. In an adventure film like *The Mark of Zorro* (Twentieth Century-Fox, 1940), a just and humane leader is replaced by an egocentric tyrant, throwing the local area into chaos. For order to be restored, this tyrant must be overthrown and the proper leader returned to his position of authority. In a screwball comedy like *The Awful Truth* (Columbia, 1937), the marriage of two lovely and well-matched young people comes apart, leading to a series of tumultuous experiences until the main characters return to their senses, reunite and agree to settle down together again. In a horror film like *Frankenstein* (Universal, 1931), a scientist's monomaniacal quest to create life spawns a monster who brings death and destruction to the local community before its villagers apparently destroy the "thing." In a musical like *Swing Time* (RKO, 1936), a series of mistakes and misunderstandings cause a man and a woman who are "made for each other" to nearly marry the wrong mates. But, just in time, they see things clearly and dance off together in the end.

As always, there are exceptions. The Marx Brothers comedies made in the early 1930s at Paramount, such as *Horse Feathers* (1932) and *Duck Soup* (1933), are surrealistic declarations of the fatuous nature of modern life. As such, they lionize the verbal non sequitur and the visual incongruity. Disorder reigns from beginning to end in these films. Indeed, one of the reasons the Paramount Marx Brothers efforts still stand out today was the decision by their makers to work against the accepted narrative and stylistic norms of the period. (Figure 5.1)

Manipulation of time

The presentations of these Hollywood allegories of order are not hampered by any significant temporal restrictions. Though the running time of features was fixed at plus or minus 90 minutes, each story could encompass days, or months, or even years. By making sure audience members always knew approximately when the action was taking place (through such devices as superimpositions, intertitles, montages, dialogue, make-up, costumes, etc.), filmmakers were free to manipulate time in a variety of ways. Usually, this meant condensing time by focusing only on the most important narrative "moments" and omitting all material that did not have a direct bearing on the development of the tale. *The Conquerors* (RKO, 1932), for example, is an episodic story that begins in 1873 and concludes in the early 1930s, encompassing several economic crises, World War I and numerous familial triumphs and tragedies – all conveyed to the audience in 84 minutes of screen time.

Figure 5.1   The anarchic Marx Brothers (*left to right*, Chico, Zeppo, Groucho and Harpo) in *Duck Soup* (Paramount, 1933). Courtesy of the USC Cinema-Television Library.

Although this happened less frequently, filmmakers could also elongate time, causing the on-screen action to take place over a longer period than might have been the case if the actions had occurred in real life. Parallel action (the juxtaposing of two or more scenes that are supposed to be taking place simultaneously), pioneered by D.W. Griffith, was employed in many westerns and other genre films to increase the excitement of a climactic scene. A good example may be found near the end of *Union Pacific* (Paramount, 1939). Two men (Joel McCrea and Robert Preston) and a woman (Barbara Stanwyck), holed up in a wrecked railroad car, fight a seemingly hopeless battle against a band of Indians. But intercut with their last stand are shots of a train full of soldiers roaring through a fiery trap set by another group of Indians and arriving just in time to save the three principal characters. Similarly, such filmmakers as Alfred Hitchcock would "stretch" time to increase the suspense of a scene like the Statue of Liberty finale of *Saboteur* (Universal, 1942) in which hero Robert Cummings tries to save villain Norman Lloyd from plunging to his death.

Omniscient point of view

Another important feature of the special worlds created in American cinema was their presentation from an omniscient point of view. Though there are exceptions, most filmed stories originating in Hollywood were told from a "god's eye" narrative perspective. This enabled the audience to experience what is happening to a number of different characters at different times and in different locations, rather than confining them to the point of view of one of the characters. In *Anthony Adverse* (Warner Bros., 1936), the eponymous hero is a foundling raised by nuns who, after growing up, attempts to find out about his lineage. Several of the other characters know who his parents were and the audience does as well, having been introduced to his mother and father in the early section of the movie. But Anthony never learns the secret nor, for that matter, does he discover that the man who has been his employer for many years is actually his grandfather.

Occasional films were produced that contained a more limited point of view. Among these were tales told by a single narrator. But, at least until the end of the period when a new kind of narrator emerged in film noir (see below), films of this sort do not maintain a consistent narrative point of view. For example, *The Power and the Glory* (Fox, 1933) and *How Green Was My Valley* (Twentieth Century-Fox, 1941) both contain narrators who are not present during a number of the events they describe. Even *Citizen Kane* (RKO, 1941), one of the most intricate narrative experiments to emerge during the period, contains shots that eschew the limited perspectives of the film's several narrators. In other words, audience members see things that no particular character in the film is seeing. Among these reversions to the omniscient point of view are the film's famous concluding shots of the burning sled, "Rosebud."

Characterization

One can detect the pattern of order–disorder–order, plus the manipulation of time and the omniscient point of view operating in the narratives of nearly all American films during the Classical Period, but it would be a reductive oversimplification to boil their cinematic stories down to just these three characteristics. The studios offered a wide variety of stories and each one presented narrative challenges that had to be overcome. Anecdotes from Hollywood insiders offer plenty of evidence of how difficult it was to fashion an exciting popular movie. *Gone with the Wind* (Selznick/MGM, 1939) required the efforts of more than a dozen screenwriters before an acceptable script was produced, and the precise resolution of *Casablanca* (Warner Bros., 1942) was so in doubt that its writers were still laboring deep into the actual shooting to determine how to wrap up the story.

Nevertheless, there are principles of characterization and structure that governed most screen stories produced during the 1930s and 1940s. Because these principles were viewed as necessary prerequisites to a successful film by studio production heads, as well as producers, screenwriters and directors, their works often did seem to be predictably formulaic. However, there were exceptions and deviations from the norm, as we will see.

With respect to characterization, Hollywood films were constructed around a protagonist, or main character. While there might be other characters of nearly equal importance, one individual tended to be the focal point of the drama or comedy. This person did not necessarily have to be sympathetic – e.g., Tony Camonte in *Scarface* (Caddo/United Artists, 1932) or Regina Giddens in *The Little Foxes* (Goldwyn/RKO, 1941) – but he or she did have to be charismatic. In most instances, the protagonist was a sympathetic, often heroic, force in the story. In addition, this person would usually be an active rather than passive character – someone who instigated the action instead of allowing others to determine his or her fate.

Even in "ensemble" films containing several important characters and plot lines, such as *Grand Hotel* (MGM, 1932) and *Dinner at Eight* (MGM, 1933), one individual would usually emerge as the protagonist. In *Grand Hotel*, this person is the Baron, played by John Barrymore. Although he is killed shortly before the film ends, his actions strongly affect the lives of all the other important characters.

The main character usually "grows" or "changes" in important ways during the course of the narrative. The events presented in the story bring a kind of maturation or enlightenment to the individual which shapes his or her actions in the concluding section of the film. In *Dark Victory* (Warner Bros., 1939), Judith Traherne, played by Bette Davis, is a spoiled, frivolous narcissist in the early scenes. But the onset of a terminal cancer and her love for and eventual marriage to a doctor (George Brent) who attempts to cure her, transform Judith into a mature, responsible and caring woman able to face death with courage and dignity. Rick Blaine (Humphrey Bogart) in *Casablanca* is a cynical, apolitical saloon keeper unmoved by the devastating effects of the World War on the lives of many of the people who surround him. But a series of interactions with the other characters, including the woman he loves, provoke a change in Rick; at the end, he relinquishes his hold on this woman (Ingrid Berman) in order to further the Allied cause, shoots a German officer and becomes a "patriot" who evidently will continue to fight against the Nazis. It should be noted that there are important exceptions to this emphasis on character growth and change. For example, the protagonists in "B" films like the "Charlie Chan," "Hopalong Cassidy" and "Torchy Blane" pictures remain essentially the same throughout the run of each series.

Another important character is the antagonist – an individual determined to frustrate the goals of the protagonist. This individual may be a positive, respectable figure such as Flaherty (Thomas Jackson), the sarcastic policeman who labors to bring Rico to justice in *Little Caesar*. He will kill the gangster at the end. But, in most cases, the antagonist is an evil presence, dangerous not only to the main character but to others as well. In *Sherlock Holmes and the Voice of Terror* (Universal, 1942), Holmes (Basil Rathbone) matches wits with the mysterious "Voice of Terror" whose radio broadcasts are frightening the British public and undermining their efforts to defeat the Nazis. A worthy antagonist to the brilliant Holmes, the "Voice" turns out to be a master spy, a trusted member of the British Intelligence Inner Council named Sir Evan Barham (Reginald Denny). Aided by a woman (Evelyn Ankers) whose husband has been murdered by the Nazis, Holmes unmasks the villain who is killed when he attempts to escape.

A great many films contain romance as a crucial ingredient. Consequently, the romantic partner of the protagonist is generally a major character who sometimes also functions as the chief antagonist, especially in comedies. In certain instances, the duo are so well-matched that it is difficult to determine who the main character actually is. In *Bringing Up Baby* (RKO, 1938), Susan Vance (Katharine Hepburn) would seem to be the protagonist since she initiates all the action. But Dr. David Huxley (Cary Grant), the initially passive young man she bedevils, is the one who finally changes, tossing aside his repressed fiancée and his stuffy scientific pursuits for a roller coaster life of adventure with Susan. The fact that David changes and that Susan represents the antagonistic force throughout much of the narrative, causing him to endure a series of humiliating and ultimately dangerous experiences, indicates that David Huxley is the actual protagonist of the picture. In most cases, however, the protagonist will be clearly defined. This is true even in films in which romance is an essential element. In *The Thin Man* (MGM, 1934), *The Adventures of Robin Hood* (Warner Bros., 1937) and *Ball of Fire* (Goldwyn/RKO, 1941), the protagonist is the male half of the romantic couple. In *Back Street* (Universal, 1932), *The Palm Beach Story* (Paramount, 1942) and *Cover Girl* (Columbia, 1944), the protagonist is the female half.

Stories told in Hollywood movies always require a number of supporting characters. These characters may be interesting and distinctive individuals, but their position in the narrative is secondary and functional with respect to the development of the plot. They may be helpful to the protagonist (friends, sidekicks, admirers) or they may be in league with the antagonist and represent impediments the main character must overcome. Sometimes, they pop up simply to provide information that moves the story forward. In a film like *The Letter* (Warner Bros., 1940), there are a small number of supporting characters but some of them are extremely important to the story's development. In others, such as *Wilson* (Twentieth Century-Fox, 1944), a screen biography of the 28th President of the US, the supporting cast is huge, though only a few of these characters have a major impact on the narrative.

Like the protagonist and other major characters, the secondary characters may also grow and change as the story unfolds. But such changes are usually triggered by their relationship with the protagonist or another major character. In *Mr. Deeds Goes to Town* (Columbia, 1936), hard-boiled press agent Cornelius Cobb (Lionel Stander) jettisons his sarcastic façade and becomes a sympathetic supporter of the gospel of common sense and generosity espoused by Longfellow Deeds (Gary Cooper). In *Crime School* (Warner Bros., 1939), a gang of young toughs sent to a reformatory are rehabilitated and directed toward productive lives by enlightened government official Mark Braden (Humphrey Bogart). And in *The Shop Around the Corner* (MGM, 1940), the clerk Pirovitch (Felix Bressart) is so upset when the film's protagonist (James Stewart) is fired that he challenges the boss, telling him, in effect, that he has made a terrible mistake. Up to this point in the story, Pirovitch has been so terrified of Mr. Matuschek (Frank Morgan) that he would go into hiding whenever the head man asked for an opinion.

The actions of characters in Hollywood movies are supposed to be clearly motivated. They are expected to make sense, based on the character's values, beliefs, attitudes, psychological make-up and goals. Thus, even when a character's decision may seem, on the surface, to be crazy or contrary, the audience is usually given enough information to comprehend (and appreciate) his or her motivation. Longfellow Deeds in *Mr. Deeds Goes to Town*, for example, may appear insane for deciding to give away most of the $25 million fortune he has inherited, but the theatergoers understand why he decides to do so; the money has messed up his formerly happy and stable life. And when Stella (Barbara Stanwyck) in *Stella Dallas* (Goldwyn/United Artists, 1937) pushes her beloved daughter away from her, we understand why she pretends not to care about her anymore; she wants Laurel (Anne Shirley) to enjoy a better life among the privileged class, a social set that Stella could never be part of.

Occasionally, the reasons why an important character acts in a certain way are withheld from the audience, creating a tension that will be released later in the narrative. In *Destry Rides Again* (Universal, 1939), the new deputy sheriff of Bottleneck (James Stewart) refuses to wear a gun, making him the local laughingstock. Eventually, the audience will learn why he has such an antipathy to guns and appreciate the magnitude of his decision when he chooses to strap them on.

Similarly, a pleasing dramatic or comedic tension can be created when an individual acts "out of character." In this instance the audience understands the motivation, but other characters in the story do not. In *Queen Christina* (MGM, 1934), Don Antonio (John Gilbert), a dashing Spanish envoy to the throne of Sweden, finds himself snowbound in a mountain inn where all the rooms are occupied. There he meets and befriends a handsome and aristocratic young man, eventually asking if he may share the fellow's room for the night. The young man instead insists that the Don take his room, which the envoy interprets as polite but somewhat insulting. Eventually the young man relents and agrees to spend the night with the Don. This sets up two very powerful surprises. For what the audience knows, but the Don does not, is that the young man is actually a beautiful woman (Greta Garbo) who also happens to be the Queen of Sweden. Another example occurs in *The Awful Truth* when Lucy Warriner (Irene Dunne), posing as her husband's sister, feigns drunkenness and behaves outrageously. The humor in this very funny scene is heightened by the audience's recognition that her act is just a ploy to prevent the breakup of her marriage. With the exception of her husband (Cary Grant), the characters who witness her exhibitionistic behavior do not understand it and are deeply offended, which is precisely what Lucy hoped their reaction would be.

Structure

A Hollywood film that lacked interesting characters whose behavior was convincingly motivated was doomed to failure. Similarly, a film in which the elements of the plot were not organized according to certain dramatic principles first enunciated, in part, by the Greek philosopher Aristotle was unlikely to engage an audience. Hollywood motion pictures employed an organizational structure designed to involve spectators in the on-screen events and to elicit emotional responses based on their characters and plot developments. Indeed, the studio heads felt that it was crucial to affect the customers emotionally – to scare them, thrill them, stir them, make them feel giddy, make them laugh or cry. If patrons were totally unmoved by their visit to the theater, they almost certainly left it feeling they had not been properly entertained, had not gotten their money's worth.

Introduced in the early scenes of each film would be an obligatory structural element of Hollywood storytelling: conflict. Without conflict, there could be no drama or comedy. Without conflict, there could be no audience interest or involvement. Indeed, screenwriting manuals from the period constantly advise budding writers to devise a structure in which order is thrown into disorder via conflict.

The most obvious conflicts would pit one character against another or one group of characters against another. In *The Adventures of Robin Hood*, Robin (Errol Flynn) and his band of outlaws oppose Prince John (Claude Rains) and the supporters of his Norman regime. Personal conflict is equally ubiquitous and important in comedies. In *Holiday* (Columbia, 1938), for example, free spirits Johnny (Cary Grant) and Linda (Katharine Hepburn) gravitate toward each other as their opposition grows to Linda's status- and money-fixated sister (Doris Nolan) and father (Henry Kolker).

Though all Hollywood movies included individualized conflicts, many also contained a variety of other, more generalized conflicts. Some examples: conflicts between humans and the natural world (*The Big Trail*, Fox, 1931), between humans and the law (*I Am a Fugitive from a Chain Gang*, Warner Bros., 1932), between humans and machines (*Modern Times*, Chaplin/United Artists, 1936), between humans and society (*You Only Live Once*, Wanger/United Artists, 1937), between humans and tyranny (*Hitler's Children*, RKO, 1943).

It was also not unusual for internal conflicts to become crucial to a screen story. These conflicts create doubts in a character's mind about an important decision or action. In *Camille* (MGM, 1937), French courtesan Marguerite Gautier (Greta Garbo) struggles to resolve an internal conflict concerning her relationship with her true love Armand Duval (Robert Taylor). After deciding that his life will be irreparably harmed if their affair continues, she makes the anguished decision to sever the relationship and return to a rich baron who was formerly her "keeper."

While all films contain multiple conflicts, some of these conflicts go through a reversal process as the stories develop. In *The Adventures of Robin Hood*, Robin is initially involved in physical conflict with both Little John (Alan Hale) and Friar Tuck (Eugene Palette), but their disagreements are quickly reversed and both men join Robin's band of outlaws. The conflict between Robin and Maid Marian (Olivia de Havilland) who initially sides with her uncle, Prince John, and Sir Guy of Gisbourne (Basil Rathbone) against the men of Sherwood Forest, takes longer to reverse. Eventually, she recognizes the honorable nature of Robin's actions, falls in love with him and helps him to achieve his goals. This particular reversal – in which future lovers are, at first, antagonistic toward one another – is quite common in comedies, musicals and other genres as well.

Hollywood stories always had a beginning, a middle and an ending. The screenwriter's job was to write scenes that propelled the story forward in dynamic fashion, increasing the audience's interest and involvement in the tale as it unfolded. Some of these scenes might be very short, lasting only seconds, while others might take 30 minutes or more of screen time.

A filmed story typically was told in chronological sequence. Whether its duration was only a few hours or covered many years, the plot would develop in A–B–C–D fashion with section A preceding section B, section B preceding section C and section C preceding section D in a straightforward linear progression. The major exception to this structural principle was the introduction of one or more flashbacks into the narrative. Audiences were quite comfortable with this device despite the fact that it disrupted the normal continuity, transporting them backwards in time. Flashbacks usually functioned to help explain relationships, behavior and the motivations of the characters, and thus helped to clarify the story for the spectator. Flashbacks in *Casablanca* and *Laura* (Twentieth Century-Fox, 1944), for example, add immeasurably to the dramatic impact and, as previously mentioned, *How Green Was My Valley* was, essentially, one extended flashback. Even in a film like *The Power and the Glory*, in which the multiple flashbacks are not chronologically sequential, screenwriter Preston Sturges was careful to make certain that audience members were always clear about where and when the action was occurring. Since the story recounts the life of one man – railroad tycoon Tom Garner (Spencer Tracy) – and each flashback is related by a single narrator, Garner's friend and associate Henry (Ralph Morgan), the jigsaw puzzle of a story may be easily pieced together by the audience.

Three-act organization

The writer of a film organized its scenes into larger units which roughly corresponded to the acts of a play. The plots of most films made during this time could be divided neatly into three acts.

The first act would introduce the principal characters and contain all the expository material. It would quickly establish the world in which the story was set, pinpointing the time and place and identifying the salient personal and psychological traits of the characters. Very quickly, the audience would begin to comprehend the motivations for their actions and, most importantly, the key conflicts would be "locked" into place. These conflicts would drive the narrative forward. By the end of the first act, the audience should be keenly aware of what is at stake in the story and have a rooting interest in the efforts of the main character to accomplish his or her goals.

In the second act, additional conflicts would be introduced and the lives of the characters would become more complicated and unstable. In this section of "rising action," the audience should become fully invested emotionally in the difficulties of their favorite characters who are often forced to cope with a series of frustrations and reversals of fortune which make it seem they will never achieve the desired outcome. It was normal for the protagonist and/or other characters to begin to change and show growth in this section.

The third act completed the process of personal growth in the characters, some of whom view life very differently at the end of the story than they did at the beginning. Though generally the shortest of the three sections, it also contained a climax, or series of climaxes, in which the major conflicts are resolved and the key characters fulfill their destinies. When the final climax occurred, the story was essentially over, but there might be some loose ends involving other characters or plot strands that must be tied up so that the audience can depart feeling that a state of order and equilibrium has returned to the imaginary world they have visited. If this is the case, a short "denouement" section would be included to "wrap up" these matters before "THE END" flashes up on the screen. In Classical Period movies, the ending was usually a happy one – though there may be surprises along the way, most films provided closure in a manner that patrons appreciated and found reassuring.

Stylistic Techniques

Hollywood filmmakers favored a stylistic approach that would animate the scripts assigned to them. For most, the myriad techniques at their disposal were simply a means to an end; these techniques were useful insofar as they could be deployed to tell the story in a way that audiences would deem entertaining. Dazzling stylistic effects were always possible, but if these effects did not help to put the story across effectively, they could be a hindrance to the overall goal.

Motion picture style is the sum total of staging (including acting, costuming, make-up and art direction), cinematography (including special effects), editing, and sound (including musical scoring). Taken together these components determine the look of a film, the rhythm of a film, the tone of a film, the ambiance of a film and, ultimately, the impact of a film. The studios employed an army of experts, organized along departmental lines, in these specialty areas. Their work would be overseen by directors and producers with a knowledge of how all the elements should fit together. The departments worked together collaboratively, and many different individuals made important creative contributions to each project.

Ironically, their contributions were not supposed to be noticed by the spectators. Rather, they were intended to appear so integral to the story that patrons would leave theaters talking about the "great" film they had just witnessed – not about the bravura acting, the spectacular production design, the exquisite lighting, the dynamic editing or the impassioned musical score. In fact, the intricacies of the filmmaking process in Hollywood were, to a large extent, concealed from the public during this period so as not to spoil the "magic" of the viewing experience. Like the famous wizard who lives in Oz, Hollywood's creative talent operated behind an opaque curtain that hid their bag of tricks, making their work seem spontaneous and effortless.

Staging

Staging included acting, make-up, costuming and art direction. All were important but acting took precedence.

The preferred acting style of the period was naturalistic. Though many performers, such as Janet Gaynor and Greta Garbo, made the transition from silent to sound films, the emphasis on facial expressions, body language and stylized gestures which characterized performance in the former era gave way to a more straightforward approach that placed a premium on an actor's ability to deliver dialogue in a convincing and expressive manner. This is not to suggest that the subtleties of silent film acting were abandoned. While the more histrionic aspects of silent performance quickly became unfashionable, the best actors, whether trained in silent acting techniques or not, used their bodies and, especially, their faces to communicate with audiences in ways that were subtle but strikingly effective.

Because of their expert ability with spoken dialogue, many actors made the move from Broadway to Hollywood during this period. Those who became successful quickly learned to act "for the camera," toning down a performance style necessary to reach patrons sitting in the back rows of large "live theater" houses. With the assistance of directors and studio acting teachers, they developed a character-driven approach which enabled them to play a wide variety of parts convincingly. Stanislavsky's "method" acting had an impact on American theater during the 1930s, but its influence in Hollywood was not significant until after the end of World War II. Nevertheless, the work of Spencer Tracy, Fredric March, Barbara Stanwyck, Bette Davis, Paul Muni, Katharine Hepburn, Laurence Olivier, Vivien Leigh, Edward G. Robinson, Henry Fonda, James Cagney, Olivia de Havilland, Humphrey Bogart, Orson Welles, James Stewart, Greer Garson and Walter Huston, among others, has stood the test of time. Even though most of these actors had no training in the "method," they still managed to create some of the most memorable characters in film history.

An actor's ability to deliver a good performance was abetted by the work of studio costumers and make-up experts. These individuals designed the characters' clothes and transformed actors' physical features to fit the requirements of their roles. For example, the wardrobe created by costume designers Adrien and Gile Steele and the make-up devised by Jack Dawn were critical in establishing the ambiance of Victorian England and making the transformations between the protagonist (Spencer Tracy) and his doppelgänger both frightening and believable in *Dr. Jekyll and Mr. Hyde* (MGM, 1941).

Superior art direction, which determined the look of the sets and exterior environments in which a film's action took place, was another essential aspect of the style of every film. For example, art director Van Nest Polglase, working with associate Carroll Clark and set dresser Thomas Little, produced a dazzling re-creation of Venice which helped to free the musical *Top Hat* (RKO, 1935) from the realm of the ordinary and point it in the direction of the sublime. An opposite approach was adopted by art directors Hans Dreier and Bernard Herzbrun and interior decorator A.E. Freudeman on *Make Way for Tomorrow* (Paramount, 1937). To make certain that the problems of an aging couple (Victor Moore and Beulah Bondi) were taken seriously, Dreier, Herzbrun and Freudeman grounded the story in environments that were simple and mundane, thereby heightening the authenticity of the drama.

The art direction and costume design of many movies from the Classical Period were influenced by the intertwined art nouveau, art moderne and streamline moderne styles (now generally lumped together under the rubric "art deco") in architecture, decor, costuming and graphics. A film like *My Man Godfrey* (Universal, 1936) is a kind of time capsule showcasing these contemporary styles in everything from Charles D. Hall's sparkling art direction to Travis Banton's resplendent gowns.

Cinematography

The director of photography (cinematographer, an all-male fraternity during this period) was responsible for capturing the images that would eventually flicker across the movie screens of the world. An expert on lighting, framing, lenses, film stocks and the development process, among other things, he approached every shot with the understanding that there were many different ways to execute it. He and the director were expected to make the most fitting choice.

Among the questions that a cinematographer would ponder: should the shot be still or contain movement (panning, tracking, tilting, swooping, zooming)? Should the camera be a substantial distance from the subject (long-shot), or positioned closer (medium-shot) or be placed snug to the subject (close-up)? What angle should the shot employ – low, eye-level, high above the subject or some other position? What lens should be used – a wide-angle (typically less than 35 mm) which produced a "fish-eye" effect but facilitated greater depth in the image, a normal (35–50 mm) which most closely simulated the optics of the human eye, or a telephoto (over 50 mm, usually 75 mm in Hollywood features) which magnified objects in the distance but tended to produce a flattened image? What lighting approach should be employed – high-key which meant that everything in the shot would be brightly and evenly illuminated with minimal shadows, or low-key which produced extreme contrasts between light and dark and evocative shadow effects? (Most lighting fell somewhere in between these two extremes.) How much backlighting and/or spotlighting should be employed? How should the shot be framed? Should the composition be balanced or unbalanced? Would the shot employ any special effects, such as matte paintings, or miniatures or process photography?

Most importantly, every director of photography was expected to make certain his imagery was in focus and consistent in its lighting and, with the director's guidance, provided adequate coverage of every scene so that the editor would have ample footage to assemble the story into a seamless and coherent whole.

One of the most interesting stylistic evolutions that occurred during this period was the cinematographic movement from a soft pictorial style to a sharp-edged approach. The soft style, which was popular during the silent era, used various methods (including Vaseline-smeared plates placed in front of the camera lens) to create fuzzy, impressionistic images with shallow depth of field that were felt to "beautify" the production. This approach was almost always employed for close-ups of the prominent actresses, but numerous silent filmmakers also strived for and achieved a consistent soft look throughout their films.

Though the soft style became less prominent during the sound era, a moderate amount of diffusion is still apparent in many 1930s films. Backgrounds were often rendered in soft focus so that actors would stand out against them. Additionally, the images of women were generally softer than those of men. In *It Happened One Night* (Columbia, 1934), director Frank Capra and cinematographer Joseph Walker consistently photographed Ellie (Claudette Colbert) more softly than her romantic counterpart Peter (Clark Gable). They even risked destroying the audience's engagement with the story and characters by including a heavily gauzed, practically indistinct close-up of Ellie just before she finally confesses that she loves Peter and wants to share his adventures with him. The amount of diffusion in the shot was so extreme that it called attention to the technique.

In 1938, Eastman Kodak introduced its Plus X film stock. This faster film was quickly embraced as the industry standard and it, along with other superior emulsions from Agfa, Du Pont and Kodak, plus the introduction of better lighting units and lenses, paved the way for a major change in cinematographic style. While the preference for the fuzzy look did not give way immediately, a growing partiality for imagery that was distinct and hard-edged and for compositions in depth became discernible. Director Orson Welles and cinematographer Gregg Toland demonstrated the extraordinary expressive potential of this approach in *Citizen Kane* and, within a short time, many Hollywood filmmakers had embraced their deep-focus style. Two byproducts of this change were an increasing interest in "realistic" images and a growing fondness for the incorporation of long takes into cinematic narratives. Even though the soft style did not totally disappear – e.g., diffuse imagery is employed quite effectively in the "transformation" section of *The Enchanted Cottage* (RKO, 1945) – it is considered somewhat antique by the end of the period.

Editing

Hollywood editors were crucial members of the storytelling team, and there are many tales of films being "saved" by clever editorial manipulations. Like the cinematographers, they also had innumerable decisions to make concerning shot selection, pacing, the duration of each shot, how each scene could be best constructed from the available footage, which transitional devices should be used to move from one scene to the next or to indicate a passage of time, etc.

Editors were experts in "continuity cutting." They understood how to build a feature film so that it seemed to be a continuous, uninterrupted flow of images and sounds that told a story in a comprehensible and compelling fashion. In fact, there was nothing continuous or "flowing" about the process at all – every film was composed of hundreds of different shots, taken from many points of view and stitched together to create constantly changing, multiple perspectives that bear no relationship whatsoever to the normal perceptual experience of human beings. Yet editors understood that if they followed certain principles which audience members had come to accept and expect – the principles of continuity editing – movie fans would not notice the bumpy, discontinuous nature of the process. Those principles included respect for the 180-degree axis (the camera shots remain on one side of the action in order to maintain consistent screen direction from shot to shot); the 30-degree rule (camera position must change at least 30 degrees from shot to shot to avoid a jarring jump cut); the pattern of shot/reverse shot (crosscuts, mainly used in scenes of conversation and often framed over the shoulders of the different characters); eyeline matching (a cut from a person looking off-screen to a shot of what the person sees); parallel editing (shots from different locations cut together in such a way that the audience understands the actions are taking place simultaneously); cutting on action or at appropriate moments in the dialogue (to "mask" or camouflage the cuts); and the use of dissolves, fades, wipes, montages or intertitles to mark important transitions and to keep the spectator always comfortably grounded within the story.

The editing process contained infinite opportunities for confusing audiences and/or calling attention to the completely synthetic nature of moviemaking. But the work of skillful Hollywood editors, such as Margaret Booth (*Mutiny on the Bounty*, MGM, 1935), Ralph Dawson (*The Adventures of Robin Hood*), Hal C. Kern (*Rebecca*, Selznick/United Artists, 1940), Robert Wise (*Citizen Kane*), Daniel Mandell (*Pride of the Yankees*, Goldwyn/RKO, 1942), Barbara McLean (*Wilson*) and George Amy (*Objective, Burma!*, Warner Bros., 1945), surmounted the potential trouble. They were masters at cementing shots together in ways that caused audiences to become completely absorbed in the filmed story, noticing nothing except what was happening to the characters on the screen.

Sound

The recording of dialogue on the set was one of the primary functions of the sound experts who labored on studio movies. But even more important was the creative sound work that took place during post-production. Just as each film's visual information was constructed by the editor, each film's sound track was assembled by members of the sound crew who were expected to deliver a myriad of sound effects – everything from the creaking doors of a "haunted" house (*The Cat and the Canary*, Paramount, 1939) to the "spitting" of a tommy gun (*Scarface*) to the windy fury of a catastrophic storm (*The Hurricane*, Goldwyn/United Artists, 1937) to the fantastical roars of two giant beasts engaged in deadly combat (*King Kong*, RKO, 1933). Sounds could be manipulated in any number of ways. They could be louder or softer than they would be in the real world or have a different pitch or timbre, or even be "subjective" (the audience hears what a character is thinking inside his or her head), but they had to seem "right" – appropriately modulated and "in synch" with the action and dialogue.

Working closely with each film's sound team would be the composer of the musical score. Early in the sound era, films typically contained little or no underscoring, but this began to change around 1932. After that, the "A" films would usually feature a score performed by a full orchestra, and this score would underpin most of the scenes in the picture. The score had several functions, including magnification of the emotional quotient of scenes, setting and maintaining a mood and propelling the story forward rhythmically. Scoring was a special art and such respected film composers as Max Steiner (*Gone with the Wind*), Alfred Newman (*The Grapes of Wrath*, Twentieth Century-Fox, 1940), Erich Wolfgang Korngold (*The Adventures of Robin Hood*), Miklos Rozsa (*Double Indemnity*, Paramount, 1944) and Dimitri Tiomkin (*Mr. Smith Goes to Washington*, Columbia, 1939) added immeasurably to the impact of many of the most beloved films of the era.

After picture editing was complete and the dialogue, sound effects and musical score were finished, all the different auditory elements would be combined in a final sound mix. This painstaking job brought the post-production process to an end and, barring additional changes that might be deemed necessary after the movie was previewed, meant that a new filmed story was ready for acceptance or rejection by the public.

A "romantic" style

The foregoing description of the elements of the Classical Style makes no attempt to define the overriding stylistic approach of the era. Perhaps the best word to describe this approach is "romantic," referencing the broadest meaning of the term.

Sustaining the narrative inclinations of Hollywood in the 1930s and 1940s, which favored stories in which courage, sacrifice, benevolence, justice, freedom, optimism, individualism and, above all else, love were figured as sacrosanct qualities, the prevailing style deftly amplified the triumphs of the human spirit. The principal actors and actresses were costumed, made up and photographed to emphasize their beauty and physical perfection, their aspirations were presented as noble and important but nearly impossible to achieve and the usually positive outcome of their struggles pointed toward a utopian world in which all things great and good were possible. Of course, one can name any number of important films (e.g., *I Am a Fugitive from a Chain Gang, You Only Live Once, Citizen Kane*, various examples of film noir) that directly challenged the romantic mythology of the period. But the majority of Hollywood filmmakers fervently embraced this "larger than life" approach, employing a style that magnified the idealistic nature of their stories.

Narrative in *Stagecoach*

In order to demonstrate how these principles were typically deployed in Classical Hollywood Cinema, let us take a detailed look at the famous western, *Stagecoach*. This 1939 film, adapted to the screen by Dudley Nichols from a short story by Ernest Haycox and produced by Walter Wanger, was atypical in that it contained more major characters than most other films and, thus, was propelled forward by a dizzying array of conflicts. Nonetheless, like *Grand Hotel, Dinner at Eight, Week-end at the Waldorf* (MGM, 1945) and other "omnibus" narratives, it conformed nicely to the storytelling principles that have been discussed so far in this chapter. To begin, we will synopsize the story according to its three-act structure.

Act I

The world of this story is the old west, some time after the end of the American Civil War. It begins in Tonto, in the Arizona Territory, where members of the military learn that the dangerous renegade Geronimo has jumped the reservation and gathered his Apache brethren to wage all-out war against the white interlopers.

The stagecoach arrives and we meet Lucy Mallory, a pregnant southern gentlewoman determined to find her husband who is serving in the cavalry. Taking special notice of her is a gambler named Hatfield. The driver of the stage, a nervous, garrulous fellow named Buck, stops by the marshal's office to find out who will be riding shotgun with him on the rest of his journey. Curley, the marshal, informs Buck that the Ringo Kid has broken out of the penitentiary and will undoubtedly be determined to get even with the Plummer brothers who were responsible for his incarceration. When Buck tells Curley that Luke Plummer is in Lordsburg, the final destination of the stagecoach, Curley decides to take over the shotgun position himself.

Meanwhile, the town banker, Gatewood, accepts and signs a receipt for a local payroll that totals $50,000. Gatewood's wife and a number of the town's other female citizens are, at the same time, escorting a prostitute named Dallas to the stagecoach. They do not want undesirables like Dallas corrupting their town. Dallas is soon joined by Doc Boone, a physician whose fondness for the bottle has caused his practice to decline to a point where he cannot pay his rent. He, too, will decide to leave Tonto via the stage. Doc stops by the saloon for one last drink. There he meets Mr. Peacock, a lamblike whiskey drummer who arrived on the coach and plans to continue his journey aboard it.

Just before the stage departs, troops ride up and warn the passengers about the Apache threat. All of them decide to proceed with the dangerous journey, although Mr. Peacock is shamed into continuing by Doc who intends to take full advantage of the drummer's whiskey samples along the way. Learning of the danger, Hatfield joins the group with the clear though unstated intention of protecting Mrs. Mallory. The passengers are relieved to learn that the soldiers will follow the stage to its first stop, Dry Fork, where another contingent of soldiers should be available to protect them on the remainder of their journey.

On the outskirts of town, the banker Gatewood hails the coach, claiming that he just received a message ordering him to come to Lordsburg. Curley wonders about this, since the soldiers had told him that the Indians had cut the telegraph wires. In fact, Gatewood received no telegram; he has decided to steal the payroll money and is attempting to flee the territory.

Farther out in the wilderness, the stage comes upon the Ringo Kid whose horse has broken down. He is immediately arrested by Curley and joins the other passengers inside the coach. As they continue, Curley and Buck talk and it is clear both think Ringo is a "fine boy," despite his outlaw status. Inside the coach, Doc and Hatfield, who were on opposite sides in the Civil War, spar verbally, and it is revealed that Ringo's brother was killed by the Plummers.

At the first stop, Dry Fork, the passengers find no troops to accompany them on the remainder of the journey. The other soldiers have orders to return and cannot be of further assistance, despite the outraged entreaties of banker Gatewood. Ignoring the danger, the occupants of the stage vote to keep going despite the objections of Peacock and Buck. During lunch, Mrs. Mallory, Hatfield and Gatewood snub Dallas and Ringo by moving away so they won't have to eat with them.

They depart Dry Fork with the cavalry taking the road back to Tonto and the stagecoach the road to Lordsburg.

Act II

Curley and Buck continue to discuss the conflict between Ringo and the Plummers. It turns out that the Plummers are pure evil and are causing lots of problems in the territory. Nevertheless, Curley does not want Ringo to get into a skirmish with them because he feels certain the kid will be killed. The safest place for Ringo, he believes, is back in the pen. Inside the coach, Mr. Peacock is unable to stop Doc from swigging his liquor. Mrs. Mallory's health is clearly declining, yet she won't accept any help from Dallas.

They arrive at the next rest stop, Apache Wells, where a Mexican named Chris and his Apache wife are in charge. Not only are there no troops there, but Chris tells Mrs. Mallory that he believes her husband might have been badly injured in a confrontation with the hostiles. Again, Dallas offers to help Lucy Mallory but is rebuffed. Soon afterward, Mrs. Mallory faints. Dallas immediately orders hot water, and the drunken doctor is called upon to minister to her. Doc drinks plenty of coffee, sobers up and prepares to deliver Mrs. Mallory's baby. Dallas will assist while the men remain in another room.

After the baby girl is born and Mrs. Mallory is on the road to recovery, the relationship between Dallas and Ringo ripens from friendship into love. Eventually, Ringo proposes and Dallas agrees to meet him at his ranch across the border if he will escape from Curley and forgo his quest for revenge against the Plummers.

Meanwhile, Gatewood pressures the others to depart immediately, but Doc tells him that Mrs. Mallory is not strong enough to travel. Now Hatfield sides with the Doc, who has renewed his love affair with the bottle, and so do the others.

Ringo decides to make a break and Curley chases after him, despite Dallas' efforts to impede the marshal. But Ringo spots something that causes him to stop – smoke signals that confirm the Indian menace. Despite Mrs. Mallory's condition, it is too dangerous to remain. Leaving Chris behind, they board the stagecoach and head toward Lordsburg.

Act III

On board the coach, the passengers are understandably scared and fractious. Gatewood, in particular, has become increasingly difficult and mean-spirited. He insults several of his fellow travelers. Peacock asks them all to have "a little Christian charity – one for the other."

The next stop is Lee's Ferry, a burned-out encampment where, once again, there is no sign of any soldiers. But there are signs of a massacre, including a dead woman whom Hatfield covers with his coat. Because the ferry has been destroyed, the men tie huge logs to the coach and float it across the river. The characters then resume their journey toward Lordsburg.

Just as the passengers begin to relax, the Indians attack. Peacock is shot in the arm by an arrow and Buck is also shot as the coach attempts to outrace the Indian ponies. The cowardly Gatewood tries to jump out of the coach, forcing Doc to punch the banker which knocks him out. Curley and Ringo shoot several of the Indians and Ringo jumps on the horses and guides the coach after Buck is disabled. Still, the chance of escape looks very dim when the men run out of ammunition. Hatfield saves one bullet and is about to use it on Mrs. Mallory (not wanting her to fall into the Indians' hands) when he is shot. As Mrs. Mallory prays, the sound of bugles is heard and the cavalry arrive, rout the Indians and save the stagecoach. However, the passengers' jubilation is tempered by the death of Hatfield.

In Lordsburg, Mrs. Mallory learns that her husband is all right. After Dallas returns her baby, the gentlewoman looks up at the prostitute she had formerly shunned and says, "If there is ever anything I can do for you . . ." Peacock is also okay. While being carted off on a stretcher, he invites Dallas to visit him and his family in Kansas City, Kansas.

Word quickly spreads through Lordsburg that the Ringo Kid is in town. It reaches Luke Plummer in a saloon where he is playing cards.

Back at the stagecoach, Gatewood is arrested by the local sheriff for stealing the payroll. It seems the telegraph was repaired before he made it to Lordsburg.

Ringo has three bullets left. Surprisingly, Curley allows Ringo to walk away with Dallas, knowing that Ringo will find the Plummers and engage them in a gunfight. But before this happens, Dallas takes Ringo on a short tour of the red-light district to make sure that he comprehends what she has been. Ringo understands but indicates that he still wants to marry her.

By now, Luke Plummer has summoned his two brothers and they nervously prepare to face Ringo. Luke orders the bartender to give him a shotgun for the confrontation but before he can leave with it, Doc tells him he will have Luke indicted for murder if he uses the gun against Ringo. Luke angrily gives up the weapon.

The local newspaper editor prepares a headline announcing Ringo's demise, but Ringo prevails in the shoot-out, apparently killing all three of the Plummers.

Returning to Dallas, Ringo is soon joined by Curley and Doc who drive up in a buckboard. They invite the two lovers to "ride a ways" and Ringo, believing he's headed back to prison, says his goodbyes to Dallas. But Curley and Doc surprise them, shooing the horses and sending Ringo and Dallas off into the night, headed toward freedom. Though he hasn't followed the letter of the law, the marshal seems quite pleased with his decision to let Ringo go and offers to buy Doc a drink. "Just one," Doc replies.

Three-act structure

The plot of *Stagecoach* is divided neatly into three acts. In the first act, all the important characters are introduced and given distinctive personalities, the two major conflicts that will propel the story forward are established (see below), and a number of other minor conflicts are "locked" into place. In addition, the expository information necessary for an audience to understand the story is provided. We quickly gather that *Stagecoach* will take place in the wild west at a time when newcomers (mostly with European roots) are endeavoring to build a safe environment in which to raise their families and prosper. We also understand that this project won't be easy because there exist antagonistic forces (represented principally by the Indians and the Plummer brothers) who oppose their goals. They are the main destabilizing forces in the story; until the Indians and heinous individuals like the Plummers are overcome, there will be no peace or order in this new land.

In the second act, the lives of the characters become more complicated and their situation more perilous. The outlaw and the prostitute fall in love, the doctor overcomes his alcoholism and ministers to Mrs. Mallory whose baby is born, the Indian threat to the undefended coach increases and a number of other conflicts are introduced, heightening the tension for characters and audience alike. The action is definitely building toward a crescendo.

The third act includes two major climaxes and a number of smaller ones which resolve all the conflicts that have been developing. These events bring closure and a sense of order to the story and suggest that there is hope for the civilizing efforts of the white settlers.

Conflicts and climaxes

Screenwriter Dudley Nichols injected so many conflicts into *Stagecoach* that it would be numbing to attempt to isolate and discuss each one. However, I will point out several of them, beginning with the two overriding conflicts mentioned above. Each of these conflicts will be resolved in a major third-act climax:

1. The white settlers vs. the Indians – the film opens with the information that Geronimo has provoked the Apache tribe to go on the warpath. Though Geronimo never becomes a fully developed character, he and his fellows represent a powerful, destructive force that menaces the passengers of the stagecoach throughout their journey. This conflict is resolved during the climactic Indian attack in which the Indians are defeated, though Buck and Peacock are wounded and Hatfield is killed.

2. Ringo vs. the Plummers – we also learn, early in the film, about the bad blood between Ringo and the Plummer brothers. Soon enough the audience meets Ringo and discerns that the comments made by Curley and Buck about him are accurate: he is a "fine boy," not a despicable outlaw. The despicable character is Luke Plummer. As Buck says, "There'd be a lot more peace in the territory if that Luke Plummer was so full of lead he couldn't hold his liquor." We are made to understand that this new land will not be a safe and stable place until Luke and his brothers are no longer a threat. Therefore, Ringo's quest represents something more than simple revenge. The climactic gun battle which resolves this conflict, just like the victory over the Indians, helps to bring peace and order to the territory. Thus, both of the major conflicts and the climaxes which resolve them relate directly to the overriding theme of the western genre during this period: the carving of a vibrant new civilization out of the wilderness. (See chapter 6.)

While a great deal of the film's energy and tension are fueled by these overriding conflicts, we should also briefly survey some of the other conflicts that contribute to the dramatic impact of the story:

1. Mr. Peacock vs. Doc who is intent on draining all Peacock's whiskey samples.
2. Hatfield vs. Doc – a complicated conflict that initially arises out of their respective allegiances to the South and the North in the Civil War.
3. The conflict between the passengers who want to continue on to Lordsburg (most of them) and those who want to return to Tonto (Buck and Peacock).
4. The class conflict between the "aristocratic" citizens (Mrs. Mallory, Hatfield, Gatewood) and the "dregs" (Ringo, Dallas, Doc).
5. The conflict between Ringo and Dallas concerning his possible escape or continuation on to Lordsburg to face the Plummers.
6. The conflict between the hypocritical and disagreeable Gatewood and the soldiers.
7. The conflicts between Gatewood and several of his fellow passengers over a variety of topics.

In addition to these personalized conflicts, the film also contains such general conflicts as:

1. The passengers of the stagecoach vs. nature – the smallness and vulnerability of the coach in the vast, forbidding landscape is emphasized and, in the final section, the men must devise a way to get the coach across the river when they find the ferry has been destroyed.
2. Gatewood vs. the law – though the other passengers are unaware that he has stolen the payroll, the audience knows what he has done and hopes for the banker's arrest.
3. Dallas vs. society – her "expulsion" from Tonto early in the film is based on societal notions of her undesirability and carried out by the "respectable" women of the town. Doc is also branded as an undesirable because of his alcoholism and both, along with Ringo, are stigmatized during the journey (see 4 above).
4. Doc vs. the bottle – though Doc Boone's alcoholism is presented in a comic light throughout much of the story, it is clear that his performance and reputation as a physician have suffered because of it. However, at a crucial point in the story, Doc is able to sober up and successfully deliver Mrs. Mallory's baby.

Finally, the film contains several notable internal conflicts as well:

1. Hatfield's tortured soul – while the audience is never given enough information to fully understand the gambler's personal demons, there are enough clues to suggest that they relate directly to the defeat of the South in the Civil War, to his relationship with his father and to his current vocation as a "notorious gambler." For Hatfield, the trip to Lordsburg seems to be a journey of redemption. His selfless protection of Mrs. Mallory helps restore his pride, and he appears to die contented.
2. Dallas' past life – after she and Ringo fall in love, she wrestles with the question of whether to let him know about her life as a prostitute or hide it from him. Despite her fear that she will lose him, Dallas shows Ringo where she "comes from" in Lordsburg and he accepts her anyway.
3. Curley's duty – it is Curley's duty as a peace officer to send Ringo back to the pen. But he is torn internally by the knowledge that Ringo should never have been imprisoned in the first place. Curley finally decides to follow his own ethical compass rather than the abstract one required by the law, setting Ringo free so he and Dallas can start a new life together.

The question of what will become of Ringo and Dallas, which Curley determines, is the only unresolved strand of the plot after the second major climax (the shoot-out). It occurs during the final "denouement" section of the film. When the two lovers take off for Ringo's ranch "across the border," all the conflicts have been resolved, order has been achieved and the film can end. The audience leaves the theater with a satisfied sense of closure – no loose ends or nagging questions remain.

Characterization

Because of its "omnibus" approach, *Stagecoach* contains more major characters than most Hollywood movies. Indeed, it could be argued that all the passengers on the coach are major characters, though some are less important (Peacock, Buck, Hatfield, Gatewood, Mrs. Mallory) than others (Ringo, Dallas, Curley, Doc). The salient point is that each of these characters is interesting, adroitly developed and skillfully integrated into the plot.

It is difficult to determine who the protagonist is in this film, but a strong argument could be made for Ringo. He plays a crucial part in both of the major conflicts/climaxes. His bravery helps to save the passengers during the Indian attack and his shoot-out with the Plummers eliminates a destructive presence in the territory. Even though he seems not to change as much as some of the other characters, he sets an example which helps elevate the behavior of several of them.

A number of the others do grow and change. Dallas goes from outcast and prostitute to selfless nurse and loving bride-to-be; Hatfield from cynical gambler to chivalrous protector; Mrs. Mallory from snobbish aristocrat to tolerant appreciator of those less fortunate than she. The film also contains several reversals, such as Mrs. Mallory's ultimate recognition of the innate nobility of Dallas, Hatfield's newfound respect for Doc Boone after Doc delivers the baby and Curley's decisions to allow Ringo to fight the Plummers and then to go free rather than back to prison. In addition, a sly ironic reversal occurs when Peacock, the whiskey salesman who has been repeatedly mistaken for a clergyman by his fellow passengers, finally seems to accept the role, entreating the others to have "a little Christian charity – one for the other."

With respect to motivation, the actions of the characters all seem clear and plausible. No one in the film does anything that strikes us as strange or out of character. Even when the others don't understand why an individual acts as he or she does, the audience is privy to the reasons. The motivation for Gatewood's bullying insistence that they push on to Lordsburg as quickly as possible may be obscure to his fellows, but we know why he is in such a hurry. The filmmakers even provide enough hints about the mysterious Hatfield's background to enable a moviegoer to view the gambler's behavior as consistent and motivated.

The film contains only a few minor characters because so much of its time is given over to the major figures. These secondary parts would include the lieutenant who leads the first contingent of cavalry, Gatewood's wife, Doc's landlady in Tonto, a few Tonto and Lordsburg women who know Lucy Mallory, several bartenders, Chris, Chris' wife and the sheriff in Lordsburg. Each has a function within the plot but none could be described as a developed character. The rest of the large cast is composed of extras, most of them dwellers of Tonto or Lordsburg or members of Geronimo's raiding party.

Time, chronology, point of view

Little need be said about time, chronology or point of view. By concentrating on the most important and dramatic events, the story, which appears to cover about two days in the lives of the characters, is effectively told in 96 minutes of screen time. Its chronology is straightforward and sequential with some parallel action but no flashbacks. And it maintains an omniscient point of view throughout most of its telling.

Summary

Stagecoach provides an excellent illustration of Hollywood's Classical approach to narrative. But before we move ahead to a discussion of the stylistic techniques employed by the filmmakers to bring depth, texture and vividness to the road map provided by the screenwriter and producer, it seems important to pause for a moment in order to underline one important point: the narrative strategies elucidated thus far were neither monolithic, nor inflexible, nor prescriptive. Many Hollywood films, among them some of the most popular and critically esteemed of the period, did not conform perfectly to the Classical narrative formula, just as many violated the rules of the Classical style which we will now begin to investigate. Herewith, a few examples of plot resolutions that disregard expectations, rupturing the usual patterns of closure: even though the formerly blind girl (Virginia Cherrill) in *City Lights* (Chaplin/ United Artists, 1931) finally recognizes that her benefactor is the little tramp, the ending leaves the audience "hanging," offering no suggestion that these characters will ever develop a relationship of any kind; despite the conspicuous dramatic requirement (reinforced by the Hollywood censors) that evildoers must be punished, the villain Rupert of Hentzau (Douglas Fairbanks Jr.) escapes unfettered at the end of *The Prisoner of Zenda* (Selznick/United Artists, 1937); instead of settling down together to rebuild their lives like Dallas and Ringo, Rhett Butler abandons Scarlett O'Hara near the finale of *Gone with the Wind*; and no last-minute rescue takes place to prevent the lynching of three innocent men in *The Ox-Bow Incident* (Twentieth Century-Fox, 1943). Shockingly, *I Am a Fugitive from a Chain Gang* contains no closure at all. At the end, the innocent protagonist (Paul Muni) is still a fugitive fleeing from the authorities. While paying a quick visit to the fiancée (Helen Vinson) he will probably never be allowed to wed, he is asked, "How do you live?" Retreating into the darkness, he replies, "I steal," and the film is over.

Style in *Stagecoach*

The style of *Stagecoach* is carefully calibrated to deliver the story to movie audiences in humorous, dramatic and "romantic" fashion. Director John Ford and his collaborators adhere to the accepted norms of Classical filmmaking throughout much of the film, but they are not afraid to make "mistakes" or break the "rules." Rather than attempt to provide a scene-by-scene analysis, it seems best to isolate the different components of the style and discuss them in the context of the overall production.

Staging: acting

Stagecoach is a well-cast film. It contains a number of recognizable western "types" such as the rugged hero, the whore with a heart of gold, the shifty gambler, the thoughtful marshal, the gentlewoman from the east, the drunkard, etc., and the actors chosen to play the parts were well-suited physically to their roles. But with Ford's help, most of these actors were able to elevate their characters beyond standard western stereotypes. One of the reasons this film continues to be highly regarded more than 60 years after it was released is the quality of the performances.

The acting of the main characters ranges from the the boisterous (Andy Devine as Buck) and the blustery (Berton Churchill as Gatewood) to the emotionally restrained (Louise Platt as Lucy Mallory) and introspective (John Carradine as Hatfield). The performances of the two leads are particularly impressive. John Wayne brings precisely the right combination of strength and

Figure 5.2 Louise Platt (*left*) as Mrs. Mallory, John Carradine as Hatfield and Claire Trevor as Dallas in *Stagecoach* (produced by Walter Wanger for United Artists, 1939). Courtesy of the USC Cinema-Television Library.

forcefulness plus naiveté and mannerliness to the role of the Ringo Kid. And Claire Trevor's impersonation of Dallas communicates, often without words, the pain and humiliation she endures when the "respectable" characters ostracize her, as well as the mental anguish she feels while struggling to decide whether to tell Ringo about her past. (Figure 5.2)

Some of the other performances contain satisfying surprises. The aptly named Donald Meek is perfect for the role of Peacock, a man so unassuming that his fellow passengers never get his name straight. But we also know Peacock has five children; thus, when he "shushes" the other men, telling them to be quiet out of respect for the infant and Mrs. Mallory, his newfound assertiveness seems both motivated and a pleasant surprise. Likewise, Curley's decision to release Ringo rather than return him to prison may be unexpected but seems "right" because George Bancroft's acting has conveyed his fondness for the boy and sympathy for his plight from the very beginning of the picture. Finally, Doc Boone's transformation from bombastic dipsomaniac to capable physician is believable since, even in his most inebriated state, Doc's education and intelligence are apparent. Thomas Mitchell won an Academy Award for this performance.

Only in the supporting characters does true stereotyping exist. Chris Martin, for example, is unable to bring any depth to Chris, the overseer of the station at Apache Wells. His buffoonish mangling of the English language and low spirits brought on by the loss of his horse (not his wife who runs away with the horse) are typical of the Mexican characters one finds in many lesser westerns of the period. Geronimo and his Apache warriors are not characterized at all. They are simply the stereotypic savages menacing the progress of white civilization on the frontier. We do spend a bit of time with Luke Plummer and his brothers, but we don't discover anything about them either. They are standard-issue bad men whose extermination is necessary to make towns like Lordsburg safe.

In sum, the naturalistic acting in *Stagecoach* is one of the movie's strengths, adding to the feeling of verisimilitude which the filmmakers wish to convey. Most of the performers flesh out their characters in ways that make them more interesting, attractive and affecting, and their ensemble efforts add weight and shading to the narrative.

Staging: costume, make-up, art direction

The costumes by Walter Plunkett and make-up (uncredited) contribute to the personas of the characters and the performances of the actors. One of the most obvious examples of this can be seen in a comparison of the two main female characters. Mrs. Mallory wears attractive, understated clothing befitting her aristocratic upbringing and status as the wife of an army officer. Her make-up is subdued. Dallas' costume, on the other hand, is much more colorful and flamboyant. Her clothes, combined with the heavy, "painted lady" quality of her make-up, make it quite clear why the female members of the Law and Order League force her to leave Tonto. Interestingly, it is Ringo's inability to read the cues provided by Dallas' clothing and make-up that let the audience know how innocent and pure of heart he is. Ringo truly is still a "kid." (Figure 5.3)

Ringo's costume and make-up help to convey his adolescent nature as well. Although John Wayne was in his early 30s when *Stagecoach* was shot, he is made to appear at least 10 years younger. His clothing shows off his height and rawboned physicality and, from his white hat down to his suspenders and boots, accentuates the fact that he will be the true hero of the tale. Likewise, the clothing and make-up help to reinforce the character traits of each of the other characters, e.g., Peacock's business attire which makes him look like a minister;

Figure 5.3 Claire Trevor as Dallas and John Wayne as the Ringo Kid in *Stagecoach* (produced by Walter Wanger for United Artists, 1939). Courtesy of the USC Cinema-Television Library.

Doc's shabby outfit and disheveled appearance; Hatfield's natty gambler's duds and well-manicured features.

The art direction contributes to the verisimilitude. Two of the most important interiors are the way stations at Dry Fork and Apache Wells. These interiors were planned and executed by art director Alexander Toluboff and his associate Wiard B. Ihnen in the southwestern style with adobe or stucco walls, period furniture and other simple props. Comparing the two, one notes that the Apache Wells set seems less spacious and open than the station at Dry Fork. Since there is considerably more tension and drama in the scenes that take place in Apache Wells, the claustrophobic feeling conveyed by the art direction (and the lighting) helps to reinforce the growing sense of danger that all the characters are feeling at that point in the story. It should be noted that ceilings are rare in Hollywood films from this period since interior sets generally were left open to facilitate lighting. Audiences never noticed the absence because of careful framing by the director of photography. In *Stagecoach*, however, ceilings are visible in numerous scenes, increasing the naturalism of the environments and, in the case of the Apache Wells interiors, exacerbating the sense of confinement.

Cinematography

The cinematography by Bert Glennon, as overseen by director Ford who had one of the best "eyes" in Hollywood, accomplishes several different goals. First, it smoothly integrates footage shot in Monument Valley and other locations, exterior footage shot at one of the studio's "western town" sets, footage shot on exterior sets within the studio, footage shot on interior sets inside the studio, and special effects footage shot against a process screen inside the studio – all sufficiently consistent that it could be edited together without the audience realizing that there was an ongoing disconnect between the images photographed in such disparate locations and ways.

Second, the footage includes magnificent long-shots, such as images of the tiny stage dwarfed by the immensity and remoteness of the wilderness. These images not only visually communicate the human beings vs. nature conflict and the vulnerable position which the characters are in, they also use the extraordinary rock monoliths of Monument Valley to create dynamic compositions which magnify the mythic qualities of the story. In case one misses the point that this saga is intended to take on meaning that transcends its component parts, Ford and Glennon's presentation of landscape, most especially the otherworldly topography of Monument Valley which had not been widely seen in films before *Stagecoach*, separates it from other contemporary westerns and raises the film into a special category. (See Figure 5.4)

Most of the story is told in medium-shots that are carefully balanced compositionally. They typically feature the most important characters in the foreground and center of the frame. When a composition becomes unbalanced, the usual response is to cut away quickly, reframe the image, or move the actors around so that a better composition results. A prime example of the latter solution occurs in the saloon in Lordsburg after Luke Plummer's brothers join him. At the beginning of the shot Luke is on the far left side of the frame with his brothers standing at the bar next to him. The composition is unbalanced with too much visual information on the left side and a sizable gap on the right. For no discernible reason (other than to make the composition more balanced), Luke suddenly walks behind his brothers and repositions himself at the bar, filling in the dead space in the composition.

The film features fewer close-ups than long- or medium-shots. They are saved for intense moments in the narrative, such as the developing love relationship

Figure 5.4 The stagecoach ferries its passengers through the beautiful but dangerous Monument Valley in *Stagecoach* (produced by Walter Wanger for United Artists, 1939). Courtesy of the USC Cinema-Television Library.

between Ringo and Dallas. Their growing affection is partially communicated to the audience in shot/reverse-shot sequences featuring close-ups of the two faces. Other examples of the film's use of dramatic close-ups include the shot of Mrs. Mallory praying as Hatfield prepares to shoot her in the head and the shot of Doc as he stands up to Luke Plummer, preventing Luke from arming himself with a shotgun for the shoot-out with Ringo.

From the standpoint of pictorial style, this film was ahead of its time in its preference for sharp focus and numerous compositions in depth. Ford and Glennon will often position characters close to the camera, characters in middle depth and characters in the background of a shot. While these individuals are not all in perfect focus, the effect is quite close to the deep focus style of the 1940s. A good example of this may be seen in the Dry Fork section. At the lunch table, just before Hatfield, Mrs. Mallory and Gatewood move away from Dallas and Ringo, there is a shot of Lucy Mallory sitting close to the camera on the right side of the frame with Hatfield standing to her left and slightly behind her, Gatewood positioned in the middle distance on the left side and Doc and Billy in the left middle background at the bar. While the focus is sharpest on Mrs. Mallory, all the characters are in relatively distinct focus. Orson Welles claimed that he learned everything he needed to know about making movies from watching *Stagecoach*, and the influence on *Citizen Kane* seems quite apparent in Ford and Glennon's efforts to bring greater depth to the images of their western.

Even though the pictorial style looks forward rather than backward, the filmmakers do not completely abandon "softness" in their imagery. In the last half of the movie, they use more diffusion in photographing the women than the men. This is particularly true of Dallas; as her generosity, essential goodness and love for Ringo become more and more evident, her image grows a bit softer. It's almost as if the camera is changing its opinion of her, just as Mrs. Mallory does.

In an approach that parallels the judicious use of the close-up, Ford and Glennon move their camera when necessary but do not overdo this technique. There are several outstanding examples of camera movement, such as the far-shot looking down on the stage in Monument Valley which then pans left and up to reveal the Indians about to attack, as well as numerous shots from a moving camera car as the Indians chase the coach. But the most spectacular camera movement in the film is the forward tracking shot which introduces John Wayne as the Ringo Kid. Beginning with a medium-shot and quickly moving in to a close-up of Ringo's face, this famous shot provides a striking contrast to the simple, non-theatrical introductions of the other characters and lets the audience know immediately that this young fellow is going to be a very important character. The use of sound adds to the impact of this shot, as I will point out in a subsequent section.

Finally, Glennon's approach to lighting evolves gradually from light to dark. The initial scenes in Tonto are shot primarily in high-key with bright illumination and little in the way of shadows. As the stagecoach proceeds, a mid-key look predominates which includes some shadow effects but favors even illumination. This changes at Apache Wells where numerous low-key shots are included in both the evening and morning images. The low-key look will culminate in Lordsburg during Ringo's "tour" of the red-light district with Dallas and his subsequent shoot-out with the Plummers. This shift does not seem accidental or arbitrary. As the pressure builds in the story, the lighting becomes more stylized and dramatic. One obvious example occurs during the introduction of Luke Plummer. He is playing poker in the Lordsburg saloon when he hears that Ringo is in town. Preparing to dispatch one of his amigos to fetch his brothers, Luke stands up and his upper torso is suddenly so obscured by shadows that we cannot even see his face. We don't really need to know that Ringo's antagonist drew aces and eights in his final hand; the lighting tells us that Luke Plummer is a "dead man walking."

Editing

John Ford was known for "cutting in the camera." Unlike most directors, he typically shot a minimum amount of footage, thus guaranteeing that the film would be put together, during the post-production process, as he envisioned it. Nevertheless, producer Walter Wanger employed three people, Otho Lovering, Dorothy Spencer and (uncredited) Walter Reynolds to edit *Stagecoach*. In all likelihood, they worked on different sections in order to finish the film as rapidly as possible. For the most part, their work conforms to the principles of Hollywood continuity editing, though they and their superiors were not afraid to junk those principles when they felt it necessary.

The most glaring example of this is the abandonment of respect for the 180-degree axis during the Indian attack scene. This chase scene includes numerous cuts from a camera position on one side of the stagecoach to a position on the opposite side. This causes screen direction to become completely jumbled, making the coach appear to move right to left in one shot and then left to right in the next. It is, of course, possible to make this kind of transition smoothly if a neutral shot (from in front of the coach as it proceeds toward the camera, for example) is used to bridge the cut, but the editors generally don't bother with the bridge. They (and probably Ford) seem to believe that the excitement of the scene and the rapidity of the cutting style used to heighten that excitement will carry the customers along without causing them to become confused or disconnected from the story.

This particular editing "mistake" has been mentioned in numerous film history books. What is not often noted is that other examples of the filmmakers' disdain for the 180-degree axis occur earlier in the film. For example, back in Tonto when the passengers first board the coach there is a shot of Dallas getting in and sitting on the right side and as far from the camera as she can get. This is followed by a shot from the other side wherein she appears to be sitting on the left side closest to the camera. Screen direction is so jumbled throughout the remainder of this scene that it is practically impossible to figure out the geographical relationships of the characters to each other by the time they have all entered the coach. But, again, the editors evidently feel the audience will never notice these continuity "bumps" because they will be so engrossed in the story.

Two other interesting "violations" occur in the initial scenes featuring Gatewood. In this case, the editors include two odd but purposeful jump cuts. In the first scene, we are introduced to Gatewood in his office at the bank. After the men who have brought in the payroll money leave, the editors cut in a closer shot of Gatewood, taken from an angle that is less than 30 degrees different from the previous shot, which causes it to appear to "jump" on the screen. A short time later we return to Gatewood's office for a short scene in which his demanding wife orders him to do certain things. After she departs, the editors jump cut to almost exactly the same shot of the glowering banker that they used in the first scene. Thus, before we even watch Gatewood transfer the $50,000 to his traveling bag, we sense that there is something shady about this character. The jump cuts inform the audience that Mr. Gatewood is not the model citizen he pretends to be.

Another odd moment in the film that might have left audience members scratching their heads occurs just before the Ringo Kid is introduced. The stagecoach has left Tonto with a cavalry escort. At some point and for reasons that are not explained, the soldiers no longer accompany the coach. We see the coach traveling ahead in isolation when suddenly there is an awkward cut to a short shot of the troops crossing a river. Since the stagecoach has been traversing arid ground, we wonder where this river is and how the coach got around it. Then the filmmakers cut back to the introduction of Ringo – a scene that ends with the soldiers rejoining the coach. There might be any number of explanations for this strange sequence, including the elimination of one or more scenes that would have shown why the cavalry became separated from the coach and what they were doing in the river. As it stands, the sequence plays as if somebody "goofed," and the editors felt that cutting in the river shot was the only way to explain why the troops are not present when Ringo is first introduced.

I do not mean to imply that *Stagecoach* is, by Hollywood standards, either an editorial mess or some sort of experimental film. Throughout most of its running time, the editing is faithful to continuity principles, respecting the 180-degree axis and the 30-degree rule. There are some excellent examples of shot/reverse-shot sequences (already mentioned), cutting on action (e.g., Doc Boone's introduction to Peacock with the cut coming in the middle of Doc's move to shake the whiskey drummer's hand) and eyeline matches (a nice one occurs in Lee's Ferry where Hatfield looks off-screen and the cut shows us what he sees – signs of the hostile Indians in the surrounding hills). The editors employ standard transitional devices, including a good many dissolves to mark short passages of time and a few fade-outs to suggest longer time ellipses or major turning points in the story. They eschew intertitles, wipes or montage sequences.

One of the film's great triumphs is the aforementioned Indian attack scene. Setting aside the 180-degree axis issue for a moment, the overall editorial design of this scene is a model of how to invigorate movie chases. The editors interlace many moving camera shots with low-angle shots in which the stage and Indians ride directly over the camera, shots of Buck and Curley driving the stagecoach forward and fending off the Apaches, shots of Ringo shooting the Indians and then leaping on the horses and guiding them after Buck loses the reins, shots of the passengers inside as some fight while others cower, etc. This sequence even includes point-of-view shots, such as the moment in which we see an Indian on horseback fire his rifle at Hatfield through Hatfield's eyes. The rapid pacing of the shots helps to increase the breathless nature of the action. The fact that the chase includes many studio and process shots joined together in fluid fashion with shots made on exterior locations at the dry lake bed and elsewhere is a testament to the editors' ability to squeeze every bit of potential excitement out of the footage without losing the audience in the process. Indeed, even the numerous continuity "mistakes" seem not to have bothered the customers or the professionals. The film was nominated for an Academy Award for best film editing.

Sound and music

The sound work credited to Frank Maher is professional throughout *Stagecoach* and dynamic at various moments in the narrative. The film contains a good deal of important dialogue which is crisply recorded and mixed together felicitously with the sound effects and musical score. At certain points, sound is used to increase the impact of a scene. As already mentioned, one of the memorable moments in the film is the rapid tracking shot that introduces Ringo. But even before the audience sees Ringo, we hear him fire his rifle and yell, "Hold it!" which prepares us for the introduction of this crucial character. Likewise, the beginning of the Indian attack is "announced" by the sound of an arrow which will end up in Mr. Peacock's shoulder. Other examples of important creative sound work would include the segue from the baying of a coyote to the similar-sounding cries of the newborn baby, and the sounds of the bugles during the Indian attack, which appear to be part of the musical score but turn out to be real bugles blown by soldiers who have arrived just in time to save the stagecoach. The filmmakers even allow sound to carry the final climax. After Ringo and the Plummer brothers advance toward each other on the Lordsburg street, the editors cut to a shot of Ringo lunging forward and firing the first shot from his rifle. They then cut away to a shot of a very worried Dallas, allowing the battle to be communicated solely by the noise of the gunshots. This serves to increase suspense because the audience remains unsure of the outcome until it sees Luke collapse on the floor of the saloon and Ringo, who is apparently not seriously injured, reunite with Dallas.

The musical score is quite unusual in that five different individuals (Richard Hageman, Franke Harling, Louis Gruenberg, John Leipold and Leo Shuken) are credited for adapting American folk songs (such as "Bury Me Not on the Lone Prairie" and Stephen Foster's "Jeanie with the Light Brown Hair"). With Boris Morros also listed as Musical Director it is impossible to determine who knitted the different songs together into the final score and who wrote the connective music that gives the score coherence. As might be expected, the result is a potpourri of different thematics (there are Indian and Mexican motifs as well as the flavorful Americana theme which predominates). However, the basic thrust of the music is epochal; like the other aspects of this "romantic" style, its function is to magnify the characters and their tribulations into a story of greatness – great courage, great love, great achievement. As a consequence, the music hyperbolizes the many different moods of the story. At one moment, it enlarges the satiric march of Doc and Dallas to the "guillotine" in Tonto; at another, it simulates the cold wind chilling the passengers as they pass through higher ground on the coach; at several others, it embellishes the increasingly ominous threat posed by the Indians; at another, it plaintively mourns the death of the woman whom Hatfield covers with his coat at Lee's Ferry; and at the end it swells triumphantly, reprising some of the earlier themes and heralding the happy ending of this mythic tale. The score received an Academy Award.

Summary

The Classical style of Hollywood filmmaking conformed to a more pliable, less restrictive model than has generally been recognized. While an unwritten compendium of rules and principles may be deduced from contemporary stylistic practices, filmmakers often set aside this "text" when it did not serve them well. Sometimes their determination to defy convention was clearly intentional. Director Ben Hecht and cinematographer Lee Garmes on *Crime Without Passion* (Hecht-MacArthur/Paramount, 1934), director Fritz Lang and cinematographer Charles Lang Jr. on *You and Me* (Paramount, 1938) and director Orson Welles and cinematographer Gregg Toland on *Citizen Kane* trespassed well beyond traditional stylistic boundaries in their attempts to expand the expressive possibilities of the medium. Though their experiments were all highly ambitious, only *Citizen Kane* ended up having a major impact on the aesthetic development of cinema. And it, like the others, was not embraced by the general public. All three films were financially unsuccessful.

However, as the analysis of *Stagecoach* demonstrates, one also finds a multitude of stylistic "infractions" in highly popular films. Director Frank Capra and his editors, for example, were not overly impressed by the 30-degree rule. His movies, including *Mr. Deeds Goes to Town* and *Mr. Smith Goes to Washington*, contain numerous jump cuts which, unlike the ones in *Stagecoach*, appear to be motivated by nothing more than a desire to bring the spectators a bit closer to certain characters. It seems that Capra's audience did not find these unusual cuts bothersome; both *Deeds* and *Smith* were highly profitable. A closer look at many other highly regarded films from the era would reveal similar departures from the dominant style.

Once again, I should re-emphasize the overriding theme of this chapter. Style was supposed to serve storytelling. Its job was to carry the story forward in a way that was clear, concise and compelling. Sometimes this meant that the style had to be as simple and invisible as possible (*Wild Boys of the Road*, Warner Bros., 1933). On other occasions, a more flamboyant, exhibitionistic style could be fitting (*Love Me Tonight*, Paramount, 1932). The possibilities were infinite, but the most talented filmmakers of the 1930s and 1940s understood how to bend and shape the malleable ingredients of the Classical style to accomplish their ultimate objective: the creation of cinematic stories that would galvanize the moviegoing public.

A Note on "Studio" Style

In his seminal study of film history, *The Liveliest Art*, Arthur Knight wrote: "Until fairly recently, almost any movie fan, after a few moments of gazing at a Hollywood film, could make a fairly accurate guess as to which company produced it without seeing either titles or trade-marks ... By and large it is the studio that leaves the strongest imprint on its films." In fact it was a studio's stars, not its stylistic propensities, that would have signaled which studio made the picture. Audience members recognized that Gable and MGM, Temple and Twentieth Century-Fox, Crosby and Paramount, Bogart and Warner Bros., etc. were practically inseparable. But they would have had no sense that studios imposed particular stylistic signatures on their products.

While a good deal of research has been done by scholars since Mr. Knight published *The Liveliest Art* in 1957, and some of this work suggests that different companies did have certain stylistic "tendencies," disparities among the products from the major studios are so subtle that making a case for the "mark" of each studio is neither tenable nor particularly useful. In fact, stylistic variations appear to have had more to do with the specific genres that studios favored than any other single factor, and so let us briefly turn our attention to the topic of genre style.

A Note on Genre Style

Audience expectations concerning the "look" of a film and the amount of stylistic embellishment that viewers would tolerate were conditioned by genre. The horror film, for example, is one of the most interesting in this regard. In addition to employing a low-key, shadowy, night-world look and generally accelerated pacing compared to other genres, these pictures allowed for an excessive amount of stylistic exaggeration. The creation sequence in *Bride of Frankenstein* (Universal, 1935) contains all manner of bizarre camera angles and outlandish lighting effects that heighten the impact of the scene but would have been unthinkable in most other genres. Similarly, the set design of *Son of Frankenstein* (Universal, 1939) is completely out of scale; it literally dwarfs the characters, helping to create the impression of a malignant environment not suitable for the raising of children. Finally, the "sound shocks" injected into the swimming pool and bus scenes in *Cat People* (RKO, 1943) are unnaturally magnified in order to ratchet up the fright level of this thriller.

While other genres that favored the imaginary over the realistic, such as fantasies, musicals, and certain comedies, also allowed for a good deal of stylistic exaggeration, most genres offered more limited possibilities. Still, one can detect certain general tendencies that help differentiate one genre from another. The preferred low-key look of some (horror, detective, gangster) may be contrasted to the more mid-key and high-key look of others (westerns, woman's films, biographies, comedies, musicals). And the so-called "action pictures" (westerns, adventure films, war movies) are typically paced more swiftly than musicals, biographies, woman's pictures and social consciousness films.

Without question, genre influenced style in ways that are reasonably predictable. And yet it must be re-emphasized that one can always find exceptions to the general tendencies. Stylistic decisions were made on a picture-by-picture basis, and these decisions took into account a broad spectrum of possibilities. (See chapter 6 for further discussion of genre styles.)

A Note on Film Noir

One of the most celebrated developments in 1940s American cinema was the film noir movement. Though it had antecedents, including German Expressionism in the 1910s and 20s and French Poetic Realism in the 30s, as well as a few silent and sound films made in Hollywood, film noir began to take shape in the early 40s and continued to gain momentum after the conclusion of the war. French critics first noticed this strange new development when they were flooded with American movies after their country's liberation. They gave the movement its name.

There is an ongoing debate whether film noir is a genre or a style. While acknowledging that even the adherents of the latter position often discuss these pictures in terms of their characters, themes and world view (basic genre ingredients), I prefer to treat film noir as a stylistic development.

One of the justifications for examining film noir as a style is the many established genres which were affected by it. Indeed, contemporary journalistic reviewers began to note that there was something different about these pictures, but they had difficulty connecting them together because they cut across so many genres: the detective film (*Murder, My Sweet*, RKO, 1945), the spy film (*Ministry of Fear*, Paramount, 1944), the woman's film (*Mildred Pierce*, Warner Bros., 1945), the social problem film (*The Lost Weekend*, Paramount, 1945), the gangster film (*High Sierra*, Warner Bros., 1941), the horror film (*The Leopard Man*, RKO, 1943), even the musical (*Blues in the Night*, Warner Bros., 1941).

The key elements that allow us to classify these pictures into a coherent group are their style and, in many cases, their unusual approach to narrative. Let us examine narrative strategies first. The point of view in a number of noir films is limited to a single character. Thus, unlike the omniscient point of view which is practically ubiquitous in Hollywood movies before the advent of film noir, these films rely on one individual to guide the audience through the story. This can be true whether the character is the actual narrator "telling" the story via a series of flashbacks (*Double Indemnity*) or simply appears in every significant scene (*The Maltese Falcon*, Warner Bros., 1941), confining the audience to his perspective throughout. This strategy sets up a different dynamic within the relationship between spectators and story because the central character is often not only a fallible individual who does not view the unfolding events clearly but also may be something less than an objective observer.

Not every example of film noir shuns the omniscient point of view or creates a narrative tension between the protagonist and the audience. But the filmmakers who created these works did approach style differently than their predecessors. Determined to portray a less "romantic" vision of the world, they pushed the possibilities of low-key cinematography farther than they had been pushed before. Such directors of photography as Nicholas Musuraca (*I Walked with a Zombie*, RKO, 1943), John F. Seitz (*Double Indemnity*), Woody Bredell (*Phantom Lady*, Universal, 1944), Milton Krasner (*The Woman in the Window*, International/RKO, 1945) and Benjamin H. Kline (*Detour*, PRC, 1945) rationed light as if it were one of the precious commodities of the war years, creating a cinema rich in the shadows of suggestive malevolence. The chiaroscuro lighting, combined with claustrophobic, often unbalanced compositions and unusual camera angles, conveyed a sense of entrapment, alienation, psychological instability and paranoia that was out of "synch" with the majority of Hollywood productions.

The odd fact that the film noir movement began during World War II, a time when Americans were extraordinarily unified, determined and hopeful about the future, can be partially explained by European influences. Most of the directors who set out to make these pictures were European expatriates sickened by the devastation wreaked on their friends, their families and their homelands by the war. They had good reason to be more cynical, less optimistic than the typical American, and they used their Hollywood clout to push these idiosyncratic projects into production. To compound the irony, some of their films, such as *Double Indemnity*, directed by Billy Wilder, and *Laura*, directed by Otto Preminger, were so fresh that they flourished both critically and commercially, paving the way for the production of more films of this kind. Other European directors who emigrated to Hollywood in the 1930s and subsequently helped to create film noir included Alfred Hitchcock (*Shadow of a Doubt*, Universal, 1943), Robert Siodmak (*The Spiral Staircase*, RKO, 1945), Fritz Lang (*Scarlet Street*, Diana/Universal, 1945), Edgar G. Ulmer (*Detour*) and John Brahm (*Hangover Square*, Twentieth Century-Fox, 1945).

A Note on Directorial Style

This book has avoided the privileging of directors which still characterizes many studies of Hollywood film history. While outstanding directors worked in the American cinema in the 1930s and 1940s, very few had "final cut," the ability to guarantee that their work reached the screen in the form they wished. Instead, producers and studio executives determined all the final details of their products, which is only one of several reasons the "auteur" theory is of limited usefulness for the study of American cinema during this period.

Still, it must be acknowledged that certain directors were able to emboss films with their own personality and vision. I have already noted this with some of the film noir directors, but it is also evident in the works of Charles Chaplin, Ernst Lubitsch, John Ford, Frank Capra, Howard Hawks, Frank Borzage, Preston Sturges, Orson Welles and others. However, the personal visions of these filmmakers have often been referenced as a function of style when, in most cases, the stylistic differences between their films are not dramatic. Rather, the directors' thematic preoccupations make their works stand out and give them coherence and personality: Chaplin's concern for the vagabonds of society and his growing political sensibility; Hawks' fascination with adventure, professionalism and the battle of the sexes; Ford's veneration of the family and of the traditions and rituals that cement human beings together; Capra's belief in the heroic possibilities of the common man; Lubitsch's sly and sophisticated deconstruction of the European class system; Borzage's sentimental faith in the transcendental power of love. It would be wrong to state that there was nothing distinctive about the style of these filmmakers. They were both artists and exceptional craftsmen and their works were usually more interesting, on every level, than those of most studio directors. No one in Hollywood had a better compositional sense than Ford, for example, and Hitchcock instinctively recognized how to shoot a film so that it could be edited to produce maximum suspense. And yet these filmmakers never forgot the dictum that style must always be in the service of story. They understood that a good story could be told with a minimum of stylistic ornamentation, but no amount of stylistic razzle-dazzle could compensate for a weak, uninvolving narrative.

Josef von Sternberg did not recognize this truism, and his career suffered as a consequence. One of the filmmaking titans of the early 1930s, the director helped mold Marlene Dietrich into an international star and gave Paramount several hits before his obsession with style began to overwhelm his interest in story. Though Sternberg may not have been wholly conscious of this, *The Scarlet Empress* (Paramount, 1934) and *The Devil Is a Woman* (Paramount, 1935) appear to be exercises in stylistic extravagance perversely designed to antagonize audience members hoping to witness an involving story. Indulging his love of scrims, veils, nets, fog, smoke and striking costuming and symbolic decor, Sternberg captured a plethora of luminescent and striking images in these two pictures. But most movie patrons did not appreciate their beauty and evocative qualities. Not only were the films major commercial failures, they also tarnished Ms. Dietrich's star image and sent her career into a tailspin. Not surprisingly, Josef von Sternberg was soon expelled from the elite cadre of Paramount contract directors, and he had difficulty securing and keeping jobs as a director for the rest of his life. Sadly, the career of Orson Welles, another distinctive stylist, would have a similar trajectory.

6

Genres

Genres, or distinct types of films, were a crucial component of the creative and economic strategies of Hollywood entertainment companies during the Classical Period. The basic idea of diversifying a studio's production output developed out of the dynamic relationship between film producers and their customers. Early in the history of cinema as a commercial enterprise, the people who made movies realized that one of the key elements needed to attract audiences was an interesting story. The quality of the story was of primary importance, but these pioneers also recognized that spectators gravitated to certain, specific types of narratives while remaining indifferent to, or less enthusiastic about, other types. By the time sound movies became the norm, genre-thinking as a production philosophy had been embraced by every studio.

Each company specialized in certain genres (see chapter 2). Decisions were based upon the strengths of the contract talent (especially the actors), as well as the preferences of the production head who naturally had to consider the perceived audience that the company was attempting to reach. Universal, for example, became the leading producer of horror films because of such actors as Boris Karloff, Bela Lugosi and Lon Chaney Jr., directors James Whale and George Waggner, writers Garrett Fort and John L. Balderston and, initially, production chief Carl Laemmle Jr. who favored their production. Likewise, Paramount made exceptional comedies throughout the 1930s and 40s, thanks to the efforts of the Marx Brothers, Mae West, Carole Lombard, Claudette Colbert, W.C. Fields, Barbara Stanwyck, Bob Hope, Paulette Goddard, Bing Crosby and Fred MacMurray, plus behind-the-camera talent that included Ernst Lubitsch, Preston Sturges, Billy Wilder and Mitchell Leisen.

A studio's "B" picture program would be conceptualized almost exclusively along genre lines. A well-rounded "B" program involved the release of a predictable number of low-budget westerns, detective films, crime pictures, comedies and woman's pictures each year. The advertising of these movies graphically emphasized their genre elements; the studios understood there was a reliable audience for genre films and made sure those customers were readily able to find the entertainments they preferred.

At the "A" level, the star was considered the primary enticement (see chapter 7). "A" programs were planned around stars and well-regarded literary material – which oftentimes did not fit neatly into genre pigeonholes. Still, most stars had established, identifiable screen personas which tended to mesh well with certain genres. This realization certainly came into play in production planning and subsequent marketing campaigns: Fred Astaire confined himself exclusively to the musical during the Classical Period; Errol Flynn was the biggest star of the adventure film; Bette Davis became identified with the woman's film, as did John Wayne with the western and Carole Lombard with the screwball comedy. James Cagney, a dancer by training and inclination, found himself associated with the gangster film after the success of *The Public Enemy* (Warner Bros., 1931).

Some genres were considered almost exclusively "A" level undertakings. Musicals, because of cost and complexity, were predominently "A" pictures. So were adventure films and screen biographies. The horror film was considered the perfect "B," because it required no stars. Boris Karloff, for example, was clearly the biggest name in the horror films of the 1930s, but his actual status is indicated by the supporting roles he played in such "A" films as *Scarface* (Caddo/United Artists, 1932), *The Lost Patrol* (RKO, 1934) and *The House of Rothschild* (Twentieth Century/United Artists, 1934). The vast majority of westerns were "B" films (or some lesser category, see chapter 2), and most detective films also fell into the "B" niche. Nevertheless, all genres offered both "A" and "B" examples, and most were able to move back and forth between the two categories easily.

While most Hollywood productions were generic, it is important to recognize the existence of non-genre films as well. Whereas genre films incorporated a predictable set of characters, settings, costumes, plot situations, themes and iconography (visual elements such as the horse in the western and the gun in the gangster film), non-genre productions usually placed special emphasis on their characters and did not include the formularized elements that one expected to find in the typical genre production. Sometimes a film transcends genre categorization because of its sheer size and scope. *Gone with the Wind* (Selznick/MGM, 1939), for example, contains elements of the woman's film, the adventure film and the war film, but it seems more accurate to describe this epic as a non-genre production. Similarly, labeling *Casablanca* (Warner Bros., 1943) an espionage film does not seem adequate, for spying is actually an insignificant component in this classic example of Hollywood romanticism. Some other major films that resist genre labels are *Grand Hotel* (MGM, 1932), *The Informer* (RKO, 1935), *Dodsworth* (Goldwyn/United Artists, 1936), *The Good Earth* (MGM, 1937), *The Long Voyage Home* (Wanger/United Artists, 1940), *How Green Was My Valley* (Twentieth Century-Fox, 1941) and *Citizen Kane* (RKO, 1941).

The bulk of this chapter will be given over to examinations of the most important genres of the Classical Period. Suffice it to say that each was popular during certain historical periods and less appealing to audience members at other times. And each was affected by the most significant extra-cinematic and cinematic influences of the time. The Depression and World War II represent particularly powerful shaping forces, as were the coming of sound and the establishment of the Production Code Administration. These factors, and others that sometimes awakened genres . . . or put them to sleep, pushed them in new directions . . . or caused them to marry with other genres and form interesting hybrids, will be discussed in the remainder of this chapter.

The Western

The western became a popular genre early in the history of cinema. By the beginning of the sound era, thousands of westerns had already been produced – films which ran the gamut from expensive epics to the cheapest shorts, from realistic depictions of life in the old west to the most fanciful versions of how that life had been lived. While the genre would continue to be a staple throughout the Classical Period and would incorporate a wide variety of characters, settings, plot situations, themes, etc., perhaps the most distinctive aspect of its existence was the consistency of its core mythic elements and the general message it communicated to viewers.

The overwhelming majority of westerns took place between the end of the Civil War (1865) and the dawn of the twentieth century. They dealt with America's "manifest destiny" – the winning of the west, the transformation of the beautiful but dangerous western wilderness into a safe and civilized environment. Most were set on the frontier, the pressure point where the representatives of civilization are fighting to get a foothold against wild nature.

Thus, these films provided the dominant culture (white men and women of European extraction) with a vision of a heroic past, the belief that their forefathers were giants who bent and shaped a beautiful but difficult land to their wills and then handed it down to them for safekeeping. Along with the land, they passed down a tradition of honor, fair play, justice and democratic ide-alism. The western became a foundation myth for American culture; for audiences of the 1930s and 40s, it was much more powerful and resonant than the tales of Paul Revere, George Washington, the Boston Tea Party, the Revolu-tionary War and the actual founding of the United States.

The films were constructed around a hero figure who is the frontier equiv-alent of a chivalric knight. This man lives by a generally unverbalized code which requires him to treat everyone fairly, to be especially solicitous to women and to use the strength and skills he has developed in the wilderness to defend those who are most vulnerable in this dangerous new world. More than anything else, he stands for justice, for what is right.

He fulfills his narrative function as bringer of justice to the new land through his relationship with the conventional settlers. In most cases, he is an out-sider, not a member of their society. The insiders are the pioneer townspeople, newly come to America and willing to work hard to carve out better lives for themselves and their burgeoning families. But these people are farmers and mer-chants and innkeepers – men and women of peace, not war, who are incapable of protecting themselves against a variety of villains determined to cheat them, exploit them, steal from them or (in the case of the Indians) annihilate them.

The hero becomes their savior. He ends up protecting them, restoring order, making the world safe for their civilizing goals. At the end of the films, this hero often seems ready to put aside his love affair with the wilderness and become one of them because of a developing romantic relationship with a pioneer woman. However, the films never treat the less exciting stories sug-gested by such a domestic union.

Finally, the western hero is a populist hero, a democratic hero. The audience generally knows little about his background. Unlike the knights of medieval legend, the great leaders of the Bible or the swashbuckling adventurers of romantic literature, the westerner has no special status bestowed upon him by God or royalty or social class. He achieves his heroic status through his beliefs and his actions, the things he stands for and the way he conducts himself. This has nothing to do with where he comes from, who his parents are, what outside forces are steering his actions. Thus, the western figure becomes the embodi-ment of the American myth that anyone – whether rich or poor, cultured or uncultured, privileged or without prospects – can become great.

In sum, the Hollywood western contained mythic roots that penetrated deep into the American psyche. Its stories celebrated a heroic past, established a strong, democratic male hero as the rightful leader of civilization and empha-sized justice and freedom as the cornerstones of the country's system of beliefs.

A number of the accepted genre elements – the WASP hero, the emphasis on violence, the racist stereotyping of Native Americans, Hispanics and other non-white characters, the chauvinist treatment of women – would occasion revisionist analysis in post-World War II westerns. But during the Classical Period, the genre remained consistent and unwavering. For years, America's young people grew up convinced that Hollywood westerns told the whole truth about their country's history.

Development

The genre passed through several phases between 1929 and 1945. The coming of sound offered special challenges because many scenes – particularly in "A" films – were shot on location to take advantage of the pictorial grandeur of natural settings. Location sound equipment presented initial difficulties, but in a short time most were overcome. Two reasonably successful early sound efforts were *The Virginian* (Paramount, 1929) starring Gary Cooper and *In Old Arizona* (Fox, 1929) with Warner Baxter.

Before long, studio executives grew satisfied with location sound quality and decided to make the western one of the showcase genres for the next techno-logical breakthrough: wide-screen (see chapter 3). Both *Billy the Kid* (MGM, 1930) and *The Big Trail* (Fox, 1930) were made in similar wide-screen proc-esses. *The Big Trail*, the saga of a wagon train journey across the continent, took special advantage of the new technology, emphasizing the panoramic beauty of the west. But audiences, beginning to feel the pinch of the worsening Depres-sion, were not impressed by either film, and both studios decided to drop their wide-screen experiments.

In 1931, the recently formed RKO attempted to establish itself as an im-portant studio by releasing an epic treatment of Edna Ferber's novel *Cimarron* about the history of the Oklahoma Territory. The huge budget ($1,433,000) which the studio lavished on the production seemed justified when the film received the Best Picture Academy Award for 1931. However, the film was a financial disaster, losing more than a half million dollars, and its weak box office, combined with the desultory performances of *Billy the Kid* and *The Big Trail*, convinced production heads that "A" budget westerns were not a good investment.

Though few "A" westerns would be made between 1932 and 1935, the genre hardly faded away. "B" westerns continued to be produced in profusion, star-ring such recognizable cowboys as Buck Jones, Tim McCoy, Hoot Gibson, Ken Maynard, Randolph Scott, Tom Keene and John Wayne. The films were short (usually less than one hour), cheaply and quickly made and targeted at rural audiences and the "Saturday Matinee" crowd of young people. They received limited foreign distribution. Small companies like Monogram, Republic and, later, PRC were best known for these pictures, but the larger studios, such as Warner Bros., Paramount, RKO, Columbia and Universal, produced them as well. They remained a standard component of their production agendas throughout the Classical Period.

Later in the decade, the "singing cowboy" took the "B" western by storm. This musical–western hybrid alternated action sequences with interludes of "crooning" by such up-and-coming cowboy stars as Gene Autry, Dick Foran, Tex Ritter and Roy Rogers. When the protagonist was incapable of performing the necessary western tunes, he generally had a sidekick to handle the duties. By the early 1940s, it was unusual to find a "B" western that did not offer at least some moments of singing and guitar strumming.

In 1936, Cecil B. DeMille made *The Plainsman* at Paramount. A fictionalized account of the exploits of Wild Bill Hickok (Gary Cooper), Buffalo Bill Cody (James Ellison) and Calamity Jane (Jean Arthur), the film was a hit and so were two other "A" productions released in the same year: *The Texas Rangers* (Paramount) and *Ramona* (Twentieth Century-Fox). Nevertheless, it took two more years before the major budget western returned to its former prominence. The year 1939 marked the beginning of a short but important revitalization period during which a number of major stars became associated with the genre. Some of the most important 1939 westerns were *Stagecoach* (Wanger/United Artists) starring John Wayne, *Union Pacific* (Paramount) starring Joel McCrea and Barbara Stanwyck, *Destry Rides Again* (Universal) starring James Stewart and Marlene Dietrich, and two Technicolor specials, *Jesse James* (Twentieth Century-Fox) starring Tyrone Power and Henry Fonda and *Dodge City* (Warner Bros.) starring Errol Flynn and Olivia de Havilland.

Patriotic sentiment inspired by the deteriorating situation in Europe seeped into the western in various ways during this pre-war period. A particularly obvious example was *Let Freedom Ring* (MGM, 1939) in which greedy railroad tycoon Edward Arnold and his minions are determined to take control of Clover City. Following a stirring speech about tyranny by hero Nelson Eddy and a ringing rendition of "My Country 'Tis of Thee" led by heroine Virginia Bruce, the townspeople rise up and overthrow the oppressor. Few westerns were as explicit as *Let Freedom Ring*, but many became vessels for the expression of high ideals and reminders of the passion for fair play and democracy that had, according to the genre's conventions, underpinned the efforts of the country's pioneers.

During this time period, even the notorious western outlaws were excused for their bad behavior in another popular hybid: the western biography. *Jesse James*, *The Return of Frank James* (Twentieth Century-Fox, 1940), *Billy the Kid* (MGM, 1941) and *The Outlaw* (Hughes/United Artists, filmed 1940 but not released until 1943) attempted to convince audiences that even the worst Americans were basically good-hearted people. The period also glorified Sam Houston (*Man of Conquest*, Republic, 1939), Wyatt Earp (*Frontier Marshal*, Twentieth Century-Fox, 1939), George Armstrong Custer (*They Died with Their Boots On*, Warner Bros., 1941) and other famous historical figures who could be role models at a time of growing crisis.

After America was swept into World War II, the production of "A" westerns again fell off, though the output of "Bs" remained steady and substantial. Most continued trends established before the war, including the singing cowboy, but some also accomplished the remarkable task of yoking together western elements with contemporary concerns. *Texas Man Hunt* (PRC, 1942), *Texas to Bataan* (Monogram, 1942), *Black Market Rustlers* (Monogram, 1943), *Cowboy Commandos* (Monogram, 1943) and *Riders of the Northland* (Columbia, 1942) were fanciful films which demonstrated that the up-to-date technical expertise of America's enemies stood no chance against the old-fashioned toughness and fighting skills of the country's western heroes.

One "A" western made during the war years was well ahead of its time. *The Ox-Bow Incident* (Twentieth Century-Fox, 1943) dealt with the lynching of three innocent men accused of cattle rustling. It called into question American justice, a cornerstone of the genre. While well-made and powerful in its dramatic presentation, the film was poorly received by audiences. Moviegoers were clearly in no mood to doubt the righteousness and higher purpose of American life at this time. Even though it was not "in synch" with its historical moment, *The Ox-Bow Incident* became a precursor of many revisionist western films that would be produced in Hollywood after the end of the war.

The Gangster Film

Gangster films dealt with the contemporary urban environment – specifically, the criminal underbelly of big-city life. Like westerns, they focused on a violent, action-oriented character, but this figure exhibited antisocial attitudes which one might think would have been off-putting to most audience members. Yet they were not. Spectators demonstrated a fascination for tough guys who lived on the edge.

To audiences in the 1930s, the gangster figure represented the ultimate rebel. Unlike most citizens, he refused to accept Depression-imposed privations. Quick with a gun and unafraid to use it, he aggressively pursued power and wealth at a time when most Americans felt powerless and deprived.

Movie gangsters were ethnic, mainly Italian Americans and Irish Americans. When they found obstacles placed in their way because of their ethnicity, or for any number of other reasons, they kicked them aside, taking the shortcut to success. Their dream was, of course, commonplace; it had lured many immigrants to American shores in the first place. As expressed by Rico (Edward G. Robinson) in *Little Caesar* (Warner Bros., 1931), these young men were determined to "be somebody": wealthy, respected, powerful. However, they chose a more rapid, direct, unlawful path to this American Dream than the heroes of the popular Horatio Alger novels who represent their law-abiding counterparts. This decision is costly; most movie gangsters die violent deaths while still young men.

The gangster's home is the modern city, a mecca of fun and excitement and opportunity. But the metropolis is also figured in the films as a place where someone can lose his moral compass and, ultimately, his soul. Although the films contain politicians and police officers and law-abiding city dwellers, the gangster rules the city of these films, a world of nightclubs, taverns, plush apartments and businesses that mask the criminal's true underground activities. The protagonist is a voracious hedonist whose all-consuming desire for flashy, expensive clothes and jewelry, large, powerful automobiles and beautiful women drives him forward. One charts his rise to the top of the gangland hierarchy through his acquisition of these iconographic markers.

Real-world gangsters were a dangerous societal menace who threatened the very lives of all honest citizens, so why did moviegoers flock to their films? Some of their appeal certainly related to the mobsters' embrace of wealth and power which were sadly lacking in the lives of so many during the Depression. But the films also gained popularity because the screen gangster died or, in some instances, was incarcerated at the finale. The importance of this reassuring closure, a convention of the genre even before the Production Code Administration cracked down on it in 1934, should not be overlooked. It is doubtful that contemporary spectators would have been so enthusiastic about Hollywood gangsters if they had emerged triumphant at the fade-out. Viewers remained fascinated with these avatars of the dark side of the American Dream so long as they were able to leave movie theaters feeling that no one in the modern world really gets away with such outrageous disregard for the law.

Development

The gangster film existed at both the "A" and "B" levels. While more "B" productions than "A" productions were made, the genre was more balanced than the western. The genre became established during the silent period, which culminated with such successful and well-regarded examples as *Underworld* (Paramount, 1927) and *The Racket* (Caddo/Paramount, 1928). However, it quickly gained maturity and entered one of its most exciting periods once sound was possible. *Lights of New York* (Warner Bros., 1928), the first "all-talking picture," was a gangster film and a blockbuster hit. Soon enough, similar films would take advantage of the dynamic possibilities of sound to provide audiences with squealing tires, police sirens, machine gun blasts, rumbling explosions and, most importantly, the special urban dialogue of the characters. Such slang terms as "molls" and "mugs," "gats" and "heaters," and "taking someone for a ride" quickly became recognized elements of the American language.

Other factors contributed to the popularity of the gangster genre during the early years of the Depression. The continuation of prohibition (it would be abolished in 1933) caused the gangster, in his bootlegger incarnation, to take on a Robin Hood persona in the minds of liberal-minded filmgoers. If one were patronizing a bootlegger, it was difficult to view him as a hardened criminal or danger to society.

This was also the era when actual criminals, such as Al Capone, John Dillinger, "Baby Face" Nelson and "Pretty Boy" Floyd, became celebrities, their exploits chronicled in newpapers, magazines, radio programs and newsreels. Audiences eagerly awaited stories about the latest St. Valentine's Day massacre or the latest bank job pulled by Bonnie and Clyde or the "Ma" Barker gang. Film producers were, of course, paying attention. They modeled many of their on-screen scofflaws after the real-life law breakers.

Over 50 gangster films were produced between 1930 and 1933. Of these, the most influential were *Little Caesar*, *The Public Enemy*, and *Scarface*. Each made a star of its lead actor: Edward G. Robinson, James Cagney, Paul Muni. Each told essentially the same story: the rise and fall of the gangster figure. And each featured snappy dialogue, memorable male and female secondary characters, shocking violence and punchy sound design, all of which would be benchmarks of the genre for years to come. To a certain extent, future gangster pictures would be measured against these early successes.

Even before enforcement of the Production Code began in mid-1934, the gangster genre started to lose its hold on the audience. The constant criticism of reformers, the national shock over the kidnapping and subsequent death of the Lindbergh baby in 1932 which was initially blamed on underworld types, the end of Prohibition and the over-production of gangster pictures all contributed to the genre's decline. Clearly, however, the *coup de grâce* was delivered when Joseph Breen took charge of the Production Code Administration. Breen let it be known that sympathetic gangsters would no longer be tolerated. Realizing that spectators would be unlikely to patronize films featuring thoroughly repellent protagonists, the studio heads turned away from the genre.

In 1935, Warner Bros. found a way to inject new life into the form. Relegating the criminal to secondary status, the studio focused instead on the crime fighter who attacks or infiltrates a gang and brings the villains to justice. *G-Men* (1935) and *Bullets or Ballots* (1936) cast James Cagney and Edward G. Robinson in the main parts. They exhibited many of the same characteristics that had made them stand out in their earlier roles – toughness, cynicism, rebelliousness, a penchant for violence; in short, they were still gangsters, only now they were sporting badges and acting for the public good. In *G-Men*, Cagney joins the FBI to get even with gangsters who murdered an unarmed friend. But even though the film was quite violent and clearly violated the Production Code ("Revenge in modern times shall not be justified"), Breen let it go because the hero was on the right side of the law.

Other films of this type, such as *Special Agent* (Warner Bros., 1935), *Racket Busters* (Warner Bros., 1938), *Smashing the Rackets* (RKO, 1938) and *Smashing the Money Ring* (Warner Bros., 1939) also received a boost from the public's growing fascination with the achievements of high-profile law enforcement officials, particularly J. Edgar Hoover of the FBI and New York Special Prosecutor Thomas E. Dewey. In 1936, Dewey engineered the conviction of Lucky Luciano on 61 different criminal charges.

Dead End (Goldwyn/United Artists, 1937) ushered in a new strain of socially aware gangster pictures which wrestled with the question of how criminal behavior can be minimized in the United States. Drawing on contemporary social science research, *Dead End* dramatized the thesis that environmental factors are the principal cause of antisocial behavior, and advocated the eradication of poverty and slum conditions as the necessary antidote. *Dead End* and other similarly-themed pictures that followed in its wake, such as *Angels with Dirty Faces* (Warner Bros., 1938), *Crime School* (Warner Bros., 1938), *Mutiny in the Big House* (Monogram, 1939) and *Men of Boys Town* (MGM, 1941), also emphasized the failure of penal institutions and reform schools whose brutalizing conditions were much more likely to turn individuals into hardened criminals than regenerated citizens. (Figure 6.1)

Figure 6.1   Humphrey Bogart (*left*) and James Cagney play two gangsters in *Angels with Dirty Faces* (produced by Sam Bischoff for Warner Bros., 1938). Courtesy of the USC Cinema-Television Library.

Another group of these sociological gangster films depicted the problems of the ex-convict, an individual who has made mistakes but "paid his debt to society" and now wishes to live a normal existence. However, the stigma attached to the incarceration makes it impossible to find or hold a decent job, so he or she is pushed back in the direction of crime. *You Only Live Once* (Wanger/United Artists, 1937) and *You and Me* (Paramount, 1938), both directed by Fritz Lang, were exemplary films that dramatized the plight of the parolee, as did *Youth on Parole* (Republic, 1937) and *Invisible Stripes* (Warner Bros., 1939).

By the late 1930s, the Production Code Administration had eased its position, allowing sympathetic gangsters to once again appear on movie screens. Some of the best films of the pre-war years dealt, in nostalgic fashion, with the Prohibition Period and, ironically, its sober aftermath. The gangster protagonist is now split into good and bad variants with the positive figures presented as tragic anachronisms. In *The Roaring Twenties* (Warner Bros., 1939), James Cagney plays a man whose battle experiences in World War I and subsequent inability to land a decent job drive him into the underworld. Nonetheless, he retains his basic decency and, after passing through a rise and fall phase during the Prohibition years, commits a socially redeeming act before dying. The bad gangster killed by Cagney in *The Roaring Twenties* was played by Humphrey Bogart, who assumed the lead role two years later in *High Sierra* (Warner Bros., 1941), another nostalgic film about a man of honor and principle whose death, like Cagney's, signals the end of an era when a crook might still have a heart of gold.

Once the US became a participant in World War II, the genre went into an immediate decline. Of the limited assortment of gangster films produced during the war years, most presented the transformation of the criminal into a patriot, as a consequence of the contemporary crisis. *Mr. Lucky* (RKO, 1943) was a good example. In the narrative, con man Cary Grant sets up an evening of casino gambling to help war relief, fully intending to abscond with the proceeds. But the influence of a beautiful woman (Laraine Day) summons forth his latent patriotism and, at the climax, he turns his posh gambling ship into a vessel for the transport of medical supplies. Similar gangster reformations occur in *All Through the Night* (Warner Bros., 1942), *Lucky Jordan* (Paramount, 1942) and *Seven Miles from Alcatraz* (RKO, 1943).

The Adventure Film

Another heavily mythic genre, the adventure film chronicled the eternal battle between good and evil. It featured gentlemanly heroes and despotic villains, romance, exoticism, suspense and spectacle.

Unlike the more contained western and gangster genres, adventure was wide-ranging, encompassing stories that took place in a variety of historical periods and settings. Its heroes might be medieval knights or eighteenth-century pirates, Renaissance explorers or Victorian defenders of empire, European kings or charming soldiers of fortune. The adventure category also subsumed a number of related sub-genres including the African primitivism of the Tarzan films, exotic fantasies such as *The Thief of Bagdad* (Korda/United Artists, 1940) and pictures dealing with the ancient worlds of Greece and Rome and usually depicting the early stirrings of Christianity, such as *The Sign of the Cross* (Paramount, 1932) and *The Last Days of Pompeii* (RKO, 1935).

The elements that give the genre coherence were a remarkably consistent hero figure and a political mythology which provides the ideological foundation for most of the narratives. The adventure hero was crucial, an exceptional specimen of manhood in every sense. He had to be handsome, polished, athletic, intelligent, shrewd, witty, strong, charismatic, a born leader. These films were expensive to produce, but perhaps the main reason there are fewer examples of adventure than most other genres is that only a handful of actors had the requisite qualities to portray an adventure film hero. Errol Flynn and Tyrone Power were the most potent embodiments of this hero, with such performers as Clark Gable, Gary Cooper, Ronald Colman, Fredric March, Douglas Fairbanks Jr., Cary Grant and Louis Hayward leaving lesser marks on the genre.

Since romance was a near obligatory element, the principal female role also required an actress of special talents. Naturally, she had to be beautiful and elegant, but she, too, had to be smart, clever and brave – someone capable of becoming an active, rather than passive, participant in the hero's quest. These roles were filled by Olivia de Havilland, Madeleine Carroll, Maureen O'Hara, Loretta Young, Linda Darnell and others.

When one distills most of the adventure narratives to their essence, the political dimension becomes apparent. The proper relationship between those who govern and those who are governed is at the heart of the genre. The films often begin with an enlightened political system in peril . . . or already displaced by an unfair, tyrannical regime. The hero's function is to protect the just ruler or overthrow those who have usurped his position and then return him to power. The stakes are high, for the happiness and well-being of all citizens depend on his success.

One tellingly American aspect of these pictures involves their settings and social structures. They usually take place in Europe or the colonies of Europe where the divine right of kings and a clearly delineated class system still prevail. Yet, while recognizing the importance of royalty and social class and presenting audiences with a hero who is from the aristocracy, the filmmakers overlay these elements with an egalitarian, populist ideology. The good of the whole is of paramount importance, and the hero willingly joins others from lower social positions to fight for freedom, justice and the enlightened political leadership that will guarantee these values. The 1930s adventure film, produced against a backdrop of the growing power of belligerent totalitarian regimes in Europe and Asia, ritualistically reminded audiences of the dangers of arrogant despotic leaders and of the value of a government devoted to protecting the rights of every individual.

Development

The early sound era saw a decline in the production of adventure pictures. Partly, this resulted from the faltering career of the first great adventure film star, Douglas Fairbanks. No one stepped forward to carry on the vigorous tradition established by Fairbanks in such silent films as *Robin Hood* (Fairbanks/United Artists, 1922), *The Thief of Bagdad* (Fairbanks/United Artists, 1924) and *The Black Pirate* (Fairbanks/United Artists, 1926), and the early, primitive sound equipment also presented problems in a genre dependent on movement and action. Still, the major impediment was the Depression. Adventure films have always been expensive undertakings because of the large casts, enormous sets, elaborate costumes and expensive talent required. Considering the uncertain future of the movies in a financially ravaged world, the genre seemed too great a risk.

In 1934, with economic conditions beginning to brighten, the studios started to make moderately budgeted adventure films. MGM offered audiences *Treasure Island* with Wallace Beery; RKO, *The Lost Patrol* with Victor McLaglen; and Small/United Artists, *The Count of Monte Cristo* with Robert Donat. *Treasure Island* became a big hit (profit: $565,000) and the others were also successful, prompting all the studios to begin contemplating the production of similar films.

In 1935, two films cemented their resolve. *Mutiny on the Bounty* (MGM), starring Clark Gable and Charles Laughton, won the Best Picture Academy Award while a remake of the silent *Captain Blood* (Warner Bros.) introduced a new actor who would immediately become the Fairbanks of the 1930s: Errol Flynn. (Figure 6.2)

The next six years turned out to be perhaps the most active and successful period in the genre's sound history. Among the noteworthy productions: *Captains Courageous* (MGM, 1937), *The Crusades* (Paramount, 1935), *The Lives of a Bengal Lancer* (Paramount, 1935), *The Buccaneer* (Paramount, 1938), *Beau Geste* (Paramount, 1939), *The Prisoner of Zenda* (Selznick/United Artists, 1937), *The Adventures of Marco Polo* (Goldwyn/United Artists, 1938), *The Man in the Iron Mask* (Small/United Artists, 1939), *Captain Fury* (Roach/United Artists, 1939), *The Son of Monte Cristo* (Small/United Artists, 1941), *The Charge of the Light Brigade* (Warner Bros., 1936), *The Adventures of Robin Hood* (Warner Bros., 1938), *The Sea Hawk* (Warner Bros., 1940), *Gunga Din* (RKO, 1939), *Under Two Flags* (Twentieth Century-Fox, 1936), *Kidnapped* (Twentieth Century-Fox, 1938), *The Mark of Zorro* (Twentieth Century-Fox, 1940), *The Black Swan* (Twentieth Century-Fox, 1942) and *Son of Fury* (Twentieth Century-Fox, 1942).

The adventure film was a rare commodity during America's World War II period. The necessity of fending off villains who were frighteningly real undoubtedly made such historical epics seem frivolous and irrelevant to

Figure 6.2 Olivia de Havilland and Errol Flynn in the adventure film *Captain Blood* (produced by Harry Joe Brown and Gordon Hollingshead for Warner Bros., 1935). Courtesy of the USC Cinema-Television Library.

war-fixated audiences. However, adventure sagas made toward the end of the conflict, such as *The Spanish Main* (RKO, 1945), pointed the way toward a new, fulsome chapter in the genre's history which began almost immediately in the post-war period. Like *The Spanish Main* and a few other earlier examples (*The Adventures of Robin Hood*, *The Black Swan*), most of the late 1940s and 50s films would be made in color which had been deemed stylistically fitting for these exuberant, larger-than-life entertainments.

The Horror Film

Like the gangster film, the horror genre was stimulated by the possibilities of the new sound medium. Many horror pictures had been made during the silent era and one of its biggest stars, Lon Chaney, had become identified with the genre, but the early 1930s still represent perhaps the most fertile and important

period in its history. While sound was not the only reason for the creative out-
burst, its introduction made it possible for audiences to hear the monster's
grunts and the victim's screams, plus howling winds, claps of thunder, the electrical buzzing and chemical bubbling of the scientist's laboratory and many
other creative effects that added to the gothic atmosphere of the films.

As mentioned earlier in the chapter, horror films were primarily "B" films
without stars. However, their sensationalistic elements offered special exploitation opportunities which occasionally enabled studio distribution departments
to sell them as "As." A few horror productions were unquestionable "As," such
as the two versions of *Dr. Jekyll and Mr. Hyde* (Paramount, 1932, and MGM,
1941), *King Kong* (RKO, 1933) and *The Phantom of the Opera* (Universal,
1943), but these were clear exceptions to the standard approach.

During the 1930s, the genre emphasized foreign (usually European) settings and characters. Such films as *Dracula* (Universal, 1931), *Frankenstein*
(Universal, 1931), *The Old Dark House* (Universal, 1932), *The Murders in the
Rue Morgue* (Universal, 1932), *The Invisible Man* (Universal, 1933), *The Black
Cat* (Universal, 1934), *The Werewolf of London* (Universal, 1935) *Mystery of
the Wax Museum* (Warner Bros., 1933) and *Dr. Jekyll and Mr. Hyde* all took
place in Europe and, for the most part, featured European-born actors and
behind-the-camera talent from the Continent. Evidently, American audiences were more willing to accept tales of the grotesque and the fantastic if
they were rooted in foreign legends and superstitions rather than the dynamic
new world of America. By the 1940s, however, the United States had become
an equally appropriate setting, as evidenced by *Cat People* (RKO, 1943), *The
Leopard Man* (RKO, 1943), *The Seventh Victim* (RKO, 1943), plus three sequels
to *The Mummy* (Universal, 1932) – *The Mummy's Tomb* (Universal, 1942), *The
Mummy's Ghost* (Universal, 1944) and *The Mummy's Curse* (Universal, 1945)
– in which the creature terrorizes inhabitants of the southern US.

Horror film narratives worked their way through a group of psychological
myths based upon universal human fears. These included fear of death, fear of
science, fear of losing control and fear of rejection.

Death in the films is personified by the various monsters – vampires, mum-
mies, Frankenstein's creation – who are not only bringers of death but are
also dead themselves in the sense that they should be dead (the vampire) or
have been unnaturally resurrected from the dead (mummy, Frankenstein's
creature). At the same time, these movies suggest that death is not something
ghastly, not something to be feared, but rather a condition to be welcomed at
the right time. As Dracula says in the 1931 film, "There are far worse things
awaiting man than death."

The scientist whose quest for knowledge reaches a catastrophic conclusion is perhaps the most ubiquitous figure in the horror films of the period. The fear of science upon which this character is based may result from a number of factors, including the theories of Charles Darwin and Sigmund Freud, which challenged cherished, traditional beliefs about the human condition, and the creation of powerful killing machines whose capacity for wholesale slaughter was amply demonstrated during World War I. *Frankenstein, The Mummy, The Invisible Man* and *Dr. Jekyll and Mr. Hyde*, among many others, feature Faustian scientists whose god-complex propels them into areas of knowledge that are figured as beyond human comprehension, particularly the creation of life and dispensing of death. The scientist's experiments disrupt the natural order and chaos and destruction, generally personified by some grotesque monster, result. Playing this "mad scientist" character in multiple films were such actors as Bela Lugosi, Boris Karloff, John Carradine and, most especially, Lionel Atwill.

The fear of rejection is dramatized by the interplay between the "abnormal" characters in these films and members of society. The thing that makes the monster monstrous and motivates his mayhem is his rejection by others; he is shunned, tormented, treated as a "thing" rather than a human being. It is the hunchback's abuse of Dr. Frankenstein's creation that angers him and leads to his murderous spree. In *Bride of Frankenstein* (Universal, 1935) where the monster can speak, he tells his blind friend, "Friends, good; alone, bad." Likewise, the anguish of the werewolf and Dr. Jekyll results, at least partially, from the realization that they can never lead normal lives again, never establish natural relationships with their fellow humans. *Freaks* (MGM, 1932) pushes this theme to its ultimate conclusion. Here, the true evil is represented by the physically attractive "normal" people who take brutal advantage of the circus freaks until these sad, vulnerable people finally turn upon them and exact their revenge. In many horror pictures, the filmmakers are careful to establish a modicum of identification between audience members and the abnormal beings, thereby making one more sympathetic to their hopelessly alienated conditions.

Dr. Jekyll and the werewolf, as well as the invisible man, also lose control over their minds and their actions. And the vampire and the mummy (at least in the 1932 Universal prototype film) can impose their wills upon their victims, causing these mortals to lose the wherewithal to resist. Dracula, for example, has the power to transform pure, virginal young women into wanton sexual predators. Thus, horror films also recognize and dramatize the possibility that humans can "snap," i.e., lose control and become aliens capable of committing heinous acts, sometimes directed at their own family and friends.

This fear of losing control is generally "explained" in the films as the result of ego-besotted arrogance or the devil's work, thus providing a measure of reassurance to all those people in the dark. Obviously, it couldn't happen to them . . . could it?

Development

The prominence of the genre was given a significant boost by the excitingly fertile period between 1931 and 1935. Universal quickly established itself as the dominant house of horror, thanks to *Dracula*, *Frankenstein*, *The Mummy* and *The Invisible Man*, plus *The Old Dark House*, *The Murders in the Rue Morgue*, *The Black Cat* and *The Raven* (1935). Most of the other studios were also active. MGM offered *Freaks*, *Kongo* (1932), *The Mask of Fu Manchu* (1932), *Mark of the Vampire* (1935) and *Mad Love* (1935); RKO, *The Most Dangerous Game* (1932), *The Monkey's Paw* (1933), *King Kong* and *The Son of Kong* (1933); Warner Bros., *Doctor X* (1932) and *Mystery of the Wax Museum*; Paramount, *Dr. Jekyll and Mr. Hyde*, *The Island of Lost Souls* (1932), *Murders in the Zoo* (1933) and *Supernatural* (1933); Fox, *Chandu the Magician* (1932) and *Almost Married* (1932); Columbia, *Night of Terror* (1933) and *The Black Room* (1935); United Artists, *White Zombie* (1932).

Despite Universal' s initial attempts at sequels, *Bride of Frankenstein* and *Dracula's Daughter* (1936), the horror film entered a dormant phase in 1936 which lasted for two years. A new regime at Universal was skeptical of horror films, and none of the other studios seemed interested either. In addition, the British aversion to the genre, as manifested by the special "H" category which their censorship authorities created in 1937 (preventing young people under the age of 16 from attending), may also have discouraged production, given the importance of the country as a foreign market for American films.

In 1939, however, the genre reawakened. Universal produced *Son of Frankenstein*, then followed it with a giddy array of sequels to its earlier classics. Among these productions were *The Invisible Man Returns* (1940), *The Invisible Agent* (1942) and *The Invisible Man's Revenge* (1944); *The Mummy's Hand* (1940), *The Mummy's Tomb*, *The Mummy's Ghost* and *The Mummy's Curse*; *The Ghost of Frankenstein* (1942) and *House of Frankenstein* (1944); *Son of Dracula* (1943) and *House of Dracula* (1945). The studio also added a new monster to its menagerie in *The Wolf Man* (1941). It had tried out the werewolf in the mid-1930s (*The Werewolf of London*) without notable success, but *The Wolf Man*, starring the dominant horror film actor of the decade, Lon Chaney Jr., captured the audience's interest and spawned its own sequel, *Frankenstein Meets*

Figure 6.3 Basil Rathbone is amazed to find several bullets lodged in the still-beating heart of his father's monstrous creation (Boris Karloff) in *Son of Frankenstein* (produced by Rowland V. Lee for Universal, 1939). Courtesy of the USC Cinema-Television Library.

the Wolf Man (1943). The wolf man also took part in Universal's all-inclusive monster roundups, *House of Frankenstein* and *House of Dracula*. (Figure 6.3)

The late 1930s also featured a new genre hybrid, the horror-comedy. There had been injections of macabre humor in earlier films, particularly the James Whale-directed *The Old Dark House*, *The Invisible Man* and *Bride of Frankenstein*. Taking advantage of the fact that audiences were now totally familiar with the genre's conventions, various comedians launched a full-fledged assault on the horror movie, producing spoofs that were designed to elicit an equal measure of chills and laughs. The Paramount remake of *The Cat and the Canary* (1939), starring Bob Hope, was so successful that the studio quickly brought the comedian back in the similarly-themed *The Ghost Breakers* (1940). Other examples included the Ritz Brothers in *The Gorilla* (Twentieth Century-Fox, 1939), John Barrymore in *Invisible Woman* (Universal, 1940), Bela Lugosi and the East End Kids in *Spooks Run Wild* (Monogram, 1941), Wayne Morris and Brenda Marshall in *The Smiling Ghost* (Warner Bros., 1941), Arthur Lake in *The Ghost That Walks Alone* (Columbia, 1944), Ole Olsen and Chic Johnson in *The Ghost Catchers* (Universal, 1944) and Alan Carney and Wally Brown in *Zombies on Broadway* (RKO, 1945).

World War II had less of an impact on the horror film than on most other genres. Many continued to be made, with a small number injecting genre ingredients into the contemporary crisis. *The Invisible Agent*, for example, offered Jon Hall as a descendant of the original invisible man. Utilizing the magic formula, he disappears in Germany and eventually disrupts the plans of both the Nazis and Japanese (embodied by Cedric Hardwicke and Peter Lorre, respectively). Other absurd films that attempted a similar merger of elements included *Black Dragons* (Monogram, 1942) which featured Bela Lugosi performing plastic surgery on Japanese saboteurs to make them appear to be Caucasian Americans; *The Gorilla Man* (Warner Bros., 1943) in which Nazi agents attempt to discredit British operative John Loder by having him declared insane; *Revenge of the Zombies* (Monogram, 1943) wherein John Carradine creates zombies to provide the Third Reich with an invincible army; and *The Return of the Vampire* (Columbia, 1944) in which a German bomb blasts vampire Bela Lugosi out of his London grave, prompting two air raid wardens to extract the stake from his heart with predictable consequences.

Most of the horror productions made during the war years did not reference the conflict. The period exhibited a strange fascination with apes; these films generally featured mad scientists fiddling around with evolutionary theory (e.g., *Captive Wild Woman*, Universal, 1943, and its two sequels, *Jungle Woman*, 1944, and *Jungle Captive*, 1945), or transplanting a human brain into a gorilla's body (*The Monster and the Girl*, Paramount, 1941).

The most significant genre development of the decade came from RKO where producer Val Lewton launched a series of literate, atmospheric, psychologically complex horror pictures. Featuring more interesting and developed characters than was typical in the genre, the Lewton pictures probed the world of human emotion for their effects, eschewing traditional monsters. *Cat People, I Walked with a Zombie* (1943), *The Seventh Victim, The Ghost Ship* (1943), *The Curse of the Cat People* (1944), *The Body Snatcher* (1945), *Isle of the Dead* (1945) and *Bedlam* (1946) prospected for evil deep within the human psyche and, through their restrained and often ambiguous approach, invited audience members to conjure up horrific effects in their own minds rather than visualizing the scary moments for them in the usual fashion. Lewton and his collaborators pointed the genre in the direction of the horror of personality, a strain that would dominate the form after Alfred Hitchcock made the landmark *Psycho* (Paramount, 1960).

The Detective Film

If the horror genre emphasized the potential dangers of science, the detective film suggested its positive qualities. These films pivoted around the exploits of an intelligent, shrewd, calculating protagonist who uses deductive reasoning to unmask the perpetrator(s) of a crime, usually a murder or series of murders. Although not a chemist, physicist or other practitioner of the hard sciences, the detective employs the scientific method to arrive at the truth of the situation.

Like horror films, detective pictures showcased the human capacity for evil and its ability to unleash chaos on the world, but they provided a strong dose of reassurance via the detective figure, a moral redeemer who prevents the evil from triumphing. The workings of his/her logical mind frustrate and unmask the forces of greed, lust, violence and sundry other sins which threaten the well-being of civilization itself. The efforts of the detective ultimately return the world to a state of safety, stability and equilibrium.

Detective films are structured as puzzles which the audience members, as well as the characters, are invited to piece together. A crime (or series of crimes) is committed which threatens the social order, whereupon the principal questions become "whodunit?" and "why?" The hero ultimately puts the pieces together, answering the key questions by sorting through a confusing thicket of clues and sizing up a daunting number of suspects. In addition, while "on the case" the detective often finds himself, and/or those to whom he has a powerful personal attachment, in danger and must respond to the threats in active, forceful fashion.

The genre's stock characters generally include a sidekick, in attendance to provide comic relief and to foreground the brilliance of the detective; the authority figures – typically members of the local police – whose bumbling efforts to solve the crime are ineffectual and often interfere with the hero's more dynamic approach; one or more beautiful women who provide romantic temptation for the detective and are either suspects in the case or potential victims of the malefactor; and the villain, a clever individual of unbridled ruthlessness, whose determination and intelligence are nearly equal to the hero's.

Like comedy and the western, this genre was extremely prolific. All the studios made detective films, and there were both "A" and "B" examples. Most were "B" pictures, parts of series built around a well-known detective figure. Many of the detective characters (e.g., Bulldog Drummond, Ellery Queen, Perry Mason) first appeared in popular fiction, then took on new lives in the movies and on radio.

Several performers became linked to the genre. Basil Rathbone, a fine actor who played an assortment of parts in both "A" and "B" pictures, is best remembered for portraying Sherlock Holmes in a series that began at Twentieth Century-Fox in the 1930s, then moved to Universal in the 40s. Warren William was cast in important roles in such films as *Gold Diggers of 1933* (Warner Bros., 1933), *Imitation of Life* (Universal, 1934) and *Cleopatra* (Paramount, 1934), then settled into a detective persona and never quite pulled free of it. He was Philo Vance for Warner Bros. in 1934 and Paramount in 1939, Perry Mason for Warner Bros. from 1934 to 1936 and the Lone Wolf for Columbia from 1939 to 1943. Warner Oland and Sidney Toler, two Caucasian actors, each played Charlie Chan more than 15 times in a series that originated at Fox in the early 1930s and ended up at Monogram in the post-war period. Other actors who became linked in the public's mind with their sleuthing characters were Peter Lorre with Mr. Moto (Twentieth Century-Fox, 1937–39); Edna May Oliver with Hildegarde Withers (RKO, 1932–34); William Powell with Nick Charles, "The Thin Man" (MGM, 1934–47); George Sanders with Simon Templar, "The Saint" (RKO, 1939–41); Tom Conway with Gay Lawrence, "The Falcon" (RKO, 1942–47); and Chester Morris with Boston Blackie (Columbia, 1941–49).

The structure of the detective film derived from a tradition of detective literature stretching back to Edgar Allan Poe. It began with a mysterious crime and proceeded through a series of suspenseful adventures to the surprising solution to the crime. The detective, who arrives at the solution, is always a person of superior moral and intellectual stature, but he or she may come from a variety of nationalities, backgrounds and social classes. On one end of the spectrum were the polished, gentlemanly Englishmen, such as Sherlock Holmes (*The Adventures of Sherlock Holmes*, Twentieth Century-Fox, 1939), Lord Peter Wimsey (*Haunted Honeymoon*, MGM, 1940) and Simon Templar (*The Saint Strikes Back*, RKO, 1939). At the other extreme were two-fisted American tough guys, often suspected of crimes themselves and closer in character to the criminals they unmask than the debonair Britons mentioned above: Michael Shayne (*Michael Shayne, Private Detective*, Twentieth Century-Fox, 1940) and Boston Blackie (*Meet Boston Blackie*, Columbia, 1941). Between these two poles, one could find the wily, aphorism-spouting Charlie Chan (*Charlie Chan Carries On*, Fox, 1931), the polite but purposely vague Mr. Moto (*Think Fast, Mr. Moto*, Twentieth Century-Fox, 1937), the shy orchid-cultivator Nero Wolfe (*Meet Nero Wolfe*, Columbia, 1936) and the suave reformed criminals Arsene Lupin (*Arsene Lupin*, MGM, 1932) and the Lone Wolf (*The Lone Wolf Returns*, Columbia, 1936). Also worthy of mention were a trio of female detectives, for whom the solving of mysteries was a hobby rather than a vocation: schoolteacher Hildegarde Withers (*The Penguin Pool Murder*, RKO, 1932), schoolgirl Nancy Drew (*Nancy Drew, Detective*, Warner Bros., 1938) and newspaper reporter Torchy Blane (*Torchy Blane in Chinatown*, Warner Bros., 1939).

Development

Like most of the other genres, the detective film was a well-established commercial form when sound arrived. *Sherlock Holmes Baffled* (Biograph, 1900) is believed to be the first example, and Boston Blackie, Bulldog Drummond, Charlie Chan, Nick Carter, the Lone Wolf and Philo Vance were all introduced in silent films before becoming even more recognizable figures during the sound era. Sound added considerably to the impact of the pictures; the right sound effects and musical underscoring could magnify the thriller elements, and dialogue, which the best writers of detective scripts orchestrated carefully, helped to make the detective hero seem both omniscient and a masterful manipulator of language.

The most successful private eye series of the period was launched by *The Thin Man* (MGM, 1934). Based on a Dashiell Hammett novel, the film starred William Powell and Myrna Loy as Nick and Nora Charles, a sprightly pair of married sophisticates whose screwball relationship complemented the smooth ratiocination of Nick the sleuth. MGM wisely spaced out the sequels, offering one each in 1936, 1939, 1941, 1944 and 1947. These films' marriage of murder mystery and romantic mirth resonated throughout Hollywood, provoking such baldfaced imitations as *Star of Midnight* (1935) and *The Ex-Mrs. Bradford* (1936), both starring William Powell, from RKO; *Fast Company* (1938), *Fast and Loose* (1939) and *Fast and Furious* (1939) from the "Thin Man" studio, MGM; and *There's Always a Woman* (1938), *There's That Woman Again* (1939) and *A Night to Remember* (1943) from Columbia.

The detective genre was strongly impacted by the entry of the US into the war. Overnight, the protagonist's mission switched from fingering murderers to foiling the diabolical schemes of the nation's enemies. Whether spies, saboteurs, smugglers or war bond thieves, the minions of the Axis powers were no match for Sherlock Holmes in *Sherlock Holmes and the Voice of Terror* (Universal, 1942), the Falcon in *The Falcon's Brother* (RKO, 1942), Michael Shayne in *Blue, White and Perfect* (Twentieth Century-Fox, 1941), the Lone Wolf in *Counter-Espionage* (Columbia, 1942), Ellery Queen in *Enemy Agents Meet Ellery Queen* (Columbia, 1942) and Charlie Chan in *Charlie Chan in the Secret Service* (Monogram, 1944). Growing anti-Japanese sentiment had a good deal to do with the cancellation of the "Mr. Moto" series in 1939. By 1942, Warner Bros. would poke fun at rival Twentieth Century-Fox for producing the series in the first place. In the Warner film *Air Force* (1943), the bomber crew adopts a canine mascot who "hates Japs" and barks furiously whenever the name "Mr. Moto" is mentioned.

While formula detective films would continue to be made throughout the 1940s, a film released in 1941 heralded a new direction the genre would take in the post-war period. Based on another Dashiell Hammett novel, *The Maltese Falcon* had been made twice before with indifferent results by Warner Bros. This time, however, the film was a hit, boosting the status of its lead actor, Humphrey Bogart, and its first-time director, John Huston.

The Maltese Falcon had the trappings of a standard murder mystery. Near the beginning, someone knocks off protagonist Sam Spade's partner, Miles Archer. Spade uses his smarts and experience to deduce the murderer and turn her over to the authorities. But Spade's victory is at best equivocal, since he didn't really like his partner in the first place and has fallen in love with the culprit, Bridget O'Shaughnessy (Mary Astor). The audience's uneasy realization that Spade's accomplishments have not set the world back on an orderly course is compounded by the escapades of a group of ruthless cutthroats and psychotics determined to possess the falcon, a bejeweled statue of enormous value. In *The Maltese Falcon*, one is left with the feeling that greed, violence and treachery are the way of the world and little can be done to change things.

Spade, himself, is not untainted. He has been having an affair with his partner's wife whom he coldly rejects after Archer's death, and he makes sure that he emerges from the "black bird" caper unscathed and with a tidy sum of money in his pocket. Still, he is the solitary voice of professionalism and existential morality in this nest of vipers.

The evolution of the detective into a hard-boiled cynic begun in *The Maltese Falcon* would be abetted by a growing fascination with the film noir style of the 1940s (see chapter 5). This style visually communicated the danger, duplicity, corruption and fatalism of the new world of the detective. *Murder, My Sweet* (RKO, 1944) also represented a harbinger of things to come. Unlike John Huston, who presented *The Maltese Falcon* narrative in rather traditional stylistic terms, director Edward Dmytryk employed a variety of expressionistic camera and lighting effects to dramatize the descent of private eye Philip Marlowe (Dick Powell) into a murky netherworld of malignant humanity. The disorientation an audience feels as it watches the labyrinthine story unfold, then draw to its abrupt, uneasy conclusion, is altogether different from the standard visual experience and clean, orderly solutions offered by most previous detective pictures. The puzzle has been solved, but the pieces don't fit neatly together and the vision of life they depict is quite disturbing.

The War Film

This genre depicted members of the military waging war in the twentieth century. It was especially popular during the World War II years, providing audiences with some sense of what it was like for American soldiers to be swept up in modern technological combat. The genre was closely related to other types of films that focused on men and women in uniform, such as comedies, love stories and musicals, and often mixed elements from them into its battlefield tales.

War films usually fell into one of two broad categories: the pacifistic indictment of war, or the war film of glory and adventure. Most of the 1930s films, reactions to the disillusionment of World War I and to contemporary isolationist sentiments, were examples of the first category. They emphasized the futility, waste and frightful carnage of modern, mechanized warfare. However, as the decade drew on and it became probable that there would be more global hostilities, the emphasis changed. First came a series of preparedness films which glamorized the image of the man in uniform and were effective recruiting tools for the different branches of the military. Next, the studios made a few pictures that reminded audiences of the importance of fighting and defeating Germany in the first global conflict; these swept aside any lingering pacifist sentiments in favor of the heroic possibilities of "doing one's duty." After Pearl Harbor, the studios embraced the genre enthusiastically, pouring considerable resources into the making of propagandistic combat films.

Filmmakers who labored on war films in the early 1940s faced several obstacles. Many studio employees, including such major stars as James Stewart, Clark Gable, Tyrone Power and Robert Montgomery, went into the service, reducing the available talent pool for these large-scale undertakings. And, of course, the war refused to move ahead in an orderly, predictable fashion, forcing writers either to celebrate battles of the recent past or set their stories in a vague time and place that would not be rendered anachronistic by the course of future events. On the positive side, the US government recognized the unifying value of such films and cooperated with the studios in their making. They provided advisors and sometimes loaned hardware and even military personnel to the studios.

These films represent an important vehicle for understanding the American

mindset during the war years, especially in the ways they attempted to rear-
range some of the basic tenets of Hollywood storytelling. For example, a
concerted effort was made to displace the American love of individualism by
emphasizing that the individual in wartime is a menace to an all-out effort
which must be based on conformity, coordination and team performance. The
conversion of the lone wolf into a productive, functioning member of a successful unit is a recurring plot motif in several films, including *Flying Tigers*
(Republic, 1942), *Air Force* and *A Guy Named Joe* (MGM, 1943). Still, individualism dies hard on the American screen, and some of the films featured
individualistic feats of derring-do which would have been altogether familiar
to fans of westerns, adventure pictures and classical detective stories. In *Crash
Dive* (Twentieth Century-Fox, 1943), Tyrone Power, Dana Andrews and James
Gleason each took full advantage of their opportunities for singular heroics.

Most World War II military films centered on small groups of fighting men
– infantry platoons, tank crews, flying groups, submariners – who demonstrate
what can be achieved through collective action. These groups were calculatedly
diverse; they incorporated rich and poor, urban and rural, educated and illit-
erate, experienced and innocent. The men hailed from various sections of the
nation and brought different sets of ethnic roots with them. Polish Americans
fought beside Mexican Americans, Greek Americans, Swedish Americans,
Russian Americans, Native Americans. Occasionally, African Americans
were part of the team, though the films reflected the segregated nature of most
segments of the military at this time. Even German Americans and Italian
Americans were offered opportunities to recuperate their respective ancestries,
though Japanese Americans were absent from the proceedings. The abilities
of these very different men to rise above any perceived prejudices and bond
together, forming a fearsome military team, offered an emphatic rejoinder to
the Nazi belief that only Teutonic "supermen" were strong and smart and pure
enough to rule the world.

The war movies also attempted to redefine male star images. Though such
unquestionable stars as Robert Taylor, John Wayne and Errol Flynn appeared
regularly, they were required to repress and deglamorize their star personas. The characters they portrayed were generally strong but quiet leaders,
important to the group effort but lacking the charisma they radiate in most
of their other genre roles. Some of the genre efforts (*Wake Island*, Paramount,
1942; *Air Force*; *Guadalcanal Diary*, Twentieth Century-Fox, 1943) eschewed
stars altogether, placing additional emphasis on the importance of every
member of the team.

Though the films valorized the group rather than the individual and attempted to tone down the centrality of the star, they were hardly realistic depictions of the actual fighting. Formally repudiating the messages inherent in pre-war pacifist films, most of the World War II pictures glorified duty, sacrifice, courage and heroism. Over and again, they emphasized the importance of victory; otherwise, future Americans would surely inhabit a world in which freedom, justice, opportunity and other cherished tenets of "Americanism" would have no meaning.

The propaganda was reinforced by the depiction of the enemy. In truth, the Japanese and German armies were formidable opponents, but in the movies their soldiers were usually depicted as arrogant, stupid and incompetent. Often faceless foes, they were easily overcome by the better-trained, better-equipped, better-led Americans. Even when US troops lost a battle, as in *Bataan* (MGM, 1943) or *Wake Island*, the enemy victory would require the deaths of many more of their soldiers than Americans.

The war films of the era provided a measure of pride and reassurance for those actually engaged in the hostilities, as well as those on the home front. The real soldiers, who often viewed these films in 16 mm prints not far from the action, recognized that they bore little relationship to the actual fighting. Yet studies revealed that most enjoyed the fantasy and approved of the Hollywood approach.

Development

The evolution of the genre was given an expected boost by sound, which added the noise of technological warfare to plot patterns already well-established in silent films. *All Quiet on the Western Front* (Universal, 1930) was quickly acknowledged as the most famous and important of early sound efforts. Based on a novel by Erich Maria Remarque, it depicted World War I from the German point of view. The film documented the lives of several young men, their imaginations fired by visions of adventure, glory and patriotism, who proceed from the safety of their schoolrooms to the slaughter of the killing fields. The indictment of war in *All Quiet* was arguably the most forceful that had ever been seen on the screen, but its sentiments were neither fresh nor unusual. Rather, they were in keeping with the genre's dominant ideological position, a position that had been well-established since the early 1920s.

Even the aviation epics that comprised the dominant strain of the war film in the early 1930s, following the success of *Wings* (Paramount, 1927), adopted an anti-war stance, albeit compromised by an emphasis on the camaraderie of the flyers and the individual heroics of daredevil pilots, locked in gladiatorial battles far above the earth. *The Dawn Patrol* (Warner Bros., 1930) was the best of these efforts, which also included the spectacular and very expensive *Hell's Angels* (Caddo/United Artists, 1930), the depressing *The Last Flight* (Warner Bros., 1931) and the tragic *The Eagle and the Hawk* (Paramount, 1933). Among the notable earthbound versions of the pacifist manifesto were *The Case of Sergeant Grischa* (RKO, 1930), *The Man I Killed* (aka *Broken Lullaby*, Paramount, 1932) and *A Farewell to Arms* (Paramount, 1932).

Few war films were produced during the middle years of the Depression. When they returned in the later 1930s, the examples often seem awkward attempts to reposition the genre. While not fully committed to an abandonment of the "war is hell" thesis, these films offered a more positive depiction of the experience in order to prepare Americans for possible remobilization. *The Road to Glory* (Twentieth Century-Fox, 1936) showed some of the horrific aspects of war, but also preached the importance of nationalism, a concept that had been witheringly denounced in *All Quiet*. Likewise, the remake of *The Dawn Patrol* (Warner Bros., 1938) paid lip service to the "slaughterhouse" emphasis of the original, but placed more emphasis on the adventurous and heroic possibilities of the situation. Among the other films that began to erase *All Quiet* from the minds of moviegoers were *Sea Devils* (RKO, 1937), *Submarine D-1* (Warner Bros., 1937), *Submarine Patrol* (Twentieth Century-Fox, 1938), *Men with Wings* (Paramount, 1938), *The Real Glory* (Goldwyn/United Artists, 1939), plus a number of military-themed comedies, dramas and musicals. *Hold 'Em, Navy!* (Paramount, 1937), *Give Me a Sailor* (Paramount, 1938), *Pride of the Marines* (Columbia, 1936), *Devil's Playground* (Columbia, 1937), *Coast Guard* (Columbia, 1939), *The Duke of West Point* (Small/United Artists, 1938), *The Singing Marine* (Warner Bros., 1937), *Wings of the Navy* (Warner Bros., 1939), *Navy Blue and Gold* (MGM, 1937) and *Come On, Leathernecks* (Republic, 1938) glamorized military life and served to prepare spectators for another time period when men and women in uniform would be the most important members of American society.

In the early 1940s, Warner Bros. took a leadership position, making two unapologetic pro-war pictures. Although set in World War I, the films were aimed at isolationists, strongly suggesting that it was time for them to change their attitudes. Both were conversion narratives. *The Fighting 69th* (1940) featured James Cagney as a man who neither appreciates the achievements of the storied division of the title nor is able to stand up to the pressures and terrors of the battlefield. At the end, he finds his courage and sacrifices his life for the cause, becoming one more example of the bravery exemplified by the "Fighting 69th." Even more important was *Sergeant York* (1941), a biography of a World War I hero who, at first, refused to bear arms because of his religious convictions.

Eventually Alvin York (Gary Cooper) came to believe that war is a necessary evil and, drawing upon skills developed in the hills of Tennessee, killed many enemy soldiers and took a whole battalion of Germans prisoner. This film was an enormous popular success, generating almost $7 million in film rentals (more than double the take of any other Warner picture during the 1941–42 release year). The popularity of *Sergeant York* suggests that even though public opinion polls showed the American people still committed to an isolationist position, most understood the country could not stay out of the world fray much longer and were preparing themselves psychologically for the inevitable. Other films that aided the readiness project were *A Yank in the RAF* (Twentieth Century-Fox, 1941), *I Wanted Wings* (Paramount, 1941), *Flight Command* (MGM, 1941) and *International Squadron* (Warner Bros., 1941).

As mentioned earlier, the war film became a high priority after the US became a participant. Films were made glorifying every branch of the service, plus the contributions of the Merchant Marine (*Action in the North Atlantic*, Warner Bros., 1943), construction engineers (*The Fighting Seabees*, Republic, 1944) military nurses (*Parachute Nurse*, Columbia, 1942; *So Proudly We Hail*, Paramount, 1943; *Cry Havoc*, MGM, 1943) and female pilots ferrying military aircraft overseas (*Ladies Courageous*, Universal, 1944). A few, such as *Wake Island* and *Guadalcanal Diary*, retained some semblance of realism, but most were wish-fulfillment propaganda. *Desperate Journey* (Warner Bros., 1942), *Sahara* (Columbia, 1943), *Crash Dive*, *A Guy Named Joe* and *Mr. Winkle Goes to War* (Columbia, 1944) were typical examples. Each featured American heroic achievements of the most amazing sort. In retrospect, these films seem about as believable as contemporaneous efforts that featured the invisible man (*The Invisible Agent*), Tarzan (*Tarzan Triumphs*, Principal Artists/RKO, 1943) and a dog (*Son of Lassie*, MGM, 1945) pummeling the country's enemies.

Only when Allied victory was no longer in doubt would a more honest presentation of modern warfare and some sense of its madness reappear in the genre. *The Story of G.I. Joe* (Lester Cowan/United Artists, 1945), *They Were Expendable* (MGM, 1945) and *A Walk in the Sun* (Twentieth Century-Fox, 1945) provided audiences with a more accurate portrait of men at war, battling its fatigue, pressures, absurdities, dirty business, even its boredom and psychological trauma. These films continued to celebrate the strength and resilience of the fighting forces and, ironically, by grounding their narratives in a more realistic combat environment, made the men's achievements seem even more extraordinary.

Comedy

Hollywood was rife with comedies during the Classical Period. Studio executives recognized the appeal of these amusing entertainments and produced more examples of the form than of any other genre. In essence, comedy was a "super-genre" with a family of sub-forms. Each studio made comedies, though some specialized in these films (Paramount, MGM, Columbia) while others made an effort but were less successful (Warner Bros., Twentieth Century-Fox).

Each company signed up actors who were particularly adept comedians. Remembering that these individuals might not remain with one organization throughout the Classical Period, the following listing is indicative: MGM (Jimmy Durante, Buster Keaton, Marie Dressler, Wallace Beery, Marion Davies, Jean Harlow, Frank Morgan, Mickey Rooney, Robert Benchley, Ann Sothern, Red Skelton), Paramount (Mae West, Cary Grant, Carole Lombard, the Marx Brothers, Claudette Colbert, George Burns and Gracie Allen, Jack Benny, Bob Hope, Fred MacMurray, Jack Oakie, Fred Allen, Paulette Goddard, Barbara Stanwyck, Joel McCrea), Warner Bros. (Joe E. Brown, Frank McHugh, Aline MacMahon, Joan Blondell, Allen Jenkins, Hugh Herbert), Twentieth Century-Fox (Will Rogers, the Ritz Brothers, Don Ameche, Slim Summerville, Jed Prouty, Spring Byington, Jack Haley, Arthur Treacher), RKO (Bert Wheeler and Robert Woolsey, Edgar Kennedy, Ginger Rogers, Lucille Ball, Joe Penner, Lupe Vélez, Guy Kibbee, Harold Peary, Wally Brown and Alan Carney), Columbia (Jean Arthur, Rosalind Russell, Ralph Bellamy, Melvyn Douglas, Walter Connolly, Arthur Lake, Penny Singleton, the Three Stooges), Universal (Bud Abbott and Lou Costello, W.C. Fields, Margaret Sullavan, ZaSu Pitts, Mischa Auer, Andy Devine) and Republic (Judy Canova, James Gleason, Roscoe Karns). In addition, many high-profile performers generally associated with other genres starred in important comedies, e.g. Clark Gable (*It Happened One Night*, Columbia, 1934), Gary Cooper (*Ball of Fire*, Goldwyn/RKO, 1941), Greta Garbo (*Ninotchka*, MGM, 1939), Bette Davis (*The Bride Came C.O.D.*, Warner Bros., 1941), Henry Fonda (*The Lady Eve*, Paramount, 1941) and Katharine Hepburn (*Bringing Up Baby*, RKO, 1938).

Similar to the detective and western genres, comedy films were often parts of series built around actors or characters with established comic personas. "Buddy films" featuring Abbott and Costello, the Marx Brothers, the Ritz Brothers, Laurel and Hardy, Wheeler and Woolsey and Hope and Crosby became episodes in a continuing series of misadventures based on the eccentric natures of their featured performers, while the "Blondie" films (Columbia, 1938–50), the "Maisie" films (MGM, 1939–47) and the "Andy Hardy" films (MGM, 1937–58) chronicled the wide-ranging activities of their amusing main characters.

Most comedies were contemporary, topical and dependent on dialogue, pacing and action. Many featured romantic relationships, focusing on mating rituals and the eternal battle of the sexes. Character was especially important; without agreeable, amusing characters placed in interesting situations, there was little hope of making audiences laugh.

Cinematic influences such as censorship, business practices, star and style certainly affected the genre, but it was profoundly shaped by two extra-cinematic factors, the Depression and World War II. Titles such as *Laugh and Get Rich* (RKO, 1931), *Pack Up Your Troubles* (Roach/MGM, 1932), *The Poor Rich* (Universal, 1934), *We're Rich Again* (RKO, 1934), *The Richest Girl in the World* (RKO, 1934) and *Make a Million* (Monogram, 1935) suggested the genre's lighthearted attempt to grapple with the economic calamity of the 1930s. And the desire to release some of the pent-up tension of the war years was reflected in such topical romps as *A Guy, a Girl and a Gob* (RKO, 1941), *Caught in the Draft* (Paramount, 1941), *The Daring Young Man* (Columbia, 1942), *Hillbilly Blitzkrieg* (Monogram, 1942) *Princess O'Rourke* (Warner Bros., 1943), *The More the Merrier* (Columbia, 1943), *Up in Arms* (Goldwyn/RKO, 1944) and *Abroad with Two Yanks* (Small/United Artists, 1944). The comedic possibilities presented by patriotic women working in formerly all-male, hard-hat occupations were addressed in *Swing Shift Maisie* (MGM, 1943), *I Love a Soldier* (Paramount, 1944) and other films.

The remainder of this section will be devoted to brief discussions of the most important comedy sub-genres. Previous texts have given primary, often exclusive, emphasis to screwball comedy. While this sub-genre is certainly important and many of the most fondly remembered comedies of the 1930s and 40s are of the screwball variety, it is important to provide an overview of the full range of the genre during the Classical Period.

Farce

Farce (or slapstick) comedy depends heavily on ridiculous characters and physical humor, emphasizing horseplay, prat falls, sight gags, chase scenes and unrelenting action that usually demolishes any pretentions to civility, decorum and other orderly, civilized pursuits. The pie-in-the-face is the signature act of farce, elements of which often turn up in other types of comedy as well. The

Three Stooges shorts, made by Columbia from 1934 to 1955, are perhaps the best-known examples of farce produced during the period. *Gold Dust Gertie* (Warner Bros., 1931) with Ole Olsen and Chic Johnson, *Three Men on a Horse* (Warner Bros., 1936) with Sam Levene, Frank McHugh and Joan Blondell, *Room Service* (RKO, 1938) with the Marx Brothers, *Charley's Aunt* (Twentieth Century-Fox, 1941) with Jack Benny and *My Sister Eileen* (Columbia, 1942) with Rosalind Russell and Janet Blair were feature-length examples of the form.

Racial and ethnic

Humor which arises from the supposed stereotypic character traits of different racial or ethnic groups, very much out of fashion today, was acceptable to audiences during the time period. This sort of comedy also provided supporting humor in family comedy, screwball comedy and other forms. Whenever African American actors Stepin Fetchit (*Judge Priest*, Fox, 1934) or Willie Best (*Kentucky Kernels*, RKO, 1934, where he is billed as "Sleep 'n' Eat") appeared in a film, for example, they typically exhibited lazy and stupid behavior which contemporary filmgoers thought was funny but later audiences would find profoundly offensive.

Many films included this sort of humor. Numerous musicals featured white performers like Eddie Cantor and Al Jolson doing blackface routines, and *Check and Double Check* (RKO, 1929) introduced radio favorites Amos 'n' Andy (Freeman Gosden and Charles Correll, two white men in blackface make-up) to movie audiences. They were also featured in *The Big Broadcast of 1936* (Paramount, 1935). "The Cohens and the Kellys," a Universal series which lasted from 1926 to 1933, pivoted around the urban cultural clash of Jewish and Irish families. Another series featured Lupe Vélez as the "Mexican Spitfire," a volatile, hot-tempered Hispanic woman whose dizzying adventures and creative mangling of the English language entertained RKO customers from 1939 to 1943. And Chico Marx always portrayed a cartoonish Italian in the Marx Brothers pictures.

Satire and parody

A brand of comedy that sometimes combined farcical elements with racial and/or ethnic humor, satire flourished in Hollywood during the Classical Period. Filmmakers who favored satire aimed their barbs at the pretentions and ridiculous behavior of many targets. Among their primary goals: to unmask the world's charlatans, to expose the folly of the most serious human pursuits, to puncture as many inflated egos as possible.

Approaches to satire varied widely. In such Paramount films as *Horse Feathers* (1932) and *Duck Soup* (1933), the Marx Brothers adopted an iconoclastic style that bordered on surrealism to lampoon the fatuous pretensions of academia and the lunacy of international politics and modern warfare. Renowned directors Charles Chaplin (*The Great Dictator*, Chaplin/United Artists, 1940) and Ernst Lubitsch (*To Be or Not to Be*, Korda-Lubitsch/United Artists, 1942) employed a more restrained, character-centered approach in their respective dismemberments of Nazism.

One of the favorite targets of Hollywood filmmakers was Hollywood itself. Many studios made parody films about the "dream factory" featuring pompous moguls, packs of "yes men," hyperbolic publicity flacks, star and directorial prima donnas, hungry young aspirants, etc. Examples include *Once in a Lifetime* (Universal, 1932), *Movie Crazy* (Lloyd/Paramount, 1932), *Bombshell* (MGM, 1933), *Boy Meets Girl* (Warner Bros., 1938), *The Affairs of Annabel* (RKO, 1938) and *Sullivan's Travels* (Paramount, 1941).

The formula plots and stock characters of genre movies were tailor-made for parodic ribbing. Wheeler and Woolsey at RKO, for example, had fun with the gangster film (*Hook, Line and Sinker*, 1930), the adventure film (*Cockeyed Cavaliers*, 1934) and the western (*Silly Billies*, 1936) as well as other genres. Indeed, the western and the horror film were favorite targets. Laurel and Hardy (*Way Out West*, Roach/MGM, 1936), W.C. Fields and Mae West (*My Little Chickadee*, Universal, 1940), the Marx Brothers (*Go West*, MGM, 1940) and Abbott and Costello (*Ride 'Em Cowboy*, Universal, 1941) all transplanted their special comic personas to western settings with agreeable results. A few of the numerous horror film spoofs have already been discussed in the horror section.

Sex

Sex comedies enjoyed considerable popularity in the early 1930s, but were snuffed out by the Production Code Administration in 1934. Mae West, who appeared in such Paramount films as *She Done Him Wrong* (1933) and *I'm No Angel* (1933), was the key figure. Her oft-stated gusto for men, provocative costuming, double entendre dialogue, suggestive songs and unique walk created an immediate sensation, made sizable profits for her studio and brought rapid, apoplectic reactions from the moral watchdogs of the screen (see chapter 4). Jean Harlow (*Red Headed Woman*, MGM, 1932; and *Red Dust*, MGM, 1932), Barbara Stanwyck (*Baby Face*, Warner Bros., 1933) and Ruth Chatterton (*Female*,

Warner Bros., 1933) also played sexually-liberated women in films that were rather awkward combinations of comedy and melodrama. Unlike Ms. West and her collaborators, the creators of the latter titles appear to have been uncomfortable about presenting a straightforward celebration of active female sexuality.

Sophisticated

Sexual behavior was also usually an issue in sophisticated comedies. These urbane pictures emphasized questions of class, status, wealth and social decorum, as well as sexual politics. Set primarily in Europe, the sophisticated films developed out of the "comedy of manners" tradition. The writers, directors and, often, the stars of sophisticated comedies generally hailed from Europe, and their tales reflected a sensibility that American filmgoers sometimes found artificial and uninvolving. The sub-genre enjoyed some success in the early 1930s, then tailed off and practically disappeared in the 40s. Some of the best examples were *The Guardsman* (MGM, 1931), *Private Lives* (MGM, 1931), *Trouble in Paradise* (Paramount, 1932), *Design for Living* (Paramount, 1933), *Our Betters* (RKO, 1933), *Widow from Monte Carlo* (Warner Bros., 1936), *Café Metropole* (Twentieth Century-Fox, 1937), *Tovarich* (Warner Bros., 1937), *The King and the Chorus Girl* (Warner Bros., 1937), *Bluebeard's Eighth Wife* (Paramount, 1938) and *Midnight* (Paramount, 1939). Two of the best sophisticated comedies with American settings were *Holiday* (Columbia, 1938) and *The Philadelphia Story* (MGM, 1940).

Family

One of the most popular strains of comedy from the period depicted a world far removed from the European salons and mansions of sophisticated comedy. Family comedies were strictly American and strictly "down-home." They documented the ebb and flow of the highly recognizable lives of ordinary, generally rural, people. Though the films contained an assortment of eccentric characters and slapstick humor, they were also designed to pluck the heartstrings, combining tears and laughter into a folksy melody that audiences found pleasing.

MGM specialized in this kind of sentimental picture. In the early 1930s, it presented Marie Dressler and/or Wallace Beery in such box office winners as *Min and Bill* (1930), *The Champ* (1931) and *Tugboat Annie* (1933). In 1937, it offered *A Family Affair* which launched the most lucrative series of the Classical Period, the "Andy Hardy" films featuring Mickey Rooney. This series would continue to pay dividends for the studio through the war years.

Fox also made important contributions to the family comedy, initially with audience favorite Will Rogers. His "aw shucks" personality and cracker-barrel philosophizing were effectively showcased in *State Fair* (1933), *Handy Andy* (1934) and *Judge Priest*. Rogers was killed in an airplane accident in 1935, but Twentieth Century-Fox would continue to mine the form, most obviously in the "Jones family" "B" series which pre-dated MGM's Andy Hardy, running from 1936 to 1940, and in such titles as *Banjo on My Knee* (1936), *Tobacco Road* (1941) and *Home in Indiana* (1944).

Most of the other studios also attempted to feed the domestic appetite for these simple, apple pie entertainments. A few examples were Republic's "Higgins family" series (1938–41), Paramount's "Henry Aldrich" series (1939–44), *Way Back Home* (RKO, 1931), *The Stranger's Return* (MGM, 1933), *Little Women* (RKO, 1933) *Anne of Green Gables* (RKO, 1934), *M'liss* (RKO, 1936), *Down in "Arkansaw"* (Republic, 1938), *Jeepers Creepers* (Republic, 1939), *Comin' Round the Mountain* (Paramount, 1940), *Penny Serenade* (Columbia, 1941) and *I'm from Arkansas* (PRC, 1944).

Buddy

The conflictual interplay of two radically different personalities provided some of the most memorable comedy of the 1930s and 40s. Buddy pictures varied widely. Some were farcical, others satirical; some depended heavily on verbal humor while others stressed the physical; some took place in the present, others in the fictional past. But the key ingredient that made them funny was the combustible yet endearing relationship of their main characters.

The biggest stars to appear in these films were Bob Hope and Bing Crosby whose *Road to Singapore* (Paramount, 1940) launched a series of exotic adventure comedies that continued into the 1960s. Other major practitioners of the buddy film were Bert Wheeler and Robert Woolsey (*Half Shot at Sunrise*, RKO, 1930), Stan Laurel and Oliver Hardy (*Sons of the Desert*, Roach/MGM, 1933) and Bud Abbott and Lou Costello (*Buck Privates*, Universal, 1940).

Screwball

The most well-known and critically acclaimed comedy form of the 1930s and 40s was screwball, though its lifespan was actually shorter than any of the aforementioned sub-genres except sex comedy. Screwball comedy appeared in 1934, in response to the Depression and to the stifling of sexually titillating humor effected by the industry's internal censorship machinery. In one sense, screwball replaced sex comedy, but it is important to remember that the pro-totype example (*It Happened One Night*) was released before the Production Code Administration was firmly established.

Screwball films were, in essence, romantic comedies which focused on the pursuit of the opposite sex (usually the woman chasing the man, e.g., *Bringing Up Baby*) or, a favorite variant, the perfectly matched couple whose marriage is on the rocks (*The Awful Truth*, Columbia, 1937). Screwball charac-ters were typically "daffy"; most had a "screw loose" and behaved in ways that were bizarre and unpredictable, rather like the baseball pitch from which the descriptive term for the genre was derived.

The humor in the films developed from these wacky characters, breakneck pacing, witty dialogue and eruptions of slapstick which punctuated the narra-tives. Most of the films dealt with the tribulations of the idle rich, thus allowing contemporary filmgoers to spend time with characters for whom the Depres-sion was, at most, a minor inconvenience while, at the same time, inviting audience members to poke fun at the dopey behavior and affectations of these well-heeled madcaps.

As mentioned, the film that launched screwball comedy was *It Happened One Night* in which gruff newspaper reporter Clark Gable tamed and ulti-mately fell in love with spoiled heiress Claudette Colbert. The film swept the Academy Awards and soon became one of the most imitated movies of all time. (Figure 6.4) Two similar 1934 productions also contributed to industry enthusiasm for the form: *Twentieth Century* (Columbia) with John Barry-more and Carole Lombard and *The Thin Man* (MGM) with William Powell and Myrna Loy. From this point until America entered World War II, all the major studios made both "A" and "B" examples. Besides the already mentioned titles, the following were highlights: *My Man Godfrey* (Universal, 1936), *Easy Living* (Paramount, 1937), *Nothing Sacred* (Selznick/United Artists, 1937), *My Favorite Wife* (RKO, 1940), *His Girl Friday* (Columbia, 1940), *The Lady Eve*, *Ball of Fire* and *The Palm Beach Story* (Paramount, 1942).

Screwball comedy declined rapidly after the bombing of Pearl Harbor. Its emphasis on the rather frivolous carryings on of wealthy, immature Ameri-cans struck audience members as inappropriate and insensitive when the world was aflame and the stakes of the conflict were so high. Efforts to revive screwball were made after the war ended, but the US did not become mired in a new Depression and, perhaps as a consequence, the genre never regained its momentum. Though occasional examples have been produced up to the present day, the years of prominence for the screwball comedy lasted only from 1934 to 1942.

Figure 6.4   Clark Gable and Claudette Colbert in the highly influential *It Happened One Night* (produced by Harry Cohn for Columbia, 1934). Courtesy of the USC Cinema-Television Library.

Other types of comedy

While the foregoing survey does not pretend to be exhaustive, brief mention should be made of three other comedy forms that existed in the 1930s and 40s.

The mime comedy perfected during the silent era persisted after the coming of sound largely because of the infrequent but highly regarded efforts of producer-director-writer-star Charles Chaplin. His *City Lights* (Chaplin/United Artists, 1931) and *Modern Times* (Chaplin/United Artists, 1936) were brilliant continuations of the adventures of the "tramp" character he had introduced many years before. Even *The Great Dictator* (Chaplin/United Artists, 1940), Chaplin's first true "dialogue" film, contained numerous examples of his exceptional non-verbal wizardry. Sadly, two other pioneers of silent comedy did not fare as well in the sound era. Buster Keaton's career fell apart quickly at MGM in the early 1930s, thanks to such inferior efforts as *The Sidewalks of New York*

(1931), *The Passionate Plumber* (1932), *Speak Easily* (1932) and *What! No Beer?* (1933). Harold Lloyd lasted longer, starring in *Movie Crazy* (Lloyd/Paramount, 1932), *The Cat's-Paw* (Lloyd/Fox, 1934), *The Milky Way* (Paramount, 1936) and *Professor Beware* (Lloyd/Paramount, 1938). Nevertheless, like Keaton, his best work had been completed before the Depression began.

Though few in number, the "populist" comedies of Frank Capra had a potent impact on their time and are still exerting influence many years after they were filmed. Often erroneously called screwball comedies, these films had quite different objectives. Rather than presenting the less-than-earth-shattering difficulties of the nouveau riche, the populist films took on the most pressing social and political issues of the period. And while they contained eccentric characters and humorous situations, included romantic elements which came to appropriate fruition in the course of events and ended on a satisfyingly up-beat note, the films were altogether serious and might just as usefully be described as social message dramas containing comedic moments. *Mr. Deeds Goes to Town* (Columbia, 1936), *Mr. Smith Goes to Washington* (Columbia, 1939) and *Meet John Doe* (Capra/Warner Brothers, 1941) were all grounded in the belief that the average American was smart, principled and kindhearted and that these character traits would enable him/her to win out no matter the resources of the adversaries or the seeming hopelessness of the predicament. Capra's films and those of his imitators were inspired efforts to help Americans ride out the Depression and make ready to take on Fascist opponents in World War II.

Finally, brief mention should be made of the early stirrings of black comedy, i.e. comedy which renders absurd and laughable the most serious and frightening aspects of modern life. James Whale's Universal horror films, particularly *The Old Dark House*, *The Invisible Man* and *Bride of Frankenstein* reveal an affinity for this approach, as does the Marx Brothers' madly satiric *Duck Soup* and the wacky *Arsenic and Old Lace* (Warner Bros., 1944). However, American audiences during this period were still relatively innocent and uncynical in their outlook; consequently, even a marvelous film like *Duck Soup* proved to be a flop. This subversive sub-genre will play a more significant role in post-war Hollywood comedy.

The Musical

Musicals during the Classical Period were often described as musical comedies. The term is apropos, for nearly all these pictures were comedies with interludes of singing and/or dancing. In fact, the omnipresence and importance of

Figure 6.5 Ginger Rogers dances with Fred Astaire in *Swing Time* (produced by Pandro S. Berman for RKO, 1936). Courtesy of the USC Cinema-Television Library.

music in sound films creates definitional problems. The Crosby–Hope "Road" pictures, Mae West's *She Done Him Wrong* and *I'm No Angel* and the Marx Brothers' *Horse Feathers* and *Duck Soup* all contain sections of musical performance. Are these films, then, actually musicals? *The Oxford Companion to Film* contains a helpful definition of the form: "A musical is a film in which the elements of song and/or dance are so essential that to remove them would leave little or nothing." Excising the musical numbers from the aforementioned pictures would certainly damage them, but the core narrative elements and much of the humor would remain. One, therefore, feels confident in defining them as comedies. Cutting the musical numbers from *Love Me Tonight* (Paramount, 1932), *Swing Time* (RKO, 1936), *The Wizard of Oz* (MGM, 1939) or *Meet Me in St. Louis* (MGM, 1944), on the other hand, would be catastrophic, eliminating the most enjoyable elements in the pictures, rendering the behavior of their characters odd, even contradictory, and causing their stories to seem incoherent. Without question, these are musicals; in fact, they represent some of the best examples of the genre produced during the period. (Figure 6.5)

The musical was, essentially, an "A" genre. This does not mean that "B" musicals didn't exist; in fact, the studios probably made more that would be classified "B" than "A." However, it was extremely difficult to conjure forth the quality that fans of the genre expected on a less-than-fulsome budget. In addition to all the talented individuals needed to make most films, musicals required lead actors who could also sing and/or dance, composers and lyricists to provide the songs, choreographers to design and execute the important musical numbers, directors familiar with the unique demands of the form, etc. In short, the musical was the most complex, demanding and, often, financially draining of motion pictures, and it took an army of specialists working together productively to make films that were both critically and commercially successful.

As with comedy, the musical had several different sub-types. The musical revue generally offered a thin plot which provided an excuse to showcase the performances of a variety of musical and comic talents. The related backstage musical focused on the show business world where the characters work feverishly to put on a successful show. A great deal is at stake on the outcome. The operetta was akin to sophisticated comedy, featuring romantic stories (often set in Europe) and principal characters who express their feelings most poignantly in the swelling tones of light opera. The singer's musical typically was set in America and offered more comedy than the operetta. It also depended heavily on romance and the more contemporary singing styles of its principals. Dancer's musicals usually featured songs by the stars, though the main attraction was their dancing. These films also placed heavy emphasis on humor and romance. Juvenile musicals showcased the talents of exceptional children capable of singing and/or dancing in breathtaking fashion. And a few studios (especially Republic) made "hayseed" musicals, aimed at rural audiences and featuring plenty of country music and corn pone humor. Finally, the integrated musical, perfected by MGM in the 1940s, was a seamless production in which every element (the story, music, singing, dancing, staging, etc.) complemented and reinforced every other element. The integrated films represent the genre's highest artistic achievement.

Musicals were among the most stylized and romantic of Hollywood genres. They were celebrations, first and foremost, of the magical power of music to elevate the human spirit. They were also celebrations of romantic love. In the world of the 1930s and 40s musical, one always finds the perfect mate; love does, in fact, conquer all; and people's dreams do come true. In short, the musical offered audiences a utopian myth. In addition, the genre had a liberating quality; it invited audience members to bury their cares and allow their imaginations to take flight. For many, the best musicals offered a sublime form of entertainment which no other movie genre could match.

Development

The development of the musical is particularly interesting because, unlike other prominent genres, this one had no silent prototypes to build on. Many of the "A" musicals released in the late 1920s and early 30s were adaptations of stage shows (e.g., *Show Boat*, Universal, 1929; *Good News*, MGM, 1930; *Hit the Deck*, RKO, 1930) or revues featuring large casts of performers (*The Show of Shows*, Warner Bros., 1929; *Paramount on Parade*, Paramount, 1930; *Happy Days*, Fox, 1930). Though there were exceptions such as *King of Jazz* (Universal, 1930), most of these films were cinematically static and uninvolving, yet the novelty of the new genre carried them to box office success anyway. Much more dynamic were Paramount's operettas made by directors Ernst Lubitsch (*The Love Parade*, 1929, *Monte Carlo*, *The Smiling Lieutenant*, 1931) and Rouben Mamoulian (*Love Me Tonight*). These films married the potentials of the medium to the genre's special qualities; they were more imaginatively shot and edited than most other films made at the time and used the musical numbers to advance the plot and develop the characters. *Love Me Tonight*, in particular, was a witty textbook of cinematic technique (see chapter 3).

As the Depression worsened and the novelty of musicals wore off, the public lost its enthusiasm for the genre. *Dixiana* (RKO, 1930), designed as a follow-up to the highly successful *Rio Rita* (RKO, 1929; profit: $935,000) and employing practically the same cast and crew, posted a loss of $300,000. Most other musicals released in late 1930 and 1931 suffered similar fates, causing the studios to cut back on production.

In 1933, *42nd Street* (Warner Bros.) and *Flying Down to Rio* (RKO) helped revive the form. The former, a backstage tale, grounded its narrative firmly within the economic distress of the time. The picture was a hit and the Warner studio followed it up with a series of similarly-themed pictures (*Gold Diggers of 1933*, *Footlight Parade*, 1933, *Dames*, 1934) in remarkably short order. All featured the innovative choreography of Busby Berkeley whose slyly sexual, geometric musical numbers became the signature elements of the films. The Berkeley approach was often copied, but never really duplicated, by other dance directors.

One can find some ersatz-Berkeley moments in *Flying Down to Rio*, the first of the RKO Fred Astaire–Ginger Rogers pictures. Though Astaire and Rogers played supporting parts in *Rio*, the eight starring pictures that followed became the first great dancers' musicals. The Warner Bros. films had sometimes showcased Ruby Keeler's tap-dancing abilities, but the big Berkeley numbers often contained little dancing, generating their style and rhythm through choreographed camera movement, camera angles, cutting, etc. After abandoning the Berkeley appoach, RKO adopted a much simpler style. Its cameramen concentrated on the beautiful, complex interaction of Astaire and Rogers dancing, presented in the most straightforward fashion imaginable. The dancers were shot full figure, in the center of the frame and in uninterrupted takes if possible.

The Astaire–Rogers films were escapist fantasies, filled with screwball comedy characters and situations. Unlike the Warner pictures, they blithely disregarded the bad news of the Depression, preferring to focus single-mindedly on romantic misunderstandings. The Shirley Temple pictures which competed with the Astaire–Rogers series to be the most popular musicals of the 1930s, occupied a middle ground between the Warner and RKO productions. Temple could sing and she could dance, but she also inhabited a world where people do have their share of problems. She, naturally, exhibits more common sense and wisdom than the grown-ups and is constantly required to solve their dilemmas for them. Though Shirley's solutions were awfully pat and her pictures syrupy sweet, no one could argue with the prodigious talent of this remarkable youngster, especially when she sang numbers like "On the Good Ship Lollipop" (*Bright Eyes*, Fox, 1934) and "When I'm with You" (*Poor Little Rich Girl*, Twentieth Century-Fox, 1936) or danced with Bill "Bojangles" Robinson (*The Little Colonel*, Fox, 1935) or Buddy Ebsen (*Captain January*, Twentieth Century-Fox, 1936) or George Murphy (*Little Miss Broadway*, Twentieth Century-Fox, 1938).

Pictures starring teenaged Deanna Durbin from Universal adopted a similar pattern. Beginning with *Three Smart Girls* (1936), Durbin's light soprano voice sang everything from opera classics to contemporary tunes in a series of popular films. In *One Hundred Men and a Girl* (1937), the persistent and innately good Miss Durbin prevailed upon renowned maestro Leopold Stokowski to sponsor an orchestra made up of out-of-work musicians, among them her own father. The film ended with Stokowski conducting the new orchestra as Durbin sings "The Drinking Song" from Verdi's *La Traviata*. Independent producer Sol Lesser (releasing through RKO) tried to wrap similar box office magic around the singing talents of boyish tenor Bobby Breen (*Rainbow on the River*, 1936) and Universal attempted a similar experiment with 11-year-old Gloria Jean (*A Little Bit of Heaven*, 1940), but neither was able to approach the level of stardom enjoyed by Miss Temple and Miss Durbin.

Rather surprisingly, Columbia Pictures was able to elevate opera diva Grace Moore to stardom for a time during the mid-1930s. Her biggest hit was *One Night of Love* (1934), followed by *Love Me Forever* (1935), *The King Steps Out* (1936), *When You're in Love* (1937) and *I'll Take Romance* (1937). Columbia's breakthrough with Miss Moore caused other studios to import such leading figures of the grand opera world as Lily Pons (*I Dream Too Much*, RKO, 1935), Nino Martini (*Here's to Romance*, Fox, 1935), Lawrence Tibbett (*Metropolitan*, Twentieth Century-Fox, 1935) and James Melton (*Stars over Broadway*, Warner Bros., 1935), but none could replicate the success that Harry Cohn had for a few years with Grace Moore.

Enjoying an even longer period of public acclaim was the MGM operetta team of Jeanette MacDonald and Nelson Eddy (*Naughty Marietta*, 1935, *Rose Marie*, 1936, *Maytime*, 1937, and others). When MacDonald and Eddy began to lose their drawing power at the beginning of the 1940s, MGM launched its own youth movement featuring Judy Garland and Mickey Rooney. Garland had already established her presence in *Broadway Melody of 1938* (MGM, 1937), *Everybody Sing* (MGM, 1938) and, of course, *The Wizard of Oz*, and Rooney was everyone's favorite teenager, thanks to "Andy Hardy." But the Rooney–Garland teaming in *Babes in Arms* (1939), *Strike Up the Band* (1940) and *Babes on Broadway* (1942) elevated the star status of both. Directed by Busby Berkeley, these films featured an energetic, kid-oriented version of the backstage plot with the youngsters "puttin' on a show" to support such worthy causes as out-of-luck parents, injured friends and underprivileged children. In his MGM efforts, Berkeley depended more on the singing and dancing abilities of his two young prodigies than on his signature kaleidoscopic visual patterns and camera pyrotechnics, though the climactic shows always turned out to be spectacular.

At Twentieth Century-Fox, Darryl Zanuck did not try to find another juvenile star when Shirley Temple grew older and less endearing to audiences. By that time, he had developed several grown-up musical stars and practically taken out a patent on "nostalgic" musical biographies and backstage stories set in the nineteenth or early-twentieth centuries. Such productions as *Alexander's Ragtime Band* (1938), *Rose of Washington Square* (1939), *Swanee River* (1939) and *Lillian Russell* (1940) proved highly appealing to audiences and advanced the careers of Alice Faye, Don Ameche, even Tyrone Power. Zanuck continued to mine this mother lode during the war years when audiences seemed even more pleased to visit a simpler, more innocent and affirmative world than the one they were confronting. He chose to make most of the 1940s musicals in Technicolor and welcomed the emergence of pin up queen Betty Grable as his biggest star in *Coney Island* (1943), *Sweet Rosie O'Grady* (1943) and *The Dolly Sisters* (1945). One of Grable's few competitors with the men-in–uniform also became a major figure in the musical around the same time. This was beautiful Rita Hayworth who was paired effectively in Columbia films with Tony Martin

(*Music in the Heart*, 1940), Fred Astaire (*You'll Never Get Rich*, 1941, and *You Were Never Lovelier*, 1942) and Gene Kelly (*Cover Girl*, 1944).

The war years naturally provoked a cascade of patriotic musicals. One of the best and most popular was another nostalgic look backward, *Yankee Doodle Dandy* (Warner Bros., 1942), in which James Cagney portrayed all-American singer-songwriter George M. Cohan. Among the most prevalent types of war years musicals were revues designed to raise money for the cause (*Thousands Cheer*, MGM, 1943; *This Is the Army*, Warner Bros., 1943; *Hey, Rookie*, Columbia, 1944), stories of men on leave trying to pack as much fun and romance as possible into their short holidays (*Seven Days' Leave*, RKO, 1942; *When Johnny Comes Marching Home*, Universal, 1943; *The Sky's the Limit*, RKO, 1943) and backstage pictures chronicling tours by show business personalities to entertain the troops (*Around the World*, RKO, 1943; *Four Jills in a Jeep*, Twentieth Century-Fox; 1944; *Follow the Boys*, Universal, 1944). Several musicals also dealt with the new breed of female defense plant workers, including *He's My Guy* (Universal, 1943) and *Rosie the Riveter* (Republic, 1944).

After years of rising steadily in box office clout, Bing Crosby hit the pinnacle during World War II. While his popularity was very positively affected by several films that were not, strictly speaking, musicals, such as the "Road" pictures, *Going My Way* (Paramount, 1944) and *The Bells of St. Mary's* (Rainbow/RKO, 1945), Crosby was best known for his singing on records, on radio and in the movies. Thus, such Paramount musicals as *Birth of the Blues* (1941), *Holiday Inn* (1942), *Dixie* (1943) and *Here Come the Waves* (1944) contributed mightily to his success.

Finally, during this period MGM began to assemble the greatest team of musical talents in Hollywood history. Performers Judy Garland, Gene Kelly, Fred Astaire, Frank Sinatra; directors Vincente Minnelli, George Sidney, Stanley Donen and Charles Walters (Donen and Walters were choreographers who quickly graduated to directing); producers Arthur Freed, Joe Pasternak and Jack Cummings were among the key individuals who took up residence at the studio and would make some of the greatest musicals in film history after the end of the war. A taste of things to come was *Meet Me in St. Louis*. Challenging the specialty of rival Twentieth Century-Fox, MGM focused Technicolor cameras on mid-western Americana, circa 1902-03. The film's brilliant orchestration of story, dialogue, musical numbers, performances, sets, costumes, art direction, color design, etc. demonstrated the quality that was possible when creative artists like Arthur Freed, Vincente Minnelli and Judy Garland collaborated. The film's emphasis on family and the importance of home also struck a resonant chord with audiences longing for a return to the values it depicted. *Meet Me in St. Louis* demonstated how far and how fast the musical had grown from its origins in *The Jazz Singer* (Warner Bros., 1927) and *The Broadway Melody* (MGM, 1929).

The Woman's Film

The woman's film represented a very important genre to Hollywood executives for it clearly targeted female patrons as its audience. While most genres (westerns, gangster films, horror pictures) were thought to appeal primarily to male viewers and a few (comedy, musical, adventure) were aimed at both sexes, the woman's film was the only genre that set its sights unabashedly on female spectators. Studio officials did hope, of course, that the women would drag along their husbands or boyfriends and/or children.

The woman's film was a melodramatic genre which focused on the life of a female protagonist. Its main objective was to engage the audience on an emotional level in ways that were always moving and often sentimental. But it is probably a mistake to use the generic term "melodrama" to describe the pictures, for other Hollywood genres – even westerns, war movies and gangster films – were often "melodramatic" as well.

The woman's film surveyed a variety of subjects deemed to be of special interest to its intended spectators. Preeminent among those subjects were romance, family and career. Over and over, the films forced their main characters to make difficult choices . . . choices that lead to considerable suffering and unhappiness. Members of the audience were encouraged to identify with the female leads, feeling their pain and shedding tears for their sad situations. Though often used pejoratively, the slang descriptions for films of this kind – "tearjerkers," "weepies," "three-hanky pictures" – were appropriate. Studio chiefs believed that the more tears a picture evoked, the better its box office performance would be.

The woman's film was another genre with "A" and "B" examples, though many films fell into the "in-between" category described in chapter 2. Nearly all the major female stars participated, and every studio made these pictures.

Like the male-dominated, action-oriented genres already discussed in this chapter, the woman's film made heroes out of its protagonists. However, the nature of heroism was quite different for the woman's film than for the male genres. A woman's heroism was measured by her ability to suffer the most heartbreaking reversals of fortune with dignity and to make the most painful sacrifices, giving up her own happiness for the happiness of others.

The genre dealt with life's universal problems: affairs of the heart, family relationships, career decisions, health problems, class barriers, one's reputation, secrets and lies, the effects of gossip. While everyone wrestles with such matters in his or her life, the films' dramatic conflicts were magnified and the responses to them mythified by the extraordinary strength of the characters and the star power of the actresses who played them. A good deal has been written about the effects these films had on both male and female viewers during the period. Without question, the movies helped to define the place of women in a pressure-cooker America, and they provided role models that colored the expectations of young and old, male and female alike. It is probably overstating the case to say that real women were expected to exhibit the selfless, undying love of Irene Dunne in *Back Street* (Universal, 1931), the monumental courage of Bette Davis in *Dark Victory* (Warner Bros., 1939), the sacrificial determination of Barbara Stanwyck in *Stella Dallas* (Goldwyn/United Artists, 1937) and the inner strength of Ginger Rogers in *Tender Comrade* (RKO, 1943). But the saintly behavior of these and many other heroines of the woman's film certainly hovered over and affected the lives of American females in the 1930s and 40s. (Figure 6.6)

Development

The woman's film was a well-established genre when sound entered the cinematic equation. A number of the stories that would be told again and again had already been filmed as silents, such as *Madame X* (MGM, 1929, 1937), *So Big* and *Stella Dallas*. Nonetheless, the genre was given a boost by the possibility of dialogue, for "talk" in a woman's film is of considerable importance. It is in dialogue that the deepest of secrets are usually revealed and through dialogue that the most powerful confrontations take place. Perhaps because of the possibilities of sound, as well as the societal ruptures caused by the Depression, the woman's film was extremely active and important in the late 1920s and early 30s.

The films of the period placed special emphasis on sex and on money. Free love, infidelity, adultery, even prostitution wreaked havoc on relationships in *Susan Lenox (Her Fall and Rise)* (MGM, 1931), *The Easiest Way* (MGM, 1931), *Illicit* (Warner Bros., 1931), *Back Street, Bed of Roses* (RKO, 1933) and many other titles. For a number of the characters in Pre-Code films, sexual activity led to children, often illegitimate children, and the sad compromises that the mothers must make to assure these children the best possible life. *Madame X*, *The Sin of Madelon Claudet* (MGM, 1931), *Only Yesterday* (Universal, 1933),

Figure 6.6   Irene Dunne with a picture of her lover, John Boles, in *Back Street* (produced by Carl Laemmle Jr. for Universal, 1932). Courtesy of the USC Cinema-Television Library.

Jennie Gerhardt (Paramount, 1933), *The Life of Vergie Winters* (RKO, 1934) and other contemporary pictures were object lessons in the depth and breadth of mother love. Despite their apparent mistakes and condemnation from the square-jawed (usually hypocritical) members of a cold, repressive society, the protagonists were typically presented as figures of nobility. Moviegoers were privy to the truth about the enormity of their love and the full extent of their sacrifice, information that is often hidden from many of the characters in the stories. In sum, the audience understood these remarkable women and was moved by the pain and indignities they suffered.

Given the hard times in which these films were produced, it might be expected that financial problems would play a part in the women's difficulties. And so they did in *Blonde Venus* (Paramount, 1932), *Bad Girl* (Fox, 1931) *Tarnished Lady* (Paramount, 1931), *Faithless* (MGM, 1932), *The Crash* (Warner Bros., 1932), *Man's Castle* (Columbia, 1933) and *Mills of the Gods* (Columbia, 1934).

The contrast between the haves and have-nots of American society continued to be an element in some woman's films made later in the 1930s, but the emphasis on economic problems lessened considerably as the decade wore on. Likewise, the emphasis on female sexuality and illegitimate children of the "fallen woman" pictures disappeared immediately after Joseph Breen was placed in charge of the Production Code Administration in mid-1934.

Although a definite reduction in the number of woman's films occurred after 1934, the genre continued to be prominent, especially at the "A" level. Sacrifice remained the key ingredient: a woman (Barbara Stanwyck) gives up her child, who is the center of her life, for the child's own good (*Stella Dallas*); a woman (Greta Garbo) spurns the man she truly loves for his own good (*Camille*, MGM, 1937); a woman (Ann Harding) gracefully steps aside, allowing her husband's romance with a younger woman to play itself out before he comes to his senses and returns to her (*The Lady Consents*, RKO, 1936); a woman (Ingrid Bergman) gives up her married lover for his own happiness and the happiness of his family (*Intermezzo*, Selznick/United Artists, 1939); a woman (Kay Francis) marries a man she does not love to try to save him from the law (*Stolen Holiday*, Warner Bros., 1937); a woman (Carole Lombard) takes the blame for her sister's nursing negligence which has resulted in the death of a patient (*Vigil in the Night*, RKO, 1940).

During this period, women were also required to cope valiantly with their own health problems (*Magnificent Obsession*, Universal, 1935; *Dark Victory*) or the illnesses and afflictions of loved ones (*Jezebel*, Warner Bros., 1938). And they had to make very difficult decisions about the right man to love (*Kitty Foyle*, RKO, 1940), about the right man to marry (*I Met My Love Again*, Wanger/United Artists, 1938), about pursuing a career (*Next Time We Love*, Universal, 1936), about being a nonconformist (*A Woman Rebels*, RKO, 1936), even about the proper dress to wear to the ball (*Jezebel*). All of the decisions (even the one about the ball gown) have monumental consequences within the fabric of the films.

When the United States became embroiled in the war, the genre faded a bit more and adopted some new emphases. Given the gravity of the situation, women were expected to rise to greater heights, to sublimate their personal needs completely. With the future of the world hanging in the balance, men alone would not determine the future. In such films as *Flight for Freedom* (RKO, 1943), *First Comes Courage* (Columbia, 1943) and *Paris Underground* (Constance Bennett/United Artists, 1945), women were more than equal to the challenge.

Another important wartime theme was separation. The principal characters watch as their husbands or fiancés or children march off to battle, knowing full well that they may never see them again. Their loneliness, compounded by unceasing concern about the welfare of their loved one(s), provided a range of dramatic possibilities in *Since You Went Away* (Selznick/United Artists, 1944), *Tender Comrade* and other films.

One of the social changes occasioned by the war effort was the wholesale entry of women into the workforce. The new expectations for women were well documented in comedies, musicals and in woman's films like *Tender Comrade* where Ginger Rogers, Ruth Hussey, Patricia Collinge, Kim Hunter and Mady Christians, most of whom have husbands or boyfriends or children in the service, bond together while working in a Douglas Aircraft plant.

The newfound independence of working women and the threat it posed to some men began to impact the genre during the war. Suddenly and oddly, considering the "accentuate the positive" quality of most World War II-era films, very dangerous women started appearing. There had, occasionally, been evil protagonists in earlier woman's pictures, such as Marlene Dietrich in *The Devil Is a Woman* (Paramount, 1935) and Bette Davis in *The Little Foxes* (Goldwyn/RKO, 1941). But they were anomalies, sharply contrasted to the noble heroines who mainly populated the genre. Thus, in *Mildred Pierce* (Warner Bros., 1945), *Guest in the House* (Stromberg/United Artists, 1945) and *Leave Her to Heaven* (Twentieth Century-Fox, 1945), a new vision of the genre's protagonist seemed to be taking shape. No longer victims, the central figures in these pictures were victimizers whose unhealthy obsessions result in disaster. The films treated the usual subjects of the genre – overpowering romance, mother love, etc. – but in a twisted, considerably more disturbing fashion. They thrust possessive, neurotic, threatening women at audiences, laying the groundwork for the emergence of the noir woman's film and the ascendence of the femme fatale in post-war American cinema.

Other Genres

The bulk of this chapter describes the most significant Hollywood genres during the Classical Period. In addition, several other types of productions deserve brief mention.

Biographies

The screen biography (also known as the "biopic") was considered to be an important star vehicle which, if properly produced, might garner both critical plaudits and box office success. While "B" examples of the form occasionally appeared (e.g., *Daniel Boone*, RKO, 1936; *The Flying Irishman*, RKO, 1939; *Roger Touhy, Gangster*, Twentieth Century-Fox, 1944), most of the biography films employed the studios' major talents. Warner Bros. made the most prestigious biography films of the 1930s, winning numerous Academy Awards for such productions as *The Story of Louis Pasteur* (1936), *The Life of Emile Zola* (1937) and *Juarez* (1939). All three films starred Paul Muni and were directed by William Dieterle. Twentieth Century-Fox also favored the form, turning out *The Story of Alexander Graham Bell* (1939), *Young Mr. Lincoln* (1939) and several musical biographies, including *Lillian Russell, My Gal Sal* (1942) and *The Dolly Sisters*. MGM unleashed its formidable star contingent in *Rasputin and the Empress* (1932), *The Gorgeous Hussy* (1936), *Boys Town* (1938) and *Madame Curie* (1943), while the other studios engaged in this type of filmmaking on a less regular basis.

Biopics were, by definition, historical, treating the lives of famous people. And even though the studios expended considerable energy and money researching the subjects and the various worlds in which they lived, the resultant films placed greater emphasis on dramatic situation than historical fact. Most biographies were tales of achievement, featuring protagonists who overcome formidable adversaries and difficult situations and, in so doing, demonstrate the qualities of greatness. In some cases, they find themselves pitted against the accepted wisdom and traditions of society itself, whose members believe them to be dangerous threats to the body politic. But, of course, the subject's vision of what is best for society is always more perceptive than that of his/her antagonists. Films of this sort were typically lauded by politicians, business leaders and educators. They were thought to have a beneficial effect on viewers, especially the younger members of the audience who might be inspired to pursue greatness by the lives of men and women who had already achieved it.

The majority of late-1920s and 1930s biographies focused on major figures from European history, including Disraeli (*Disraeli*, Warner Bros., 1929), Voltaire (*Voltaire*, Warner Bros., 1933), Catharine II of Russia (*The Scarlet Empress*, Paramount, 1934), Benvenuto Cellini (*The Affairs of Cellini*, Twentieth Century/ United Artists, 1934), Queen Christina of Sweden (*Queen Christina*, MGM, 1934), Mary, Queen of Scots (*Mary of Scotland*, RKO, 1936), Charles Stewart Parnell (*Parnell*, MGM, 1937) and Marie Antoinette (*Marie Antoinette*, MGM, 1938). However, as the political climate deteriorated in Europe and the US grew more nationalistic, the focus switched to homegrown heroes. Studios celebrated the lives of presidents (*Abe Lincoln in Illinois*, RKO, 1940), inventors (*Edison, the*

Man, MGM, 1940), religious leaders (*Brigham Young, Frontiersman*, Twentieth Century-Fox, 1940), football legends (*Knute Rockne – All American*, Warner Bros., 1940), even misunderstood outlaws (*Billy the Kid*). The trend continued throughout the pre-war period and war years. Among the subjects for patriotic biographies were World War I hero Alvin York (*Sergeant York*), all-American showman George M. Cohan (*Yankee Doodle Dandy*), heroic Navy doctor Corydon M. Wassell (*The Story of Dr. Wassell*, Paramount, 1944), legendary westerner Bill Cody (*Buffalo Bill*, Twentieth Century-Fox, 1944) and President Woodrow Wilson (*Wilson*, Twentieth Century-Fox, 1944).

As should be clear from earlier sections of this chapter, the biography was easily adapted into a hybrid. Musical biographies (*The Great Ziegfeld*, MGM, 1937; *The Story of Vernon and Irene Castle*, RKO, 1939; *Swanee River*, Twentieth Century-Fox, 1940) were the most popular, but there were also numerous western biograhies (*Annie Oakley*, RKO, 1935; *Jesse James*; *When the Daltons Rode*, Universal, 1940), adventure biographies (*Clive of India*, Twentieth Century/United Artists, 1935; *The Buccanneer*, Paramount, 1938) and sports biographies (*Harmon of Michigan*, Columbia, 1941; *Gentleman Jim*, Warner Bros., 1942).

Espionage

The roots of the espionage genre stretch well back into the silent era. Closest in form and content to detective films, spy stories emphasized suspense, adventure, romance, patriotism, politics, loyalty and treachery. During the Classical Period, most dealt in ethical absolutes and clearly defined good guys and bad guys. In later years, the genre would grow more complex, but there was little interest in fully developed characters or moral ambiguity at this time.

Espionage films enjoyed some popularity in the early sound era, with most of the plots fused with elements of the woman's film. Greta Garbo (*Mata Hari*, MGM, 1931), Marlene Dietrich (*Dishonored*, Paramount, 1931), Helen Twelvetrees (*A Woman of Experience*, RKO, 1931), Constance Bennett (*After Tonight*, RKO, 1933), and Fay Wray (*Madame Spy*, Universal, 1934) all played agents whose love affairs compromise their missions. Most die tragically at the end. Set during World War I, these hybrids favored romance over suspense, which is generally the most important element in the genre.

By the mid-1930s, the espionage picture had receded so completely that it was barely alive. However, the unraveling European situation revived it, and spy movies remained prominent through the remainder of the period. A "hot," contemporary genre, the late-1930s espionage films were primarily "Bs" and

"B" hybrids in which enemy spies were outmaneuvered and foiled, often by the studios' well-established master detectives (*Mr. Moto Takes a Chance*, Twentieth Century-Fox, 1938; *The Lone Wolf Spy Hunt*, Columbia, 1939; *Nick Carter, Master Detective*, MGM, 1939).

The year 1939 saw the release of *Confessions of a Nazi Spy* (Warner Bros.), the most controversial and important espionage film of the Classical Period. Sidestepping various censorship problems (see chapter 4), this daring attack on Hitler and his accolytes portrayed the Nazis as unredeemed figures of evil at a time when most Americans were committed to neutrality and trying to keep an "open mind" on the European crisis. Some of the other pre-war espionage films were *Espionage Agent* (Warner Bros., 1939), *They Made Her a Spy* (RKO, 1939), *Navy Secrets* (Monogram, 1939) *Foreign Correspondent* (Wanger/United Artists, 1940), *Enemy Agent* (Universal, 1940), *Murder in the Air* (Warner Bros., 1940), *One Night in Lisbon* (Paramount, 1941) and *Scotland Yard* (Twentieth Century-Fox, 1941).

After Pearl Harbor, the espionage film became even more prominent. Constantly reminded that "loose lips sink ships," Americans began to think that enemy agents were all around them, and the genre fed their paranoia directly. While most of the productions were "Bs," there were plenty of "A" films as well, including *Across the Pacific* (Warner Bros., 1942), *Saboteur* (Universal, 1942), *Above Suspicion* (MGM, 1943), *Watch on the Rhine* (Warner Bros., 1943), *Hangmen Also Die* (Pressburger/United Artists, 1943), *Secret Command*, (Columbia, 1944), *Ministry of Fear* (Paramount, 1944) and *The House on 92nd Street* (Twentieth Century-Fox, 1945).

The genre also was yoked to comedy during the war. As might be guessed from their principal performers, the following hybrids combined humor with the usual thrills and suspense: *My Favorite Blonde* (Paramount, 1942) and *They Got Me Covered* (Goldwyn/RKO, 1943) starring Bob Hope; *The Daring Young Man* (Columbia, 1942) starring Joe E. Brown; *Ship Ahoy* (MGM, 1942) starring Red Skelton and *Joan of Ozark* (Republic, 1942), a musical comedy starring Judy Canova.

Fantasy

It would not be accurate to define fantasy films as a free-standing genre. Fantasy elements were injected into other film forms to produce fantasy adventures (*The Thief of Bagdad*; *Tarzan's Desert Mystery*, Principal Artists/RKO, 1943), fantasy comedies (*Topper*, Roach/MGM, 1937; *I Married a Witch*, Paramount/United Artists, 1942), fantasy musicals (*The Wizard of Oz*; *Cabin in the*

Sky, MGM, 1942), even fantasy war films (*A Guy Named Joe*). And genres such as science fiction, which did not become important in Hollywood until after World War II, horror and feature-length animation, were totally dependent on elements of the fantastic.

Nevertheless, it seems important to note that audiences during this period willingly embraced the full realm of the imaginary, including ghosts (*The Canterville Ghost*, MGM, 1944), angels (*Here Comes Mr. Jordan*, Columbia, 1941), fairies (*The Blue Bird*, Twentieth Century-Fox, 1940), genies (*Turnabout*, Roach/United Artists, 1940), death personified (*Death Takes a Holiday*, Paramount, 1934), the devil (*All That Money Can Buy*, RKO, 1941), a magical dwelling where ugliness is transformed into beauty (*The Enchanted Cottage*, RKO, 1945), and an uncharted land whose inhabitants never age (*Lost Horizon*, Columbia, 1937).

Social consciousness

The standard definition of a film genre involves a predictable matrix of characters, settings, thematic material and iconography. This conception would exclude socially conscious productions from genre consideration. However, the Hollywood studios made a surprising number of films that did not have consistent genre elements, but were linked together by a kind of educational, public service agenda. These movies attempted to call attention to contemporary problems, to create drama out of the significant social issues of the time.

Although they never quite broke free of the usual Hollywood narrative patterns, the writers, producers and directors of social consciousness films tried to offer a more realistic and thought-provoking cinema, a cinema that could potentially lead to social change. Some studio heads were not particularly interested in this type of production, but others – especially the executives at Warner Bros. and Twentieth Century-Fox – believed that social consciousness could translate into good box office as well as good citizenship and regularly gave green lights to films of this kind. Among the more famous and effective examples: *Five Star Final* (Warner Bros., 1931) focusing on the human damage wrought by tabloid jornalism; *I Am a Fugitive from a Chain Gang* (Warner Bros., 1932) concerning deplorable penal conditions in the southern US; *Our Daily Bread* (Viking/United Artists, 1934) which offered a collectivist answer to the problems of the unemployed; *Black Legion* (Warner Bros., 1936) which unmasked xenophobic hate groups like the Ku Klux Klan; *Fury* (MGM, 1936) and *They Won't Forget* (Warner Bros., 1937) dealing with lynching and the mob mentality; *Make Way for Tomorrow* (Paramount, 1937) about old age and the generation gap; *The Grapes of Wrath* (Twentieth Century-Fox, 1940) chronicling the sad plight of dust bowl farmers forced to journey west in hopes of finding salvation; *The Male Animal* (Warner Bros., 1942) which touched on the issues of free speech and censorship in American universities; and *The Lost Weekend* (Paramount, 1945) which portrayed the horrors of alcoholism. The latter film won the 1945 Best Picture Academy Award and helped to spark a renewed interest in this sort of filmmaking which characterized the immediate post-war period.

Sports films

The American love affair with sports and sporting events was reflected in a number of pictures in which athletic contests were featured. However, it is also difficult to ascribe genre status to the "sports film," for most were examples of other genres which simply incorporated the sporting contest into their pre-existing narrative patterns. And, unlike some other hybrids, these films were not a true marriage of equally weighted elements; rather, they used sports as a background against which to situate comedies, biographical tales, gangster films, etc.

The sports film which comes closest to achieving genre status essayed the world of boxing. The studios produced at least 50 of these during the Classical Period. Many were comedies (*The Milky Way*), biographies (*The Great John L.*, Crosby/United Artists, 1945), woman's films (*Bad Girl*, Fox, 1931), musicals (*Swing Fever*, MGM, 1943), and gangster films (*Kid Galahad*, Warner Bros, 1937). Still, in *Golden Boy* (Columbia, 1939) and a few other boxing films from the period, the filmmakers grapple with certain thematic dichotomies that will be explored and more fully developed in post-World War II productions: brutality vs. artistry; competition vs. corruption; career vs. family; fame vs. conscience.

Other sports films fell well short of genre status. Though numerous football pictures were produced, for example, none really investigated or analyzed the sport in serious fashion. Most were comedies (*Hold 'Em Jail*, RKO, 1932; *The Gladiator*, Columbia, 1938; *Mr. Doodle Kicks Off*, RKO, 1938), musicals (*College Coach*, Warner Bros., 1933; *Pigskin Parade*, Twentieth Century-Fox, 1936; *Rosalie*, MGM, 1937) or biographies. With some exceptions, such as *Knute Rockne – All American* and *The Iron Major* (RKO, 1943), the biographies tended to feature the actual football hero playing himself. Tom Harmon starred in *Harmon of Michigan*, Bruce Smith in *Smith of Minnesota* (1942) and Frankie Albert in *The Spirit of Stanford* (1942), all made by Columbia Pictures.

None of these Hollywood neophytes made the transition from playing field to sound stage with aplomb.

Despite the claim that baseball was the "national pastime," fewer baseball movies were made than boxing or football pictures. Again, most were comedies. Joe E. Brown, a former player, enjoyed a successful run of nutty baseball pictures at Warner Bros. in the early 1930s: *Fireman, Save My Child* (1932), *Elmer the Great* (1933) and *Alibi Ike* (1935). Perhaps the most highly regarded of all the sports films of the period was producer Samuel Goldwyn's biography of Lou Gehrig, *The Pride of the Yankees* (Goldwyn/RKO, 1942). An iron man who set a record by playing in 2,130 straight games, Gehrig's life was cut short by an incurable disease which was later named after him. The humility, strength and courage displayed by Gehrig (Gary Cooper) struck a chord with many American males facing their own impending crisis: participation in a terrifying global war.

Other sporting events which were showcased in films of the period included wrestling (*The Sport Parade*, RKO, 1932), swimming (*Bathing Beauty*, MGM, 1944), automobile racing (*The Crowd Roars*, Warner Bros., 1932), hockey (*King of Hockey*, Warner Bros., 1936), track and field (*Local Boy Makes Good*, Warner Bros., 1931), horse racing (*National Velvet*, MGM, 1944), skiing (*Ski Patrol*, Universal, 1940), rowing (*Million Dollar Legs*, Paramount, 1939) and ice skating (*One in a Million*, Twentieth Century-Fox, 1937).

7

Stars and the Star System

Actors who become intense objects of public fascination are called stars. Their personal magnetism and ability to captivate audiences make these performers crucial ingredients in the film business recipe for success. Because of the many volumes of superficial, gossipy (and often partially fictitious) material that have been published about them, stars from the Classical Period have only recently been taken seriously as legitimate subjects for academic scrutiny. Star scholarship is, in actuality, both a daunting and potentially rewarding avenue of historical inquiry. By mapping star careers against the backdrop of a mercurial industry as well as a nation (and world) passing through major social changes, it is possible to gain a greater understanding of both cultural history and film history. One might argue, in fact, that stars are cultural barometers whose popularity speaks volumes about their times and the psychological needs of the fans who worshiped them.

The Star as Business Commodity

At the dawn of the sound era, movie stars were well known throughout the world. To the studios, they represented a scarce and very precious commodity. If showcased properly, a star could generate revenue for many years, though star development and nurturing were recognized as inexact sciences. Even the biggest box office names were subject to the changing whims and tastes of the public. Mary Pickford and Douglas Fairbanks defined the meaning of stardom, but neither managed to survive the transition from silent cinema to sound. Yet their loss of status, evidently, had little to do with their voices or their ability to recite dialogue convincingly. The reasons for the declining careers of Pickford and Fairbanks are complex, but they are clearly related to the aging process and the inability of the actors to continue embodying the sorts of characters that made them public favorites in the first place. Like so many stars, Pickford and Fairbanks found it imperative, but impossible, to alter their screen personas – the unique cinematic images which moviegoers adored. With such salutary examples as Fairbanks and Pickford to learn from, studio executives recognized that a premium would always be placed on youth and, therefore, were constantly on the lookout for fresh personalities who might be molded into stars.

For the public, stars meant two things above all else: a reliable kind of entertainment and an assurance of superior production values. Audiences who attended a Shirley Temple film, or a Mae West film, or a Bing Crosby–Bob Hope film had a very good idea of the sort of diversion they would experience. If the picture lived up to their expectations, they would likely return when the next production featuring their favorite(s) arrived at a convenient theater. Spectators also realized that studios tended to support stars with money and talent that would not be expended on "B" films and shorts. To most patrons, a star-driven movie represented the highest level of Hollywood production.

The star was also the most important element in each studio's marketing efforts. "A" pictures were sold to exhibitors and ultimately to the public based primarily on "star power." Exhibitors in the early 1930s who agreed to play blocks of MGM product knew very little about the stories and genres which they would later be presenting and even less about the quality and appeal of those productions, but they they did know that Clark Gable, Joan Crawford, Norma Shearer, Jean Harlow, Wallace Beery, Marie Dressler, Greta Garbo and other crowd-pleasers would be featured. The exhibitor, therefore, bet his or her livelihood on the ability of these personalities to attract a requisite number of customers.

In their advertising and publicity campaigns for "A" pictures, the studios gave prominence to the star. Story, genre, producer, director and supporting players generally took lesser positions than the key performer, who would be featured in both the textual and graphic elements of the promotional material. "Katharine Hepburn as the lying, stealing, singing, praying witch girl of the Ozarks" (*Spitfire*, RKO, 1934 – see Figure 7.1), "Foot-Free Fred and Joyous Ginger . . . In Their Gayest, Gladdest Show!" (*Shall We Dance*, RKO, 1937 – see Figure 7.2) are examples. One need only compare the star-oriented approach in "A"-film advertising to the genre elements usually emphasized in "B"-picture advertising where the actors were often an insignificant element in the campaign (e.g., *I Walked with a Zombie*, RKO, 1943 – see Figure 7.3) to gauge the importance of the star.

Figure 7.1   An advertisement for *Spitfire* (produced by Pandro S. Berman for RKO, 1934). Author's private collection.

Figure 7.2 An advertisement for *Shall We Dance* (produced by Pandro S. Berman for RKO, 1937). Author's private collection.

Figure 7.3 An advertisement for *I Walked with a Zombie* (produced by Val Lewton for RKO, 1943). Author's private collection.

The long-term contract

A key to the star system for the studios was the long-term, exclusive contract. New performers were required to sign contracts which bound them to a specific studio for a prescribed period of time – usually five or seven years. The company's actual commitment to the performer, however, was generally six months, for the usual contract contained six-month option clauses. If studio executives decided that the actor's potential value was not substantial, they could release the individual at the end of the option period. However, if the performer was thought to have potential, his or her option would be "exercised," meaning that the relationship would continue with the actor receiving a small pay raise.

The actor did not have the same rights. Even if thoroughly dissatisfied with the parts he or she was assigned to play or the way the studio was managing his or her career, the actor remained exclusive studio property until either the executives decided not to exercise the option or the long-term contract came to an end. A typical studio contract called for 40 weeks of pay and 12 weeks of unpaid vacation. The studio had the right to determine when the vacation period(s) would begin and end.

In addition, if an irreconcilable disagreement arose between the actor and the studio (usually over the roles which the producers and studio head required the actor to play), the studio had the right to suspend the performer without pay. Suspension time was automatically added to the time frame of the original contract, lengthening it to the studio's benefit. In 1945, a film company's right to tack suspension time onto these contracts ended as the result of a historic lawsuit initiated by Olivia de Havilland against Warner Bros. From that point on, unhappy actors could "sit out" the remainder of their contracts and then start anew, as free-lance talent or with a different organization.

The standard contract also gave a studio the right to loan its contract actors to other production entities. This might occur for several different reasons. The usual justification was that the home studio did not have an appropriate property ready for the performer. Rather than pay the individual to sit idly by until a fitting vehicle was ready to go before the cameras, the studio chief would call other studios, hoping one might be able to use the actor and absorb his or her salary. A very different circumstance arose when a studio developed a script with a role that was perfect for a performer who was under contract to a competitor. In this case, the studio might be able to obtain the actor, but would usually pay dearly for the privilege. The home studio often made a handsome profit on these loan outs.

Film companies, however, were generally cautious about loan-out arrangements, especially when they involved their most popular talent. While considering requests for these individuals, the head of the studio would demand to see a script and to know the producer, director and other members of the cast with whom their star would be working. No amount of excess income would be worthwhile if the project turned out poorly, damaging the value of the star. Harry Cohn at Columbia had a very weak group of contract players, yet he was able to borrow Clark Gable from MGM for *It Happened One Night* (1934), Gary Cooper from Paramount for *Mr. Deeds Goes to Town* (1936) and James Stewart from MGM for both *You Can't Take It with You* (1938) and *Mr. Smith Goes to Washington* (1939) because each of these films was a quality production directed by highly respected Frank Capra. And, in each instance, the actor returned to his parent company a bigger star than he had been before working with Capra. The studio's investment had been enhanced by the loan out to Columbia.

Some major stars had a contractual right to do one "outside" picture a year for which they (or, typically, their agents) could negotiate a deal. Claudette Colbert, for example, exercised this provision in her Paramount contract in order to co-star with Gable in *It Happened One Night*. This was a shrewd decision; she won a Best Actress Academy Award for her work in the picture. Bing Crosby had a similar clause in his Paramount contract, enabling him to make *East Side of Heaven* (1939) and *If I Had My Way* (1940) for Universal.

Still, there was less farming out of stars than one might imagine. The practice made certain performers angry unless it involved a role and/or working relationship they coveted. More importantly, the studios recognized the value of major stars and wished to showcase them exclusively in company productions. Greta Garbo never made an American film for a studio other than MGM. Though Twentieth Century-Fox and MGM loaned stars back and forth frequently because Fox executive William Goetz was the son-in-law of Louis B. Mayer, Mayer found the door slammed in his face when he asked for Fox's biggest star, Shirley Temple, for *The Wizard of Oz* (1939). (Ironically, Mayer was forced to use his own contract employee Judy Garland as Dorothy, and the part elevated her star status.) All of Katharine Hepburn's films were made for RKO until her box office clout began to wane in the late 1930s. Only then would RKO agree to a loan out (to Columbia for *Holiday*, 1938). When Ms. Hepburn returned to the studio and refused to appear in a picture called *Mother Carey's Chickens* (1938), the studio released her from her contract.

The biggest complaint voiced by star actors was that the studios often forced them to play roles that were unsuitable or to appear in what they felt would be

bad pictures. Most acting contracts gave the studio full control over the assign-
ment of film material, though a number of big stars attained the right to refuse
an assigned part. Warner Bros., always the most contentious of studios, was
the site of numerous pitched battles between executives and such performers
as Bette Davis and James Cagney over this issue. And yet Humphrey Bogart
ascended toward stardom at Warner Bros. in roles that George Raft refused
to play: Roy Earle in *High Sierra* (1940) and Sam Spade in *The Maltese Falcon*
(1941). MGM was extremely lenient; it rarely forced one of its many stars to
take a role that he or she disliked.

Free-lance actors

Beginning in the last half of the 1930s, some stars opted to free-lance. While
the majority continued to recognize the advantages of working for a single
studio which provided career management and publicity as well as guaranteed
employment, others began to feel that they would be better off choosing each
role they would play. John Barrymore was one of the first to do this. In the early
1930s, he picked varied and challenging parts in such films as *Moby Dick* (1930)
for Warner Bros., *Grand Hotel* (1932) for MGM, *Topaze* (1933) for RKO and
Twentieth Century (1934) for Columbia. Sadly, the career of this man who was
considered one of the great actors of his time began to decline precipitously in
the mid-1930s, though Barrymore's own self-destructive behavior, rather than
poor career planning, was the fundamental problem. He continued to free-
lance for the rest of his life, but his deteriorating abilities forced him to take
less significant parts in marginal pictures such as *Hold That Co-Ed* (Twentieth
Century-Fox, 1938), *The Invisible Woman* (Universal, 1941), *World Premiere*
(Paramount, 1941) and *Playmates* (RKO, 1941). Barrymore died in 1942.

A much more positive experience involved Cary Grant. Grant enjoyed some
success while under contract to Paramount in the early 1930s, but became a
true star after he took control of his career in 1937. Grant's decisions to appear
in *The Awful Truth* (Columbia, 1937), *Topper* (Roach/MGM, 1937), *Holiday*
(Columbia, 1938), *Bringing Up Baby* (RKO, 1938), *Gunga Din* (RKO, 1939),
The Philadelphia Story (MGM, 1940), *My Favorite Wife* (RKO, 1940), *His
Girl Friday* (Columbia, 1940) and *Suspicion* (RKO, 1941), among other films,
transformed him into one of Hollywood's most coveted leading men. Others
who became free agents in the pre-war period, leaving behind exclusive con-
tracts with their former studios, included Fredric March, Carole Lombard,
Ginger Rogers, Fred Astaire, Gary Cooper, Dick Powell, John Wayne and Joan
Blondell.

Star development

Most studios invested heavily in star development. When a young actor was placed under contract, the individual received acting lessons, elocution lessons, grooming advice, physical fitness coaching, as well as voice and/or dance training when necessary. In addition, the neophyte was taught how to interact with fans, fan clubs, reporters, writers for fan magazines, gossip columnists and others. It was considered imperative that perceptions about both the on- and off-screen lives of actors be controlled by filtering them through the studio's publicity staff. If something went awry, the publicists were expected to minimize the damage.

Distilled to its essence, star development involved building up an actor's status through a series of roles which would establish, stabilize and expand upon an image or persona which moviegoers found appealing. Once the persona was fixed in the public's mind, all publicity and promotional material was designed to complement and magnify this pleasing image. Greta Garbo, for example, was perceived to be just as melancholy, mercurial and unfathomable off the screen as she was on it. Likewise, Shirley Temple was considered by the public to be the same perfect child she played in her movies – precocious, energetic, respectful of her elders, adorable.

Though everyone assumed that movie stars lived glamorous lives and made lots of money, their publicity, with some exceptions, was tailored to convince the public that they were just as normal and down-to-earth as everyone else. Clark Gable supposedly preferred to rough it on hunting and fishing trips with his chums rather than indulge in luxurious vacations to Paris or New York. And, in spite of the exotic and erotic image she projected on screen, Marlene Dietrich was featured in fan magazines as an old-fashioned hausfrau who loved to cook and clean and take care of her daughter.

Except for a special case like Garbo, it was deemed important for stars to be almost constantly before the public. During the 1930s, most appeared in three or more films a year. In addition, they were often on the radio, either in their own shows (Bob Hope, Dick Powell, Al Jolson, Bing Crosby, Jeanette MacDonald, Fred Astaire, Eddie Cantor and others) or as guests on other programs. In addition, they were used to advertise every kind of consumer product, from cigarettes and automobiles to dishwashing soap and toothpaste. Most also made personal appearances, particularly around the time that one of their films was opening. During World War II, the responsibilities of the stars expanded to include selling war bonds, entertaining the troops and "working" in USO-sponsored GI hangouts like the Hollywood Canteen. In America during this period, movie stars were ubiquitous. A veritable cottage industry of fan magazines, gossip columns and radio and newspaper reportage existed to provide the public with a continuous flow of information about their favorites.

Despite its considerable importance and the legions of professionals who played a role in the process, star development was a maddening business. The number of thunderous mistakes that would later haunt the studios' highly paid "experts" almost certainly equals the perceptive decisions made by those same individuals. Universal had Bette Davis under contract in the early 1930s, but its management did not foresee a bright future for her and let her go. Warner Bros. signed her, but she languished there until the studio loaned her to RKO for *Of Human Bondage* (1934). Her stunning performance as sluttish waitress Mildred opposite Leslie Howard's Philip Carey caused the Warner executives to realize that they had a powerhouse actress and valuable commodity in the fold.

RKO helped turn Bette Davis into a star for Warner Bros., but it made plenty of mistakes with its own personnel. It had a chance to sign Clark Gable and passed him up. The studio did have Betty Grable under contract, but eventually let her go. So did Paramount after she made an uninspiring run of films for them in the late 1930s. The third try, however, was charmed for Grable who became a huge star at Twentieth Century-Fox in the early 40s. Joan Fontaine wasted away in undistinguished RKO parts before the company finally released her in 1939. Two years later, RKO borrowed Miss Fontaine back from independent producer David O. Selznick for *Suspicion*. The studio was forced to pay a price many times that of her previous RKO salary and found its embarrassment compounded when her performance in *Suspicion* won the Academy Award for Best Actress.

Perhaps the most famous example of a botched star campaign in Hollywood history involved Russian actress Anna Sten. Independent producer Samuel Goldwyn, who had a keen eye for talent and developed numerous stars during his career, was entranced by Miss Sten and determined to turn her into a public favorite who would rival European-born stars Greta Garbo and Marlene Dietrich. Goldwyn's publicity campaign began more than a year before the actress appeared in her first American picture. Sten was labeled the "Million Dollar Discovery" and "The Brightest Star from the Northern Skies." A steady stream of articles about this amazing discovery filled newspapers and fan magazines while the actress worked to perfect her English.

Goldwyn decided to chart a "high brow" path to success. He first starred Anna Sten in *Nana* (United Artists, 1934), based on a novel by Emile Zola. The actress played a Parisian courtesan who uses men to achieve fame and money, then enters into a love affair which ends tragically. The plot of *Nana* was reminiscent of several Garbo films and even included a singing sequence that was similar in style to those found in some of Dietrich's movies. Nonetheless, audiences were unimpressed. Perhaps no one could have lived up to the hyperbolic advance publicity, but Sten's overly emphatic acting style and her dreadful singing did not help. The film was a flop.

Undaunted, Goldwyn instructed his publicists to act as if Anna Sten had become a major star in her first Hollywood film, one likely to supplant Garbo and Dietrich. For her next vehicle, Goldwyn chose *We Live Again* (United Artists, 1934), an adaptation of Tolstoy's *Resurrection*, in which she portrayed a very different sort of character. Dressed in virginal white, with a single cross around her neck, she played an innocent servant girl who is seduced and abandoned by a prince. Though director Rouben Mamoulian elicited a more controlled performance from Sten than Dorothy Arzner had in *Nana*, audiences were perhaps confused by this radical shift in her screen persona and Goldwyn soon had another money-loser on his hands.

Still, the producer refused to give up. For *The Wedding Night* (United Artists, 1935), Goldwyn paired her with Gary Cooper and attempted to "Americanize" her image. She played a Polish immigrant who falls in love with a married writer (Cooper) in Connecticut. Though Sten's performance, as guided by director King Vidor, was appealing, the story was weak and climaxed with her accidental death. The upshot – a third consecutive box office calamity – convinced the producer to give up on a woman who soon became known throughout the industry as "Goldwyn's Million Dollar Folly."

In the case of Anna Sten, the cyclonic publicity campaign boomeranged. It would have been practically impossible for any actor to live up to the advance billing that she received. Of course, one can only speculate, but a more measured approach combined with a more judicious effort to pinpoint the ideal Anna Sten screen persona – rather than an attempt to shoehorn her into the Garbo–Dietrich mold – might have yielded more positive results.

The Multiplicity of Stars

There was no dominant star persona in Hollywood during the Classical Period. The biggest stars of the 1930s ran the gamut from the very young (Shirley Temple) to the elderly (Marie Dressler), from the exotic (Garbo) to the familiar (Will Rogers), from the beautiful and glamorous (Joan Crawford) to the plain and simple (Janet Gaynor), from the tall and handsome (Gary Cooper) to the short and average (Mickey Rooney). In a way, however, all the stars did have one common quality: charisma. Their personal magnetism was difficult to describe but palpable when they were on screen. For each, the combination of physical type, acting style and roles played fixed a persona that caused contemporary audiences to seek out each new film they appeared in. Moviegoers had the opportunity to spend time with hundreds of different screen actors, but they favored certain stars above all others. These performers not only represented invaluable assets to their employers, they also provide special insights into the historical moment during which they resided at the top of the motion picture world.

As discussed in chapter 6, many stars became identified with particular genres: Charles Chaplin (comedy), Bette Davis (the woman's film), Errol Flynn (the adventure film), John Wayne (the western), Fred Astaire (the musical), James Cagney (the gangster film). Interestingly, a number of the biggest stars of the 1930s and 1940s were identified with comedy and/or the musical: Marie Dressler, Will Rogers, Abbott and Costello, Bob Hope (comedy); Shirley Temple, Betty Grable, Bing Crosby (musical); Janet Gaynor, Mickey Rooney (both). Arguably, these were the most popular genres of the Classical Period, with comedy dominating during the grim days of the Depression and the musical asserting its power just before and during World War II.

Nonetheless, most studio executives were committed to a diversified program of feature films and recognized that the customers wanted to see their favorites play a variety of different characters. The actors themselves often felt straitjacketed when they were confined to a specific genre and pressured producers to give them the opportunity to "stretch." For some, this was impossible. If a film featured the Marx Brothers, Laurel and Hardy or Joe E. Brown, it had to be a comedy. If Boris Karloff or Bela Lugosi or Lon Chaney Jr. played the lead, the audience expected a horror film. Most stars, however, did have opportunities to migrate between genres and were able to adapt their personas to the demands of differing forms.

Still, this could be a tricky business. James Cagney and Humphrey Bogart, two actors identified with contemporary urban genres like the gangster film, seemed strangely out of place, to critics and viewers alike, in *The Oklahoma Kid* (Warner Bros., 1939), a western about the opening of the Oklahoma Territory. Likewise, audiences who adored the hyper-masculine and prototypically American Clark Gable were less than enthusiastic when he made the biographical film *Parnell* (MGM, 1937), which detailed the noble efforts of an Irish patriot attempting to convince the British Parliament to grant home rule to his native land. The film was, by far, the largest financial dud of Gable's 1930s career, costing the studio $637,000 in losses. One other example involved Cary Grant. During the war years, Grant convinced RKO to let him star in *None but the Lonely Heart* (1944), the downbeat tale of a restless cockney resident of the London slums reaching out toward a better life. Grant's fans, expecting the usual urbane, sophisticated and romantic persona which had made him a star, were not pleased by this glum portrait of shattered dreams in a sordid and indifferent world. Though Grant felt Ernie Mott was a more realistic, substantial, and interesting character than he usually played, audiences stayed away and the film lost $72,000. And this during a period when other, less challenging pictures starring Grant, such as *Once upon a Honeymoon* (RKO, 1942, profit: $282,000) and *Mr. Lucky* (RKO, 1943, profit: $1,603,000) were quite successful.

Some actors knew better than to monkey around with their personas. When production head Darryl Zanuck asked Betty Grable to play the role of alcohol and drug-addicted Sophie MacDonald in *The Razor's Edge* (Twentieth Century-Fox, 1946), she refused. "I'm the truck drivers' delight," she said. "They want to see me in tights backstage. They don't want to see me doing heavy emoting." The part was eventually played by Anne Baxter who won an Oscar for it.

On occasion, self-preservation required that an actor abandon his/her persona. This was difficult for child stars such as Jackie Cooper, Shirley Temple and Deanna Durbin who grew up and out of the screen personas that audiences adored. Elizabeth Taylor, however, managed the transition. After coming to the public's attention in such juvenile roles as Priscilla in *Lassie Come Home* (MGM, 1942) and Velvet Brown in *National Velvet* (MGM, 1944), Taylor developed into a bigger star as an adult than she had been as a child.

It was also difficult for an adult to cast aside an established screen image and re-emerge in a new guise that the public would approve. One who managed the transformation successfully was Dick Powell. Powell enjoyed considerable success as a breezy male ingenue in *42nd Street* (1933), *Gold Diggers of 1933* (1933), *Dames* (1934) and other musicals made by Warner Bros. By the early 40s, however, his career as a song-and-dance man was in decline. He appeared in several comedies and musicals for Paramount, Universal, MGM and United Artists, none of which was a roaring success, and even accepted a secondary part in the Abbott and Costello vehicle *In the Navy* (Universal, 1941). Then, RKO took a chance, casting him as hard-boiled private eye Philip Marlowe in an adaptation of Raymond Chandler's novel *Farewell, My Lovely*. Fearing that audiences would perceive the film to be just another half-baked Powell musical, the studio changed the title to *Murder, My Sweet* (1944) and ran an aggressive advertising campaign (see Figure 7.4) that invited audiences to come and see the new Dick Powell: "TWO-FISTED . . . HARDBOILED . . .

Figure 7.4 A title card meant to be displayed in theater lobbies for *Murder, My Sweet* (produced by Adrian Scott for RKO, 1945). Author's private collection.

TERRIFIC . . . MEET the year's biggest movie surprise . . . Dick Powell playing a new kind of role . . . in a murder-mystery that packs as big a punch as the NEW Dick Powell." The title card graphics feature Powell in a clinch with femme fatale Claire Trevor and fighting with giant Mike Mazurki. *Murder, My Sweet* was a hit and Powell's career was rejuvenated. He would continue to portray tough guys into the next decade.

Another actor who managed to reinvent herself was Joan Crawford. In such films as *Our Dancing Daughters* (MGM, 1928), *Our Modern Maidens* (MGM, 1929) and *Our Blushing Brides* (MGM, 1930), she epitomized the jazz baby, an energetic girl on the make determined to challenge, if not fracture, the tenets and taboos of her elders. In the early 1930s, she started to play ambitious working-class women who slide into romantic relationships which are often without benefit of marriage (e.g., *Possessed*, MGM, 1931; *Rain*, Feature Productions/United Artists, 1932; *Sadie McKee*, MGM, 1934; *Chained*, MGM, 1934). These roles, in particular, seemed well suited to Crawford whose publicity had always emphasized her difficult upbringing and her driving desire to triumph over personal adversity. At the same time, Crawford was one of the sexiest actresses of the period, and reports that she was named corespondent in several divorce actions reinforced the persona that she was building on screen. However, most likely because of the influence of the Production Code Administration, Crawford soon found herself playing characters who were more refined and wealthy in standard-issue MGM woman's films and comedies, such as *No More Ladies* (1935), *I Live My Life* (1935) and *Love on the Run* (1936). While the parts enabled the actress to showcase a dazzling array of designer clothes (most provided by resident MGM designer Adrian), they were not received with unbridled enthusiasm by the public. After years of consistent profits, her films began to lose money: *The Bride Wore Red* (MGM, 1937, $271,000 loss); *The Shining Hour* (MGM, 1938, $137,000 loss); *The Ice Follies of 1939* (MGM, 1939, $343,000 loss); *The Women* (MGM, 1939, $262,000 loss). She had been a top-rated star in the early 1930s, but by the end of the decade, she was branded "box office poison" by the Independent Theater Owners Association, along with Garbo, Dietrich, Katharine Hepburn, Edward Arnold and others. Part of the problem almost certainly related to Crawford's own maturation process. Though she remained a beautiful woman, her appearance changed so radically between the early and late 1930s that it was difficult to believe that the youthful, romantic stenographer of *Grand Hotel* (MGM, 1932) and the hard-bitten, conniving man trap of *The Women* were played by the same person.

Crawford blamed her declining popularity on MGM, feeling the studio executives had not furnished her with the sort of roles that would reverse the downward spiral. Following the failure of *A Woman's Face* (MGM, 1941, $131,000 loss) and a loan out to Columbia for *They All Kissed the Bride* (1942), she left the company, signing with Warner Bros. There she was offered the part that would revitalize her career: Mildred Pierce in the eponymous 1945 film. The story of a mother (Crawford) who loses one child and thoroughly spoils a second, it also presented the star as a determined, independent woman who builds a business empire from nothing. Thus, the film hearkened back to that earlier period of the actress' success when she had played a younger version of the same driven character. The public must have approved of this "reversion to type"; *Mildred Pierce* garnered film rentals of more than $5.6 million and Crawford won the Academy Award as Best Actress.

On occasion, an actor's career could be strongly affected by his or her off-screen life. If a fissure opened between the public's perceptions of a star and the individual's actual behavior, the results were sometimes disastrous. Perhaps the most famous example occurred during the silent era when popular comedian

Roscoe "Fatty" Arbuckle was accused of raping and then murdering starlet Virginia Rappe during a wild party in a San Francisco hotel suite. Although ultimately acquitted of the charges (after three trials), Arbuckle never recaptured his audience. The public simply could not laugh with or at him again. Though he managed to surmount his difficulties better than Arbuckle, Errol Flynn's career was also affected by legal proceedings concerning his sexual relationships with young women in the 1940s. And Charlie Chaplin's affair with Joan Barry, the subsequent paternity suit and his marriage to 18-year-old Oona O'Neill during World War II certainly had a negative effect on his popularity.

Changing historical realities could also affect a star's career. European-born actors such as Greta Garbo, Marlene Dietrich, Maurice Chevalier, Elissa Landi and Luise Rainer saw their box office power decline in the last half of the 1930s, at least partially because of the American public's feelings of discomfort about the growing crisis on the other side of the Atlantic. The loss of various foreign markets in the late 1930s and early 1940s, owing to the war, also impacted Garbo, Dietrich and others, whose films had always garnered more than the usual percentage of revenues from abroad. Similarly, attempts in the last half of the decade to make stars out of such European newcomers as Francis Lederer, Simone Simon, Richard Greene, Annabella, Anton Walbrook, Danielle Darrieux, Isa Miranda, Nino Martini, Sigrid Gurie, Heather Angel, Brian Aherne, Binnie Barnes, Vera Zorina and Margot Grahame did not meet with success. There were exceptions; Norwegian ice skating champion Sonja Henie became a big star at Twentieth Century-Fox and French-born Charles Boyer emerged as a dependable leading man during the period. Once the United States entered the war, the uneasiness seemed to dissipate. The sincere patriotic efforts of Dietrich helped to rejuvenate her career, and such European-born performers as Ingrid Bergman, Paul Henreid, Hedy Lamarr, Ray Milland, Greer Garson and Paul Lukas thrived.

Any actor whose commitment to the American crusade against Germany and Japan appeared to be less than total placed his or her career in immediate jeopardy. Lew Ayres, for example, was a reliable leading man throughout the 1930s. In 1938, he settled into the role of Dr. Kildare in the popular MGM series; he also starred in MGM films opposite such female luminaries as Joan Crawford, Lana Turner, Jeanette MacDonald and Greer Garson. However, in 1942 he became a figure of nationwide controversy. Perhaps influenced by his starring role in the most powerful anti-war film of the 1930s, *All Quiet on the Western Front* (Universal, 1930), Ayres declared himself a conscientious objector. Exhibitors throughout the country announced that they would no longer show his pictures and even studio mogul Louis B. Mayer initially scorned him, though company president Nicholas Schenck later took a full-page ad in *Variety* defending the actor. Lew Ayres served four years as a non-combatant in the US Army Medical Corps and was cited for gallantry on the battlefield. However, when he returned from the war and began acting again, he was cast primarily in supporting parts. It is plausible to suggest that Ayres' career was never able to rebound from the public charges of cowardice and unpatriotic behavior that swirled around him for a time in 1942.

Even Charlie Chaplin, one of the biggest and most beloved stars in film history, suffered. Chaplin's decision to make a film denouncing the Nazis and Fascists (*The Great Dictator*, Chaplin/United Artists, 1940) before Pearl Harbor did not sit well with the nation's powerful isolationist faction. In addition, the news that he had never become an American citizen, despite living for many years in the US and making his fortune in the country, plus his left-wing pronouncements on numerous subjects and the aforementioned relationships between the mid-50s star and much younger women, transformed Chaplin's image from lovable rascal into suspicious character in the early 40s. Suspicion turned to downright hostility during the redbaiting McCarthy period that arrived after the end of World War II, and Chaplin eventually elected to abandon the United States, his career and reputation in tatters.

In sum, stardom during the Classical Period was a precarious business, subject to a large number of vicissitudes, some of which were beyond the individual's (or even the studio's) ability to control. With the exception of a few special cases, such as Clark Gable, Gary Cooper and Bing Crosby, most top stars were not able to sustain a high level of popularity for more than a few years. Movie spectators are a fickle lot who embrace certain favorites, then move on in the proverbial blink of an eye.

The Star as Actor

Stars were, first and foremost, actors. Though some critics have maintained that most stars are not really actors at all, simply magnetic personalities who play themselves over and over again, closer scrutiny reveals a different picture. Many stars, were, in fact, accomplished performers whose screen images were quite different from their off-screen personalities. Their ability to embody a figure whom spectators embraced and looked forward to seeing on screen in future roles required considerable acting talent.

At the same time, most of the top-rated stars were "types" who could not (or did not) play a wide range of parts. Will Rogers, Mickey Rooney and Abbott and Costello were certainly stars, but no one would ask them to play Oedipus Rex or Hamlet. Similarly, the public adored Marie Dressler, Shirley Temple and Betty Grable, but they wouldn't be cast as Lady Macbeth or Hedda Gabler.

A number of Hollywood actors did consider themselves capable of portraying a broad range of characters and pressured producers and studio executives to seek properties that would enable them to showcase their thespian abilities. While recognized as the true artists of the American cinema, these performers rarely approached the upper echelons of stardom. Paul Muni left an indelible mark on the gangster film (*Scarface*, Caddo/United Artists, 1932), the social problem film (*I Am a Fugitive from a Chain Gang*, Warner Bros., 1932) and the screen biography (*The Story of Louis Pasteur*, Warner Bros., 1936), among other genres, yet he was never a public favorite, never a box office star. George Arliss, Edward G. Robinson, Luise Rainer, Fredric March, Pat O'Brien, Claude Rains, Herbert Marshall and others had similar careers.

Two exceptional actors who did become top-ranked stars were Spencer Tracy and Bette Davis. Like Muni, Tracy excelled in a broad spectrum of genre roles: gangster (*Twenty Thousand Years in Sing Sing*, Warner Bros., 1932), comedy (*Libeled Lady*, MGM, 1936), social problem (*Fury*, MGM, 1937), biography (*Stanley and Livingstone*, Twentieth Century-Fox, 1939), horror (*Dr. Jekyll and Mr. Hyde*, MGM, 1941), war (*Thirty Seconds over Tokyo*, MGM, 1944). He reached the peak of his popularity in the late 1930s and early 1940s when he won two consecutive Academy Awards as Best Actor for *Captains Courageous* (MGM, 1937) and *Boys Town* (MGM, 1938). His portrayal of Father Flanagan in *Boys Town* and its sequel *Men of Boys Town* (MGM, 1941) resulted in two of the biggest hits of the period while, at the same time, he was appearing in such action-oriented fare as *Test Pilot* (MGM, 1938), *Northwest Passage* (MGM, 1940) and *Boom Town* (MGM, 1940). Tracy's teaming with Katharine Hepburn in a series of MGM films beginning in the early 1940s helped to solidify his popularity and elevate hers.

Bette Davis enjoyed her highest audience approval around the same time. An actress of substantial range and, at times, extraordinary power, she was forced to play a number of indifferent roles by Warner Bros. executives but managed to excel whenever given a challenging part. Though flexible enough to work in the studio's detective films (*Satan Met a Lady*, 1936), biographies (*The Private Lives of Elizabeth and Essex*, 1939), comedies (*The Bride Came C.O.D.*, 1941) and other genre pictures, Davis' stardom was based on her towering presence in the woman's film. After winning Best Actress Academy Awards for *Dangerous* (Warner Bros., 1935) and *Jezebel* (Warner Bros., 1938), she played the leading roles in such other Warner hits as *Dark Victory* (1939),

All This and Heaven Too (1940), *The Great Lie* (1941) and *Now, Voyager* (1942). The most surprising aspect of Bette Davis' stardom was her willingness to play roles that were thoroughly unsympathetic. As previously mentioned, it was the reprehensible Mildred in *Of Human Bondage* that had elevated her initially; later, she agreed to play such villainesses as Leslie Crosbie in *The Letter* (Warner Bros., 1940), Regina Gibbons in *The Little Foxes* (Goldwyn/RKO, 1941) and Stanley Timberlake in *In This Our Life* (Warner Bros., 1942). Arguably the most unusual of movie stars, Bette Davis was surely the most fearless, and the public's fascination with her is a testament to her contrary nature, as well as her extraordinary talent.

The Most Popular Stars

Beginning in 1932, Quigley Publications, the publisher of such influential trade journals as *Motion Picture Herald* and *Motion Picture Daily*, began to release its annual "Top 10 List of Money Making Stars." In order to determine the most popular personalities, the Quigley staff polled independent and circuit exhibitors throughout the United States on the theory that theater owners were in the best position to identify the stars who attracted a disproportionate number of their customers. Though not conducted in scientific fashion, the Quigley Poll was taken seriously – both inside and outside the industry – and its results seem to accord with fan-oriented polls, as well as available studio records which indicate the financial performances of different actors' films.

The results of the Quigley survey were as follows:

1932　1. Marie Dressler 2. Janet Gaynor 3. Joan Crawford 4. Charles Farrell 5. Greta Garbo 6. Norma Shearer 7. Wallace Beery 8. Clark Gable 9. Will Rogers 10. Joe E. Brown

1933　1. Marie Dressler 2. Will Rogers 3. Janet Gaynor 4. Eddie Cantor 5. Wallace Beery 6. Jean Harlow 7. Clark Gable 8. Mae West 9. Norma Shearer 10. Joan Crawford

1934　1. Will Rogers 2. Clark Gable 3. Janet Gaynor 4. Wallace Beery 5. Mae West 6. Joan Crawford 7. Bing Crosby 8. Shirley Temple 9. Marie Dressler 10. Norma Shearer

1935　1. Shirley Temple 2. Will Rogers 3. Clark Gable 4. Fred Astaire and Ginger Rogers 5. Joan Crawford 6. Claudette Colbert 7. Dick Powell 8. Wallace Beery 9. Joe E. Brown 10. James Cagney

1936　1. Shirley Temple 2. Clark Gable 3. Fred Astaire and Ginger Rogers

4. Robert Taylor 5. Joe E. Brown 6. Dick Powell 7. Joan Crawford
8. Claudette Colbert 9. Jeanette MacDonald 10. Gary Cooper

1937   1. Shirley Temple 2. Clark Gable 3. Robert Taylor 4. Bing Crosby
5. William Powell 6. Jane Withers 7. Fred Astaire and Ginger Rogers
8. Sonja Henie 9. Gary Cooper 10. Myrna Loy

1938   1. Shirley Temple 2. Clark Gable 3. Sonja Henie 4. Mickey Rooney
5. Spencer Tracy 6. Robert Taylor 7. Myrna Loy 8. Jane Withers 9. Alice
Faye 10. Tyrone Power

1939   1. Mickey Rooney 2. Tyrone Power 3. Spencer Tracy 4. Clark Gable
5. Shirley Temple 6. Bette Davis 7. Alice Faye 8. Errol Flynn 9. James
Cagney 10. Sonja Henie

1940   1. Mickey Rooney 2. Spencer Tracy 3. Clark Gable 4. Gene Autry
5. Tyrone Power 6. James Cagney 7. Bing Crosby 8. Wallace Beery
9. Bette Davis 10. Judy Garland

1941   1. Mickey Rooney 2. Clark Gable 3. Bud Abbott and Lou Costello
4. Bob Hope 5. Spencer Tracy 6. Gene Autry 7. Gary Cooper 8. Bette
Davis 9. James Cagney 10. Judy Garland

1942   1. Bud Abbott and Lou Costello 2. Clark Gable 3. Gary Cooper.
4. Mickey Rooney 5. Bob Hope 6. James Cagney 7. Gene Autry 8. Betty
Grable 9. Greer Garson 10. Spencer Tracy

1943   1. Betty Grable 2. Bob Hope 3. Bud Abbott and Lou Costello 4. Bing
Crosby 5. Gary Cooper 6. Greer Garson 7. Humphrey Bogart 8. James
Cagney 9. Mickey Rooney 10. Clark Gable

1944   1. Bing Crosby 2. Gary Cooper 3. Bob Hope 4. Betty Grable 5. Spencer
Tracy 6. Greer Garson 7. Humphrey Bogart 8. Bud Abbott and Lou
Costello 9. Cary Grant 10. Bette Davis

1945   1. Bing Crosby 2. Van Johnson 3. Greer Garson 4. Betty Grable
5. Spencer Tracy 6. Humphrey Bogart/Gary Cooper 7. Bob Hope
8. Judy Garland 9. Margaret O'Brien 10. Roy Rogers

Before discussing the major stars of the period, a few general remarks should be made. First, the polls confirm the dominant position of Metro-Goldwyn-Mayer with respect to stars. Of the 43 actors listed in the Top 10 during the years 1932–45, 17 were under exclusive contract to MGM. In second position, surprisingly, was Fox/Twentieth Century-Fox. A studio that claimed to compensate for its lack of box office personalities by making "the story the star," Fox was, in fact, quite adept at star development; the studio had nine Top 10 figures during the period. Next came Warner Bros. with six, Paramount with five, Republic (improbably) with two, then Universal, RKO and United Artists with one each. (To be accurate, both the Universal and RKO favorites were teams: Abbott and Costello and Astaire and Rogers, respectively.) Columbia was unable to place a single star in the Top 10.

Another interesting facet of the Quigley Polls relates to the importance of pairings in films. With the exception of Will Rogers, Shirley Temple and Betty Grable, all of the top stars were either members of a famous team or regularly cast with another performer whose persona and style meshed nicely with their own. In the silent era, Marie Dressler partnered with Polly Moran in a group of pictures that carried over into the early sound era. Miss Dressler's biggest hits, however, came in films with Wallace Beery as her co-star, such as *Min and Bill* (MGM, 1930) and *Tugboat Annie* (MGM, 1933). Beery also made the Top 10 during the years he and Dressler were working together, then declined in the rankings. Mickey Rooney was at the peak of popularity in the late 1930s and early 40s when he was regularly paired with Judy Garland, who occupied tenth place in the 1940 and 1941 Polls. They appeared together in *Love Finds Andy Hardy* (MGM, 1938), *Babes in Arms* (MGM, 1939) and *Strike Up the Band* (MGM, 1940), among other films. Rooney also made *Captains Courageous*, *Boys Town* and *Men of Boys Town* with Spencer Tracy, who maintained a spot in the Top 10 every year from 1938 to 1945. After years of popping in and out of the Top 10, Bing Crosby began a five-year run as the Number One star in 1944. Crosby, of course, regularly co-starred in films with Bob Hope (e.g., *Road to Singapore*, Paramount, 1940, *Road to Zanzibar*, Paramount 1941, and *Road to Morocco*, Paramount, 1942) who maintained a spot of his own in the Top 10 each year from 1941–45.

In fact, the packing of several top stars into a single film often produced scintillating box office results. MGM was especially adept at this. All-star casts were offered in such MGM productions as *Hollywood Revue of 1929* (profit: $1,135,000), *Grand Hotel* (1932, profit: $974,000), *Dinner at Eight* (1933, profit: $998,000), *Libeled Lady* (1936, profit: $1,189,000), *San Francisco* (1936, profit: $2,237,000) and *Test Pilot* (1938, profit: $967,000). While none of the other studios was capable of putting three or more Top 10 performers in a single film, they did occasionally mount a multi-star picture in a halfhearted attempt to ape the success of MGM. Paramount, for example, featured Ray Milland, Paulette Goddard, John Wayne and Susan Hayward in star producer-director Cecil B. DeMille's *Reap the Wild Wind* (1942), Twentieth Century-Fox used Tyrone Power, Alice Faye, Don Ameche and Ethel Merman in *Alexander's Ragtime Band* (1938) and Warner Bros. placed James Cagney, Olivia de Havilland, Dick Powell and Joe E. Brown in *A Midsummer's Night's Dream* (1935).

Many of the most respected and fondly remembered actors of the period were less popular than one might imagine. Greta Garbo (Number Five in 1932) made the list only once, as did Jeanette MacDonald (Number Nine in 1936), William Powell (Number Five in 1937), Errol Flynn (Number Eight in 1939) and Cary Grant (Number Nine in 1944). Among those who never penetrated the Top 10 during the Classical Period: Barbara Stanwyck, Charles Chaplin, Marlene Dietrich, Katharine Hepburn, Deanna Durbin, Olivia de Havilland, Henry Fonda, Jean Arthur, Rita Hayworth, James Stewart, Loretta Young, Ronald Colman, Fred MacMurray, John Wayne and Carole Lombard.

Another telling aspect of the listings is the odd fact that, during this period, Americans required their stars to be modest, self-effacing and without pretensions. It was a time when a number of individuals who did not fit the glamorous stereotype of the "movie star" reigned supreme in the Hollywood pyramid: Marie Dressler, Will Rogers, Shirley Temple, Mickey Rooney. If the public smelled even a whiff of egotism, snobbery or arrogance in a performer's demeanor, he or she was likely to fall quickly out of favor. (In fact, many of the villainous characters and characters who function as objects of satirical ridicule in the films of the period display these precise personality traits.) Toward the end of the 1930s, for example, the Independent Theater Owners Association began a crusade against a group of actors it labeled "box office poison." Among the targeted players were Greta Garbo, Marlene Dietrich and Katharine Hepburn, all of whom had garnered a "high hat" reputation from their on-screen roles and from reports of their off-screen behavior. Hepburn and Dietrich managed to rebuild both their personas and their careers, but Garbo retired in the early 1940s after making two films (*Ninotchka*, MGM, 1939 and *Two-Faced Woman*, MGM, 1941) designed to change her profile from dramatic to comedic actress. Embarrassed, particularly by the critical skewering of *Two-Faced Woman*, she opted to abandon the screen rather than capitulate to the public's perceived demand for a warmer, more accessible and humble Garbo.

"The King"

The dominant star in Hollywood during the Classical Period was Clark Gable. Known throughout the industry as "the King," Gable appeared in a few silent productions and then played inconsequential parts in early sound films for Warner Bros. and RKO-Pathé before signing with MGM. Despite formidable competition at this star-rich studio, Gable quickly rose to the top. While he never finished first in the Quigley Poll, he was a member of the Top 10 every year from 1932 to 1942, placing second during six years and third in two other years. Undoubtedly he would have continued at or near the top in 1944 and

1945, but he opted to enter military service and was off the screen during this time.

It could be argued that Gable was the prototype male star, an actor who transcended his time and place. He could have been a star in the silent period, and it seems plausible that he would be a star if he were working in films today. Clark Gable combined rugged good looks with a charming personality, a roguish but big-hearted persona and a powerful physical presence. Nevertheless, he was not a perfect specimen; his large, protuberant ears caused Jack Warner and Darryl Zanuck of Warner Bros. to believe that he would never gain audience acceptance. Like the RKO executives, they passed up the opportunity to sign Gable to a long-term contract.

Clark Gable was typically humble, especially about his acting ability. He once said, "I'm just a guy trying to get along. I'm not important. I stand up in front of a camera and make faces and talk some words. That's all." This lack of pretension and an unwillingness to take himself seriously clearly endeared Gable to audiences.

Gable was actually a fine actor who functioned effectively in a number of genres, including the woman's film (*Possessed*, MGM, 1932), the gangster film (*Manhattan Melodrama*, 1934), the adventure film (*Mutiny on the Bounty*, MGM, 1935) and the comedy (*It Happened One Night*). He also proved a potent romantic match for MGM's top female stars: Greta Garbo (*Susan Lenox (Her Fall and Rise)*, MGM, 1932), Joan Crawford (*Dancing Lady*, 1933), Norma Shearer (*A Free Soul*, MGM, 1931), Jean Harlow (*Red Dust*, MGM, 1932), Myrna Loy (*Wife vs. Secretary*, MGM, 1936), Jeanette MacDonald (*San Francisco*), Hedy Lamarr (*Comrade X*, MGM, 1940), and Lana Turner (*Honky Tonk*, 1941). He was considered the one indispensable ingredient in the blockbuster hit of the period, *Gone with the Wind* (Selznick/MGM, 1939), in which his Rhett Butler was memorably matched with Hollywood newcomer Vivien Leigh's Scarlett O'Hara. Gable also meshed well with established male performers, such as William Powell (*Manhattan Melodrama*), Charles Laughton (*Mutiny on the Bounty*), Spencer Tracy (*Test Pilot*) and Wallace Beery (*China Seas*, MGM, 1935).

Perhaps the key to Gable's success was his wide-ranging appeal. He was a favorite of young and old, male and female, rich and poor. The MGM publicity department emphasized his all-American roots, positioning Gable as a broad-shouldered midwesterner who had endured plenty of tough times before striking it rich in the movies. Having worked in a rubber factory in Ohio, the oil fields of Oklahoma and the lumber camps of Oregon, Gable was a figure whom Depression audiences could both empathize with and idolize.

His breakthrough role was gangster Ace Wilfong in *A Free Soul*. Gable stole the picture from its star Norma Shearer, though not from Lionel Barrymore whose histrionic performance as Shearer's father earned him a Best Actor Oscar. One scene in particular stood out, a scene in which Gable roughed up Shearer. Though initially inclined to remove it, production head Irving Thalberg left the scene in the picture and audience response convinced the MGM production chief that he had a budding star on his hands. Most of Gable's future roles would be considerably more heroic and romantic, but the animal magnetism, virility and sense of menace that Gable displayed in *A Free Soul* was always there, lurking just beneath the surface of the characters he played in *Red Dust*, *Manhattan Melodrama*, *Mutiny on the Bounty* and *Gone with the Wind*; it was buried a bit deeper in some of his other parts, such as the reporter in *It Happened One Night*.

The tragic death of Gable's beloved wife Carole Lombard in a 1942 airplane accident as she was returning from a war bond sales drive and his decision, shortly thereafter, to enter military service further endeared him to the public. For many in the 1930s and 1940s, Clark Gable was not just the king of Hollywood. Like John Wayne in subsequent years, he represented the ideal American male, a figure of strength, resilience, savvy, humor and values.

The early 1930s: sentimentality, sacrifice and common sense

According to the Quigley Poll, the top movie stars of the Depression's blackest years were an improbable trio: Marie Dressler from MGM and Janet Gaynor and Will Rogers from Fox. They had several things in common: all had made silent films but became bigger stars in sound movies; none was especially attractive or alluring; each had an everyman/woman quality and yet was larger than life. Though neither sexy nor violent, they reigned at the same time that actors like Mae West and Jean Harlow were making significant inroads in the arena of cinematic sex and James Cagney, Paul Muni and Edward G. Robinson were pushing the boundaries of acceptable screen violence. Indeed, they seem to represent a kind of conservative antidote to the more controversial aspects of Pre-Code screen content. In their films, Dressler, Gaynor and Rogers offered certain old-fashioned values, values that had come under attack before the Depression began but now had taken on renewed importance in an unhinged world.

Marie Dressler has been called the most unlikely of movie stars. Older than 60 when she reached the top, this large, awkward, plain-featured but oddly dignified woman had already enjoyed a long but bumpy career before she hit it big. Her initial foray into movies, which began with *Tillie's Punctured Romance* (Sennett Studios) in 1914, ended badly and she was out of the cinema from 1918 to 1926. Her stage work and vaudeville appearances went into a steep decline around 1919, so she bought a house and settled in, waiting for some producer or manager to call. However, the calls never came, prompting Miss Dressler to announce her retirement in 1925. Finally, director Allan Dwan offered her a small part in a film he was making in 1926 and, although she only worked for one day, it reminded the right people that Dressler still had talent. Brought back to Hollywood and provided with more substantial roles, she clicked with filmgoers in such late silent comedies as *Bringing Up Father* (MGM, 1928) and *The Patsy* (MGM, 1928). The magnitude of her comeback was unparalleled in the history of cinema to that time.

Marie Dressler's career truly blossomed after *Min and Bill*, an early talkie in which she teamed with Wallace Beery. Playing two denizens of the waterfront, Dressler and Beery engage in a rough-and-tumble relationship highlighted by a hilarious brawl that occurs after she catches him with another woman. The main thrust of the film was decidedly sentimental, however, as Dressler (Min) does everything in her power to protect a young girl (Dorothy Jordan) she has raised and make certain the girl enjoys the full range of life's advantages. In order to accomplish her goal, Min must pretend not to care for her so that the girl will go to live with a schoolmaster and his wife. She must also give up her life savings and ultimately shoot the girl's actual mother who is intent on cashing in on the neophyte's new life among the upper crust of society. While the girl knows little of Min's sacrifices, the audience is well aware of them, creating a typical sentimental comedy denouement in which the patrons leave the theater vacillating between tears and laughter. Marie Dressler was honored with the Academy Award as Best Actress for her portrayal. (Figure 7.5)

This pattern of selfless sacrifice was repeated in subsequent Dressler films, including *Emma* (MGM, 1932), *Prosperity* (MGM, 1932) and *Tugboat Annie*. Each was very successful with *Emma* and *Tugboat Annie* generating profits of $898,000 and $1,212,000, respectively.

Miss Dressler's "real" life away from the cameras also contributed to her popularity. It was well known that the actress had serious health problems during the early sound period; indeed, many fans were aware that she had been fighting cancer for several years. Yet she showed no signs of flagging spirits or diminished energy. Her determination to continue working despite her deteriorating physical condition and her unwillingness to allow the situation to dampen her comic spirits endeared her to the audiences of the time. She reminded the public of the meaning of courage and perseverance and

Figure 7.5 Marie Dressler (*center*) with Wallace Beery and Marjorie Rambeau in *Min and Bill* (MGM, 1930). Courtesy of the USC Cinema-Television Library.

hope, as well as sacrifice – qualities that many believed would enable them to survive and prevail during those dark years. When she died in 1934, Edward G. Robinson said, "Her great comeback into public favor at her age should prove an inspiration to all who today may be faced with the same despair that once assailed her."

Janet Gaynor picked up the mantle of "America's Sweetheart" after Mary Pickford could no longer wear it. Short, cute, but physically unexceptional, she possessed a highly expressive face and eyes which spoke volumes in such late silent masterpieces as *Sunrise* (Fox, 1927) and *Seventh Heaven* (Fox, 1927). Teamed with Charles Farrell in *Seventh Heaven*, *Street Angel* (Fox, 1928) and *Lucky Star* (Fox, 1929), Miss Gaynor and her co-star soon became the leading romantic couple of the early sound cinema. They worked together in nine other pictures, and Mr. Farrell occupied the Number Four position in the Quigley rankings in 1932.

Gaynor's films ran the gamut from drama and melodrama to comedies and musicals. She was often cast as a girl without prospects – an orphan or drudge or poor working girl – whose spunk, pride and character shine through and enable her to win both a good man and a better life. Her films resonate with Depression subjects: financial problems (*Merely Mary Ann*, Fox 1931; *The First Year*, Fox, 1932; *Paddy the Next Best Thing*, Fox, 1933, *Carolina*, Fox, 1934), menial labor (*Lucky Star*, Fox, 1929; *Merely Mary Ann*; *Change of Heart*, Fox, 1934; *The Farmer Takes a Wife*, Fox, 1935), class conflict (*Sunny Side Up*, Fox, 1929; *High Society Blues*, Fox, 1930; *Delicious*, Fox, 1931; *Carolina*). Even when she was cast as a wealthy and/or upper-class individual, the films' narratives provided situations that force her to understand and empathize with less fortunate members of society. In *Adorable* (Fox, 1933), for example, Gaynor is a princess who pretends to be a manicurist and in *Servants' Entrance* (Fox, 1934) she plays a spoiled young woman who becomes a servant after her wealthy father encounters financial problems.

Like Marie Dressler in her movies, Gaynor is frequently called upon to help others in ways that require great courage. In *Tess of the Storm Country* (Fox, 1932) she cares for an illegitimate child even though she knows that others, including the man she loves (Farrell), will assume it is her baby and scorn her. In *The Man Who Came Back* (Fox, 1931), she feigns drug addiction in order to force her lover (Farrell again) to stop drinking. And in *Change of Heart*, she nurses Farrell back to health even though he is in love with another woman.

While always placed in difficult positions and made to appear vulnerable in the films, the Gaynor child-woman possessed an inner strength that enabled her to triumph over adversity. Usually the adversity was of a romantic nature, but her efforts were not confined to bright, uplifting story material. Having initially gained fame as a dramatic actress in films like *Sunrise* and *Street Angel*, she pressured the Fox executives for more weighty roles and occasionally got her way, as in *The Man Who Came Back* and *One More Spring* (Fox, 1935). The latter dealt with a range of Depression horrors, including unemployment, homelessness, bank failure and attempted suicide. Members of the early-1930s audience must have felt that if this tiny, freckled, often forlorn gamin could find the wherewithal to overcome her difficulties, they could too.

Though both were employed by the same studio, Gaynor and Will Rogers worked together only once, in the popular rural comedy *State Fair* (Fox, 1933). Rogers did not have the acting aspirations of a Janet Gaynor. "I ain't smart enough to act," he said. "If they can find a role that's sorta like me, I'm okay." In fact, he did pretty much play himself in film after film which, given the fact that he was one of the best-known and best-loved men in the United States at the time, was just what his employers wanted.

Rogers' fame derived from his multi-faceted career. Born in Oologah, Indian Territory (now Oklahoma) in 1879, Rogers eventually conquered the worlds of vaudeville, journalism, publishing, radio and the movies. In his performances, newspaper columns and radio appearances, he blended down-home humor with folksy wisdom and gentle political satire into a concoction that many audience members found not only funny and trenchant but prototypically American.

Despite his multiple activities, Rogers somehow managed to carve out enough time to appear in 18 films between 1931 and 1935. He specialized in rural comedies, playing characters whose rumpled, jocular, "aw shucks" exteriors camouflage a clever resourcefulness which he marshals to overcome the multiple problems inherent in each tale. In the early sound films, the principal threat is the virulent effect of newfound riches which threaten the simple values of a country life where people are judged by the size of their hearts rather than the size of their bank accounts. *Down to Earth* (Fox, 1932) is the signature title for this cycle of pictures. In it, Pike Peters (Rogers), having struck it rich in the oil fields, finds himself at odds with his wife (Irene Rich). She revels in her ability to throw extravagant parties and hobnob with other people of "substance." A series of financial reversals force a relieved Peters back to the modest house where he and his wife lived before they became wealthy. She eventually joins him there and happiness reigns, though he predicts they will get rich a second time and go through the same craziness all over again. Other films in which Rogers takes a stand against pretension, snobbery and the corrosive nature of wealth include *Doctor Bull* (Fox, 1933), *Handy Andy* (Fox, 1934) and *In Old Kentucky* (Fox, 1935). (Figure 7.6)

Rogers' films always contained a romantic subplot, though he was rarely one of the lovebirds. Instead, his usual function was matchmaker, manipulating events to make certain that nothing derails the marriage of two young people who are, of course, "made for each other." In *State Fair*, Abel Frake (Rogers) remains on the sidelines, paying most of his attention to his prize pig Blue Boy while his daughter Margy (Janet Gaynor) sorts through her own romantic dilemmas. But this is unusual. More typical is the situation in *Life Begins at Forty* (Fox, 1935) in which Kenesaw H. Clark (Rogers) champions the cause of an ex-convict (Richard Cromwell) in his pursuit of a girl (Rochelle Hudson) who is coveted by the son of a powerful colonel. Displeased by Clark's efforts, the colonel takes over the newspaper Clark edits and forces him out. Undaunted, Clark starts a rival paper. Eventually, the proper lovers are united and Clark gets his old job back.

Though clearly designed as a role model in all his pictures, Will Rogers was

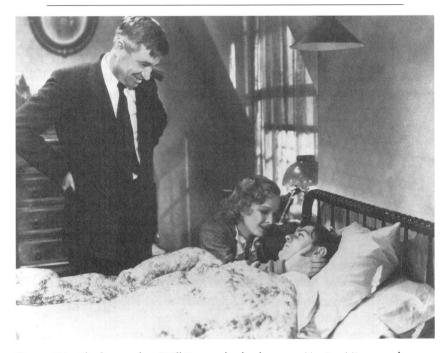

Figure 7.6 The benevolent Will Rogers looks down on Marian Nixon and Howard Lally in *Doctor Bull* (produced by Winfield Sheehan for Fox, 1933). Courtesy of the USC Cinema-Television Library.

rarely presented as perfect or a paragon of virtue. Even when he portrays a doctor or lawyer (*Doctor Bull*; *Judge Priest*, Fox, 1934), he happily mangles the English language and often displays a fondness for the bottle (*Lightnin'*, Fox, 1929; *Young as You Feel*, Fox, 1931). In *Too Busy to Work* (Fox, 1932), he plays a vagabond intent on murdering the man who stole his wife away from him. But even in this extreme case, Rogers comes to his senses and ends up doing much more good than harm.

Ultimately, this was the underlying message of most of the Rogers films – "love thy neighbor" – and help him or her or them as much as you can. Over and over, Rogers finds himself in the eye of an emotional hurricane packing enough destructive force to wreck many lives. With little more than humor, horse sense and his belief in the innate goodness of the common people, Rogers calms everything down, making sure that only those who truly deserve it are punished by the storm.

Rogers' last film, *Steamboat Round the Bend* (Fox, 1935), exemplifies the formula. In it, he plays Dr. John Pearly, a patent medicine salesman who pur-chases a broken down Mississippi River steamboat. He hopes that his nephew Duke (John McGuire) will pilot the craft, but Duke has killed a man who attacked Duke's girlfriend Fleety Belle (Anne Shirley) and is facing a murder charge. Fleety Belle has problems of her own; her father, brother and previous fiancé are determined to pry her away from Duke and take her back to the swamps where she grew up. With some assistance from his alcoholic first mate and a full-throated preacher who fancies himself the "new Moses," Doc manages to fend off Fleety Belle's pursuers, win a crucial wager in a steamboat race and save Duke from the hangman's noose. At the conclusion, peace, love and harmony envelop the mighty Mississippi thanks to the efforts of Dr. John Pearly, a dispenser of "remedies" in more ways than one.

The generosity of spirit which Rogers displayed in his movie roles was mir-rored in the actual conduct of his own life. Whenever someone staged a benefit for disaster relief – to assist the victims of a hurricane in Florida, a flood in Mis-sissippi, an earthquake in Nicaragua, etc. – Will Rogers would participate. And while he tried to keep his personal gift-giving secret, he contributed hundreds of thousands of dollars to philanthropic causes. The Red Cross and the Salva-tion Army were his favorite charities, but he opened his checkbook to many others while always demanding that his contributions be kept anonymous. Very few movie stars have ever approached the commitment to humanitarian-ism exhibited by Will Rogers.

Rogers' famous motto was, "I never met a man I didn't like." Although the phrase was surely an exaggeration (he once met Benito Mussolini, for example), Will Rogers set an open and winsome example and became a unique hero for Depression America. This kindhearted, thoughtful man, a man who socialized with presidents and kings but never lost his connection to the common folk, was the most public of public figures. In Rogers' books, newspaper articles, radio shows, live performances and films, he consistently reminded everyone to hold on to their families, their traditional values and their senses of humor. If Americans could keep their priorities straight, he believed, the Depression would soon become a memory.

In August 1935, at the very pinnacle of his career, Rogers was killed in a plane crash in Alaska. The nation mourned his loss, including President Frank-lin Roosevelt who had, on occasion, been the target of Will Rogers' satirical barbs. Later, Roosevelt would write: "There was something infectious about his humor. His appeal went straight to the heart of the nation. Above all things, in a time grown too solemn and somber, he brought his countrymen back to a sense of proportion."

The pre-war years: innocence and determination

The biggest stars of the last half of the Depression, which coincided with the increasingly tension-ridden pre-war era, were moppet Shirley Temple and teenager Mickey Rooney. While more mature actors, such as Clark Gable, Bette Davis and James Cagney, continued to be very popular with audiences, there was a definite premium placed on youth during the period. In addition to Temple and Rooney, Jane Withers and Judy Garland captured spots in the Quigley Top 10 while Freddie Bartholomew, Jackie Cooper, the Dead End Kids, Bobby Breen, Virginia Weidler, Anne Shirley, Edith Fellows and Gloria Jean also enjoyed considerable success. And, although she never made it into the Quigley Poll, Deanna Durbin became Universal's top performer in the late 30s; the public appetite for her musicals (*One Hundred Men and a Girl*, 1937; *Mad About Music*, 1938, etc.) helped the studio weather a very difficult period in its financial history.

Shirley Temple was the preeminent star of the decade, holding first position in the Quigley Poll from 1935 through 1938 and also making the Top 10 in 1934 and 1939. She literally grew up on screen, first appearing in a series of "Baby Burlesque" shorts at the age of four; by seven, she was the top-ranked star. A good deal has been written about the meaning of her stardom (see especially Charles Eckert's famous article, "Shirley Temple and the House of Rockefeller" in *Jump Cut*), but what has not been emphasized enough is the sheer magnitude of her talent. This beautiful child could hold her own with such seasoned actors as Academy Award-winner Victor McLaglen (*Wee Willie Winkie*, Twentieth Century-Fox, 1937), dance with consummate professionals like Bill "Bojangles" Robinson (*The Little Colonel*, Fox, 1935) and sing well enough to sell half a million copies of "On the Good Ship Lollipop" (introduced in *Bright Eyes*, Fox, 1934), a figure that even Bing Crosby most certainly envied. That this tiny tot could be so massively talented seemed a miracle to Depression audiences who returned again and again to sample her magic. (Figure 7.7)

The Fox Film organization placed Temple under contract during the filming of *Stand Up and Cheer!* (1934). Warner Baxter and Madge Evans were the nominal stars of the picture and Temple's role was quite small, but when she performed the "Baby Take a Bow" number the entire industry took notice.

The film that propelled her to the top was *Little Miss Marker* (1934), made as a loan out to Paramount. A far-fetched comedy based on a story by sentimental author Damon Runyon, the tale pivoted around her "adoption" by a motley assortment of gamblers and thugs with colorful names like Sorrowful, Sore Toe, Canvas Back and Bennie the Gouge. Marky (Temple) envisions them as chivalric knights and her inherent sweetness combined with a determination

Figure 7.7 Shirley Temple seems perplexed as she tries to figure a way to soften the hard heart of her grandfather (Lionel Barrymore) in *The Little Colonel* (produced by B.G. DeSylva for Fox, 1935). Courtesy of the USC Cinema-Television Library.

to idolize them, despite plenty of reasons not to, causes even Big Steve (Charles Bickford), the toughest of the lot, to rise above himself and perform acts of kindness and generosity.

The narrative pattern established in *Little Miss Marker* would be repeated in most of the films Shirley Temple made during this phase of her career. It is a pattern that bears considerable similarity to the films of Janet Gaynor (from whom she inherited Mary Pickford's symbolic crown as "America's Sweetheart") and Will Rogers. Shirley Temple's impact on most of the other characters in her films is transformative. Her innocence, openness, complete lack of pretense and unmitigated love delight and seduce even the most dour, crabby individuals, reminding them of the joy and beauty of youth and causing them to soften their rigid, dispirited views of life. Since these individuals represent the principal impediment to the happiness of all the characters in the stories, their transformation paves the way for harmony and good cheer to reign at the conclusion of each.

There were only three types of characters in a Temple film. The first are individuals immediately charmed by her. Their lives are improved (often romantically speaking) because they respond so positively to this little girl.

The second group is made up of people who initially resist or dislike her and/or the good people she loves, but eventually fall under her spell. These are the characters who generally have the potential to affect the most lives for good or ill; after they surrender to Shirley's love, their actions are always beneficent.

The third group is composed of individuals who never change, never succumb to the child's goodness. In the world of a Shirley Temple film, these people are unspeakably, irredeemably evil and the blackness of their souls is measured by the fact that they are beyond the redemptive powers of this extraordinary youngster. Naturally, their own schemes to gain wealth or power or to harm others are not successful.

In both her on-screen persona and her off-screen publicity, Shirley Temple was presented as the perfect child, the child every parent wishes were his or her daughter. However, the circumstances in which her cinematic characters find themselves are far from perfect. In most cases, she is an orphan or becomes orphaned in the course of events. In *Little Miss Marker*, her widower father commits suicide; in *Bright Eyes*, her widowed mother is killed in an automobile accident while on the way to her little girl's birthday party; in *The Littlest Rebel* (Twentieth Century-Fox, 1935), her mother dies as a result of the Civil War. In *The Little Princess* (Twentieth Century-Fox, 1939), a woman tries to sell her to gypsies; in *Now and Forever* (Paramount, 1934), her own father wants to sell her; and in *Dimples* (Twentieth Century-Fox, 1936), her grandfather almost sells her. In short, she is subjected to numerous disappointments, humiliations and tragedies and given ample opportunities to shed tears.

Yet, despite all these problems, her spirits are never dimmed. Her optimism, determination and loving attitude toward almost everyone, regardless of their age, status, race or occupation, prove an inspiration to others. In some of her films, the stakes are high. Both *Wee Willie Winkie* and *Susannah of the Mounties* (Twentieth Century-Fox, 1939) place Temple's characters in very dangerous situations, then provide her with the opportunity to intercede and prevent bloody wars. In other films, her accomplishments are more modest. She made a series of movies with show business backgrounds (*Poor Little Rich Girl*, Twentieth Century-Fox, 1936; *Dimples*; *Rebecca of Sunnybrook Farm*, Twentieth Century-Fox, 1938; and *Young People*, Twentieth Century-Fox, 1940); in each, her function is to melt away the antagonistic attitudes of hidebound, puritanical souls who do not recognize any affirmative qualities in the world of grease paint and music. Like Will Rogers, she also proves to be an adept matchmaker, steering the appropriate romantic couples together in *Bright Eyes, Our Little Girl* (Fox, 1935), *Curly Top* (Fox, 1935) and *Rebecca of Sunnybrook Farm.*

Depression difficulties are rarely foregrounded in a Shirley Temple film. Two exceptions are *Captain January* (Twentieth Century-Fox, 1936) and *Just Around the Corner* (Twentieth Century-Fox, 1938). In the former, the kindly lighthouse keeper (Guy Kibbee) who saves the aptly named Star (Temple) from a shipwreck is forced to join his fisherman friends among the ranks of the unemployed because of newfangled, automatic lighthouse equipment. In the latter, Penny's (Temple's) architect father is thrown out of work when his pet project is foreclosed upon and shuttered by a no-nonsense banker. Thanks to the Temple characters, everything turns out well in both stories with *Just Around the Corner* having an especially interesting narrative. The banker, named Samuel in the movie, bears a strong resemblance to graphic depictions of "Uncle Sam." Taking her father (Charles Farrell) literally when he tells her that things will be fine when Uncle Sam recovers from the Depression and can help business again, Penny organizes a show to aid the banker (Claude Gillingwater Sr.). Though angered at first, Samuel is eventually touched by her innocent efforts and approves the resumption of work on her father's building.

Though *Just Around the Corner* was the most explicit Depression allegory in the Temple canon, its narrative still conforms to the prototypical Temple pattern. Thus, it is possible to argue that all of her pictures suggest an approach to riding out the hard times. The approach involves a reconnection to the innocence and joy of childhood, a plea for openness and kindness toward all human beings and a determination to remain upbeat despite the disappointments and misfortunes that life inevitably provides. In spite of her diminutive size (the words "Little" or "Littlest" are used in the titles of seven of her films), Shirley Temple was a colossus. Not only did she help contemporary audiences forget their troubles for a couple of darkened hours at their local theaters, she challenged them to to stay positive and confident about their futures. How could the world in which this magical child was growing up not become a better place?

Like Shirley Temple, 5' 3" teenager Mickey Rooney, who replaced Temple at the top of the star hierarchy when the aging process swept away her elfin charm, was small in size but large in talent. He could sing, dance, play various instruments (most particularly the drums); do "spot on" impressions of individuals like Clark Gable, Lionel Barrymore and even President Roosevelt (see *Babes in Arms*); and he could act as well.

Rooney also began his movie career at a young age. At the age of six, he was hired to play the title role in a series of "Mickey McGuire" shorts for FBO (later RKO) and adopted, for a time, the character's name as his own. The series would last for several years, straddling the transitional period from silents to sound and totaling some 60 episodes in all. Modeled on producer Hal Roach's successful "Our Gang" series, the Mickey McGuires were filled with slapstick gags and featured the mischievous McGuire interacting with a menagerie of dogs, cats, birds and other animals, as well as a motley assortment of street urchins.

After the "Mickey McGuire" period ended and he changed his stage name to Rooney, the young actor's workload in features accelerated to a frantic pace. Between 1932 and 1936, Rooney appeared in 33 movies, as well as assorted shorts and serials. Mostly he played supporting parts, including a memorable performance as Puck in *A Midsummer Night's Dream*. Placed under contract by MGM in 1934, Rooney continued to work hard, but with mostly indifferent results, until 1938.

In that year, Mickey Rooney's portrayals of two characters vaulted him to the top. One was Whitey Marsh, the cigarette-puffing, card-playing hoodlum whose life is given new meaning and direction by Father Edward Flanagan (Spencer Tracy), the founder of *Boys Town*. Though Tracy certainly deserved the Oscar he received for his performance, Rooney's acting was no less impressive. He made Whitey's evolution from hardened street tough who idolizes his criminal brother to exemplary youth who idolizes Father Flanagan both real and poignant. In the end, Whitey's moral journey helped to confirm Flanagan's oft-stated belief that "there's no such thing in the world as a bad boy." *Boys Town* was a blockbuster success; made on a budget of $722,000, it earned $2,112,000 in profits for the studio.

Also in 1938, MGM's "Hardy family" series caught fire with audiences. First introduced in *A Family Affair* (1937), the Hardys lived in Carvel, a mythical small town somewhere in the midwestern US. The patriarch of the family is Judge James Hardy (played by Lionel Barrymore in *A Family Affair*, but then embodied throughout the rest of the series by Lewis Stone). A wise man and loving husband and father, Judge Hardy still makes mistakes which occasionally threaten the well-being of the clan. His spouse Emily (Fay Holden for most of the episodes) is a recognizable housewife whose good sense, as well as her good cooking, fortifies the Hardys and holds the family together. Their oldest child, daughter Marian (Cecilia Parker), is a typical teenager, unnerved by the maturation process and by her annoying little brother. That brother is Andy Hardy (Rooney), a short-fused firecracker constantly exploding in unpredictable ways and directions, though the damage he causes is always minimal.

Figure 7.8   Andy Hardy (Mickey Rooney) and his father (Lewis Stone) have one of their man-to-man talks in *Andy Hardy Gets Spring Fever* (produced by Lou Ostrow for MGM, 1939). Courtesy of the USC Cinema-Television Library.

The Hardy movies were a dream-come-true for MGM. Produced on "B" budgets, *A Family Affair* and the second installment, *You're Only Young Once* (1937), realized decent if unspectacular profits of $153,000 and $240,000 respectively. But with segment three, *Judge Hardy's Children* (1938), profits jumped to $422,000 (on a production cost of $182,000); after that the films hit a box office home run every time out. *From Love Finds Andy Hardy* (1938; cost $212,000; profit $1,345,000) through *The Courtship of Andy Hardy* (1942; cost $338,000; profit $1,319,000), the next 10 Hardy family movies were a remarkable profit center for MGM. Even when the production budget jumped up considerably in the final segment released before the end of World War II – *Andy Hardy's Blonde Trouble* (1944; cost $723,000; profit $956,000) – the financial return was still impressive. (Figure 7.8)

It was not a coincidence that the series blasted off once Andy Hardy's name began to appear in the titles. The first two Hardy movies employed an ensemble approach with Rooney's screen time rather limited. But then the MGM production team recognized that Andy should be the real focus of the series and began devoting more and more of each episode to his misadventures.

Andy Hardy is impish, impetuous, disorganized, stubborn, crass, unsophisticated, conniving, obtuse, forgetful, full of himself and totally befuddled by the opposite sex. An indifferent student who barely graduates from high school despite his expert knowledge of the latest slang terminology, Andy is also a major irritant to his sister, whom he teases unmercifully. He also occasionally locks horns with his father; in both *You're Only Young Once* and *Andy Hardy Meets Debutante* (1940), he accuses the Judge of being too old-fashioned and provincial to understand him.

Yet, despite the mistakes he makes in every story and his multiple character flaws, Andy is still overwhelmingly appealing because he is as good-hearted as he is precocious, as energetic as he is imaginative. And, ultimately, he has the right values. Andy adores his mother, nearly falling apart when he believes she is soon going to die (*Judge Hardy and Son*, 1939). Similarly, despite their disagreements, he venerates his father. Most of the films included "man-to-man" talks in which Andy seeks the Judge's counsel on a broad spectrum of topics. Often the Judge will invoke the great leaders of America's past to help his son. In *Judge Hardy's Children*, he takes Andy to Mount Vernon to learn about George Washington. In *Andy Hardy Meets Debutante*, a visit to the Hall of Fame at New York University helps Andy comprehend the real meaning of freedom and equality. Though Andy may not fully absorb these lessons or scrupulously follow his father's advice, the very fact that he feels comfortable enough to share his troubles with his dad is an endearing aspect of the films.

Another rising young star, Judy Garland, appeared in three of the Hardy family films and also partnered with Rooney in several MGM musicals made during the peak years of his popularity. These Busby Berkeley-directed movies, *Babes in Arms* (1939), *Strike Up the Band* (1940) and *Babes on Broadway* (1942), featured groups of talented youngsters who "put on a show," always for a good cause and in defiance of the most daunting odds. Needless to say, the shows which the kids manage to conjure up are hardly amateur productions; the levels of MGM professional gloss, as well as cornball Hollywood hokum, were near their all-time high in these movies. Yet audiences could not seem to get their fill of them – the pictures produced profits of at least $1.5 million each.

One of the reasons for their success was the almost frightening level of energy and determination exhibited by Mickey Rooney in the key role of each film. His drive and talent are so infectious that they seem to take possession of all the other kids and, by the end of each story, a miracle has occurred. The entire group has become a unit of "can-do kids," youngsters who believe in themselves, in their peers and, most importantly, in their country. There was a heavy overlay of patriotic propaganda in the Rooney–Garland musicals; the title *Babes in Arms* and the production numbers in that film alone leave little doubt that these kids are not simply capable of mounting a triumphant stage production; they are also fully prepared to fight for "God's Country" (the final number in the film) where "we've got no Führer, we've got no Duce" and where "every man is his own dictator."

Mickey Rooney reached the top of the movie star pyramid in the year World War II broke out in Europe and remained Number One until the US became an active participant in the war. To suggest that an American public, nervous about the possibility that its young men and women might soon be sucked into the hostilities, was reassured to have a pint-sized Mickey Rooney to unleash upon future enemies would be absurd. But that would be taking matters literally, rather than viewing Rooney for what he was – a metaphorical representative of his generation. Looked at in this way, it is not at all ridiculous to postulate that the spirit, determination, energy, respect for one's family and, by extension, one's country inherent in the Hardy pictures, the musicals and uplifting stories like *Young Tom Edison* (MGM, 1940) helped US men and women believe that the young people of Depression America would be resilient enough to handle any challenge. Mickey Rooney personified contemporary American youth as a force of nature: dynamic, unstoppable, unconquered and unconquerable.

The war years: hot, cool and wacky

The World War II era produced another unlikely cadre of preferred stars. Given the national obsession with the armed conflict and the rapid emergence of the war film as a major genre, one might have expected broad-shouldered action heroes to dominate the popularity polls. However, John Wayne, Errol Flynn, Randolph Scott, Dana Andrews, Anthony Quinn, Bruce Bennett, John Ridgely and Barry Nelson, all of whom were featured in contemporary war pictures, took a backseat to bumbling comedians Bud Abbott and Lou Costello, pin up queen Betty Grable and silky crooner Bing Crosby. Moviegoing became a national pastime during the war, and the folks at home particularly favored performers who demonstrated the ability to lift spirits and boost morale during arguably the most nerve-racking years of the century.

Like Shirley Temple, the team of Bud Abbott and Lou Costello shot to the top of the Quigley Poll in remarkably short order. Veterans of burlesque, vaudeville, nightclubs and the stage, the duo became household names on radio, where they continually repeated and refined stand-up routines that would also become important elements in their subsequent movies. Abbott and Costello signed with Universal in 1939, first appearing in secondary roles in *One Night in the Tropics* (1940), a tepid musical starring Allan Jones and Nancy Kelly. Despite the lackluster performance of the film, the studio executives upped the screen time of the two funny men in *Buck Privates* (1941), which turned out to be one of the best decisions in Universal's history.

Buck Privates was a topical offering that dealt with the new peacetime draft; it showed up in theaters less than five months after President Roosevelt signed the bill making selective service a reality. A jagged conglomeration of narrative elements, the picture not only tickled contemporary audiences but also provided a blueprint for subsequent Abbott and Costello successes. It was part musical with several lively numbers performed by the Andrews Sisters; part love story charting the competition between playboy Randolph Parker III (Lee Bowman) and his chauffeur Bob Martin (Alan Curtis) for the affections of USO hostess Judy Gray (Jane Frazee); and part contemporary message picture depicting the patriotic transformation of Parker from spoiled rich boy, determined to escape the military life, to dedicated soldier who proudly accepts a slot in Officers' Training School. Most importantly, it was also a manic comedy built around the oddball relationship of Abbott and Costello seasoned with plentiful slapstick, verbal humor and sight gags. (Figure 7.9)

The personas of the two comedians were nicely fashioned for the screen by writer Arthur T. Horman (with special material for Abbott and Costello supplied by veteran burlesque gagman John Grant) and director Arthur Lubin. In the story, slim and oily scoundrel Slicker Smith (Bud Abbott) takes full advantage of his moon-faced, dimwitted pal Herbie Brown (Lou Costello). The characters soon run afoul of the law and then blunder their way into Army uniforms and basic training. Given their breathtaking level of incompetence, the inclusion of these two buffoons in the military at this crucial moment in history would not appear to bode well for US chances in any potential armed conflict. Yet audiences clearly did not read the film in this way. The madcap antics of Abbott and Costello helped relieve the tension of a nation gearing up for a very real and very frightening war and somehow reinforced, rather than undercut, the serious, patriotic sentiments which popped up regularly throughout the film. Made for less than $200,000, *Buck Privates* became a sleeper hit and convinced the Universal executives to feature Bud and Lou in more military-themed comedies.

Before 1941 was over, the studio rushed out *In the Navy* and *Keep 'Em Flying*,

Figure 7.9 Lou Costello (*left*) and Bud Abbott in uniform in *Buck Privates* (produced by Alex Gottlieb for Universal, 1941). Courtesy of the USC Cinema-Television Library.

both sporting prominent dedications to the Navy and Air Corps while offering Abbott and Costello opportunities to inject their dubious skill sets into new branches of the military. Once again musical interludes, romantic subplots and patriotic propaganda regularly interrupted the flow of the boys' lunatic activities, but no one seemed to mind. The films brought in even more box office lucre than *Buck Privates* and, by the end of the year, Abbott and Costello had come from nowhere to claim the Number Three slot in the Quigley Poll.

The fourth Abbott and Costello picture of 1941, filmed right after *Buck Privates* but held for release until *In the Navy* had been playing in theaters for a couple of months, was *Hold That Ghost*. This parody of both the gangster and horror genres pointed the way toward another rich vein that the pair would mine for years to come – the spoof comedy. Before the end of the war, Abbott and Costello would shake up the formulaic foundations of the western (*Ride 'Em Cowboy*, Universal, 1942), the South Seas adventure (*Pardon My Sarong*, Universal, 1942), the murder mystery (*Who Done It?*, Universal, 1942), the "winter wonderland" musical (*Hit the Ice*, Universal, 1943), the Arabian Nights tale (*Lost in a Harem*, MGM, 1944), the college comedy (*Here Come the Co-Eds*, Universal, 1945) and the "Hollywood Insider" story (*Bud Abbott and Lou Costello in Hollywood*, MGM, 1945). The two funny men would continue to make this kind of movie for years, fashioning numerous parodies of famous horror films, as well as takeoffs on other genres and familiar cinematic plots.

Abbott and Costello were the box office champions of 1942. Oddly, given the huge success of the three military comedies released in 1941, they did not play servicemen in any of their 1942 releases, nor would they don cinematic uniforms again until after the hostilities were concluded. However, their commitment to the war effort continued unabated, as evidenced by the hugely successful war bond tour which they undertook that year, their regular participation in shows organized to entertain the troops and the attention paid to contemporary events on their radio programs. Their on-screen alter egos also helped foil the plans of enemy agents in two of their 1942 releases: *Rio Rita* (MGM) and *Who Done It?*. Without question, the popularity of the team was connected, in the public's mind, with the overall US commitment to winning the war.

They were also popular simply because audiences found their movies to be uproariously funny. Like the plots of their films, the Abbott and Costello approach to humor was loosely structured, broadly based and improvisational. Everything revolved around Lou, the short, portly, cowardly but lovable simpleton. It is Lou who absorbs most of the slapstick punishment, either from his "pal" Bud, who is fond of slapping and punching him in Three Stooges fashion, or from a sinister mechanical world which attacks him without provocation, as in the hotel washing machine sequence in *Rio Rita* or the hook and ladder sequence in *Hit the Ice*. It is Lou who instantly comes unglued whenever a beautiful woman appears and whose infantile approach to courtship is punctuated by a bizarre outpouring of squeaks, shrieks, whistles, whoops, gurgles, bellows and other alien noises. And it is Lou who generally gets the worst of his verbal interchanges with the wily, manipulative Bud. The famous "Who's On First" routine, perfected on radio and adapted to the screen in their first film, *One Night in the Tropics* (and again, in a more complete version, in *The Naughty Nineties*, Universal, 1945), develops because of Lou's failure to understand that the first baseman described by Bud is actually named "Who" and all of his teammates have similarly confusing names. By the end of their dialogue, Bud has effectively tied the apoplectic Lou in verbal knots and reduced the spectators to hysterics into the bargain. Most of the Abbott and Costello films contain several of these burlesque-inspired dialogue sketches.

Finally, it is significant that Abbott and Costello always played blue-collar workers in their movies, e.g. waiters (*Hold That Ghost* and *Hit the Ice*), house detectives (*Rio Rita*), soda jerks (*Who Done It?*), plumbers (*In Society*, Universal, 1944), barbers (*Bud Abbott and Lou Costello in Hollywood*). Their inability to handle any of these jobs well, sometimes leading to disaster (they foul up the plumbing of a Long Island mansion so totally during *In Society* that the entire place is flooded) and often to their firing, became a great source of amusement and, perhaps, comfort to the working men and women of a nation at war. The job of the civilian workers was a big one; just like the efforts of the soldiers, as the US government constantly reminded, their labor would make the difference between victory and defeat. Hollywood turned out a number of serious films about the heroism and sacrifice of both the fighting men and civilian workforce of the time. Though they were popular with audiences, the appeal of these morale-boosting productions paled in comparison to the appeal of films which chronicled the nonsensical adventures of two boobs named Bud and Lou. Bumbling their way to the requisite happy ending, these clowns provided a tonic of steady laughter which helped counteract the nervous disorder felt by so many Americans during those years of collective uncertainty.

If show business insiders were surprised by the rapid ascent of Abbott and Costello in Hollywood, they were positively shocked when Betty Grable became a big star; in truth, she was probably more amazed than they were. Miss Grable had been making pictures since the early sound era, mostly "Bs" with some supporting parts in "A" productions. Placed under contract at various times by Fox, Goldwyn, RKO and Paramount, she found herself, by the end of the 1930s, lumped together with hundreds of other perky, attractive women who had worked in front of studio cameras without making any notable impact. In between the movie jobs, she had also crisscrossed the country, appearing in vaudeville shows and with dance bands as a torch singer, dancer and fledgling comedienne. As per the showbiz cliche, she paid her dues . . . but did not have much to show for them.

Then Darryl Zanuck at Twentieth Century-Fox hired Grable to fill in for Alice Faye, who had to drop out of *Down Argentine Way* (1940) for medical reasons. A musical confection designed to have special appeal in the increasingly important South American market, the film allowed the actress to demonstrate her singing and dancing talents and showed that she could hold her own with well-established leading man Don Ameche and scene-stealing Latina actress Carmen Miranda. The studio chose to make the film in Technicolor, which proved especially flattering to Miss Grable's bright blue eyes, flawless complexion and sparkling smile. The process also enabled the costume department to drape her perfect figure in a variety of vibrant outfits.

Zanuck, realizing he had stumbled onto something good, made room for Grable in a number of subsequent productions. Still, he apparently did not recognize her actual potential, for in the next four movies Miss Grable's screen time was limited by the presence of bigger names: Alice Faye and John Payne (*Tin Pan Alley*, 1940), Don Ameche (*Moon over Miami*, 1941), Tyrone Power (*A Yank in the RAF*, 1941) and Victor Mature (*I Wake Up Screaming*, 1941). While her work in the last two pictures, both non-musicals, did little to distinguish her, Grable continued to shine in the musicals. This caused Zanuck to crown her his top musical star and to line up Technicolor for all of her forthcoming productions except *Footlight Serenade* (1942).

Not coincidentally, Grable's popularity peaked during the war years. She held the top spot in the Quigley Poll in 1943 and was in the top five in 1944 and 1945, despite a reduced schedule of films necessitated by maternity leave. During the war, Fox released a pin up photo of Betty Grable that would become one of the most famous images of the twentieth century. Clad in a white bathing suit and high heels, hands on hips, back to the camera, she peeks over her right shoulder, offering a smiling "come hither" glance to the invisible spectator (Figure 7.10). Hundreds of thousands of US servicemen projected themselves into the position of that unseen spectator, flooding the studio with requests for the saucy still. Approximately three million copies ultimately circulated, with some later discovered among the possessions of German and Japanese soldiers, as well as Allied military men. Other Hollywood stars, such as Rita Hayworth and Lana Turner, also became special favorites of the men-in-arms, but Betty Grable was the undisputed queen of the pin ups, her famous pose painted on the nose cones of innumerable bombers and fighter planes and, surprisingly, used to teach budding aviators how to decipher aerial maps.

In return, Grable did her part for the war effort. She made special appearances to entertain the troops, sold war bonds (in 1943, a pair of her nylon stockings were auctioned off for $40,000 worth of bonds; a kiss from Lana Turner only garnered $15,000) and appeared in *Four Jills in a Jeep* (1944) and *Pin Up Girl* (1944), both of which referenced the contemporary situation. Oddly, however, most of the Grable musicals did not include the war in their narratives. They had show business backgrounds with half set in the late nineteenth or early twentieth centuries (*Coney Island*, 1943; *Sweet Rosie O'Grady*, 1943; *The Dolly Sisters*, 1945) and the other half in the present (*Footlight Serenade*; *Springtime in the Rockies*, 1942; *Billy Rose's Diamond Horseshoe*, 1945). The repetitive plots generally involved the performer's rocky love life complicated by her efforts to gain acceptance in the world of show business.

The Grable persona remained consistent throughout the period. Though she

Figure 7.10 The famous pin up shot of Betty Grable, taken in early 1943. Twentieth Century-Fox capitalized on its popularity, producing *Pin Up Girl* in 1944. Courtesy of the Academy of Motion Picture Arts and Sciences Library.

was sometimes naughty (she played a gold digger in *Moon over Miami*; a compulsive liar in *Pin Up Girl*; a material girl who agrees to romance a man for a fur coat in *Billy Rose's Diamond Horseshoe*), a heart of gold beats within the glorious body, leading her to choose love over wealth, social status and fame in film after film. Their plots contained multiple misunderstandings, feuds and lovers' quarrels, but audience members knew how they would turn out; at the finale, Miss Grable would be back together with the only man who could make her happy – John Payne (four times) or Victor Mature or Dick Haymes or George Montgomery.

For American soldiers, the Grable pin up provided a powerful image of what they were fighting for. Her films reinforced that image, suggesting that this other-worldly specimen of American womanhood was just as honest and dependable as they were and would wait . . . wait as long as it took for Johnny to come marching home. In 1943, Miss Grable married band leader Harry James after working with him in *Springtime in the Rockies*. Soon enough, one of the soldiers' favorite tunes became an old standard with revamped lyrics: "I want a girl, just like the girl who married Harry James."

There was another reason for Grable's popularity, a reason that the Production Code Administration did its best to defuse: her not-so-latent sexuality. Would the less-than-original, less-than-memorable Grable musicals have been so successful if this had not been a time when many thousands of American men and women were kept apart by the war? Though sex may have been in the forefront of a lot of people's minds, the Grable pictures could not foreground sex in their narratives. But they did proffer the star in a variety of form-fitting, eye-catching costumes and provide generous opportunities for her to show off her perfect legs. When Twentieth Century-Fox took out a $1 million insurance policy on those legs (ironically, she had appeared in the 1939 Paramount production *Million Dollar Legs*, but the title reference was to the legs of a crew team, not those of Miss Grable), the gesture was more than a publicity stunt. Betty Grable's legs arguably earned much more than a million for the studio.

Finally, the Grable phenomenon also had something to do with her total lack of ego. People who worked with her remarked about her warmth, her consideration, her humility. She was more than adequate as an actress, a singer and a dancer, but she constantly downplayed her own talents. "I was just lucky," she would say, adding that she considered her dancing, "average, maybe a little bit below" and her voice, "just a voice." Even after the war ended, she remained in the Quigley Top 10 every year until 1952. While the famous pin up shot probably did more for her fame than any of the movies, the public's adoration of Miss Grable was also based on the belief that her on-screen and off-screen lives were one and could be extrapolated into an ideal image of womanhood: beautiful, sexy, loving and, at the same time, steadfast, funny, unpretentious. Hers was the kind of success story that Americans prized, that of a girl who worked hard, brushed aside multiple disappointments and finally made it to the top without once forgetting who she was, how she got there or how she should treat those who surrounded her, the artists with whom she worked and, most importantly, her legions of fans.

Like Betty Grable, Bing Crosby began making films in the early days of the talkies and worked primarily in the musical genre. However, he gained fame very quickly, first showing up in the Quigley Poll as the seventh ranked star in 1934. He cracked the Top 10 again in 1937, 1940 and 1943 before taking possession of the top spot in 1944. He would remain Number One for an unprecedented five consecutive years and a member of the Top 10 every year until 1955.

The American public thought of Crosby more as a singer than actor, and his screen success was inextricably interwoven with the popularity he had garnered in music and radio. Similar to Will Rogers, he was an early "crossover" talent who sold millions of records, starred in his own radio show throughout the 1930s and 40s and still managed to make two to four movies a year. His career was brilliantly orchestrated; he introduced new songs in his pictures, many of which became hot-selling records, then plugged both the movies and records on his radio broadcasts. American audiences liked him, and he never suffered a significant downturn in popularity. Later, when television replaced radio as the preferred home entertainment vehicle, Crosby moved right in and conquered the new medium in short order. Indeed, everything seemed to come easily for him, from the smooth and relaxed way he would croon a song to the unflappable self-confidence he exhibited in his movie roles.

Unlike the other stars we have surveyed in the latter portion of this chapter, Bing Crosby played quite different characters in the films that boosted him to the top. In Paramount's "Road" pictures (*Road to Singapore, Road to Zanzibar, Road to Morocco*), he traipses around the world, hatching "get rich quick" schemes that place his pal Bob Hope in jeopardy and inevitably lead to big trouble rather than big money. These loopy adventure comedies were filled with inside jokes about Hollywood, Paramount and Hope and Crosby themselves, as well as self-reflexive asides addressed directly to movie audiences. Theatergoers evidently loved them, for the series became a financial bonanza with four more installments produced after the end of the war. (Figure 7.11)

The characters played by Crosby in the "Road" films would always find opportunities to croon in the unique Crosby fashion but, as the series drew on, they became increasingly venal, mean-spirited, insulting and churlish. Though Bob Hope always lost out to Crosby in their competition for "the girl" (series regular Dorothy Lamour) and was thoroughly outsmarted by his buddy, his characters did not exactly beg for audience sympathy either. A cowardly egotist and professional "wolf," Hope earned the various moments of comeuppance

Figure 7.11   Bing Crosby (*left*), Dorothy Lamour and Bob Hope in *Road to Morocco* (produced by B.G. DeSylva for Paramount, 1942). Courtesy of the USC Cinema-Television Library.

which inevitably came his way. Bob Hope was also a big star during this era, especially on radio but also in the movies; an intriguingly anti-heroic pair in their films, he and Crosby managed to be both ahead of their time and the most potent box office tandem of the war years.

The other films that turned Bing Crosby into a top movie star were *Going My Way* (Paramount, 1944) and *The Bells of St. Mary's* (Rainbow/RKO, 1945). The figure Crosby played in these two films was saintly priest Charles Francis Patrick O'Malley, a man with a radically different purpose in life than the actor's "Road" movie characters. Though a bit of a nonconformist concerning the traditions and rituals of the Catholic Church, Father O'Malley is a pure, selfless cleric dedicated to helping his fellow men and women. In the narratives of both films, he manages to work miracles, some small, some much more significant. And, of course, he is aided in his quest by his magnificent voice which comes to seem like a special gift from God.

Spiritual solace took on especial importance in America during World War

II. It was a time when multitudes prayed for the safety of relatives, sweethearts and friends whose lives were endangered by the fighting. Sadly, thousands of families received the dreaded telegram from the government, informing them that one of their own had died in the conflict. A large percentage of the bereaved needed to believe that the loss had meaning and that there would be an opportunity to reunite with the loved one at some future time and place. Hollywood studios recognized the heightened importance of religion, featuring members of the clergy in many films and fashioning entire pictures, such as *The Keys of the Kingdom* (Twentieth Century-Fox, 1944) and *The Song of Bernadette* (Twentieth Century-Fox, 1945), that emphasized the mystery, power and importance of the religious experience.

These films were successful, both critically and financially, but their achievements pale in comparison to the two Crosby/O'Malley pictures. *Going My Way* won the Academy Award as Best Picture of 1944, plus six other Oscars (including one for Crosby as Best Actor), and both pictures were huge moneymakers. *The Bells of St. Mary's* became the most successful film in the history of RKO.

On the surface it seems odd that audiences would accept Bing Crosby's transformation from the slightly disreputable knaves he played in the various "Road" pictures into a sensitive, idealized priest. However, closer examination reveals that even though the characters were fundamentally different, the Crosby persona remained fairly consistent throughout. The key was his ever-present calm, his understated self-confidence, his grace under pressure. No matter the difficulties – man-eating cannibals in *Road to Zanzibar*, the fiery destruction of the parish church in *Going My Way*, the seemingly inevitable closing of a parochial school in *The Bells of St. Mary's* – the Crosby character overcomes them in a manner that seems especially remarkable because it appears so effortless.

Crosby did his part for the war effort, performing at numerous USO shows, devoting portions of his radio broadcasts to boosting military morale, and appearing in movies like *Star Spangled Rhythm* (Paramount, 1943) and *Here Come the Waves* (Paramount, 1944) which glorified the men and women in uniform. However, arguably his greatest contribution came via his famous rendition of the Irving Berlin song "White Christmas," introduced in the Bing Crosby–Fred Astaire film *Holiday Inn* (Paramount, 1942). Though "White Christmas" did not make any direct references to the war, its nostalgic lyrics proved especially poignant for US soldiers and civilian personnel far removed from their homes and families because of the hostilities. "White Christmas" quickly became the bestselling record in history and helped cement the country's resolve to get the fighting over as soon as possible so everyone could come home.

It is, obviously, impossible to calculate the part Bing Crosby played in the winning of the war, just as there is no formula that could accurately determine how much Betty Grable or Abbott and Costello or Bob Hope contributed. But Crosby's supreme popularity during this period, and for years afterward, suggests how needy the contemporary American public was for a figure with his specific personality traits. He was "Mr. Cool, Calm and Collected," a man whose singing and acting styles were remarkably consistent, smooth and unruffled. Though he was not a physically prepossessing individual, he radiated assurance and, in his very being, helped to reassure his fellow countrymen and women that everything would turn out for the best.

8

Conclusion

Athough the leaders of the Hollywood companies did not realize it, profound changes would affect their business in the years that followed the end of World War II. The exhilaration that accompanied victory did continue throughout much of 1946. Movie moguls celebrated as extraordinary amounts of cash flowed into their coffers. The opening of European and Asian markets that had been off-limits for years, combined with robust domestic ticket sales, generated $1.75 billion in industry gross revenues in 1946. Paramount led the way, posting unprecedented profits of $39 million. Twentieth Century-Fox (profit: $25 million), Warner Bros. (profit: $22 million), MGM/Loews (profit: $18 million) and RKO (profit: $12 million) also enjoyed their most successful financial years in history. Thus, no one could foresee the coming events that would rock the very foundations of the industry's economic model and soon bring an end to the studio system era in American film history.

These events included:

1. *The imposition of a 75 percent tax on the earnings of all foreign companies in Great Britain, beginning in 1947.* This tax would soon be rescinded, to be replaced by the old "frozen funds" concept (American movie companies could still earn large sums in Britain but were required to spend the bulk of these earnings within the country). The British decisions were the first of a number of protectionist laws instituted by foreign leaders whose countries had suffered much more than the US during the war and who were determined to control the outflow of capital from their fragile economies. These decisions, along with various incentives designed to lure filmmakers to produce movies in their lands, caused Hollywood executives to begin making movies all over the globe. The era of "runaway production" had begun, meaning that Hollywood's position as the unchallenged center of movie production was eroding.

2. *Labor problems.* The relationship between management and labor in the movie capital had been relatively harmonious throughout most of the war. But as soon as it was clear that the Allies would win, blue- and white-collar workers began demanding their share of the bounty that their employers had reaped during the previous years. A series of bitter, sometimes violent strikes and lockouts resulted between 1945 and 1947. In October 1945, for example, more than 1,000 people (picketers, scab workers, strikebreakers, police officers, studio security personnel) battled outside the gates of the Warner Bros. studio. Eventually, most of the workers were given pay raises and additional benefits, but photographs of the riotous conditions which ran in the nation's newspapers tarnished the industry's public image.

3. *Anti-Communist paranoia which enveloped Hollywood in 1947.* Convinced that the movie industry was a hotbed of subversive activity, the House Committee on Un-American Activities (HUAC) subpoenaed movie veterans to testify about the alleged injection of communist propaganda in commercial films. After a group of "friendly" witnesses informed the committee that some individuals were indeed trying to co-opt the movies for their own nefarious purposes, the politicians summoned a group of "unfriendly" witnesses who belligerently refused to answer the key question: "Are you now or have you ever been a member of the Communist Party?" This group of eight writers, one producer and one director soon came to be known as the "Hollywood Ten"; they were held in contempt of Congress, denounced by most of their fellow workers and fired by their employers. All would later serve time in prison. And so the era of the "blacklist" commenced in Hollywood. Those suspected of being Communists or harboring sympathies for left-wing causes or for the Soviet Union, soon found themselves unemployable. The period would last for more than a decade, further corroding the industry's reputation and causing some potential customers to think twice before they opened their wallets at a box office window.

4. *The end of block booking and guaranteed outlets for studio product.* The government's investigation into the distribution practices of the major studios (the "Paramount Case") was finally settled in 1948. In a "Consent Decree" the Big Five studios, in essence, admitted that the marketing of their products to independent theater owners had been handled in an unfair, monopolistic fashion. These studios agreed to sell their theater chains, thereby severing exhibition from their production–distribution operations. After the "divorcement" was complete, every studio would have to compete with every other studio to release its movies in the best theaters, at the most propitious times of the year, and on the most favorable rental terms.

5. *The growth of television.* By the early 1950s, television had become a significant competitor for the public's leisure time. Television stations were popping up all over the nation and TV sets were flying off the department store shelves. Seduced by the novelty of "free" visual entertainment in their homes, fewer and fewer people felt compelled to frequent their local movie houses.

These and other factors, such as the baby boom and the large-scale migration of American families to the suburbs, which took them far away from the first-run theaters, also contributed to an alarming decline in movie attendance. By the mid-1950s, most of the studios were releasing fewer films, had pink-slipped most of their contract employees and were moving toward the United Artists model which emphasized distribution over production. Indeed, by this time, a large contingent of independent companies had set up offices in Hollywood, and the major studios were scrambling to finance and/or release films made by the best of them.

The changes that occurred in the post-war years affected the industry in other ways. Over time, the Production Code Administration lost much of its power, opening up the screen to stories that dramatized various aspects of human experience which had been taboo for many years, such as drug addiction (*The Man with the Golden Arm*, Preminger/United Artists, 1955). And the determination to offer moviegoers a more dynamic visual and audio presentation than they could ever hope to experience on their television sets led to an increase in color productions and the development of various wide-screen formats, stereophonic sound, even movies in 3-D.

Still, by the early 1950s, the glory days of Hollywood were rapidly receding. During my initial time in Los Angeles, I was fortunate to meet and interview a number of creative people who worked in the movie business during the years covered in this book. Many of them made outstanding pictures after 1945 but, when I asked which period of their careers they preferred, a surprising number expressed an overpowering nostalgia for the heyday of the studio system. As the inimitable Billy Wilder put it, "At least you knew whose ass to kiss back then."

It is, of course, important to guard against viewing the period through rose-tinted spectacles. This was a time when several of the studios were run by iron-fisted potentates who worked their employees unmercifully hard and often exhibited callous indifference to their personal problems. It was time when thousands of Hollywood aspirants failed to achieve their celluloid dreams and slunk away from the studio gates, crushed and embittered. And a time when many of the studios' productions were mediocre at best, dreadful at worst.

And yet, history suggests that this was still the best of times: a true golden age. The extraordinary cinematic works produced during the Depression and World War II years remain vital and supremely influential. This legacy is constantly being rediscovered by new generations of film viewers and remade by new generations of filmmakers.

As proof of the superlative achievements of the era, the year 1939 is often cited. Without doubt, 1939 was an *annus mirabilis*, the year when the following classics were released: *Gone with the Wind* (Selznick/MGM), *The Wizard of Oz* (MGM), *Ninotchka* (MGM), *The Women* (MGM), *Midnight* (Paramount), *Beau Geste* (Paramount), *Dark Victory* (Warner Bros.), *The Roaring Twenties* (Warner Bros.), *Young Mr. Lincoln* (Twentieth Century-Fox), *Love Affair* (RKO), *Gunga Din* (RKO), *The Hunchback of Notre Dame* (RKO), *Mr. Smith Goes to Washington* (Columbia), *Only Angels Have Wings* (Columbia), *Golden Boy* (Columbia), *Destry Rides Again* (Universal), *Stagecoach* (Wanger/United Artists), *Wuthering Heights* (Goldwyn/United Artists), *Intermezzo* (Selznick/United Artists).

But if the reader takes a close look at almost any year from this period, he or she will find a remarkable number of films that have stood the test of time. Let's consider 1932, for example. In that year, Paramount alone released *Trouble in Paradise, Love Me Tonight, Dr. Jekyll and Mr. Hyde, Shanghai Express, Blonde Venus, One Hour with You, The Sign of the Cross* and *A Farewell to Arms*. Add to the above titles such memorable works as *Grand Hotel* (MGM), *Red Dust* (MGM), *I Am a Fugitive from a Chain Gang* (Warner Bros.), *What Price Hollywood?* (RKO), *American Madness* (Columbia), *Back Street* (Universal), *The Mummy* (Universal), *Scarface* (Caddo/United Artists), *Arrowsmith* (Goldwyn/United Artists) and *Rain* (Feature Productions/United Artists) and 1932 seems pretty miraculous as well.

Perhaps the best news of all is that many of these pictures are now readily available for viewing. Thanks to videotape and DVD releases, as well as that mecca for lovers of cinema, Turner Classic Movies, one can watch, study and enjoy Hollywood's finest with relative ease. My hope is that this book will inspire you to watch, or rewatch, these worthwhile films and help increase your comprehension and appreciation of them. For many of my readers, a brave "old" world of cinematic treasures awaits – explore it. The quest will repay your efforts many times over.

Selected Bibliography

Chapter 1 Historical Overview

Barnouw, Eric. *The Golden Web*. New York: Oxford University Press, 1968.

Barnouw, Eric. *A Tower in Babel*. New York: Oxford University Press, 1966.

Blum, John Morton. *V Was for Victory*. San Diego: Harcourt Brace Jovanovich, 1976.

Brinkley, Alan. *Voices of Protest: Huey Long, Father Coughlin, and the Great Depression*. New York: Random House, 1982.

Brockett, Oscar G. *A History of Theatre*. Fourth edition. Boston: Allyn and Bacon, 1982.

Cashman, Sean D. *America in the Twenties and Thirties: The Olympian Age of Franklin Delano Roosevelt*. New York: New York University Press, 1989.

Ceplair, Larry and Steven Englund. *The Inquisition in Hollywood: Politics in the Film Community, 1930–1960*. Urbana: University of Illinois Press, 2003.

Chafe, William H. *The American Woman: Her Changing Social, Economic and Political Roles, 1920–1970*. New York: Oxford University Press, 1975.

Chambers, John W. II and David Culbert (eds.). *World War II, Film, and History*. New York: Oxford University Press, 1996.

Couperie, Pierre and Maurice C. Horn. *A History of the Comic Strip*. New York: Crown Publishers, 1968.

Csida, Joseph and June Bundy Csida. *American Entertainment*. New York: Watson-Guptill, 1978.

Daniels, Les. *Comix: A History of Comic Books in America*. New York: Outerbridge and Dienstfrey, 1971.

Dick, Bernard. F. *The Star-Spangled Screen: The American World War II Film*. Lexington: University of Kentucky Press, 1985.

Doherty, Thomas. *Projections of War: Hollywood, American Culture and World War II*. New York: Columbia University Press, 1993.

Dolan Jr., Edward F. *Hollywood Goes to War*. New York: Smith, 1985.

Dunning, John. *Tune In Yesterday: The Ultimate Encyclopedia of Old-Time Radio*. Englewood Cliffs, NJ: Prentice Hall, 1976.

Edsforth, Ronald. *The New Deal: America's Response to the Great Depression*. Malden, MA: Blackwell, 2000.

Ewen, David. *All the Years of American Popular Music*. Englewood Cliffs, NJ: Prentice Hall, 1977.

Ewen, David. *Great Men of American Popular Song*. Englewood Cliffs, NJ: Prentice Hall, 1970.

Garrity, John A. and Robert A. McCaughey. *The American Nation: A History of the United States Since 1865*. Volume two. Fourth edition. New York: Harper and Row, 1987.

Goldman, Eric. *The Crucial Decade and After*. New York: Vintage, 1956.

Green, Harvey. *The Uncertainty of Everyday Life 1915–1945*. New York: Harper Collins, 1992.

Greene, Suzanne Ellery. *Books for Pleasure*. Bowling Green, OH: Bowling Green University Popular Press, 1974.

Hacket, Alice Payne. *Seventy Years of Best Sellers*. New York: R.R. Bowker, 1967.

Hart, James D. *The Popular Book*. Berkeley: University of California Press, 1961.

Hartmann, Susan. *The Home Front and Beyond: American Women in the 1940s*. Boston: Twayne, 1982.

Higgs, Robert J. *Sports: A Reference Guide*. Westport, CT: Greenwood Press, 1982.

Hodgson, Godfrey. *America in Our Time*. New York: Vintage Books, 1976.

Jarvie, Ian. *Movies and Society*. New York: Basic Books, 1970.

Jowett, Garth. *Film, the Democratic Art: A Social History of American Film*. Boston: Little, Brown, 1976.

Keegan, John. *The Second World War*. New York: Viking, 1989.

Koppes, Clayton R. and Gregory D. Black. *Hollywood Goes to War: How Politics, Profits, and Propaganda Shaped World War II Movies*. New York: Free Press, 1987.

Leuchtenberg, William E. *The FDR Years: On Roosevelt and His Legacy*. New York: Columbia University Press, 1995.

Leuchtenburg, William E. *The Perils of Prosperity, 1914–1932*. Chicago: University of Chicago Press, 1958.

Lingeman, Richard. *Don't You Know There's a War On? The American Home Front 1941–1945*. New York: Thunder's Mouth Press, 2003.

MacDonald, J. Fred. *Don't Touch That Dial*. Chicago: Nelson-Hall, 1979.

McElvaine, Robert S. *The Great Depression, America 1929–1941*. New York: Times Books, 1984.

Maltby, Richard. *Harmless Entertainment: Hollywood and the Ideology of Consensus*. Metuchen, NJ: Scarecrow Press, 1983.

Manvell, Roger. *Films and the Second World War*. New York: Delta, 1974.

May, Lary. *Screening Out the Past: The Birth of Mass Culture and the Motion Picture Industry*. New York: Oxford University Press, 1980.

Mitchell, Curtis. *Cavalcade of Broadcasting*. Chicago: Follett Publishing, 1970.

Mordden, Ethan. *The American Theatre*. New York: Oxford University Press, 1981.

Mott, Frank Luther. *Golden Multitudes*. New York: Macmillan, 1947.

Nash, Gerald D. *The Crucial Era: The Great Depression and World War II, 1929–1945*. Second edition. Prospect Heights, IL: Waveland Press, 1992.

Noverr, Douglas A. and Lawrence E. Ziewacz. *The Games They Played*. Chicago: Nelson-Hall, 1983.

Nye, Russel. *The Unembarrassed Muse*. New York: Dial Press, 1970.

O'Connor, John E. and Martin A. Jackson (eds.). *American History/American Film: Interpreting the Hollywood Image*. Second edition. New York: Continuum, 1988.

Polenberg, Richard (ed.). *America at War*. Englewood Cliffs, NJ: Prentice Hall, 1968.

Poteet, G. Howard. *Radio!* Dayton, OH: Pflaum, 1975.

Rader, Benjamin G. *American Sports*. Second edition. Englewood Cliffs, NJ: Prentice Hall, 1970.

Rosen, Marjorie. *Popcorn Venus: Women, Movies and the American Dream*. New York: Avon, 1974.

Settel, Irving. *A Pictorial History of Radio*. New York: Citadel Press, 1960.

Shenton, James P. *History of the United States from 1865 to the Present*. Garden City, NY: Doubleday, 1964.

Sklar, Robert. *Movie-Made America: A Cultural History of American Movies*. Revised edition. New York: Vintage, 1994.

Sinclair, Andrew. *A Concise History of the United States*. London: Lorrimer, 1984.

Solberg, Curtis A. and David A. Morris. *A People's Heritage: Patterns in United States History*. Second edition. Dubuque, IA: Kendall/Hunt, 1984.

Spaeth, Sigmund. *A History of Popular Music in America*. New York: Random House, 1948.

Susman, Warren I. *Culture as History*. New York: Pantheon Books, 1984.

Terkel, Studs. *Hard Times*. New York: Pantheon Books, 1970.

Wechter, Dixon. *The Age of the Great Depression, 1929–1941*. New York: Macmillan, 1948.

Weinstein, Allen and Frank Otto Gatell. *Freedom and Crisis, An American History. Volume two: Since 1860*. Third edition. New York: Random House, 1981.

Westbrook, Robert B. *Why We Fought: Forging American Obligations in World War II*. Washington: Smithsonian Books, 2004.

Wilson, Gariff B. *Three Hundred Years of America Drama and Theatre*. Englewood Cliffs, NJ: Prentice Hall, 1973.

Wyckoff, Peter. *Wall Street and the Stock Markets*. Philadelphia: Chilton, 1972.

Chapter 2 Film Business

Austin, Bruce A. *Immediate Seating: A Look at Movie Audiences*. Belmont, CA: Wadsworth, 1989.

Balio, Tino (ed.). *The American Film Industry*. Revised edition. Madison: University of Wisconsin Press, 1985.

Balio, Tino. *Grand Design: Hollywood as a Modern Business Enterprise, 1930–1939*. New York: Scribner's, 1993.

Balio, Tino. *United Artists: The Company Built by the Stars*. Madison: University of Wisconsin Press, 1976.

Behlmer, Rudy (ed.). *Inside Warner Bros. (1935–1951)*. New York: Viking, 1985.

Behlmer, Rudy (ed.). *Memo from David O. Selznick*. New York: Viking, 1972.

Bergan, Ronald. *The United Artists Story*. New York: Crown, 1986.

Bergman, Andrew. *We're in the Money: Depression America and Its Film*. New York: New York University Press, 1971.

Bordwell, David, Janet Staiger and Kristin Thompson. *The Classical Hollywood Cinema*. New York: Columbia University Press, 1985.

Chandler Jr., Alfred D. *The Visible Hand: The Managerial Revolution in American Business*. Cambridge: Harvard University Press, 1977.

Crafton, Donald. *The Talkies: American Cinema's Transition to Sound, 1926–1931*. Berkeley: University of California Press, 1997.

Conant, Michael. *Antitrust in the Motion Picture Industry: Economic and Legal Analysis*. Berkeley: University of California Press, 1960.

Crowther, Bosley. *The Lion's Share: The Story of an Entertainment Empire*. New York: E.P. Dutton, 1957.

Eames, John D. *The MGM Story*. London: Octopus Books, 1977.

Eames, John D. *The Paramount Story*. New York: Crown, 1985.

Fernett, Gene. *Poverty Row*. Satellite Beach, FL: Coral Reef, 1973.

Finler, Joel W. *The Hollywood Story*. New York: Crown, 1988.

Gabler, Neal. *An Empire of Their Own: How the Jews Invented Hollywood*. New York: Crown, 1988.

Gomery, Douglas. *The Hollywood Studio System: A History*. London: British Film Institute, 2005.

Gomery, Douglas. *Shared Pleasures: A History of Movie Presentation in the United States*. Madison: University of Wisconsin Press, 1992.

Hampton, Benjamin. *History of the American Film Industry*. Second edition. New York: Dover, 1970.

Haver, Ronald. *David O. Selznick's Hollywood*. New York: Bonanza Books, 1980.

Hay, Peter. *When the Lion Roars*. Atlanta: Turner Publishing, Inc., 1991.

Hirschhorn, Clive. *The Columbia Story*. New York: Crown, 1990.

Hirschhorn, Clive. *The Universal Story*. New York: Crown, 1983.

Hirschhorn, Clive. *The Warner Bros. Story*. New York: Crown, 1979.

Holliss, Richard and Brian Sibley. *The Disney Studio Story*. New York: Crown, 1988.

Huettig, Mae D. *Economic Control of the Motion Picture Industry*. Philadelphia: University of Pennsylvania Press, 1944.

Hurst, Richard M. *Republic Studios: Between Poverty Row and the Majors*. Metuchen, NJ: Scarecrow, 1979.

Izod, John. *Hollywood and the Box Office, 1895–1986*. New York: Columbia University Press, 1988.

Jacobs, Lewis. *The Rise of the American Film*. New York: Teachers College Press, 1975.

Jewell, Richard B. with Vernon Harbin. *The RKO Story*. New York: Arlington House, 1982.

Jowett, Garth. *Film: The Democratic Art*. Boston: Little, Brown, 1976.

Kerr, Paul (ed.), *The Hollywood Film Industry*. London: Routledge and Kegan Paul, 1986.

Kindem, Gorham (ed.). *The American Movie Industry: The Business of Motion Pictures*. Carbondale: Southern Illinois University Press, 1982.

Koszarski, Richard. *Universal Pictures: 75 Years*. New York: Museum of Modern Art, 1977.

McCarthy, Todd and Charles Flynn (eds.). *Kings of the Bs*. New York: E.P. Dutton, 1975.

Miller, Don. *B Movies*. New York: Ballantine Books, 1973.

Mordden, Ethan. *The Hollywood Studios*. New York: Knopf, 1988.

Okuda, Ted. *Grand National, Producers Releasing Corporation, and Screen Guild/Lippert*. Jefferson, NC: McFarland, 1989.

Okuda, Ted. *The Monogram Checklist*. Jefferson, NC: McFarland, 1987.

Roddick, Nick. *A New Deal in Entertainment: Warner Brothers in the 1930s*. London: British Film Institute, 1983.

Ross, Murray. *Stars and Strikes: Unionization in Hollywood*. New York: Columbia University Press, 1941.

Sands, Pierre N. *A Historical Study of the Academy of Motion Picture Arts and Sciences (1927–1947)*. New York: Arno Press, 1973.

Schatz, Thomas. *Boom and Bust: American Cinema in the 1940s*. Berkeley: University of California Press, 1997.

Schatz, Thomas. *The Genius of the System*. New York: Pantheon Books, 1988.

Sklar, Robert. *Movie-Made America: A Cultural History of American Movies*. Revised edition. New York: Vintage, 1994.

Slide, Anthony. *The American Film Industry: A Historical Dictionary*. New York: Limelight Editions, 1990.

Staiger, Janet (ed.). *The Studio System*. New Brunswick, NJ: Rutgers University Press, 1995.

Stanley, Robert H. *The Celluloid Empire*. New York: Hastings House, 1978.

Thomas, Tony and Aubrey Solomon. *The Films of 20th Century-Fox*. Secaucus, NJ: Citadel Press, 1979.

Thompson, Kristin. *Exporting Entertainment*. London: British Film Institute, 1985.

Tusca, Jon. *The Vanishing Legion: A History of Mascot Pictures. 1927–1935*. Jefferson, NC: McFarland, 1982.

Wasco, Janet. *Movies and Money: Financing the American Film Industry*. Norwood, NJ: Ablex, 1982.

Chapter 3 Technology

Bandy, Mary Lea (ed.). *The Dawn of Sound*. New York: Museum of Modern Art, 1989.

Basten, Fred E. *Glorious Technicolor: The Movies' Magic Rainbow*. New York: A.S. Barnes, 1980.

Belton, John. *Widescreen Cinema*. Cambridge: Harvard University Press, 1992.

Bordwell, David, Janet Staiger and Kristin Thompson. *The Classical Hollywood Cinema: Film Style and Mode of Production to 1960*. New York: Columbia University Press, 1985.

Brosnan, John. *Movie Magic: The Story of Special Effects in the Cinema*. New York: St. Martin's, 1974.

Cameron, Evan W. (ed.). *Sound and the Cinema: The Coming of Sound to American Film*. Pleasantville, NY: Redgrave, 1980.

Carr, Robert E. and R.M. Hayes. *Wide Screen Movies: A History and Filmography of Wide Gauge Filmmaking*. Jefferson, NC: McFarland and Co., 1988.

Carringer, Robert. *The Making of Citizen Kane*. Berkeley: University of California Press, 1985.

Crafton, Donald. *The Talkies: American Cinema's Transition to Sound, 1926–1931*. Berkeley: University of California Press, 1997.

Dunn, Linwood G. and George E. Turner (eds.). *The ASC Treasury of Visual Effects*. Hollywood, CA: American Society of Cinematographers, 1983.

Eyman, Scott (ed.). *Five American Cinematographers: Interviews with Karl Struss, Joseph Ruttenberg, James Wong Howe, Linwood Dunn, and William H. Clothier*. Metuchen, NJ: Scarecrow Press, 1987.

Eyman, Scott. *The Speed of Sound: Hollywood and the Talkie Revolution*. New York: Simon and Schuster, 1997.

Fielding, Raymond (ed.). *A Technological History of Motion Pictures and Television*. Berkeley: University of California Press, 1967.

Fielding, Raymond. *The Technique of Special Effects Cinematography*. Third edition. New York: Hastings House, 1974.

Fry, Ron and Pamela Fourzon. *The Saga of Special Effects*. Englewood Cliffs, NJ: Prentice Hall, 1977.

Goldner, Orville and George E. Turner. *The Making of King Kong*. New York: Ballantine Books, 1975.

Kindem, Gorham (ed.). *The American Movie Industry: The Business of Motion Pictures*. Carbondale: Southern Illinois University Press, 1982.

Koszarski, Richard. *An Evening's Entertainment: The Age of the Silent Feature Picture 1915–1928*. New York: Scribner's, 1990.

Macgowan, Kenneth. *Behind the Screen: The History and Techniques of the Motion Picture*. New York: Delacorte, 1965.

Maltin, Leonard (ed.). *The Art of the Cinematographer: A Survey and Interviews with Five Masters*. New York: Dover Publications, 1978.

Ryan, Roderick T. *A History of Motion Picture Color Technology*. New York: Focal Press, 1977.

Salt, Barry. *Film Style and Technology: History and Analysis*. London: Starwood, 1983.

Walker, Alexander. *The Shattered Silents: How the Talkies Came to Stay*. New York: William Morrow, 1979.

Watts, Stephen. *Behind the Screen: How Films Are Made*. New York: Dodge, 1938.

Weis, Elizabeth and John Belton (eds.). *Film Sound: Theory and Practice*. New York: Columbia University Press, 1985.

Chapter 4 Censorship

Adler, Mortimer. *Art and Prudence*. New York: Longmans, Green and Co., 1937.

Balio, Tino (ed.). *The American Film Industry*. Revised edition. Madison: University of Wisconsin Press, 1985.

Balio, Tino. *Grand Design: Holywood as a Modern Business Enterprise, 1930–1939*. New York: Scribner's, 1993.

Bergman, Andrew. *We're in the Money: Depression America and Its Films*. New York: Harper, 1971.

Bernstein, Matthew (ed.). *Controlling Hollywood: Censorship and Regulation in the Studio Era*. New Brunswick, NJ: Rutgers University Press, 1999.

Black, Gregory. *The Catholic Crusade Against the Movies, 1940–1970*. Cambridge, UK: Cambridge University Press, 1997.

Black, Gregory. *Hollywood Censored: Morality Codes, Catholics, and the Movies*. Cambridge, UK: Cambridge University Press, 1994.

Biesen, Sheri Chinen. *Blackout: World War II and the Origins of Film Noir*. Baltimore: Johns Hopkins University Press, 2005.

Blumer, Herbert. *Movies and Conduct*. New York: Macmillan, 1933.

Carmen, Ira H. *Movies, Censorship and the Law*. Ann Arbor: University of Michigan Press, 1966.

Conant, Michael. *Antitrust in the Motion Picture Industry: Economic and Legal Analysis*. Berkeley: University of California Press, 1960.

Couvares, Francis G. (ed.). *Movie Censorship and American Culture*. Washington: Smithsonian Institution Press, 1996.

De Grazia, Edward and Roger K. Newman. *Banned Films: Movies, Censors and the First Amendment*. New York: R.K. Bowker Co., 1982.

Ernst, Morris and Pare Lorentz. *Censored: The Private Life of the Movies*. New York: Jonathan Cape and Harrison Smith, 1930.

Facey, Paul. *The Legion of Decency: A Sociological Analysis of the Emergence and Development of a Social Pressure Group*. New York: Arno Press, 1974.

Forman, Henry J. *Our Movie Made Children*. New York: Macmillan, 1933.

Gardner, Gerald. *The Censorship Papers: Movie Censorship Letters from the Hays Office, 1934–1968*. New York: Dodd, Mead, 1987.

Hays, Will. *Memoirs*. New York: Doubleday, 1955.

Hunnings, Neville M. *Film Censors and the Law*. London: Allen and Unwin, 1955.

Inglis, Ruth A. *Freedom of the Movies: A Report on Self-Regulation from the Commission on Freedom of the Press*. Chicago: University of Chicago Press, 1947.

Jacobs, Lea. *The Wages of Sin: Censorship and the Fallen Woman Film, 1928–1942*. Madison: University of Wisconsin Press, 1991.

Jowett, Garth, Ian Jarvie and Kathryn Fuller. *Children and the Movies: Media Influence and the Payne Fund Controversy.* Boston: Cambridge University Press, 1996.

Jowett, Garth. *Film: The Democratic Art.* Boston: Little, Brown, 1976.

Koppes, Clayton R. and Gregory D. Black. *Hollywood Goes to War: How Politics, Profits and Propaganda Shaped World War II Movies.* New York: Free Press, 1987.

Leff, Leonard J. and Jerold L. Simmons. *The Dame in the Kimono: Hollywood, Censorship and the Production Code from the 1920s to the 1960s.* New York: Grove Weidenfeld, 1990.

Maltby, Richard. *Harmless Entertainment: Hollywood and the Ideology of Consensus.* Metuchen, NJ: Scarecrow Press, 1983.

Martin, Olga J. *Hollywood's Movie Commandments.* New York: H.W. Wilson, 1937.

Mast, Gerald (ed.). *The Movies in Our Midst: Documents in the Cultural History of Film in America.* Chicago: University of Chicago Press, 1982.

Miller, Frank. *Censored Hollywood: Sex, Sin and Violence on the Screen.* Atlanta: Turner, 1994.

Moley, Raymond. *Are We Movie Made?* New York: Macy-Massius, 1938.

Moley, Raymond. *The Hays Office.* Indianapolis: Bobbs-Merrill, 1945.

Nizer, Louis. *New Courts of Industry: Self-Regulation Under the Motion Picture Code.* New York: Longacre Press, 1935.

Phelps, Guy. *Film Censorship.* London: Victor Gollancz, 1975.

Powdermaker, Hortense. *Hollywood: The Dream Factory.* Boston: Little, Brown, 1950.

Production Code Administration Files. Academy of Motion Picture Arts and Sciences Library. Beverly Hills, CA.

Quigley, Martin. *Decency in Motion Pictures.* New York: Macmillan, 1937.

Randall, Richard S. *Censorship in the Movies: The Social and Political Control of a Mass Medium.* Madison: University of Wisconsin Press, 1968.

Rosten, Leo. *Hollywood: The Movie Colony, The Movie Makers.* New York: Harcourt, Brace, 1941.

Schaefer, Eric. *"Bold! Daring! Shocking! True": A History of Exploitation Films, 1919–1959.* Durham: Duke University Press, 1999.

Schumach, Murray. *The Face on the Cutting Room Floor: The Story of Movie and Television Censorship.* New York: Morrow, 1964.

Sklar, Robert. *Movie-Made America: A Cultural History of American Movies.* Revised edition. New York: Vintage, 1994.

Vizzard, Jack. *See No Evil: Life Inside a Hollywood Censor.* New York: Simon and Schuster, 1970.

Walsh, Frank R. *Sin and Censorship.* New Haven: Yale University Press, 1996.

Winkler, Allan M. *The Politics of Propaganda: The Office of War Information, 1942–1945.* New Haven: Yale University Press, 1978.

Chapter 5 Narrative and Style

Albrecht, Donald. *Designing Dreams: Modern Architecture in the Movies*. New York: Harper and Row, 1986.

Allen, Robert C. and Douglas Gomery. *Film History: Theory and Practice*. New York: Knopf, 1985.

Balio, Tino. *Grand Design: Hollywood as a Modern Business Enterprise, 1930–1939*. New York: Scribner's, 1993.

Barsacq, Leon. *Caligari's Cabinet and Other Grand Illusions: A History of Film Design*. Revised edition. New York: New American Library, 1978.

Biesen, Sheri Chinen. *Blackout: World War II and the Origins of Film Noir*. Baltimore: Johns Hopkins University Press, 2005.

Blacker, Irwin. *The Elements of Screenwriting: A Guide for Film and Television Writers*. New York: Macmillan, 1986.

Bordwell, David. *Narration in the Fiction Film*. London: Methuen, 1985.

Bordwell, David. *On the History of Film Style*. Cambridge: Harvard University Press, 1997.

Bordwell, David and Kristin Thompson. *Film Art: An Introduction*. Seventh edition. Boston: McGraw-Hill, 2004.

Bordwell, David, Janet Staiger and Kristin Thompson. *The Classical Hollywood Cinema: Film Style and Mode of Production to 1960*. New York: Columbia University Press, 1985.

Buscombe, Edward. *Stagecoach*. London: British Film Institute, 1992.

Butler, J. (ed.). *Star Texts: Image and Performance in Film and Television*. Detroit: Wayne State, 1991.

Cameron, Evan (ed.). *Sound and the Cinema: The Coming of Sound to American Film*. Pleasantville, NY: Redgrave, 1980.

Cameron, Ian (ed.). *The Movie Book of Film Noir*. London: Verso, 1992.

Crafton, Donald. *The Talkies: American Cinema's Transition to Sound, 1926–1931*. Berkeley: University of California Press, 1997.

Fell, John. *Film and the Narrative Tradition*. Berkeley: University of California Press, 1986.

Flinn, Caryl. *Strains of Utopia: Gender, Nostalgia and Hollywood Film Music*. Princeton: Princeton University Press, 1992.

Hambley, John and Patrick Downing. *The Art of Hollywood: Fifty Years of Art Direction*. London: Thames Television, 1979.

Higham, Charles. *Hollywood Cameramen: Sources of Light*. Bloomington: Indiana University Press, 1970.

Kalinak, Kathryn. *Settling the Score: Music and the Classical Hollywood Film*. Madison: University of Wisconsin Press, 1992.

Kawin, Bruce. *How Movies Work*. Berkeley: University of California Press, 1992.

Knight, Arthur. *The Liveliest Art: A Panoramic History of the Movies*. New York: Macmillan, 1957.

Krutnick, Frank. *In a Lonely Street: Film Noir, Genre, Masculinity*. London: Routledge, 1991.

La Vine, W. Robert. *In a Glamorous Fashion: The Fabulous Years of Hollywood Costume Design*. New York: Scribner's, 1980.

Maeder, Edward. *Hollywood and History: Costume Design in Films*. Los Angeles: Los Angeles County Museum of Art, 1987.

Maltin, Leonard (ed.). *The Art of the Cinematographer: A Survey and Interviews with Five Masters*. New York: Dover, 1978.

Manvell, Roger and John Huntley. *The Technique of Film Music*. New York: Focal Press, 1957.

Naremore, James. *Acting in the Cinema*. Berkeley: University of California Press, 1988.

Naremore, James. *More Than Night: Film Noir in Its Contexts*. Berkeley: University of California Press, 1998.

Neale, Steve. *Cinema and Technology: Image, Sound, Color*. Bloomington: University of Indiana Press, 1985.

Palmer, R. Barton. *Hollywood's Dark Cinema: The American Film Noir*. New York: Twayne, 1994.

Polan, Dana. *Power and Paranoia: History, Narrative, and the American Cinema, 1940–1950*. New York: Columbia University Press, 1986.

Ray, Robert. *A Certain Tendency of the Hollywood Cinema, 1930–1980*. Princeton: Princeton University Press, 1985.

Roberts, Graham and Heather Wallis. *Introducing Film*. London: Arnold, 2001.

Salt, Barry. *Film Style and Technology: History and Analysis*. Second edition. London: Starword, 1993.

Sarris, Andrew. *The American Cinema: Directors and Directions, 1929–1968*. Chicago: University of Chicago Press, 1986.

Schatz, Thomas. *Boom and Bust: American Cinema in the 1940s*. Berkeley: University of California Press, 1997.

Sennett, Robert S. *Setting the Scene: The Great Hollywood Art Directors*. New York: Harry N. Abrams, 1994.

Silver, Alain and Elizabeth Ward (eds.). *Film Noir: An Encyclopedic Reference to the American Style*. Woodstock, NY: The Overlook Press, 1992.

Staiger, Janet (ed.). *The Studio System*. New Brunswick, NJ: Rutgers University Press, 1995.

Sterling, Anna Kate (ed.). *Cinematographers on the Art and Craft of Cinematography*. Metuchen, NJ: Scarecrow, 1987.

Telotte, J.P. *Voices in the Dark: The Narrative Patterns of Film Noir*. Urbana: University of Illinois Press, 1989.

Vale, Eugene. *The Technique of Screenplay Writing*. New York: Grosset and Dunlap, 1972.

Walker, Alexander. *The Shattered Silents: How the Talkies Came to Stay*. New York: William Morrow, 1979.

Weis, Elisabeth and John Belton (eds.). *Film Sound: Theory and Practice.* New York: Columbia University Press, 1985.

Chapter 6 Genres

Altman, Rick. *The American Film Musical.* Bloomington: Indiana University Press, 1987.

Basinger, Jeanine. *A Woman's View: How Hollywood Spoke to Women, 1930–1960.* London: Chatto and Windus, 1993.

Basinger, Jeanine. *The World War II Combat Film: Anatomy of a Genre.* New York: Columbia University Press, 1986.

Baxter, John. *Hollywood in the Thirties.* New York: A.S. Barnes, 1968.

Balio, Tino. *Grand Design: Hollywood as a Modern Business Enterprise, 1930–1939.* New York: Scribner's, 1993.

Bowden, Liz-Anne. (ed.). *The Oxford Companion to Film.* New York: Oxford University Press, 1976.

Buscombe, Edward. *The BFI Companion to the Western.* New York: Da Capo Press, 1988.

Cavell, Stanley. *Pursuits of Happiness: The Hollywood Comedy of Remarriage.* Cambridge: Harvard University Press, 1981.

Cawelti, John. *Adventure, Mystery and Romance: Formula Stories as Art and Popular Culture.* Chicago: University of Chicago Press, 1976.

Cawelti, John. *The Six-Gun Mystique.* Bowling Green, OH: Bowling Green Popular University Press, 1981.

Clarens, Carlos. *Crime Movies: An Illustrated History.* New York: W.W. Norton, 1980.

Clarens, Carlos. *An Illustrated History of the Horror Film.* New York: Capricorn Books, 1968.

Doane, Mary Ann. *The Desire to Desire: The Woman's Film of the 1940s.* Bloomington: Indiana University Press, 1987.

Feuer, Jane. *The Hollywood Musical.* Bloomington: Indiana University Press, 1982.

Fordin, Hugh. *Hollywood's Greatest Musicals: The World of Entertainment.* New York: Avon, 1985.

French, Philip. *Westerns.* London: Secker and Warburg, 1973.

Gehring, Wes D. *Handbook of American Film Genres.* Westport, CT: Greenwood Press, 1988.

Gehring, Wes D. *Screwball Comedy: A Genre of Madcap Romance.* Westport, CT: Greenwood Press, 1986.

Grant, Barry K. (ed.). *Film Genre Reader.* Austin: University of Texas Press, 1986.

Grant, Barry K. (ed.). *Film Genre Reader II.* Austin: University of Texas Press, 1995.

Grant, Barry K. *Planks of Reason.* Metuchen, NJ: Scarecrow, 1988.

Harvey, James. *Romantic Comedy in Hollywood, from Lubitsch to Sturges.* New York: Alfred A. Knopf, 1987.

Haskell, Molly. *From Reverence to Rape: The Treatment of Women in the Movies*. New York: Holt, Rinehart and Winston, 1974.

Jenkins, Henry III. *What Made Pistachio Nuts? Early Sound Comedy and the Vaudeville Aesthetic*. New York: Columbia University Press, 1993.

Kaminsky, Stuart. *American Film Genres*. New York: Dell, 1977.

Kendall, Elizabeth. *The Runaway Bride: Hollywood Romantic Comedy of the 1930s*. New York: Alfred A. Knopf, 1990.

Kitses, Jim. *Horizons West: Directing the Western from John Ford to Clint Eastwood*. New edition. London: BFI Publishing, 2004.

Lagman, Larry and Daniel Finn. *A Guide to American Crime Films of the Thirties*. Westport, CT: Greenwood Press, 1995.

Lagman, Larry and Daniel Finn. *A Guide to American Crime Films of the Forties and Fifties*. Westport, CT: Greenwood Press, 1995.

Lenihan, John L. *Showdown: Confronting Modern America in the Western Film*. Urbana: University of Illinois Press, 1980.

McArthur, Colin. *Underworld USA*. London: Secker and Warburg, 1972.

McCaffrey, Donald W. *The Golden Age of Sound Comedy: Comic Films and Comedians of the Thirties*. New York: A.S. Barnes, 1973.

Mast, Gerald. *The Comic Mind: Comedy and the Movies*. New York: Bobbs-Merrill, 1973.

Roffman, Peter and Jim Purdy. *The Hollywood Social Problem Film: Madness, Despair and Politics from the Depression to the Fifties*. Bloomington: Indiana University Press, 1981.

Rosen, Marjorie. *Popcorn Venus: Women, Movies and the American Dream*. New York: Avon, 1974.

Rossow, Eugene. *Born to Lose: The Gangster Film in America*. New York: Oxford University Press, 1978.

Schatz, Thomas. *Hollywood Genres: Formulas, Filmmaking and the Studio System*. New York: Random House, 1981.

Shadoian, Jack. *Dreams and Dead Ends*. Cambridge: MIT Press, 1977.

Taves, Brian. *The Romance of Adventure: The Genre of Historical Adventure Movies*. Jackson: University of Mississippi Press, 1993.

Tudor, Andrew. *Monsters and Mad Scientists: A Cultural History of the Horror Movie*. Oxford: Basil Blackwell, 1989.

Walsh, Andrea. *Women's Film and the Female Experience, 1940–1950*. New York: Praeger, 1984.

Warshow, Robert. *The Immediate Experience*. New York: Atheneum, 1970.

Weales, Gerald. *Canned Goods as Caviar: American Film Comedies of the 1930s*. Chicago: University of Chicago Press, 1985.

Wright, Will. *Sixguns and Society: A Structural Study of the Western*. Berkeley: University of California Press, 1975.

Chapter 7 Stars and the Star System

Affron, Charles. *Star Acting*. New York: E.P. Dutton, 1977.

Balio, Tino, *The American Film Industry*. Revised edition. Madison: University of Wisconsin Press, 1986.

Braudy, Leo. *The World in a Frame*. Garden City, NY: Anchor/Doubleday, 1976.

Britton, Andrew. *Cary Grant: Comedy and Male Desire*. Newcastle upon Tyne: Tyneside Cinema, 1983.

Britton, Andrew. *Katharine Hepburn: Star as Feminist*. New York: Columbia University Press, 2003.

Brown, W.R. *Imagemaker: Will Rogers and the American Dream*. Columbia: University of Missouri Press, 1970.

Butler, J. *Star Texts: Image and Performance in Film and Television*. Detroit: Wayne State University Press, 1990.

Cooke, A. *Douglas Fairbanks: The Making of a Screen Character*. New York: Museum of Modern Art, 1970.

DeCordova, Richard. *Picture Personalities: The Emergence of the Star System in America*. Urbana: University of Illinois Press, 1990.

Durgnat, Raymond and John Kobel. *Greta Garbo*. New York: Dutton, 1965.

Dyer, Richard. *Heavenly Bodies: Film Stars and Society*. London: Macmillan, 1987.

Dyer, Richard. *The Matter of Images: Essays on Representation*. New York: Routledge, 1993.

Dyer, Richard. *Stars*. London: British Film Institute, 1979.

Gaines, Jane and Charlotte Herzog (eds.). *Fabrications: Costume and the Female Body*. New York: Routledge, 1991.

Griffith, Richard. *The Movie Stars*. Garden City, NY: Doubleday, 1970.

Haskell, Molly. *From Reverence to Rape: The Treatment of Women in the Movies*. Second edition. Chicago: University of Chicago Press, 1987.

Kerr, Paul (ed.). *The Hollywood Film Industry*. New York: Routledge and Kegan Paul, 1986.

Kindem, Gorham (ed.). *The American Movie Industry: The Business of Motion Pictures*. Carbondale, IL: Southern Illinois University Press, 1982.

Maland, Charles J. *Chaplin and American Culture: The Evolution of a Star Image*. Princeton, NJ: Princeton University Press, 1991.

McGilligan, Patrick. *Cagney: The Actor as Auteur*. South Brunswick, NJ: A.S. Barnes, 1982.

Mellon, Joan. *Big Bad Wolves: Masculinity in the American Film*. London: Film Tree Books, 1978.

Mordden, Ethan. *Movie Star: A Look at the Women Who Made Hollywood*. New York: St. Martin's Press, 1983.

Naremore, James. *Acting in the Cinema*. Berkeley: University of California Press, 1988.

Powdermaker, Hortense. *Hollywood: The Dream Factory*. Boston: Little, Brown, 1950.

Prindle, David F. *The Politics of Glamour: Ideology and Democracy in the Screen Actors Guild.* Madison: University of Wisconsin Press, 1988.

Rosen, Marjorie. *Popcorn Venus: Women, Movies and the American Dream.* New York: Avon, 1973.

Schickel, Richard. *Intimate Strangers: The Culture of Celebrity.* Garden City, NY: Doubleday, 1985.

Schickel, Richard. *The Stars.* New York: Dial, 1962.

Shipman, David. *The Great Movie Stars: The Golden Years.* New York: Hill and Wang, 1979.

Tudor, Andrew. *Image and Influence.* London: Allen and Unwin, 1974.

Walker, Alexander. *Stardom: The Hollywood Phenomenon.* New York: Stein and Day, 1970.

Weis, Elizabeth (ed.). *The National Society of Film Critics on the Movie Star.* New York: Viking, 1981.

Index

General

Note: page references in italics indicate illustrations

Film titles

Note: A and *The* are ignored in the alphabetization of titles.